MW01267977

Music, Dance, and Society

Medieval Institute Publications is a program of
The Medieval Institute, College of Arts and Sciences

 WESTERN MICHIGAN UNIVERSITY

Music, Dance, and Society

Medieval and Renaissance Studies in Memory of Ingrid G. Brainard

Edited by
Ann Buckley and Cynthia J. Cyrus

MEDIEVAL INSTITUTE PUBLICATIONS
Western Michigan University
Kalamazoo

Library of Congress Cataloging-in-Publication Data

Music, dance and society : medieval and renaissance studies in memory of Ingrid
G. Brainard / edited by Ann Buckley and Cynthia J. Cyrus.
    p. cm.
  Includes bibliographical references and index.
  ISBN 978-1-58044-166-7 (clothbound : alk. paper)
  1. Brainard, Ingrid. 2. Music--500-1400--History and criticism. 3. Music--15th
century--History and criticism. 4. Music--16th century--History and criticism.
I. Buckley, Ann (Ann I.) II. Cyrus, Cynthia J. III. Brainard, Ingrid.
  ML55.B7127 2011
  780.9'02--dc23

                                               2011034853

Contents

Interpreting the Repertory

Reevaluating the Repertory

Ingrid Karsten Brainard
November 10, 1921–February 18, 2000

A Tribute

For twenty-two years, participants at the International Congress on Medieval Studies at Kalamazoo would find Ingrid Brainard standing near the check-in area as they arrived. She would be at her best, greeting old friends and making new ones with a vivacity and enthusiasm that warmed the heart. She knew many of us indeed. After all, for quite a few of us, Ingrid had accepted and then attended our very first paper at an international conference. She had patiently organized those "Musicology at Kalamazoo" sessions, year in year out, foregoing the easy route of the word processor in favor of her old and visually distinctive typewriter. Capitalizing on this *entrée* into a sort of early music *Who's Who?*, she would strike up conversations with the new arrival, discover his or her interests, and then make introductions and begin the process of integrating this new colleague into her network of friends, a network which covered much of the Kalamazoo population. For all of her generosity in welcoming newcomers to the world of scholarly endeavors, she also savored the reappearances of old friends, and would respond with a hug and an inquiry after family, life events, and research progress. Ingrid had a prodigious memory for detail, and could often recite the names of family members faster than we could ourselves. And then the conversation would turn to the practical: "What are you going to submit next year?" became the topic of conversation over breakfast, lunch, and dinner.

Of course, Kalamazoo was not her only haunt, nor musicology her only love. Ingrid was a vibrant presence at meetings of the Society of Dance History and of the Congress on Research in Dance, a regular visitor to the American Musicological Society, and a dance instructor at gatherings both formal and informal. Ingrid negotiated with ease those false divisions between academia and the rest of the world, serving at once as consultant for the professional Waverly consort and for the local chapter of the Society for Creative Anachronism. Tellingly, Ingrid appears in the minutes of SCA meetings, but she did not bother to include those events in her own *curriculum vitae*: she shared her information with a broader public but did not claim those activities as scholarly or educational. That generosity, of giving where no return was expected, was characteristic of this remarkable woman.

Ingrid Brainard mixed the competencies of the traditional musicologist with the practical knowledge of gesture of the dance historian. In addition to her scholarly and artistic contributions through prose and through movement, she served musicology and dance history alike through the thankless but necessary tasks of book reviewer and session organizer. Her reviews, often substantial and always readable, appeared in *Notes, Die Musikforschung, American Recorder, Speculum, Dance Research Journal*, and, most regularly, in *Dance Chronicle*. Moreover, her presence as session organizer and as unofficial greeter at music and dance conferences and, especially, at the International Congress on Medieval Studies at Kalamazoo, was a given for more than two decades.[1]

Her fifteen articles in journals, *Festschriften*, collections of essays and symposia represent an admirable corpus of scholarship, especially for an active performer/choreographer and teacher. If she sometimes chose to publish in out-of-the-way venues, she nevertheless offered a polymath's perspective on whatever engaged her attention. The precisely one hundred footnotes for an article on "The Role of the Dancing Master"[2] are symptomatic of Ingrid's urge to know everything. Indeed, in a critique of translations, Ingrid explained the high standards to which she held herself and her peers:

> The translator of a fifteenth-century Italian dance manual faces a formidable task. He or she must be a paleographer, linguist, dance historian, musicologist, Renaissance scholar and editor all at once, able to deal with the language of the source, with the ambiguities of an early author's personal style and vocabulary, with the specific terminology pertaining to the theory and practice of dance and of music, as well as with a musical notation that does not always conform to the conventions of the period. The translator must be informed about early Renaissance cultural history, thought and politics and familiar with the primary sources as well as the relevant secondary literature; he or she must bring an editor's exacting care to the apparatus and the final faithful rendering of the centuries-old document in a modern language.[3]

In spite of what might possibly be mistaken for a pedant's attention to detail, Ingrid also had a lively and engaging interest in pragmatic lived experience. One of her most accessible contributions for the nonspecialist is found in "Modes, Manners, Movement,"[4] an article which discusses the kinds of resources available to reconstruct past fashions and past dances and, more significantly, provides plausible linkages between those two fields. As Ingrid shows, a change of clothing style may well limit the kinds of gestures available, and the sliding movements of one generation can be connected rather directly to the kind of footwear popular among courtiers of the time. Her thesis, that the choice of wardrobe influences the kinds of dancing that the wearer was willing and able to undertake, is commonsensical, but is also well documented in this careful yet readable scholarly reconstruction. A similarly engaging contribution in the *Early Drama and Music (EDAM) Newsletter* is cited by several scholars as the easiest introduction to Renaissance Dance manuals available in print.[5]

Ingrid knew how to woo and win her audiences. In fact, her enthusiasm was contagious, and it is characteristic of her writing, as with her conversation, that she was not afraid to approve of dances in print. "Another stunning example for the use of pattern as a storytelling device occurs in the delightful balletto *La Malgratiosa* for two (a man with his lady) which is ascribed to Domenico [da Piacenza]," she opines in one description.[6] Terms such as "stunning" and "delightful" are not objective scholarly vocabulary, but they are all the more informative for that. Who better to measure the success of a good dance than the scholar so deeply engaged with its reconstruction?

Indeed, Ingrid's broad perspective has been influential, in spite of the relatively slender portfolio of her conventional scholarly work. Her widely acclaimed, self-published *Art of Courtly Dancing* sits on the shelf of many a dancer, musicologist, and historical reenactor, and is widely cited in the secondary literature. A short volume of choreographies, *Three Court Dances of the Early Renaissance*, makes accessible some of the work based on her dissertation.[7] As several friends and colleagues have noted, Ingrid was uncomfortable with formalizing a rendition of a dance; she expressed concern over the fixity inherent in notating her momentary understanding of "how the dance goes." Dancer Patri Pugliese noted explicitly that Ingrid was always open to rethinking her interpretation of the documents. He cites the *Ballo Verceppe* which Ingrid rechoreographed, rehearsed, and had the group perform in a single week after a student drew her attention to variants between treatise and realization. Ingrid regularly performed historical works but she did not see these performances as finalized versions and was always looking for new insights. Indeed, her excitement at discovering that a particular *continenza* was performed like "treading organ bellows," and her willingness to demonstrate what that meant on tabletop at a conference meeting, shows the ways in which active scholarship intersected with Ingrid's embodied realizations.[8]

Ingrid's own depth of knowledge was perhaps most evident in the performances of the Cambridge Court Dancers, an organization which she founded in 1969 and led with enthusiasm throughout the rest of her career. She described the group in program notes: "The Cambridge Court Dancers, directed by Ingrid Brainard, specialize in the reconstruction and performance of historical dances.

Dr. Brainard has recreated the repertoire of choreographies from the original dance instruction manuals of the late Middle Ages, the Renaissance and Baroque periods."[9]

At the memorial ceremony held in celebration of Ingrid's life on April 22, 2000, Pugliese recalled his experiences in the Cambridge Court Dancers: "The Cambridge Court Dancers were in part Ingrid's guinea pigs for working out new choreographies. As such we were the recipients—the first recipients—of the benefits of her research and also of her great care and attention, for she was always very attentive to the details of the dance and to her dancers."[10] His comments acknowledge Ingrid's twofold contribution. She worked hard to reconstruct dances which adhered as closely as possible to the surviving documentary descriptions. But she also loved working with the people who brought those dances to life. It is one of Dr. Ingrid Brainard's major legacies to have introduced so many individuals to historical dance—both those who took it up professionally and those who had merely a single evening's opportunity to experience for themselves the joys of moving step by step according to her careful instructions.

It may have been her urge to serve the nonspecialist that motivated Ingrid's extensive contributions to encyclopedias in dance and in music. She wrote for eight different reference resources, including the *Harvard Dictionary of Music* (2/1969), *The New Grove Dictionary of Music and Musicians*, *Die Musik in Geschichte und Gegenwart*, *Handbuch des Musiktheaters*, *The Companion to the Medieval Theatre*, and *The Encyclopedia of Dance*. If work of this sort, like that of reviewing books or that of organizing conference sessions, is largely thankless, Ingrid Brainard nevertheless received public recognition for her many contributions. She was Artist-in-Residence at Northeastern University in 1975–76 and Lecturer in Dance for Aston Magna in 1991. She served as board member of CORD (Congress on Research in Dance) in 1970–76 and as its chair during 1978–80; she was also a founder and member of the first board for the Society of Dance History Scholars. Ingrid Brainard held a number of positions as dance advisor (to the Waverly consort, the MIT Shakespeare Ensemble, the Massachusetts Council on Arts and Humanities), and spent a fruitful two years as Fellow of the Radcliffe Institute for Independent Studies, Cambridge, Massachusetts, in 1962–64. Perhaps most tellingly, after her death in 2000 from a heart attack, there were numerous memorials and tributes to her in the form of conference sessions, concerts, a volume of dance essays, and this, a gift of scholarly contributions from friends and admirers from across several disciplines.

Important as such public recognition is, it does not capture the whole person, for Ingrid Brainard was at heart a generous soul, ready with a laugh, a smile, a hug, and an open and accepting camaraderie. Ingrid was always a mentor, offering time, encouragement, and opportunities to innumerable scholars- and dancers-to-be.

She was a colleague, sharing in triumphs and consoling setbacks, meeting and greeting conference acquaintances with an enthusiasm that lifted the spirit. Above all, she was a lover of life, of music, and of movement:

> The dance has many faces, fulfills many functions, satisfies many needs; it is magic and theatre, service of Deities and delight of man; it is an outlet for surplus energies, a supreme means of expression; it is vigorous and health-giving exercise; it is, in the words of the 16th-century clergyman and dancing master Thoinot Arbeau, "both a pleasant and a profitable art which confers and preserves health, proper to youth, agreeable to the old and suitable to all provided fitness of time and place are observed and it is not abused" (*Orchésographie*, 1589). (Ingrid Brainard, West Newton, MA, January 1971)[11]

The essays included in this volume testify to the impact of this singular scholar. They are expression of our personal and professional need to acknowledge the far-reaching influence of a figure whose area of specialization took her outside of the at times artificial and constricting disciplinary boundaries of modern day academia. Our call for papers went out to dance historians and musicologists; to American, European, and Australian scholars; to friends, pupils, colleagues, and intellectual comrades of this scholar/dancer and world-class mentor. The broad array of topics in the resulting collection reflects, but far from encompasses, Ingrid Brainard's own broad interests and enthusiasms. This volume is lovingly dedicated to her memory.

Notes

1. Ingrid Brainard first organized musicology sessions for the International Congress on Medieval Studies at Kalamazoo in 1977, and was the driving force behind those sessions until her death in February 2000.
2. "The Role of the Dancing Master in 15th-Century Courtly Society," *Fifteenth-Century Studies* 2 (1979): 21–44.
3. Ingrid Brainard, "Translating Cornazano," *Dance Chronicle* 7 (1984): 107.
4. "Modes, Manners, Movement: The Interaction of Dance and Dress from the Late Middle Ages to the Renaissance," *Society of Dance History Scholars Conference Proceedings*, 6th Annual Conference (1983): 17–36.
5. "The Dance Manuals of the Late Middle Ages and Renaissance: A Survey," *EDAM [Early Drama, Art and Music] Newsletter* 6/2 (Spring 1984): 28–35.
6. The full passage evokes the visual design of the dance: "Another stunning example for the use of pattern as a storytelling device occurs in the delightful balletto *La Malgratiosa* for two (a man with his lady) which is ascribed to Domenico [da Piacenza] in the RVBRI-CA of the Siena Guglielmo codex. With utter economy of design—straightforward passages by the man, each ending in a reverence, and half turns by the lady—the misfortunes

of an ardent suitor in his relationship with his 'ungracious' lady are depicted. He struts and bows, she turns away from him. He tries again, getting himself into her line of vision; she responds with another disdainful half turn. More angrily he advances a third time, meeting with the same reaction. Finally he abandons all *cortezia* in favor of a more direct approach: he catches the lady, who is trying to move away from him once more, and hand in hand they finish the dance." Ingrid Brainard, "Pattern, Imagery and Drama in the Choreographic Work of Domenico da Piacenza," in *Guglielmo Ebreo da Pesaro e la danza nelle corti italiane del XV secolo*, ed. Maurizio Padovan (Pisa: Pacini, 1990), p. 90.

7. Ingrid Brainard, "Die Choreographie der Hoftänze in Burgund, Frankreich und Italien im 15. Jahrhundert" (Ph.D. diss., Georg-August-Universität, Göttingen, 1959); Brainard *The Art of Courtly Dancing in the Early Renaissance*, vol 2., *The Practice of Courtly Dancing,* 1st preliminary edition (West Newton, MA: I. G. Brainard, 1981); Brainard, *Three Court Dances of the Early Renaissance*, with labanotation by Ray Cook (New York: Dance Notation Bureau, 1977).

8. The description of the dance comes from the Nürnberg Germanisches National-museum MS 8842, and the anecdote is recorded in Patricia Rader, "In Memoriam," *Dance Research Journal* 31/1 (Summer 2000): 173.

9. Program notes, "Guglielmo Ebreo and His Contemporaries," Sept. 22, 1986. It should be pointed out that Brainard counted the fifteenth century as part of the late Middle Ages.

10. This anecdote, like other reminiscences cited elsewhere in this tribute, was included in the memorial ceremony of April 22, 2000; a videotape of the ceremony is available at the Dance Division of the New York Public Library for Performing Arts with the title "A Celebration of Ingrid G. Brainard, Ph.D." Some of the testimonies were published in slightly revised versions as "In Memoriam: Ingrid Brainard," *Dance Research Journal* 32/2 (Winter 2000/2001): 158–66; other testimonies are bound together in a typescript volume in the NYPL Clippings file: "Ingrid Brainard: Nov. 10, 1925–Feb. 18, 2000," compiled by Patricia W. Rader, NYPL PerfArts-Dance, Call number MGZR (Brainard, Ingrid Kahrstedt, 1925– [clippings]). Unless otherwise noted, transcripts from the video are by Cynthia Cyrus.

11. The passage comes from the preface to Brainard, *Three Court Dances of the Early Renaissance*, p. vii.

Introduction

In her long and varied career—as dancer/choreographer, as dance historian, and as session organizer for Musicology at Kalamazoo—Ingrid Brainard demonstrated a creative ability to see the connections between diverse kinds of evidence, between disciplinary approaches, and between topics, that bespeaks the interconnectedness of humanistic endeavors. The breadth of her interests is reflected in the essays gathered here to honor her memory. They range in chronological scope from the Carolingian Empire through the later Renaissance. Moreover, there is, as might be expected, a rough threefold division which reflects the rich variety of her accomplishments: performative dance and dance history; social history; and musicological issues. This diversity testifies to the rich life of the mind of a scholar/dancer who helped to shape and steer the careers of many an early music scholar as well as many a professional dance colleague.

It was one of Ingrid Brainard's strengths that she engaged with colleagues and addressed issues from a variety of disciplines. This volume is intended both to honor and to continue that legacy by combining the fields of dance and music history in a mutually illuminating dialogue. In this same inclusive spirit, the editors present three interconnected themes, examining first of all the creation and the interpretation of the repertory, and concluding with a section devoted to questions of re-evaluation.

In the opening contribution, Vincent Corrigan discusses the development of the Office of St. James. He examines two northern French services and, comparing them to the more famous office from the Codex Calixtinus, offers a plausible chronological ordering of the various contributions to the liturgy. Clyde Brockett continues this comparative approach in his examination of Old Roman and Carolingian recensions of the processional antiphons. Brockett, like Corrigan, then uses stylistic evidence to help to date the repertories in question. In a detailed examination of the Feast of Candlemas, and of one processional chant in particular, Joseph Dyer suggests that the "creative phase" of Old Roman practice, previously thought to have ceased in the early eighth century, may have continued for at least another generation, to the mid 700s.

This initial section continues with essays evaluating the contexts—social and political as well as musical and liturgical—for musical creation. Barbara Walters explores the Liégeois context for the sequence "Laureata plebs fidelis," focusing particularly on the veneration of the Eucharist and the establishment of the Feast of Corpus Christi in Liège at the instigation of the circle surrounding an Augustinian nun, Juliana Mont Cornillon. Julia Shinnick identifies polyphonic passages in a *Liber generationis* setting from the thirteenth-century troper-proser, Assisi MS 695. She places the *Liber generationis* in a liturgical context and speculates on how and when the polyphonic rendition might have been performed; she also wrestles with the problematic notation of the added voice. Alice Clark discusses fourteenth-century citations, taking as her corpus the motets which draw their tenors from other motets. As the closing article in this section, Richard Agee addresses the Tridentine reforms of plainchant and Palestrina's role therein; he evokes the lively personal and political debates that surrounded the various projects, describing an environment not unlike modern-day academia where personal alliances help to shape scholarly and editorial choices.

Introducing the second section, Interpreting the Repertory, Cathy Ann Elias turns to the topic of performance, investigating Italian *novelle* for fictionalized accounts of music making undertaken during travel. She documents the kinds of events that elicited musical performances, the kinds of music said to have been performed, and the characters deemed by their authors to be capable of such performance. In a parallel discussion, Eleonora Beck uses literary and iconographical sources with dance scenes to address questions of where and when dance might be depicted, who engaged in its production, and what social implications those practices held. The Italian fresco, like the Italian *novella*, has much to tell us about the place of music and dance in an idealized version of what society could be. Addressing a repertory from a century earlier, Elizabeth R. Upton examines the Machaut-related works in the Chantilly codex, works which intersect with the master's own repertory through allusion, citation, and paraphrase. Like the two preceding articles, this analysis engages not just with the creators of the poems and songs but also with the audience, evoking the rich cultural milieu in which these chansons circulated.

Nona Monahin resumes the theme of dance and social meaning, but switches focus to the meaning within individual dances. Her careful elucidation draws on gestural vocabulary, social class, and gender stereotypes to offer a plausible interpretation for each of three Renaissance dances.

Concluding this section, in her paper Jennifer Nevile studies the repertory of fifteenth-century dances. For Nevile, the question is how a fifteenth-century audience might have differentiated between French, Italian, and German dances. She argues that dance was a vehicle for constructing "a larger, communal identity." Given the many constraints on travel and the distances from one center to another, it should come as little surprise that liturgical practice and dance are both bound up with geographic identity.

Returning to the religious sphere, and engaging questions of reevaluation, William Peter Mahrt demonstrates how acoustical phenomena guided the placement of singers and influenced the choice of a particular repertory or style for a particular spatial environment. Mahrt takes as his point of departure the differences between the choir stalls in the nave of the church and the more acoustically resonant Lady Chapels in medieval English cathedrals; he then discusses the kinds of repertoire linked to these spaces and the processionals which navigate the spaces between them.

Greta-Mary Hair—like Shinnick in the first section—considers transcription difficulties, taking as her focus the melody for the monophonic trope, "Haec est nimis." Hair's conclusion is broadly applicable: to understand the notation one must understand the scribe's writing habits. Richard Rastall investigates compositional techniques of a somewhat later period, those of Martin Peerson, whose fifteen Latin motets are lacking a cantus. Rastall discusses several strategies for reconstructing the missing voices, demonstrating the end results with a number of musical examples.

To conclude, we return to the dance-historical endeavor that was Ingrid Brainard's first love. Barbara Sparti reevaluates *Le Balet Comique de la Reine*, questioning the sometimes overblown claims of previous historians. In spite of the *Le Balet*'s reputation as "seminal", it has not heretofore received the kind of close critical scrutiny that a work of such importance demands. Sparti enhances her source-based findings by placing the *Balet comique* into the context of other dance publications of the 1580s.

Yvonne Kendall moves from the realm of a single work to the investigation of an entire genre. Her study of variation form evaluates seventy choreographies and over seven hundred tunes. Her article is emblematic of the project undertaken in this volume as a whole, for Kendall seeks to understand the ways in which the disciplines of dance and music approached a single genre held in common. The art of movement and the art of sound share genres, venues, and social contexts. It is our job as scholars, dancers, and performers to seek out the connections and, yes, the differences between music and dance.

Overall, the contributions attest to the manifold ways in which music and dance accrue meanings as a single piece or an entire repertory moves from place to place or is transmitted through time. Context matters, and recovering the context for these musical works and dances can teach us something about what the works can and should mean to us. We hope that it will be received as a small though fitting tribute to this remarkable woman, scholar, colleague, mentor, and all-around warm human being. May the light of her fierce yet gentle spirit and scholarly integrity continue to illumine our work and our lives.

Creation of the Repertory

The Codex Calixtinus and the French Connection: The Office for St. James in Northern France

Vincent Corrigan

The rituals for St. James, intended for the Cathedral of Santiago de Compostela and recorded in the mid-twelfth-century manuscript Codex Calixtinus,[1] are well known and have been studied by many scholars for some time. The Codex Calixtinus was assembled, so the author says, to replace existing liturgies based on apocryphal texts, or liturgies drawn from inappropriate Common sources.[2] The result is a service that uses scriptural or other authoritative texts, set to music that was either newly composed or drawn from preexisting sources.[3] This activity was part of a general liturgical reform at Compostela imposed by the Council of Burgos in 1080 in which the older ritual, which celebrated James on December 30, was replaced by the Roman rite in which his feast fell on July 25. In addition to masses, processions, and the famous collection of polyphonic pieces, the Codex contains music for all of the offices for the vigil and feastday for both major and minor hours, a total of sixty-one pieces (See table 1).[4]

This is the most familiar of the services for James, but there were several others.[5] Two additional services from northern France, spanning the fourteenth through the sixteenth centuries, shed light on the creation of Proper services in general, and on the history of Proper service for James in particular. The first is a secular service from the Parisian church of St. Jacques de la Boucherie, and the second is a monastic service from the Monastery of St. Vedastus (or St.-Vaast) in Arras. This paper will describe these two French office liturgies and relate them to the Codex Calixtinus. It will show that the Parisian liturgy is the oldest, that the Calixtine service represents a first wave of revision, and that the Arras service is the most recent.

Paris

The church of St. Jacques de la Boucherie[6] was one of the earliest Parisian churches dedicated to St. James, and a major landmark on the northern French pilgrimage

Table 1. Office for St. James at Compostela, Codex Calixtinus

	Title	Function	Service	Mode
			Vigil	
1.	Regem regum	Invitatory	Matins	(2)
2.	Psallat chorus celestium	Hymn	Matins	(8)
3.	O venerande Christi	Antiphon	Matins	1
4.	Redemptor imposuit	Responsory	Matins	1
5.	Vocavit Ihesus	Responsory	Matins	2
6.	Clementissime Deus	Responsory	Matins	7
7.	Imposuit Ihesus	Antiphon	Lauds	1
8.	Vocavit Ihesus	Antiphon	Lauds	2
9.	Sicut enim	Antiphon	Lauds	3
10.	Recte filii	Antiphon	Lauds	4
11.	Iacobus et Iohannes	Antiphon	Lauds	5
12.	Ascendens	Benedictus ant.	Lauds	8
13.	Ad sepulchrum	Antiphon	Vespers	1
14.	O quanta sanctitate	Antiphon	Vespers	2
15.	Gaudeat plebs Gallecianorum	Antiphon	Vespers	3
16.	Sanctissime apostole Iacobe	Antiphon	Vespers	4
17.	Iacobe servorum	Antiphon	Vespers	5
18.	Felix per omnes	Hymn	Vespers	(4; 1)
19.	Honorabilem eximii	Magnificat ant.	Vespers	8
20.	Alleluia Iacobe sanctissime	Antiphon	Compline	5
21.	Alma perpetui	Nunc dimittis ant.	Compline	6
			Feast	
22.	Venite omnes	Invitatory	Matins	(1)
23.	Iocundetur et letetur	Hymn	Matins	(1)
24.	Ihesus Dominus vidit	Antiphon	Matins	1
25.	Venite post me	Antiphon	Matins	2
26.	Iacobus et Iohannes	Antiphon	Matins	3
27.	Ihesus vocavit Iacobum	Antiphon	Matins	4
28.	Eduxit Ihesus	Antiphon	Matins	5
29.	Dixerunt Iacobus et Iohannes	Antiphon	Matins	6
30.	Ihesus autem ait	Antiphon	Matins	7
31.	Iam nos delectat	Antiphon	Matins	8
32.	Herodes rex misit	Antiphon	Matins	1
33.	Videns Herodes	Antip	?	2
34.	Regis vero facinus	Antiphon	?	3
35.	Statim percussit	Antiphon	?	4
36.	Iacobe magne	Antiphon	Canticle ant.	5
37.	Salvator progressus	Responsory	Matins	1
38.	Dum esset salvator	Responsory	Matins (+ first vespers)	2
39.	Accedentes ad salvatorem	Responsory	Matins	3

Table 1 (*continued*)

Title	Function	Service	Mode
	Feast		
40. Cum vidissent	Responsory	Matins	4
41. Iam locum celsitudinis	Responsory	Matins	5
42. Confestim autem	Responsory	Matins	6
43. Hic est Iacobus	Responsory	Matins	7
44. Misit Herodes	Responsory	Matins	8
45. Huic Iacobo	Responsory	Matins	1
46. Cum adpropinquaret	Responsory	Matins	8
47. Iacobe virginei	Responsory	Matins	8
48. O adiutor	Responsory	Second vespers	1
49. Inmisit inquit	Antiphon	Lauds	1
50. His qui obtulerat	Antiphon	Lauds	2
51. Ducti sunt	Antiphon	Lauds	3
52. Cum ducerentur	Antiphon	Lauds	4
53. At Iacobus	Antiphon	Lauds	5
54. Apostole Christi	Benedictus ant.	Lauds	1
55. Ora pro nobis	Responsory	Lauds	(5)
56. Ora pro nobis	Responsory	Terce	
57. Iacobe servorum	Responsory	Terce	(6)
58. Imposuit Ihesus	Responsory	Sext	
59. Iacobe pastor	Responsory	Sext	(6)
60. Occidit autem	Responsory	None	
61. O lux et decus	Magnificat ant.	Vespers	3

route to Compostela (Shaver-Crandell and Gerson 1995, 266–68). The church began life as a chapel dedicated to St. Anne in the middle of the tenth century, but by the early twelfth century it had assumed the patronage of St. James (Mathieu 1843, 289–304).[7] Because of this, it needed a service proper to the saint. There was such a liturgy, first described by Alejandro Planchart (Planchart 1976, 26–53). He found two fifteenth-century manuscripts—a missal, BnF, lat. 17351, and an antiphonary, BnF, lat. 1051—which contain services for the vigil and the feast day of the saint.

The missal transmits vigil and feast day masses identical to those in the Codex Calixtinus; the office hours in the antiphonary, on the other hand, differ completely. They begin on folio 192r with a complete first vespers, including a commemoration to St. Christopher, and continue with matins and the beginning of lauds for the feast (fols. 194v–206v). Unfortunately there is a gap in the manuscript at this point,[8] for folio 207 starts with an incipit for the first psalm of the second nocturn of matins for the feast of St. Joachim (July 26), and it continues with the second antiphon for that service.

Table 2. Office for St. James at St. Jacques de la Boucherie
Paris: BnF lat. 1051 with additions from ODO(*)

	Title	Function	Service	Mode
		Vigil		
1.	Adest dies iocunditatis	Antiphon	First vespers	(8)
2.	Sancte et dilecte	Antiphon	First vespers	(4)
3.	Christe nobis	Antiphon	First vespers	(5)
4.	In celesti regno	Antiphon	First vespers	(3)
5.	Flos pietatis	Antiphon	First vespers	(6)
6.	Dum vero sanctus	Responsory	First vespers	(1)
7.	Adnue gregi pater	Hymn	First vespers	(4)
8.	O pastor benigne	Magnificat ant.	First vespers	(1)
9.	Bonus athleta Christoforus	Commemoration	First vespers	(1)
10.	Miserere mihi	Antiphon*	Compline	(8)
11.	Te lucis ante terminum	Hymn*	Compline	(1)
12.	Pastor Bone	Nunc dimittis ant.*	Compline	(8)
13.	Gregem tuum	Nunc dimittis ant.*	Compline	(3)
14.	Salva nos	Nunc dimittis ant.*	Compline	(3)
15.	Vigilate et orate	Nunc dimittis ant.*	Compline	(3)
16.	Lucem tuam	Nunc dimittis ant.*	Compline	(4)
17.	Evigilia super nos	Nunc dimittis ant.*	Compline	(4)
18.	O rex gloriose	Nunc dimittis ant.*	Compline	(3)
		Feast		
19.	Adoremus regem sempiternum	Invitatory	Matins	(4)
20.	Exultet chorus omnium	Hymn	Matins	(1)
21.	Nobilissimo genere	Antiphon	Matins	(1)
22.	Postquam Ihesum	Antiphon	Matins	(2)
23.	Pudoris palmam	Antiphon	Matins	(3)
24.	Confessus Dei	Responsory	Matins	(1)
25.	Secutus est	Prosa*	Matins	(1)
26.	Operibus plebem	Responsory	Matins	(2)
27.	Quadam die	Responsory	Matins	(3)
28.	Auro presentis	Antiphon	Matins	(4)
29.	Innocenter secularia	Antiphon	Matins	(5)
30.	Gloriam Dei	Antiphon	Matins	(6)
31.	Audiens sanctum	Responsory	Matins	(4)
32.	Qui cum audissent	Responsory	Matins	(5)
33.	Beatus Iacobus	Responsory	Matins	(6)
34.	Pontificis anni	Antiphon	Matins	(7)
35.	Sanctus Dei	Antiphon	Matins	(8)
36.	Muneribus sumptis	Antiphon	Matins	(1)
37.	Summi Dei	Responsory	Matins	(7)
38.	Servus Dei	Responsory	Matins	(8)

Table 2 (*continued*)

	Title	Function	Service	Mode
		Feast		
39.	Ex eius Christe	Responsory	Matins	(1)
40.	Sospitati datum	Prosa	Matins	(1)
41.	Beatus apostolus (incomplete)	Antiphon	Lauds	(1)
41.	Beatus apostolus	Antiphon*	Lauds	(1)
42.	Ecclesie statum	Antiphon*	Lauds	(2)
43.	Iuste et pie	Antiphon*	Lauds	(4)
44.	Amicus sancte	Antiphon*	Lauds	(6)
45.	O per omnia	Antiphon*	Lauds	(8)
46.	Exultet celi curia	Hymn*	Lauds	(2?)
47.	Copiose bonitatis	Benedictus ant.*	Lauds	(3)
48.	Viva Christi	Commemoration*	Lauds	(3)
49.	In omnem terram	Responsory*	Terce	(6)
50.	Constitues eos	Responsory*	Sext	(6)
51.	Nimis honorati	Responsory*	None	(6)
52.	Iuravit Dominus	Antiphon*	Second vespers	(7)
53.	Collocet eum	Antiphon*	Second vespers	(8)
54.	Dirupisti Domine	Antiphon*	Second vespers	(7)
55.	Euntes ibant	Antiphon*	Second vespers	(8)
56.	Confortatus	Antiphon*	Second vespers	(7)
57.	O Christe Salvator	Magnificat ant.*	Second vespers	(6)
58.	O Martyr invincibilis	Commemoration*	Second vespers	(8)
59.	Gloriosum sydus	Commemoration*	Second vespers	(4)
		Translation		
60.	Tecum principium	Antiphon*	First vespers	(1)
61.	Redemptionem misit	Antiphon*	First vespers	(7)
62.	Exortum est	Antiphon*	First vespers	(7)
63.	Apud Dominum	Antiphon*	First vespers	(4)
64.	De fructu	Antiphon*	First vespers	(8)
65.	Alleluia	Antiphon*	Compline	(8)
66.	Nuncium vobis	Hymn*	Compline	(4)
67.	Alleluia. Adorate	Nunc dimittis ant.*	Compline	(5)
68.	Ante luciferum genitus	Commemoration*	Lauds	(2)

Fortunately the church published its rituals in 1581 in a volume entitled *Ordo divini officii beati Iacobi Apostoli Maioris* (ODO), which completes and expands on the service in MS 1051[9] (see table 2). It gives not only the Proper items for the office service, but much of the Ordinary as well. We can thus complete lauds and add the remaining feast day office hours through second vespers (nos. 41–57). Furthermore, ODO gives us the antiphon and hymn for compline (nos. 10 and 11), a complete week of "Nunc dimittis" antiphons for compline on the vigil (nos. 12–18), a new prosa "Secutus est" (no. 25), and three memorial antiphons for lauds and vespers, two for St. Christopher ("Viva Christi hostia"; "O martyr invincibilis," nos. 48 and 58) and one for St. Marcellus ("Gloriosum sydus," no. 59), both of whose feasts also fall on July 25, and who are commemorated in the James Office. Finally, it gives office services for the Feast of the Translation, which the Church celebrated on the first Sunday after the Epiphany,[10] including the normal series of second vespers antiphons for the Christmas season (60–67),[11] and a commemoration of the Epiphany to be sung at lauds (68).[12] We thus have a detailed and comprehensive view of the Parisian Jacobean liturgy.

Modal ordering is clear in the matins antiphons and responsories. Both run from mode 1 through mode 8, returning to mode 1 at the end. There is also a chronological structure to the antiphon and responsory texts. The antiphons of the first nocturn describe James's heritage, his calling, and his decision to become an apostle. In the first nocturn responsories James is called, begins preaching, and converts Hermogenes. The second nocturn antiphons describe the preaching of both Hermogenes and James. In the responsory texts James is arrested and preaches to the bystanders. The third nocturn deals with James's martyrdom. In the antiphons he is bound and taken by Josias to Herod. In the responsories he is taken before Herod and sentenced to death. The final responsory refers to his death: James, taken up to heaven, is now revered throughout the world.

Despite its late date, the ODO contains a version of a very early service for St. James, a reworking of the Office for St. Nicholas; the melodies and textual cue words are the same as those in the Nicholas Office, but the texts are reworked to refer to James.[13] The Office for St. Nicholas was old when the Codex Calixtinus was written. It was composed, or assembled, sometime before 966 by Reginold of Eichstätt. Over the course of the next century it spread throughout continental Europe and England, collecting accretions as it went (see Jones 1963, 118–20).

A service related to the Nicholas Office is mentioned in the introduction to the Codex Calixtinus where the author, stressing the importance of singing the correct service for the saint's feast, relates the story of Johannes Rudricus, an archdeacon at Compostela at the end of the eleventh century and the beginning of the twelfth. Here is the story:

> A certain canon of St. James, a cantor of his [James's] very cathedral [Santiago de Compostela] by the name of Johannes Rudricus, was filling his purse from the altar offerings, and when his turn came to sing in the office, he commemorated himself, because in a particular response of St. Nicholas there is sung "He knows how to offer fitting gifts to

his servants." Accordingly, it was the custom, in the choir of St. James
on his feast day, to sing this same responsory, but removing the name
of the confessor [St. Nicholas] and rather saying "Blessed James, now
having attained his triumph, knows how to offer fitting gifts to his
servants."[14]

The responsory Johannes reportedly sang is the third responsory in the second
nocturn of matins (no. 33 in table 2). Both the Parisian responsory and the Sarum
version of the Nicholas responsory are shown in example 1.[15] The two texts are
closely related. They often share the same or similar words (indicated in bold face),
and where the texts differ, they often use nearly the same number of syllables. This
allows the new text to fit the old melody quite easily.

The important point to note is that the passage Calixtus cites ("Novit suis
famulis prebere presentia commoda"—see the second system of ex. 1) is the Latin
text from the Nicholas liturgy, not the Parisian one for James. This Nicholas-based
service must have predated the Codex Calixtinus, and was one of the services that
Calixtus hoped to replace with his own.[16] Furthermore, in Paris the readings at
matins begin with the text "Iacobus Apostolus domini nostri Ihesu Christi, frater
beati Iohannis evangeliste, omnem Iudeam et Samariam visitabat, ingrediens per
synagogas." This is the opening of the passion of St. James which, as Calixtus says,
was considered by some to be apocryphal. Compostela thus had a service for St.
James, which it celebrated on December 30, that used the music from the Office
for the Feast of St. Nicholas (which had just been celebrated on December 6), but
with James's name replacing that of Nicholas. The lections for this service used the
apocryphal Passion of St. James. The office by Calixtus was intended to supersede
this one.

But the older Nicholas-based service did not disappear. Its texts were
reworked until there developed an alternative Proper cycle for James, with readings retained from the apocryphal passion and music from the Nicholas Office.
This is the liturgy recorded in Paris in the fifteenth century, which was still in use
in 1581.

Arras

The second service to be considered is found in a fourteenth-century breviary
from the monastery of St. Vedastus (Arras, Bibliothèque municipale, MS 465
[893][17]). The monastery of St. Vedastus has a history that extends back to the
middle of the sixth century.[18] Its founding is dated to approximately 680, when a
small group of monks built the first abbey on lands donated by Thierry III,[19] and
it was well established by the middle of the ninth century. The abbey grounds
contained a chapel dedicated to St. James, still in use in 1170, and the Hôpital

Example 1. "Beatus Iacobus intrepidus" and
"Beatus Nicholaus iam triumpho."

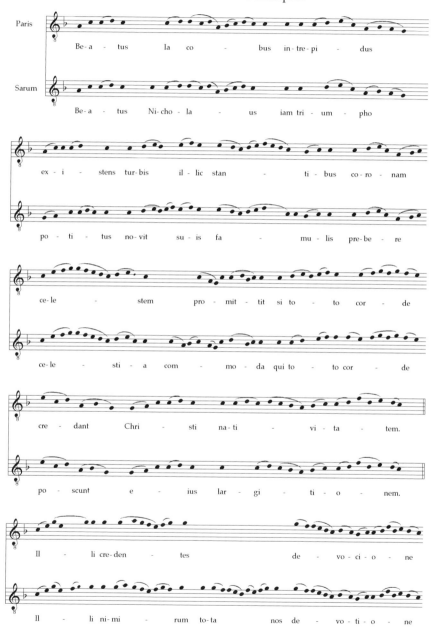

Paris

Be - a - tus Ia - co - bus in - tre - pi - dus

Sarum

Be - a - tus Ni - cho - la - us iam tri - um - pho

ex - i - stens tur - bis il - lic stan - ti - bus co - ro - nam

po - ti - tus no - vit su - is fa - mu - lis pre - be - re

ce - le - stem pro - mit - tit si to - to cor - de

ce - le - sti - a com - mo - da qui to - to cor - de

cre - dant Chri - sti na - ti - vi - ta - tem.

po - scunt e - ius lar - gi - ti - o - nem.

Il - li cre - den - tes de - vo - ci - o - ne

Il - li ni - mi - rum to - ta nos de - vo - ti - o - ne

Example 1 (*continued*)

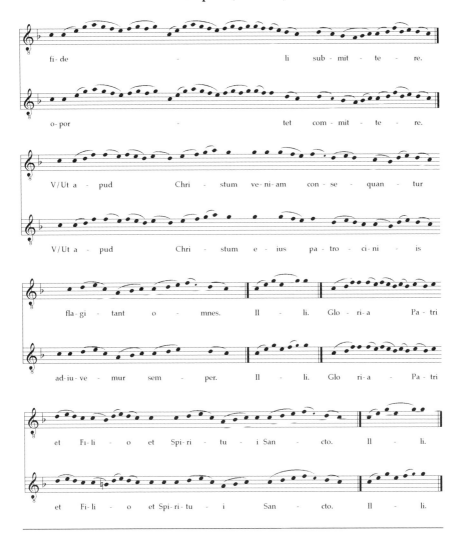

Paris

R. **Beatus Iacobus** intrepidus existens turbis illic stantibus coronam **celestem** promittit **si toto corde** credant Christi nativitatem. **Illi** credentes **devocione** fideli **submittere**. V. **Ut apud Christum** veniam consequantur flagitant omnes.

Sarum

R. **Beatus Nicholaus** iam triumpho potitus novit suis famulis prebere **celestia** commoda **qui toto corde** poscunt eius largitionem. **Illi** nimirum tota nos **devotione** opportet **committere**. V. **Ut apud Christum** eius patrociniis adiuvemur semper.

Table 3. Office for St. James at the Monastery of St. Vedastus
Arras, Bibl. mun. MS 465 (893)

	Title	Function	Service	Mode
1.	Gloriosa splendit	Antiphon	First vespers	(1)
2.	Congaudendum est	Magnificat ant.	First vespers	(1)
3.	Veneremur Christum	Invitatory	Matins	(4)
4.	Ut celestis	Antiphon	Matins	(1)
5.	Corde mundus	Antiphon	Matins	(2)
6.	Verbo Dei	Antiphon	Matins	(3)
7.	Laudabitur	Antiphon	Matins	(4)
8.	Quod a Deo	Antiphon	Matins	(5)
9.	Gloriosus princeps	Antiphon	Matins	(6)
10.	Fulget sole	Responsory	Matins	(1)
11.	Dum tropheum	Responsory	Matins	(2)
12.	Ab Iosia	Responsory	Matins	(3)
13.	Ducebatur	Responsory	Matins	(4)
14.	Hereditatem tu	Antiphon	Matins	(7)
15.	Intellexit Dei	Antiphon	Matins	(8)
16.	Quam beatus	Antiphon	Matins	(1)
17.	Istius iusti	Antiphon	Matins	(2)
18.	Per Iacobum	Antiphon	Matins	(3)
19.	Christo cuius	Antiphon	Matins	(4)
20.	Admirans Christi	Responsory	Matins	(5)
21.	Quanta refulsit	Responsory	Matins	(6)
22.	Iam addictum	Responsory	Matins	(7)
23.	O caritas	Responsory	Matins	(4)
24.	Cum prece	Canticles ant.	Matins	(6)
25.	Immenso Salvatoris	Responsory	Matins	(8)
26.	Egregiis fratribus	Responsory	Matins	(2)
27.	Fraterna mens	Responsory	Matins	(4)
28.	Insignis athleta	Responsory	Matins	(1)
29.	Auctori celebres	Antiphon	Lauds	(2)
30.	Cuius in ecclesia	Antiphon	Lauds	(3)
31.	Ad Christi vocem	Antiphon	Lauds	(4)
32.	Cum facies	Antiphon	Lauds	(5)
33.	Sacra voce	Antiphon	Lauds	(6)
34.	Iam signis	Benedictus ant.	Lauds	(7)
35.	Rogat Ihesum	Responsory	Second vespers	(7)
36.	O beate Dei athleta	Magnificat ant.	Second vespers	(8)
		Octave		
37.	In nomine	Antiphon	Lauds	(4)
38.	In virtute	Antiphon	Second vespers	(5)
39.	Magnificet	Magnificat ant.	Second vespers	(1)
40.	Dum celestis	Magnificat ant.	Second vespers	(1)

Saint-Jacques, established in the early thirteenth century, was located two blocks from the abbey's main gate down the Rue de Grauchon. Thus, the veneration of St. James seems to have flourished in Arras from at least the twelfth century, and was closely tied to the monastery itself.

Details of the Arras Office are shown in table 3. There are many differences between this service and the other two. In the first place, at forty items, it is much shorter; the manuscript gives only matins and lauds in full. There is a small collection of items for the days within the Octave, first and second vespers have only two items, and there is no music for compline or any of the day hours. Secondly, it is a rhymed office. The modes are organized in a manner similar to the other two services, but the texts consist of rhymed, rhythmic poems. Finally, it is a monastic service, with thirteen antiphons and twelve responsories laid out in performance order.

Blume and Dreves (1897, 124–26) published a secular version of this office, compiled from twenty-five sources from the thirteenth century through 1516 (AH 26, no. 42). As the editors point out, this is one of the most widespread and varied of James's rhymed offices. Individual poems come and go, change liturgical assignment, and contain many little differences in word choice and line structure. As a result, it is very difficult to point to an original version of the service. In some ways the Arras service would seem to be it. The modes are organized in the manner appropriate for monastic services. In matins the antiphons run from modes 1 through 8, and then repeat modes 1 through 4, concluding with mode 6 for the canticle antiphon. The responsories begin in the same way, but the numerical sequence is interrupted after mode 7. The antiphons at lauds continue the modal sequence begun with the last responsory of matins, moving from mode 2 through mode 7 (see Hughes 1983, 36–37).

On the other hand, the narrative is topsy-turvy, freely mixing scriptural and apocryphal elements, and is only loosely connected with the structure of the services. Antiphons in the first nocturn describe James's preaching, his rescue of Philetus from Hermogenes, the Transfiguration (which James witnessed), the encounter with the magicians whom he converted, and his sentencing and martyrdom by Herod.[20] Responsories in the first nocturn describe the Transfiguration, James's preaching and conversion of the magicians, Josias leading James to martyrdom, and the healing of the paralytic. In the second nocturn responsories, Josias begs forgiveness of James, is tortured and martyred, baptized, and given the kiss of peace. Responsories in the third nocturn refer to James and John's request to sit at the right and left of Jesus in the Kingdom, the topic of the gospel for the day, and of Bede's sermon on the subject.[21]

Some of the lauds antiphons also allude to incidents in the saint's life. No. 3 refers to the calling of James, and no. 4 to the episode of the healing of Jairus's daughter, something no other office service mentions.[22] The last makes reference

Example 2. "Ab Iosia fune vinctus."

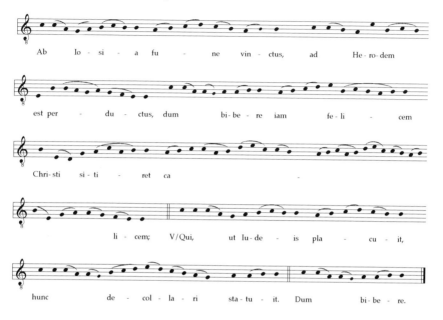

to James's nickname, the Son of Thunder. Thus, there is no clear chronological order to these texts.[23]

One example can show the difference in musical style between this office and the Parisian liturgy. Example 2 shows "Ab Iosia fune vinctus," the third responsory of the first nocturn at matins (table 3, no. 12). The musical material reinforces the structure of the poem. The first text line is divided into two parts, each of which carries a musical phrase cadencing on *b*, which serves as the dominant in this third mode antiphon, instead of the more usual *c*. The second line is also divided into two parts; the first, recalling the first phrase of the piece, cadences on *b*, while the second descends to the final. The melisma to the last word of the responsory, in a three-part *aab* form, is reminiscent of the music to the end of the first and third lines. The music to the verse is an abbreviated version of the music to the same first two text lines. The overall effect is one of varied melodic repetition of a single idea, in which reiterated cadences to *b* serve to delay and strengthen the two cadences to the final *e*. There are some fine melodic touches: the short melisma emphasizing the word "felicem," and the unexpected upward leap of a fifth on "Herodem" balanced by the equally unexpected descending fifth on "Christi." One cannot help but be reminded of secular song from the late thirteenth century.

Conclusions

These services show three different approaches to constructing a Proper Office. The first involved original composition in both text and music; the Nicholas service may have been such an office. The rhymed Office of James used at Arras is another. Here rhymed, rhythmic poetry necessitated original musical composition. The other two approaches involve some sort of borrowing. In the case of the Parisian Office, the entire Nicholas Office was taken over. The texts were rewritten to refer to James and the events in his life, but the structure and cue words of the original text were retained, allowing the music to fit to the new text with relatively little difficulty. The Calixtine Office shows the third process, one in which scriptural, or at least authoritative, texts are set to original or borrowed music.

On the basis of this information, it is possible to formulate a provisional history of office services for St. James. The center of the veneration of St. James was Santiago de Compostela, supposedly the saint's final resting place. Because of its importance as a pilgrimage destination, the cathedral needed its own unique liturgies. The first office service to develop was an adaptation of the Office for St. Nicholas, in which James's name replaced that of Nicholas. Perhaps this was the first service to be constructed for James after the Council of Burgos. Or it may, in fact, be the original service for James in the Spanish churches. In any event, the Parisian church of St. Jacques de la Boucherie preserves the music to this earliest Jacobean Office (but with texts adapted to James), one that predates the twelfth-century Codex Calixtinus.

The Codex Calixtinus itself constitutes a second stage, undertaken sometime between 1080, when the Council of Burgos mandated the Roman service for Compostela, and the third quarter of the twelfth century, by which date the Codex Calixtinus had been completed. It contains a compilation of liturgical items whose text sources were scriptural and whose music was either newly composed or drawn from preexisting sources. Perhaps the Parisian service was part of this second stage as well, in which the older service was modernized. We cannot yet be certain when the revision for St. Jacques de la Boucherie took place, but we do know that it consisted of reworking the older texts while retaining the music.

The Arras service seems to be the most recent. It originated somewhere in the mid to late thirteenth century and achieved a significant degree of popularity over the next two hundred years. The textual style is very different—rhymed, rhythmic poetry replaces prose texts or scriptural passages. The music accompanying these texts is newly composed. The differences among the manuscripts suggest that it never achieved the sort of stability that the Nicholas-based office enjoyed.

Notes

1. Reaney 1966, 238–41.

2. The apocryphal source was the passion of St. James from the Apostolic History of Abdias, which began with the text "Apostolus Christi Iacobus per sinagogas ingrediens." James (1924, 463–64) provides a summary of this history. The liturgical sources Calixtus mentions as inappropriate are the Common of Martyrs or Apostles ("Sancte Iacobe Christi apostole audi rogantes servulos"), the liturgy for St. John the Baptist ("O speciale decus"), and one for St. Nicholas which he does not name.

3. As an example, the Vigil Matins responsory "Redemptor imposuit" uses a modified version of Mark 3:13, 16 as its text. The melody is similar to "Medicinam carnalem corpori" in the Worcester Antiphonary, fol. 275, for the feast of St. Agatha, the first responsory of third nocturns.

4. The modes are specified in the Codex Calixtinus. When the mode is not specified, the number appears in parentheses in the table. This applies also to tables 2 and 3. A beautiful facsimile of the Codex Calixtinus was published in 1993 by Kaydeda Ediciones, replacing the older one (Whitehill 1944).

5. Hughes (1994) lists six, IA11–16. Neither the office in the Codex Calixtinus nor the Parisian office is among these, because they fall outside of his time frame. The Arras office *Gloriose splendet orbi* is IA12.

6. Its name derives from its close proximity to the butcher shops and tanneries relegated to the suburbs of Paris, and also possibly from the donations made by the butchers to the church. Wolinski (1999a and b) has shown the importance of other Parisian institutions (hospitals, confraternities) in the preservation of liturgies for St. James.

7. Mathieu (1843, 290) cites a bull of Calixtus II dated "14 des calendes de décembre 1119" (November 18) carrying the phrase "in suburbio parisiacae urbis ecclesiam Sti-Jacobi cum parochia."

8. The guide at the end of fol. 206v does not coincide with the initial pitch on fol. 207r, the mode changes, and the psalm incipit ("Eructavit") is not the correct one for Lauds ("Dominus regnavit").

9. This volume too was mentioned by Planchart (1976, 29). I am indebted to Prof. Planchart for allowing me to study his copy of the ODO.

10. Dates for James's feasts are embedded in the continuation of ODO's title: *Cuius dies festus celebratur vigesima quinta mensis Julii: Translationis autem, semper prima Dominica post festum Epiphanie.* Compostela celebrated the Translation on December 30.

11. See *Liber usualis*, 412.

12. In fact, this commemoration antiphon, "Ante luciferum genitus," is the first antiphon at second vespers on the Epiphany. See *Liber usualis*, 463.

13. Planchart remarks (1976, 29) that: "Given the liturgical customs of the fifteenth century, one of the most remarkable traits of the Parisian liturgy is the virtual absence of rhymed or metric texts beyond that of the prose." The reason for this is now clear: the office service is a contrafactum of the much earlier liturgy for St. Nicholas which makes little use of rhymed or metrical texts.

14. Codex Calixtinus, fol. 2r–v. "Canonicus quidam sancti Iacobi, cantor eiusdem basilice, nomine Iohannis Rudrici, dum vice quadam ebdomidam suam faceret, et ex oblacionibus altaris marsupium suum impleret, sibimet ipsum commemoravit, quod in quodam responsorio sancti Nicholai canitur 'Novit suis famulis prebere presentia commoda.'

Qua propter usus est cantare in choro sancti Iacobi die festo idem R. auferens confessoris nomen; e converso dicens 'Beatus Iacobus iam triumpho potitus novit suis famulis prebere presentia commoda.'"

15. For the Sarum facsimile, see Frere 1901–25, 358.

16. See above, p. 1.

17. An inventory of the manuscript may be found in Leroquais 1934, 1:53–54. The second manuscript, Arras, B. m. 229 (905) is described on 39–42. This manuscript also contains services for St. James, including one on fols. 421v–424v for the "Relatio capitis s. Iacobi" (Jan. 3). An index of MS 893 [olim 465] is now available through the efforts of the CANTUS project <http://bach.music.uwo.ca/cantus> under the direction of Ruth Steiner, who allowed me to work with the microfilm.

18. The following history is drawn from Gruy (1967, 33–37), and Berger (1981, 35, 59–61, 80–81).

19. Thierry III (654–91) was a member of the Merovingian dynasty, king of Neustria and Burgundy (673; 675–79), and king of the Franks (679–91).

20. Antiphons in the second nocturn contain various praises of James and have no biographical content.

21. A paraphrase of Mark 10:35–38, not Matthew 20:20–22.

22. Mark 5:37–42 and Luke 8:49–55. The miracle is also covered in Matthew 8:18–26 but without mention of James.

23. Hughes (1983, 31) points out that nonchronological narrative is characteristic of some medieval texts.

References

Antiphonaire monastique XIIIe siècle: Codex F. 160 de la Bibliothèque de la Cathédrale de Worcester. 1971. Paléographie musicale XII. Bern: Herbert Lang.

Berger, Roger. 1981. *Littérature et Société Arrageoises au XIIIe Siècle*. Arras: Imprimerie Centrale de l'Artois.

Blume, Clemens, and Guido M. Dreves, eds. (1897) 1961. *Historiae rhythmicae: Liturgische Reimofficien des Mittelalters*. Vol. 26 of *Analecta hymnica*. Leipzig. Reprint, New York: Johnson Reprint Corp.

CANTUS: A Database for Latin Ecclesiastical Chant. http://publish.uwo.ca/~cantus.

Frere, Walter Howard. (1901–25) 1966. *Antiphonale Sarisburiense*. London. Reprint, Farnborough, Hants, England: Gregg Press.

Gruy, Henry. 1967. *Histoire d'Arras*. Arras: Doullens, impr. Dessaint.

Hughes, Andrew. 1983. "Modal Order and Disorder in the Rhymed Office." *Musica Disciplina* 37:29–51.

———. 1994. *Late Medieval Liturgical Offices*. Toronto: Pontifical Institute of Mediaeval Studies.

Jacobus: Codex Calixtinus de la Catedral de Santiago de Compostela. 1993. Madrid: Kaydeda Ediciones.

James, Montague Rhodes. 1924. *The Apocryphal New Testament*. Oxford: Clarendon Press.

Jones, Charles W. 1963. *The Saint Nicholas Liturgy and Its Literary Relationships*. Berkeley: University of California Press.

Leroquais, Victor. 1934. *Les bréviaires: Manuscrits des Bibliothèques Publiques de France.* 5 vols. Paris: Macon, Protat.

Liber usualis. 1963. Tournai: Desclee Co.

Mathieu, Gustave. 1843. "S. Jacques-la-Boucherie." In *Les églises de Paris, sous le patronage et avec l'approbation de Monseigneur l'archevêque de Paris; précédées d'une introduction de M. l'abbé Pascal.* Paris: J. Martinet et G. Mathieu.

Ordo divini officii beati Jacobi Apostoli Maioris, patroni ecclesie parrochialis eiusdem sancti Jacobe de Carnificeria (ODO). 1581. Paris: Jean LeBlanc.

Planchart, Alejandro Enrique. 1976. "Guillaume Dufay's Masses: A View of the Manuscript Tradition." In *Dufay Quincentenary Conference: Papers Read at the Dufay Quincentenary Conference, Brooklyn College, Dec. 6–7, 1974,* edited by Allan W. Atlas, 26–53. New York: Brooklyn College.

Reaney, Gilbert, ed. 1966. *Manuscripts of Polyphonic Music, 11th–Early 14th Century.* RISM B IV, 1. Munich: Henle.

Shaver-Crandell, Annie, and Paula Gerson. 1995. *The Pilgrim's Guide to Santiago de Compostela.* London: Harvey Miller.

Whitehill, Walter Muir, Dom Germain Prado, and J. C. Garcia, eds. 1944. *Liber Sancti Jacobi, Codex Calixtinus.* 3 vols. Santiago de Compostela: CSIC: Instituto Padre Sarmiento de Estudios Gallegos.

Wolinski, Mary E. 1999a. "The Mass of St. James in the Middle Ages." Paper presented at the 34th International Congress on Medieval Studies, Kalamazoo, MI, May 6, 1999.

———. 1999b. "Music for the Confraternity of St. James in Paris." Paper presented at the Sixteenth-Century Studies Conference, St. Louis, MO, Oct. 29, 1999.

The Roman Processional Antiphon Repertory

Clyde Brockett

This article compares the presentation and circulation of processional antiphons in the Roman and Gregorian traditions. In both traditions these antiphons normally appear in series. These series are noncanonical, however, in that chant groups could be interchangeable, even optional. Unlike the cycles of Mass chants, which are grouped "vertically" by disparate genres, the processional pieces are grouped horizontally by feast days and are presented autonomously and separately from the Mass to correspond best to the distance and duration of the procession's traverse.

The Roman chants for processions from church to church from the seventh century onward are preserved in two graduals. The first is dated 1071, originating at St. Cecilia's in the Trastevere (hereafter abbreviated to R-C), and is incomplete; the other, dated early twelfth century, is considered to have been prepared at St. John Lateran basilica (hereafter referred to as R-R).[1] Combined they preserve the extent of the surviving repertory, which is indexed alphabetically in table 1, restricting to processional antiphons the index of all chants from Roman sources compiled by Lütolf.[2]

The Gregorian chants appear in the six complete graduals dated from the ninth century which are gathered in Hesbert's *Antiphonale Missarum Sextuplex* (hereafter, AMS).[3] They are occasionally referenced in an Ordo Romanus (hereafter, Ordo), informed in the edition of the *Ordines Romani* (hereafter, OR).[4] They were principally transmitted in the Frankish-Carolingian Romano-Germanic Pontifical (hereafter, PRG).[5] Texts 1 through 6, which follow, examine the differences in rite, selection, and order of appearance of these chants as they are prescribed for six principal festivals throughout the liturgical year and the votive occasions to which they were assigned, singly or in series. The parallel placement of the texts compares them to the northern authorities of the AMS.

The first of the Roman sets accompanies the Purification candlelight procession of February 2 (nos. 38, 8, 2, 10), compared in text 1 with the AMS, PRG, and Ordo XX texts, the last dating from 780–90. The first antiphon of this

Table 1. Alphabetical List of Roman Processional Antiphons[3]

#	Antiphon (Roman antiphoners)	R-R	R-C	non-R	Liturgical use
1.	✧Ad honorem sanctorum	135v		I-Rvat lat4770 I-NOVd G.3	In dedicatio[ne] ecclesiae
2.	Adorna		29r		Purificatio S. Mariae
3.	Ambulate sancti Dei ad locum	135v			In dedicatio[ne] ecclesiae
4.	Ambulate sancti dei ingredimini	135v			In dedicatio[ne] ecclesiae
5.	Asperges me Domine		126r		Ad processionem
6.	✦Asperges me hyssopo		125v		Ad processionem
7.	✦Aspice Domine	144v			[De tempore belli]
8.	Ave gratia plena ... ex te		28v		Purificatio S. Mariae
9.	✦Ave gratia plena...gaudium		33r		Purificatio S. Mariae/ Annuntiatio S. Mariae
10.	✧Beata es Virgo Dei genetrix		29r	CAO/E/L	Annuntiatio S. Mariae
11.	Cognovimus Domine...quia	142v			[De quacumque tribulatione]
12.	Collegerunt pontifices		69r		Dom. in Palmas
13.	Confitemini Domino	101v	94r		Letania maior
14.	✧Congregati sunt	144v		AMS 207	[De tempore belli]
15.	Convertere Domine	142v			Antiphona [de paenitentibus]
16.	*Crucifixum in carne (/73v)			found in 3 other sources, all Italian w/o Alleluias	[per totam Resurrectionem]
17.	Cum jocunditate	135v			In dedicatio[ne] ecclesiae
18.	Custodit Dominus animas	145v			In sanctorum [natalitiis]
19.	De Jerusalem	135v			In dedicatio[ne] ecclesiae
20.	Deprecamur te Domine	141v			[De quacumque tribulatione]
21.	✧Deus de coelis		126r	I-BV 34	Ad processionem
22.	Dimitte Domine peccata populi	141r			[De quacumque tribulatione]
23.	*Domine Deus noster qui (115v/89)	101r	94r		Letania maior
24.	Domine inminuti	143r			[De quacumque tribulatione]
25.	✦Domine miserere... tribulationis	142r			[De quacumque tribulatione]
26.	Domine non est alius	140v			[De quacumque tribulatione]

Table 1 (*continued*)

#	Antiphon (Roman antiphoners)	R-R	R-C	non-R	Liturgical use
27.	Domine Rex Deus	144r			[De siccitate]
28.	✦Domine tu dixisti	143r			[De quacumque tribulatione]
29.	✦Dominus qui elegit te	137r			In ordinatione [pontificis]
30.	Ecce populus	135r			In dedicatio[ne] ecclesiae
31.	Ego sum Deus	101v	94r		Letania maior
32.	✦Erit Dominus	137v			In ordinatione [pontificis]
33.	Exaudi Deus deprecationem	141v			[De quacumque tribulatione]
34.	Exaudi Domine deprecationem	141r			[De quacumque tribulatione]
35.	Exaudi nos Domine qui	142r			[De quacumque tribulatione]
36.	Exaudi nos Domine quoniam	39r	37v		Caput ieiunii
37.	Exclamemus omnes	102r	94v		Letania maior
38.	Exsurge Domine	30v	28v		Purificatio S. Mariae
39.	*In die resurrectionis (104v/74v)	85v			De tota Resurrectione ad Vesperas
40.	Iniquitates nostrae	102r	94v		Letania maior
41.	Inundaverunt aquae	143r			De nimia pluvia
42.	Lapidem quem reprobaverunt	92r			De tota Resurrectione ad Vesperas
43.	✧Memento congregationis	145v		AMS 210	In sanctorum [natalitiis]
44.	Miserere Domine plebi	141r			De nimia pluvia
45.	✦Miserere Domine populo	145r			[De tempore belli]
46.	Multa sunt	141v			[De quacumque tribulatione]
47.	✦Multitudinem dierum ... Dominus	137v			In ordinatione [pontificis]
48.	✦Multitudinem dierum ... misericordia	137r			[De quacumque tribulatione]
49.	✦Nativitas tua	126r			Nativitas S. Mariae
50.	Non in iustificationibus	142v			[De quacumque tribulatione]
51.	Non nos demergas	143v			De nimia pluvia
52.	Nos autem gloriari	104v	98r		Inventio S. Crucis
53.	Numquid est	144v			[De siccitate]
54.	Omnipotens Deus maestorum		126v		Ad processionem
55.	Omnipotens Deus supplices		126r		Ad processionem

Table 1 (*continued*)

#	Antiphon (Roman antiphoners)	R-R	R-C	non-R	Liturgical use
56.	Parce Domine	101v	94v		Letania maior
57.	Peccavimus Domine et tu	142r			[De quacumque tribulatione]
58.	✧Per memetipsum	143v		AMS 205	De nimia pluvia
59.	Plateae Jerusalem	136r			In dedicatio[ne] ecclesiae
60.	*Populus Sion (115v/89)	101r	93v		Letania maior
61.	Propitius esto Domine	33v	32v		Annuntiatio S. Mariae
62.	✦Quis novit potestatem	140v			[De quacumque tribulatione]
63.	Recordare Domine…exaruit	144r			[De siccitate]
64.	Redime Domine…tu scis	102r	94v		Letania maior
65.	Respice Domine quia	144r			[De siccitate]
66.	✦Rex regum Domine	145r			[De tempore belli]
67.	Signum salutis		126r		Ad processionem
68.	✧Sub altare Domini	136r		N	In dedicatio[ne] ecclesiae
69.	✦Super flumina	143v			De nimia pluvia
70.	*Vidi aquam (104v/75)	86r			De tota Resurrectione ad Vesperas

*In this table the following symbols are used: ✦ Unique in R; ✧ Rare (one other source found); * Located in Roman Office antiphoners, in parenthesis titles by folio numbers in I-Rvat, B79/GB-Lbl., Add. 29988; AMS: *Antiphonale Missarum Sextuplex*, (see n. 3) with rite number; CAO: *Corpus Antiphonalium Officii* (see n. 10, manuscript abbreviations in slashes); N: Nonantolan repertory.

Candlemas chant series that the Roman group presents, "Exsurge (Exurge) Domine" (no. 38 with Ps. 43:26), diverges considerably from the position it assumes in the Minor Litanies of the pre-Ascension Rogation Days where it is recorded in the PRG. The assignment of the verse "Deus auribus" (Ps. 43:2) to "Exsurge" is noteworthy because both antiphon and verse open the litaneutical processions in an Aquitanian witness, which antedates their earliest recorded codification as "Minor Litanies" in the PRG at just after the mid-tenth century.[6] There is no record of use of this antiphon in Rome for litanies. Instead, it appears in Ordo XXXVIII for the *collecta*—prayer designated for the gathering church (Greek *synaxis*)—at Ember Saturdays of the Four Seasons (*Quattuor tempora*) as well as Ordo XX for February 2. Michel Andrieu suggested that the older Ordo XX and Ordo XXI (De Litaniis Majoribus) provided the material for Ordo XXXVIII (OR IV, 262). If we look back as far as the earliest recoverable date, we should think the

Text 1. The Purification Series.

AMS	PRG	R-C	R-R
		Exsurge Domine	Exsurge Domine
		Ps. Deus auribus	Vs. Opus quod
		Vs. Opus	
	Venite et accendite lampades		
	Adorna thalamum		
		Ave gratia plena . . . ex te	
		Adorna thalamum	
		Beata es Virgo Dei	
Chaere cecaritomeni/Ave gratia plena . . . ex te	Ave gratia plena . . . ex te		
	Responsum accepit Simeon		
Chathacosmyso/Adorna	Hodie Beata Virgo		
Responsum accepit Symeon	Ecce Maria venit		
Suscipiens Jesum	En Christi Genetrix		

Ordo XX How it is done on the Purification of St. Mary

Let the *scola* begin the antiphon "Exsurge, Domine, adjuva nos" and the verse names [missing] *Gloria*

. . . Let the *scola* begin the verse at the repetition . . .

When this antiphon has finished . . . .

From there the *scola* follows the pope singing antiphons

When the *scola* finishes an antiphon the psalmist [*clerus*] who goes in front of the pope repeats [it].

reverse true: that this relatively sober chant that introduced the Purification would be a borrowing from the previous calendric Ember occasion of December from no later than the papacy of Leo I (440–61).[7] Thus, "Exsurge" with verse should have been already old when it found its way into the graduals. The more revealing testimony will be the pairing of the psalm's verse to this psalmlike antiphon prayer, discussed later.

The Marian texts "Ave gratia . . . ex te" and "Adorna" (nos. 8, 2) found in R-C are not acknowledged in R-R, which McKinnon (2000, 125) considered the more representative of the Roman *graduales*. Pope Sergius I (687–701) had inaugurated the Purification procession (McKinnon 2000, 168, 185–86) with its *collecta* prayed at St. Adrian Martyr coursing a northerly route to its station at St. Mary Major, the route also followed for the Annunciation celebration. Conceivably "Ave gratia . . . ex te" and "Adorna" were incorporated into the Purification at the pope's instigation. Since the Marian titles are not mentioned in the prescription of Ordo XX, the "zealous propagator of Roman usages" who copied this "Roman Order" could have failed to insert processional antiphons familiar to him out of a sense of obligation to his putatively papal model.[8]

The oldest of the AMS chant books, the Gradual of Monza (AMS/M)—which assigns February 2 to the biblical priest Simeon (In Sancti Simeonis) sought in the temple by Mary—could date from the whole century-wide window of the 700s, specifically the first decades (cf. AMS, x–xi). Since the latest liturgical increment supplied by Sergius I would not have been in circulation for a period long enough to be included, the Monza manuscript may have slightly antedated Ordo XX. On the other hand, these two antiphons, provided with Greek texts in the eighth- to early ninth-century Gregorian Gradual of Mont Blandin (AMS/B) and in the Messine Ordinal, suggest a Carolingian imprimatur.[9] "Ave gratia" and "Adorna," therefore, either formed part of a Purification Presentation of the Virgin solemnized in Francia, which had not migrated before 780–90 into a celebration "through the street" at Rome, or they formed part of the procession eventually assimilated into the Mont Blandin manuscript. The latter possibility might explain how (despite Ordo XX's indefinite term "antiphon," unnamed) Greek verseless processional antiphons arrived from near Charlemagne's base, where Byzantine influence is traced in the Gregorian repertory. This possibility might also be a reason for the presence of the lead antiphon "Exsurge" with its verse, not new liturgically but a carry-over from a previously celebrated outdoor procession. Further, the liturgical assignment of "Exsurge" and verse might have been situated authentically "at the gathering" rather than "on the way," since the processions appear to have postdated the institution of this feast by perhaps half a century, during which "Exsurge" could have been practiced at stasis.

The last R-C antiphon of the series, "Beata es Virgo Dei" (no. 10), finds a similarly worded text only in the earliest antiphoners of the Office recorded in the tonaries of Metz and Regino of Prüm, but not in the Roman Office antiphoners. The origin of the "Beata" as a specifically processional antiphon is indigenous to Rome.[10] Also, this processional antiphon likely is a late addition, probably newly created, certainly not for a gradual but perhaps under the aegis of the compiler(s) of R-C.

The second Roman series of the year is directed to the assembly point—*collecta* church—for the Annunciation (nos. 61, 9). This is peculiar in that the rubric in R-C directing the procession to start at St. Adrian's is attached to this day, March 25, rather than to the Purification. Sergius I is again credited with the processional complement to this feast as well as to the Assumption and the Nativity of the Virgin. Indeed, the Annunciation, along with these two other major Marian feasts, dates to only slightly later than the Purification, between 680 and 701 (McKinnon 2000, 177). The selection of music to precede the Annunciation Mass proper according to R-C and R-R is shown in text 2. The opening chant, "Propitius esto Domine" (No. 61 with Ps. 78:9, line 3–10, line 1), like "Exsurge Domine," has a penitential resonance; also like "Exsurge," this lead antiphon pertained to the quatember, specifically to a Lenten and September Saturday text drawn from Psalm 78 (McKinnon 2000, 145). Both Roman graduals follow the processional antiphon with two pericopes divided into verses 1–8 and 9–13. "Propitius" appears to be preferred over "Exaudi nos," which the governing *ordo* prescribes as the alternative to "Exsurge Domine." However, R-R reserves "Exaudi" for Ash Wednesday (Ordo XXXVII, 2). Like "Exsurge," "Propitius" is an introductory antiphon with attached verses whose *collecta* application would have paralleled that of the Purification order. R-R again omits a processional chant alluding to the Virgin, especially one like the unique "Ave gratia plena . . . gaudium" evidently composed for the ceremony at St. Cecilia's.

Only a single antiphon, "Exaudi nos" (no. 36 with Ps. 68:17), is prescribed for Ash Wednesday in both R-C and R-R, in contrast to the three processional chants sung at the onset of Lent in the AMS and throughout the PRG domain, as shown in text 3. The sole antiphon that comprises this series is "Exaudi nos . . . quoniam" (no. 36), always with psalm verse "Salvum me fac." Even though on the surface this "series" would appear a reduction in the R-C/R use of the chants found in the Gregorian cluster, the Roman Ordo XXII for Lent, dated 790–800, does not specify the customary antiphons for this rite: "Juxta vestibulum" and "Immutemur habitu." This Ordo features merely a procession from the *collecta* church with an *antiphona per viam*. Andrieu (OR 3, 259n2) claimed that "Exaudi" was the chant sung in the *secretarium* while the pope vested, and thus was not in a procession; nonetheless, he misnamed it an introit. The processional antiphon-not-introit sung through the street was to be followed by a *letania*. This

Text 2. The Annunciation Series.

AMS	PRG	R-C	R-R
missing	missing	Propitius esto Domine Ps. Deus venerunt Vs. Adjuva nos Ave gratia plena . . . gaudium	Propitius esto Domine Ps. Deus venerunt Vs. Adjuva nos

Text 3. The Ash Wednesday Series.

AMS	PRG	R-C	R-R
Exaudi nos Domine Ps. Salvum me fac Juxta vestibulum Immutemur habitu	Exaudi nos Domine Ps. Salvum me fac Juxta vestibulum Immutemur habitu	Exaudi nos Domine Ps. Salvum me fac	Exaudi nos Domine Ps. Salvum me fac

was evidently the omnipresent Kyrie eleison, giving rise to the ternary form conceivably modeled on the Major Litany series to be discussed later (see text 5). This
series structures an antiphon—probably with psalm—the *letania*, and a psalm,
perhaps sung *in directum*, that is, intoned without other accompanying chant or
vice versa. The kinship of "Exaudi nos" to "Exsurge," also prescribed in the AMS,
in that it is a brief but florid chant and bears a verse and a structure quite different
from processional antiphons as a genre, prompts one to consider the possibility of
an ancient Roman origin of both.

The fourth rite to be accompanied by processional chants is that of Easter.[11]
The legacy of this "glorious Office" that proceeded through the Lateran complex to stations at the altar, font, St. John *ad vestem*, and St. Andrew *ad crucem*
(shown in text 4), and recurred throughout Easter Week, garners interest here
for its interspersion of antiphons. The multifaceted Roman Easter Vespers Office
at St. John Lateran has passed under the musicological microscope of Bruno
Stäblein, who charted its multiple-station ritual through its Roman antecedent
Ordo XXVII, the PRG, the Roman Office antiphoners, R-R (R-C does not transmit these vespers), and various Gregorian Office antiphoners.[12] These antecedents
are dissociated from Roman fore-Mass specifications (material before the introit
"Resurrexi"), not transmitted through the AMC/C but rather through the Office
antiphoner bound into that compendious chant codex. Nor do the antecedents
occur in the *Ordo [Paschae] secundum romanos* published in the PRG (405). Still
they constituted their own processional complement for this evening ceremony
both in Rome and elsewhere.

This ritual consists of Kyrie, psalms with multiple Alleluia, processions—
each with a processional antiphon, to designated Lateran stations—and a mixture
of individual Office antiphons and *alleluiatica* with psalms. These last are of special
interest because they require the verses in both Greek and Latin, indicating the
early use at Rome of the language from Byzantium at a date probably earlier than
the putative Carolingian adoption of the Greek "Ave gratia" and "Adorna" at the
Purification. Text 4 presents excerpts that show just the subject antiphons with
their governing rubrics. For processions, R-R destines three antiphons for Easter:
"In die Resurrectionis," "Lapidem quem reprobaverunt," and "Vidi aquam" (nos.
39, 42, 70), while the Roman antiphonary prescribes "Crucifixum in carne" (no.
16; Nowacki 1980, no. 658). The procession to St. Andrew "at the Cross" is missing
from R-R, Stäblein's primary source, and from the PRG. The absence is striking
because the two earlier documents, Ordo XXVII and AMS/C, favor a quadruple
station, not the simple three processions that would discard the movement along
a Lateran porch to the hospice of St. Andrew *ad crucem*, demolished, incidentally,
by Sixtus V (1585–90). The effect of this decrease is the removal of one of the
antiphons, *Lapidem* (no. 42), in all but the earliest sources and its displacement

Text 4. Excerpt of the Easter Vespers Order.

Ordo XXVII:67–79	CAO-C, Rite 75d	PRG XCIX:411–12	R-R(MMMAE 2, 524–31)
AD VESPERAS DIE PASCHE SANCTUM	INCIPIT ORDO AD VESPEROS		
They go down to the font with the antiphon	*They go down to the font with the antiphon*	*They go down to the font with the antiphon*	
In die Resurrectionis meae	In die Resurrectionis meae	In die Resurrectionis meae	[I]n die Resurrectionis meae
oratio	[*complete text*]	oratio	[*complete antiphon*]
	oratio		
They go to Saint John "ad vestem" singing the antiphon	*They go to Saint John "ad vestem" singing the antiphon*		
			[Feria IV]
Lapidem quem reprobaverunt	Lapidem quem reprobaverunt		Lapidem quem reprobaverunt
oratio	[*complete text*]		[*complete antiphon*]
	oratio		
They go to Saint Andrew "ad crucem" singing the antiphon	*They go to Saint Andrew "ad crucem" singing the antiphon*	*They go to the cross [crossing?] singing the antiphon*	
Vidi aquam egredientem	Vidi aquam egredientem	Vidi aquam. *sive* Christus resurgens	Vidi aquam egredientem
[*complete text*]	[*complete text*]		[*complete antiphon*]

to Easter Wednesday, while Ordo XXVII and CAO/C (no. 3577) carry it over
into Easter Monday. Only the processional antiphons "In die" and "Vidi" have a
place in Roman Office antiphonaries, which happen to be contemporary to R-R
(Nowacki 1980, nos. 654, 656). R-R fails to transmit a Wednesday assignment
for "Lapidem," while both destinations *ad vestem* "at the vesture" (located in the
baptistery) and *ad crucem* are foundations of the same pope, Hilarius (461–68),
thus coexisting from the outset.[13] These internal stations show the R-R preparers'
probable interest in creating a Mass book that reflected what they knew of the
Lateran usage.

The eight antiphons (nos. 60, 23, 31, 13, 56, 40, 37, 64) for the Roman
Major Litanies of St. Mark's Day, April 25, appear with their music in a fixed
order in the two Roman sources. All carry concluding alleluias, not universally
true for processional chants but agreeable to the Gregorian taste, where alleluias
appended to penitential antiphons such as these are optional and added at random. The PRG includes an order for this endemically Roman festivity that dates
from the time of Gregory the Great and was labeled "major" in the time of Pope
Leo III, 795–816 (AMS, xcii). There is no notice of any chant for procession, nor
is any to be found in the governing Roman Ordo XXI (Ordo Letaniae Maioris),
curious since "litanies," synonymous with "antiphons," formed the centerpiece of
this all-important Roman festivity.

The music that is available is a pool of processional antiphons listed in
AMS/C, by and large found in musically notated Gregorian sources dating from
fifty years afterward. Text 5 illustrates the differences between the Roman and
Gregorian assignments by numbering the Roman collection 1 through 8 in their
Gregorian succession. Ordo XXI (9, 14, 15) explains the use of antiphons for
this solemnity. The procession takes place *after* the introit and from the altar of
the appointed church. This collectary church, named in R-C, is appropriately St.
Mark's, about half the distance between the Lateran and St. Peter's, the destination of the route. The *schola* is directed by the pope to commence the processional
antiphon while exiting to the street. Upon completion of this and the following
litany and prayer, the pope again nods to the *schola* to start a second antiphon. The
rubric continues, "let them do similarly for every church where it is the custom [to
make a station]." Only later, however, documented in the year 1140, did this route
on its generally east-west axis—Lateran to Vatican—surpass the Purification
observance in content and length. So the extension probably took effect between
1071 and this later date.

The antiphon "Exsurge," present in Ordo XX for the Purification, but now
with the verse "Deus misereatur," is found in AMS, solely in the gradual of Senlis (see note 6). The remainder of the complete AMS texts nearly parallels the
R-C and R-R ones. Only the Gregorian "Ego sum Deus" and "Exclamemus" are

Text 5. The Major Litanies Series.

AMS/C (Compendiensis)		R-C/R
Exsurge Domine Ps. Deus misereatur//		
Ego sum Deus	1	
Populus Sion	2	1 Populus Sion
Domine Deus noster qui	3	2 Domine Deus noster qui
		3 Ego sum Deus
Confitemini Domino	4	4 Confitemini Domino
Exclamemus omnes	5	
Parce Domine	6	5 Parce Domine
Iniquitates nostrae	7	6 Iniquitates nostrae
		7 Exclamemus omnes
Domine imminuti sumus		
Redime Domine	8	8 Redime Domine
Sit Dominus Deus noster		
Domine Deus noster Abraham		
Cognovimus Domine impietates nostras et		
Peccavimus Domine injuste		
Domine defecimus in ira tua		
Cognovimus Domine impietates nostras quia		
Anima in angustia posita		

displaced from their Roman counterparts in this series order. This conformity of title and order suggests that at some time following the compilation of the AMS graduals, newer repertories became current in which certain of the antiphons in the AMS sequence failed adoption or, more possibly, transmission. In fact, a number of antiphons do not survive in the PRG and pertinent manuscript sources from the third decade of the tenth century on. On the other hand, since no early Roman record of their titles exists, antiphons for the "major" litany may not have been determined or prescribed in medieval antiquity but were selected as expedient, ad hoc.

Processional music for the Invention of the Holy Cross (May 3) and the Nativity of the Virgin Mary (Sept. 8) consist of just a single antiphon apiece (53, 49). "Nos autem gloriari" (Galatians 6:14) identifies with the introit for the Invention Mass and also the masses of Maundy Thursday and the previous Tuesday (MMMAE 2, 14). McKinnon (2000, 178) dated to well after 701 the Invention with its propers that accrued to the Roman liturgical year. Indeed, the Invention was highly enough favored in both graduals to join the other non-votive festivals that merited such special antiphons, perhaps long after this date. "Nativitas tua" in its turn occurs as a Gregorian—but not Roman—Office antiphon of identical text also found in Greek.[14] However, the Roman processional text shares its melody with the Gregorian *processional* antiphon counterpart. The processional text's presence in Rome only in R-R points to a usage at the Vatican of a third principal Marian procession added to the two discussed earlier.

In their votive processional antiphon supplements the two *graduales* diverge as to content. R-C begins its series imprecisely Ad Processionem (nos. 6, 5, 67, 21, 54, 55), but the manuscript breaks off midway through the antiphon "Omnipotens Deus supplices," posing the probability of the loss of processional antiphon material (Lütolf 1987, 1:21). The R-C chants are intended for the Sundays after Pentecost, where they are destined in the Gregorian series Ab Octavis Pentecosten usque ad Adventum.[15] The R-R processional supplement starts with the Dedication In Dedicatio[ne] ecclesiae series (nos. 30, 17, 19, 1, 3, 4, 59, 68), revealed in text 6, with a history in three *Ordines Romani* (XLI, XLII, XLIII) dated between 720 and 790.[16] The initial antiphon to be prescribed in text 6, "Asperges me Domine," documented at Rome in Ordo XLI, is not the same antiphon as "Asperges me hyssopo" (no. 6) noted earlier as found in R-C (Ad Processionem). However, the second antiphon, "Ecce populus" (no. 30) with psalm verse "Fundamenta ejus" to which the clergy enter according to Ordo XLIII, adheres textually to the earliest documents; its melody in the manuscripts that transmit the thirteenth-century pontifical of the Roman curia is the Roman one.[17] The last of the R-R series, a rare "Sub altare" (no. 68)—with melody identical to the version at Nonantola, compared in example 1—is deemed "very like an Office antiphon."[18] It reflects, rather, the processional practice in Rome dating from the second half of the eighth century. This chant, which appears in Ordo XLII without a psalm but in the more detailed Ordo XLIII with an appropriate psalm benediction of "those who walk in the way" (Ps. 118:1 without *Gloria patri*), bears an affinity to the pre-lenten trio "Exurge," "Propitius," and "Exaudi," as well as to "Ecce populus" in the present series. Possibly reflecting the psalm verse, the melody of "Sub altare" seems to assume a distantly psalmodic course within the antiphon itself.

The procession for papal coronations In Ordinatione [Pontificis] that ensues in R-R (nos. 29, 48, 32, 47) consists entirely of antiphons unknown outside the orbit of these Roman gradals. Unique as well are the attachments of verse "Via justorum" to antiphon "Dominus qui elegit" and "Erit Dominus" to "Multitudinem dierum . . . misericordia." McKinnon (2000, 131) has shown that the choices of all Gregorian Mass chants for episcopal elevations are peculiarly different from the Roman assignments "for reasons not known to me." It appears clear that these unique antiphons constitute a Roman series based upon a processional complement to the Coronation of Popes.

The supplementary Antiphanas [*sic*] that follow only in R-R are those that form the sequel to the opening series of eight antiphons In Letania Maiore (see text 5). In their succession they generally equate with antiphons for hardships,

Text 6. The Procession of Relics at the Dedication of a Church.

AMS/C	Ordo XLI	Ordo XLII	Ordo XLIII	R-C/R
	Asperges me Domine			(C) Asperges me (for Sundays after Pentcost)
Ecce populus			Ecce populus	(R) Ecce populus
Cum jocunditate		Cum jocunditate	Cum jocunditate	(R) Cum jocunditate
			Sacerdos magne [introit?]	
De Jerusalem exeunt				(R) De Jerusalem
				(R) Ad honorem sanctorum
Ingredere benedicite				
Via justorum facta est				
Ecce Sion filii				
Jerusalem civitas				
Ambulate . . . ad locum				(R) Ambulate . . . ad locum
Ambulate . . . ingredimini				(R) Ambulate . . . ingredimini
				(R) Plateae Jerusalem
		Sub altare Domini	Sub altare Domini	(R) Sub altare Domini

Example 1. The Dedication Antiphon "Sub altare Domini."

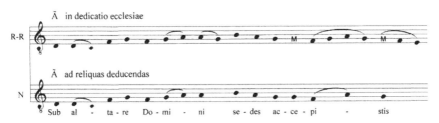

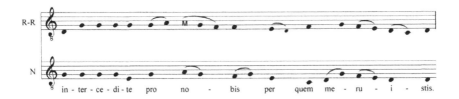

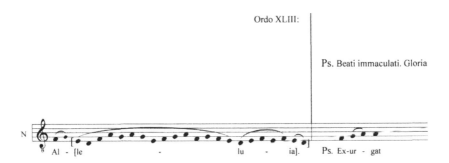

De Quacumque Tribulatione as titled in the AMS sources, the blanket title for all series that follow and not just the first. This supplement is titled Antiphanas [*sic*] in R-R. Ordo XXXVIII, 4 directs: "Once the *oratio* is finished, let the crosses with the processional candles be lifted, the choir singing an antiphon 'Concerning hardships whatever' as far as the station." Apparently an antiphon pool made possible a choice for imprecations occasioned by ephemeral hardships, and this series was separate from the specified Letania Major set. The "antiphanas" apparently provided this supplement.

Guided by the AMS we might now assume that the subsequent series, whether titled or untitled, would proceed thus: *De Misericordia* (nos. 61, 26, 34, 44, 22, 33, 46, 20, 57, 25, 35, 15, 50, 11, 24, 28); cessation of rain, titled, *De Nimia Pluvia* (nos. 41, 51, 69, 58); rain, *De Siccitate*, untitled (nos. 27, 63, 65); wartime,

De Tempore Belli, also untitled (nos. 14, 7, 45, 66, 18, 43); and saints (nos. 17, 42) titled *In Sanctorum* [Nataliis, word erased].[19] This thematic succession agrees more closely with the titular rubrics and incipits in AMS than does the Ad Processionem series in R-C. However, each Roman series admits some supernumeraries for the Letania Major of St. Mark's Day, such as the "Quis novit" that begins the R-R supplementary "Antiphons." It is likely that other such melodies that appear to be new in the two graduals, such as "Custodit Dominus animas" in the series for saints, which Kenneth Levy considered a Roman hybrid, are indeed comparatively recent.[20] But whatever their relationships or differences from Gregorian counterparts, processional antiphons might be considered some of the best indicators of Roman melody converted from Gregorian style.[21]

This article has concerned the antiphons sung during processions from *collecta* rite gathering to subsequent station. Although actual routes traced between Roman churches have lain outside its scope, the element of processing casts its own importance in constituting a link between religion and music. The sound of liturgical song by the pope's own disciplined *schola*, and movement of the pontiff in person through the streets invoking ecclesiastical traditions accompanied by impressive solemnities, exercised a singular "crowd appeal." Such an affect is attributed by sacramentarial and ordinal references to an amassed *populus*. In Rome this pageantry had the attraction that a parade in a more modern age has, and such a dynamic has indeed mustered the attention of scholars today like Ingrid Brainard, for whom events in movement through music remained ever vital.

Notes

1. On R-C, see Lütolf 1987; on R-R, Stäblein and Landwehr-Melnicki 1970 (hereafter cited as MMMAE 2). My reasons for not identifying the third medieval Roman gradual, Rome, Biblioteca Apostolica Vaticana, St. Peter F.22, are that this chant source is, first, a representative of the thirteenth century (Giacomo Baroffio, *Iter Litergicum Italicum*, Padua: CLEUP Editrice, 1999, 264), a date later than the time I project here, and, second, the repertory of this manuscript from the Vatican adds nothing of use to this article's facts and observations. On the routes of processions and Roman topography in general, I am profoundly grateful to Joseph Dyer for information he has provided that illuminates this article.

2. Not referenced on the list is the handful of processional antiphons found in the Roman Office antiphoners. See Nowacki 1980, 2: appendices 1 and 3.

3. Hesbert 1935, rites 200–214.

4. Andrieu 1960–65, v. Wherever the term *antiphonalia missarum* is used synonymously with the term "graduals" (*graduales*), it should be understood as referring to a type of liturgical book *ancestral* to the gradual that collocated musical elements of the sacramentary and the missal.

5. Vogel and Elze 1962, 1963, 1972, iii.

6. "Exsurge" heads the Major Litanies in the *antiphonalia missarum* of Corbie (AMS/K, without verse: Rite 200) and Senlis (AMS/S, with verse "Deus misereatur"); "Exsurge" heads the Rogation Days series of antiphons and supplications (*preces*) preserved in the Gregorian tradition found in the manuscript BnF lat. 1240 (customarily dated 933).

7. McKinnon 2000, 142–43. McKinnon has shown that at Rome the direction of borrowing went from certain older Ember fast days to certain newer feasts of the year.

8. OR 3, 231. The source is the comprehensive *Ordo de Saint Amand*, copied possibly in the Aquitaine, contained in BnF lat. 974.

9. Huglo 1967, 270.

10. The "Beata es Virgo Dei" that appears in the monastic antiphoner of St. Lupus of Benevento (I-BV21) and the secular antiphoner of Ivrea (I-IV106) for the Assumption is entirely distinct melodically. For the text, see Hesbert 1968, iii, (CAO) No. 1566.

11. For information on the Palm Sunday antiphons, not treated here, see Brockett 2000, 127–28.

12. MMMAE 2, 98*–99*. Note also CAO/C (cf. AMS/C dating ca. 887), CAO/M/B/S (the last monastic), and the PRG (XCIX 411).

13. OR 3, 304, 305–6, notes. MMMAE 2, 140*.

14. The text is a literal translation from the *Apolytichion* (CAO iii, no. 3852n4).

15. See Huglo 1999–2004, vol. 1, 47*.

16. Vogel 1986, 181.

17. Huglo 1952, 138. Stäblein (MMMAE 2, 77*) agreed that these three antiphons were "old-Roman."

18. Bailey 1971, 127n4.

19. The AMS series corresponding to R-R are rites 201, 202, 204, 205, 206, 207 and 210. These AMS series are followed by a number of unclassified antiphons. See Huglo 1999–2004, vol. 1, 43*–45* (tableau I).

20. Levy 2000, 100.

21. Levy 1998, 78.

References

Andrieu, Michel, ed. 1960–65. *Les "Ordines Romani" du haut Moyen Age*. 5 vols. Louvain: Spicilegium Sacrum Lovaniense.

Bailey, Terence. 1971. *The Processions of Sarum and the Western Church*. Toronto: Pontifical Institute of Mediaeval Studies.

Brockett, Clyde. 2000. "*Osanna!* New Light on the Palm Sunday Processional Antiphon Series." *Plainsong & Medieval Music* 9 (2):95–129.

Hesbert, René-Jean. 1935. *Antiphonale Missarum Sextuplex*. Rome: Herder.

———. 1968. *Corpus Antiphonalium Officii*. Rerum ecclesiasticarum documenta, Series maior, Fontes 9, 3. Rome: Herder.

Huglo, Michel. 1952. "Les antiennes de la Procession des Reliques: Vestiges du chant 'Vieux-Romain' dans le Pontifical." *Revue Grégorienne* 31:136–39.

———. 1967. "Relations musicales entre Byzance et l'Occident." In *Proceedings of the Thirteenth International Congress of Byzantine Studies, Oxford, 5–10 September, 1966*, edited by Joan M. Hussey, 267–70. London: Oxford University Press.

———. 1999–2004. *Les Manuscrits du Processionnal*. RISM B XIV, 1–2. Munich: Henle.

Levy, Kenneth. 1998. "Toledo, Rome and the Legacy of Gaul." In *Gregorian Chant and the Carolingians*, 32–81. Princeton: Princeton University Press.

——. 2000. "A New Look at Old Roman Chant." *Early Music History* 19:81–104.

Lütolf, Max. 1987. *Das Graduale von Santa Cecilia in Trastevere (Cod. Bodmer 74), Biblioteca Bodmeriana: Texte.* 2 vols. Vol 1: *Kommentar und Register.* Vol. 2: *Faksimile.* Cologny: Foundation Martin Bodmer.

McKinnon, James. 2000. *The Advent Project: The Later-Seventh-Century Creation of the Roman Mass Proper.* Berkeley: University of California Press.

Nowacki, Edward C. 1980. "Studies of the Office Antiphons of the Old Roman Manuscripts." 2 vols. PhD diss., Brandeis University.

Stäblein, Bruno, and Margareta Landwehr-Melnicki, eds. 1970. *Die Gesänge des altrömischen Graduale Vat. Lat. 5319.* Monumenta Monodica Medii Ævi, 2. Kassel: Bärenreiter.

Vogel, Cyrille. 1986. *Medieval Liturgy: An Introduction to the Sources.* Revised and translated by William G. Storey and Niels Krogh Rasmussen. Washington, DC: Pastoral Press.

Vogel, Cyrille, and Reinhard Elze, eds. 1962, 1963, 1972. *Le pontifical romano-germanique du dixième siècle.* Studi i Testi 226, 227, 269. Vatican City: Biblioteca Apostolica Vaticana.

The Celebration of Candlemas in Medieval Rome

Joseph Dyer

The feast of Candlemas on February 2, also known as the Purification or the Presentation in the Temple, retained its medieval character well into the twentieth century.[1] The observance consisted of two contrasting parts, potentially of independent origin. The first was a penitential procession during which the participants, lay and clerical, carried lighted candles. The procession might traverse the distance between one church and another, or it might make a circuit within the church or cloister. At its conclusion, a festal Mass was celebrated with singing of Gloria in Excelsis and Alleluia (unless February 2 fell after Septuagesima Sunday).

The various names attached to the feast emphasize either the visit of the infant Jesus to the Temple forty days after his birth or the purificatory ritual to which his mother submitted herself according to the Mosaic Law. The Greek names Hypapante (ὑπάντησις, "encounter") or "feast of St. Simeon," stress the soteriological dimension that links the event with the Christmas-Epiphany cycle, while "Purification" shifts the emphasis to Mary's visit to the Temple—"when the days of her purification according to the law of Moses were accomplished" (Luke 2:22), a phrase that refers to the purificatory ritual required forty days after the birth of a male child (Lev. 12:1–4).[2] Popular names for the feast in European languages—Candlemas (English), *Chandeleur* (French), *Mariä Lichtmess* (German)—evoke the most distinctive aspect of the February 2 liturgy: the candles carried in procession, then taken home to be lit in times of distress. On the following day, the feast of St. Blaise, it became the custom in Catholic parishes for priests to bless the throats of young and old with two of the candles blessed the day before and bound together in the shape of a modified letter Y.

Origin of the Feast

By the end of the fourth century, a commemoration of the presentation of the infant Jesus in the Temple and his "meeting" with Simeon and Anna was being observed at Jerusalem on February 14, forty days after Epiphany. Since in the East the birth of Jesus was commemorated on Epiphany, the calculation was correct. The date fixed in the West, February 2, was calculated from Christmas, the supposed *dies natalis* of the Savior, thereby honoring the same "forty day" principle.

The Spanish pilgrim Egeria was the first to mention this observance. In her travel journal (ca. 385) she assigned no specific name to the feast, but she claimed that it was celebrated at Jerusalem "valde cum summo honore," indeed, in a manner reminiscent of Easter ("ac si per pascha").[3] Egeria referred to the fact that there was a "processio in Anastase," i.e., in the church built over Jesus's tomb, but she offered no details about it. The service within the church consisted of extended preaching and the celebration of the Eucharist. Egeria mentions nothing about the carrying of lighted candles, a practice motivated by the aged Symeon's acclamation of the infant Jesus as the "light to enlighten the Gentiles." In the mid-fifth century, Hesychius, a priest of Jerusalem, claimed in a sermon that the day was justly called "the feast of feasts, the sabbath of sabbaths" (ἑορτῶν ἑορτήν, Σαββάτων Σάββατον)—the first phrase an epithet usually reserved for Easter, the second borrowed from that used by Jews to designate Yom Kippur.[4] Naturally, at Jerusalem the feast would have enjoyed special significance as the commemoration of the Savior's first visit to the city.

The vita of the monk Theodosius by Cyril of Scythopolis (fl. ca. 525–ca. 560) reported that the use of candles (probably implying a procession) was introduced to a church not far from Jerusalem by the deaconess Hikelia about fifty years after Egeria's pilgrimage.[5] Whereas this cannot be taken at face value as an explanation for the origin of carrying candles, it suggests that the custom was initiated not too many years into the fifth century. An anonymous mid-fifth-century homily attributed to Cyril of Jerusalem (ca. 313–86/7), alluding to the wise virgins of the biblical parable, encouraged the "daughters of Jerusalem" to meet the Lord with lamps bright with the true light.[6] Perhaps the author was speaking figuratively—the frequent recurrence of the rhetorical "today" might suggest so—but he continues with an exhortation that seems to evoke a real procession: "in company with Sion let us, people of the gentiles, meet him bearing [our] lights."[7] Later in the homily, the author exhorts his listeners: "as children of light, let us bring forward candles to the true light, Christ."[8] Cyril of Alexandria (370/80–444), citing the great popularity of the Hypapante celebration in his patriarchal see, evoked the image of the faithful gathering to celebrate the festival "with shining lamps" (μετὰ φαιδρῶν τῶν λαμπάδων).[9]

There is conflicting information about when Hypapante was introduced to Constantinople. Severus of Antioch (ca. 465–538; patriarch of Constantinople, 512–18), relying on the testimony of some "old men," thought that it began to be observed there not long before he assumed the patriarchal office.[10] His chronology appears to be unreliable, however, for he also claimed that Hypapante was not a very old feast at Jerusalem, which can scarcely have been true. Severus indicates that Hypapante was not yet celebrated at Antioch. The chronicler Theophanes claimed that Emperor Justinian (527–65) introduced the feast to Constantinople in 534 and ordered its observance on February 2.[11] This assertion follows directly upon Theophanes's report that earlier in the year (October, but the Byzantine year began in September) a plague (μέγα θανατικόν) had struck the city. It has been suggested that the penitential characteristics of the Byzantine (and later Roman) observance of Hypapante can be traced back to these circumstances.

By the beginning of the seventh century, the Constantinopolitan observance of Hypapante combined both penitential and festal elements. In 602, during the procession on the eve of the feast (celebrated on February 14), a revolt broke out against the emperor Maurice (582–602), who was walking barefoot in the procession—a distinctive sign of a penitential ritual. The emperor managed to escape and complete the evening's observance at the church dedicated to the Theotokos in the Blachernae quarter of Constantinople.[12] All the components of the Roman and Western version of the feast are present here: a penitential procession, the carrying of lights (arguably functional in the case of a nocturnal procession), and the veneration of the Virgin at the major site dedicated to her in the imperial capital. Here for the first time allusion is made to a penitential element inserted in what was hitherto a celebratory observance.

Introduction of Hypapante to Rome

The date when the feast of Hypapante and its associated procession began to be observed at Rome cannot be determined precisely, but it is clear that there were sufficient Eastern precedents for both feast and procession. The resemblance of the Roman observance to the penitential-festal profile of the Constantinopolitan ritual points to a likely place of origin. No reference to the feast's celebration at Rome is to be found in the sermons of popes Leo I (440–61) or Gregory I (590–604). Hypapante is likewise absent from the earliest Roman Epistle list, the *Comes* of Würzburg, dated slightly before the middle of the seventh century (Würzburg, Universitätsbibliothek, codex M. p. th. f. 62), as it is from the roughly contemporary list of Roman Gospel readings in the same manuscript. A reading for Hypapante was subsequently inserted in the Gospel list, but out of place and without an identifying title. Space had to be made for it by erasing the title preceding the series of readings from Septuagesima to Easter.[13] Even in the absence of a rubric, however, the pericope (Luke 2:22–32) reveals its intended destination: Hypapante.[14]

The feast of Hypapante might have been introduced to Rome from the East as early as the pontificate of Pope Theodore I (642–49), whose father had been a bishop at Jerusalem.[15] By the mid-seventh century the presence of Greek and Greek-speaking monks and secular clergy resident in Rome was strong, and this presence continued to grow through the first half of the eighth century—the result of successive waves of immigration triggered by Persian and Arab military incursions.[16] Some who decided to risk physical harm from invading armies eventually emigrated to the West, to escape persecution for their adherence to the orthodox faith in opposition to a succession of heterodox emperors and hierarchs.[17] The decree of Emperor Leo III the Isaurian forbidding the veneration of sacred images (726) introduced a severe persecution that drove many monks to the West.

Several monasteries of Eastern monks, of both Greek and Syrian origin, had already been established in Rome by the time of Pope Theodore. They settled in depopulated areas of the city and followed a quasi-eremitical existence.[18] The number of new arrivals from the East must not have been overwhelming, however, since "Greek" monasteries never represented more than a fraction of the monasteries within the walls; over time all of them became Latin. Their influence on the urban or papal liturgy cannot have been great. Few of the immigrants knew Latin, and relatively few were the Romans who understood Greek.[19] Nevertheless, the monastic presence and that of secular clergy from the East furnished conduits through which eastern liturgical observances could have become known in "old Rome."

Hypapante is mentioned for the first time at Rome in the *Liber pontificalis* biography of Pope Sergius I (687–701), a Sicilian whose family came from Antioch. He is said to have decreed that "on the day of the Lord's Annunciation, of the Dormition [i.e., Assumption] and the Nativity of St. Mary, ever-virgin Mother of God, and of St. Simeon (which the Greeks call *Hypapante*) a litany [procession] should go out from St. Hadrian's and the people should come together at St. Mary's [S. Maria Maggiore]."[20] This report does *not* say that Sergius instituted the feast just mentioned, but since all except the Assumption are absent from the earliest stratum of the Roman Epistle and Gospel lists, they cannot have been adopted at Rome much before his time.[21] Sergius revised the Mass formularies for the three Marian feasts and added processions to them after the model of Hypapante, which already had a procession.[22]

Both of these conclusions can be confirmed on the evidence of the branches of the Gregorian sacramentary, a book of prayers for use at Mass created originally for the papal liturgy. All of Sergius's revisions are found in the representative of the Gregorian sacramentary tradition known as the Hadrianum (named after Pope Hadrian, who sent this sacramentary to Charlemagne). The Hadrianum represents the papal liturgy at Rome around the first third of the eighth century, and hence after the pontificate of Sergius.[23] Two other branches of the Gregorian sacramentary tradition, one known as the Sacramentary of Padua (Paduense), the other as the Sacramentary of Trent (named after the cities where the manuscripts are preserved), are based on models that left Rome in the early 680s and hence before the pontificate of Sergius. Padua and Trent have the feasts of the Annunciation, Assumption, and Nativity of the Virgin, but they do not agree on the Mass prayers, an indication that the Roman euchological tradition for these days was not uniform before Sergius. Neither Padua nor Trent has the processions or the revised Mass formularies introduced by Sergius.

It is significant, on the other hand, that all three branches of the Gregorian sacramentary tradition are in complete agreement with respect to Hypapante (table 1). All have the prayer (Erudi quesumus domine) that precedes (and thus implies) the procession, and they have exactly the same prayers for the Mass formulary. This unanimity means that Hypapante (procession and Mass) existed before Sergius's time at Rome, and that he modified neither procession nor Mass. The collect prayer pleads that the public devotion of the faithful may gain for them the interior "light" of grace, no doubt an allusion to the candles already in their hands.[24] The first Mass prayer makes explicit reference to the day on which Jesus "in templo est praesentatus." Of the two prayers *ad completa* (post-communion), the first prays for the intercession of the Virgin; the second refers to God's promise made to Simeon that he would not see death until he had beheld the Messiah.

Bede (673–735), writing a quarter century after Sergius's pontificate, testified to the rapidity with which this innovation reached the distant British Isles. He regarded the procession of February 2 as "a model for other feasts of the blessed Virgin," and his description of the procession as he knew it ("all singing devout hymns and carrying in their hands the burning candles given them by the bishop") sounds very much like the procession known from later sources.[25] Bede was convinced that the February procession had replaced the former pagan *amburbale* observed that same month, and in this opinion he misled medieval liturgical commentators and modern scholars.[26] The Roman *amburbale* purification ritual was performed every five years and covered the entire city.

The Mass prayers for Hypapante in the Old Gelasian sacramentary indicate that the feast was most likely known in Rome before Sergius. They do not fulfill the Marian expectations raised by the title that introduces them (Orationes in purificatione sanctae Mariae), a formulation that might represent a northern revision. (This is also the title of Ordo Romanus 20, to be discussed below.) The collect of the Mass alludes to the presentation in the Temple; the secret follows closely the Gregorian prayer "super oblata" of the first Mass of Christmas, and the (generic) post-communion is similar to the prayer "ad complendum" of the last (24th) Sunday after Pentecost. Mary figures not at all, and no note is taken of the collect and procession.

Table 1. Mass Prayers for Hypapante in the Gregorian Sacramentary Tradition.

Hadrianum (27) Ypopanti ad s. Mariam	Paduense (25–26) Ypapanthi ad s. Mariam	Trent (20) Yppapanti ad s. Mariam
Or. collecta ad s. Hadrianum **Erudi q dne plebem tuam**	*Or. ad collectam* **Erudi q dne plebem tuam**	*Or ad collectam ad s. Hadrianum* **Erudi q dne plebem tuam** *Alia* Inlumina q dne populum tuum *Alia* Da q dne populo tuo involabilem
Ad missa ad s. Mariam maiorem **O s ds maiestatem tuam supplices** *Super obl.* **Exaudi dne preces nostras** *Ad compl.* **Q dne ds noster ut sacrosancta** *Alia or.* Perfice in nobis q dne gratiam	*Ad missas* **O s ds maiestatem tuam supplices** *Super obl.* **Exaudi dne preces nostras** *Ad compl.* **Q dne ds noster ut sacrosancta**	*Ad missas ad s. Mariam maiorem* **O s ds maiestatem tuam supplices** *Super obl.* **Exaudi dne preces nostras** *Ad compl.* **Q dne ds noster ut sacrosancta**

The Gelasian sacramentary is notoriously difficult to date. Its sole surviving manuscript was copied at the convent of Chelles ca. 750. Antoine Chavasse argued that it was a Roman "sacramentaire presbytéral," which he dated towards the end of the seventh century; others have argued for various degrees of northern involvement.[27] The sacramentary was compiled sometime between 628 (presumed date of the introduction of the Feast of the Holy Cross) and the beginning of the pontificate of Gregory II (715–31), who instituted Masses for the heretofore aliturgical Thursdays of Lent, which are still absent from the Gelasianum.

The Roman Hypapante Procession

As received from Constantinople in the seventh century, the observance of Hypapante at Rome was less than celebratory. The pope walked barefoot and the clergy donned dark vestments. There is no indication in the earliest description of the Roman procession (Ordo Romanus 20) that the clergy changed into white vestments for Mass, as was later the custom.[28] The solemn cortège of Roman clergy in dark vestments, illuminated by the flickering of candles, impressed Ambrose Autpert, abbot of S. Vincenzo al Volturno (d. 784). Without explicitly mentioning a procession, his apparently eyewitness account attests to the popularity of Hypapante at Rome, "where the catholic church under its first pastor chose the primacy." On that day, "which gleams with the light of candles the entire citizenry, coming together as one, celebrated Mass."[29] In fact, as Autpert explains, having a candle in one's hand was essential for admission to the stational church.

The penitential character of the procession on February 2 would not have been common to the three Marian feasts, which in this regard stood apart from the typical, normally penitential Roman *litaniae*. The processional route on all four occasions was identical, however, beginning with a collect at S. Adriano and proceeding to S. Maria Maggiore, the Marian church of Rome par excellence.[30]

The earliest description of the Roman Hypapante procession (and, argu- ably, a record of the procession as it might have existed in Sergius's own day) is preserved in Ordo Romanus 20, the work of a northern scribe characterized by Michel Andrieu as a "zélé propagateur des usages romains, [qui] travaillait sur d'authentiques documents liturgiques venus de Rome."[31] OR 20 (translated in the appendix) was probably compiled not long after Sergius's pontificate. Its title, "Ordo qualiter in purificatione sanctae Mariae agendum est," derives from the Gelasian sacramentary tradition; "Hypapante" is distinctive of the Gregorian sacramentaries (table 1). Table 2 compares OR 20 with a later Roman source, the mid-twelfth-century *Liber politicus* (to be discussed below). According to OR 20, laity and lower-ranking clergy came to S. Adriano at dawn ("aurora luscente") from the churches and diaconiae of Rome carrying lighted candles, singing anti- phons and a litany. The pope and his clergy went to the "sacristy" (the nearby church of S. Martina), where all donned dark vestments and received a candle from the hands of the pope. (No blessing of the candles is mentioned.) Appar- ently, the papal entourage walked in silence from S. Martina to S. Adriano. The collect ceremony that preceded the procession took the normal format for such gatherings. It began with the customary quasi-introit ("Exurge domine"), an anti- phon whose music is preserved in three Roman manuscripts: two Old Roman graduals (Cologny-Genève, Bibl. Bodmeriana, MS C 74; BAV, Vat. lat. 5319) and a book from St. Peter's containing various offices (BAV, Archivio San Pietro, F 11A, eleventh–twelfth century). Its simple melody, typical of the Roman chant style, cannot be far removed from what was sung in late seventh-century Rome.[32] The collect prayer (Erudi quesumus domine) was said, introduced by the deacon's "Flectamus genua/Levate" (OR 20.6). The procession then began its departure for the Marian basilica on the Esquiline.

Laity from the seven ecclesiastical regions of Rome, having gathered around their respective regional crosses, walked first in the procession (OR 20.7). The clergy (priests and deacons), next in line, were followed by two crosses and a sub- deacon carrying a censer in front of the pope. The schola cantorum took up the last place in the procession, singing antiphons (not further identified), to which the clergy responded (OR 20.8). The route taken by the procession is not described.

Table 2. Hypapante/Purification in Two Roman Sources.

Ordo Romanus 20 (early 8 c.) Ordo qualiter in purificatione sanctae Mariae agendum est [Collecta]	Liber politicus (1140) [Collecta]
1. Ipsa autem die, aurora ascendente, procedant omnes de universas diaconias sive de titulis cum letania vel an[tiphona]s psallendo et cerea accensa portantes omnes in manibus per turmas suas et veniunt in <u>ecclesia sancti Adriani martyris</u> et expectant pontificem.	29. Exeunt xviii imagines a diaconis, et cum clericis et popule veniunt <u>ad sanctum Adrianum</u> ubi fit collecta.
2. Interim ingreditur pontifex sacrario et induit se vestimentis nigris et diaconi similiter planitas induunt nigras.	Sed domnus pontifex descendit <u>ad sanctam Martinam</u> cum episcopis et cardinalibus et ceteris scolis, ubi cum omnibus induitur.
3. Deinde intrant omnes ante pontificem et accipiunt ab eo singula cera.	
4. His expletis, **incohat schola an[tiphonam]** *Exurge, domine, adiuva nos.* Et, dicto versu, egreditur pontifex de sacrario cum diaconibus dextra levaque, et annuit pontifex scola ut dicatur *Gloria*.	Archidiaconus annuit ut cantet scola. **Primicerius incipit et cantat** *Exurge, domine, adiuva nos.*
5. Deinde acedens ante altare, inclinans se ad orationem usquedum inchoat scola versum ad repetendum, surgit ab oratione, salutat altare, et diaconi similiter hinc et inde.	
6. Ipsa an[tiphona] expleta, non dicit scola *Kyrieleison*, sed pontifex stans ante altare dicit: "Dominus vobiscum," deinde "Oremus," et diaconus: "Flectamus genua," et facto intervallo, dicit iterum: "Levate," et dat pontifex orationem.	Finita antiphona, pontifex dicit "Oremus," diaconus "Flectamus genua," alius diaconus dicit "Levate," et pontifex dicit orationem. Diaconus dicit "Procedamus in pace," scola respondet "In nomine Christi."
[Procession]	[Procession]
7. Interim egrediuntur cruces VII, portantur a stauroforo permixti cum populo. Deinde presbiteri vel diaconi. Deinde pontifex cum diaconibus et duo cerea accensa ante eum portatur et thimiasterium a subdiacono et duae cruces ante ipsum.	Tunc subdiaconus regionarius levat crucem stationalem de altari, plane portans eam in manibus usque ad ecclesiam.

Table 2 (*continued*)

Ordo Romanus 20 (early 8 c.) Ordo qualiter in purificatione sanctae Mariae agendum est	Liber politicus (1140)
	Cum autem venerit foras, levat eam sursum, quam fert ante pontificem in processione usque <u>ad sanctam Mariam maiorem</u>.
	Primicerius in manu leve retro regendo pallium pontificis, cum cantoribus cantat antiphonam *Adorna thalamum*
Deinde **subsequitur scola pontificem psallendo an[tiphona]s**.	*tuum, Syon*. **Pontifex cum aliis dicit**
8. Dum finit scola [antiphonas], repetit clerus qui ante precedit pontificem.	**psalmos**, et sic procedens discalciatus <u>ante arcum Nerve</u> intrat <u>per forum Trajani</u>, exiens <u>ad arcum auree in porticu absidiata</u>, ascendit <u>per clivum iuxta Eudoxiam</u>; et transiens <u>per silicem iuxta domum Orphei</u>, ascendit
9. Cum autem adpropinquaverint <u>atrium sanctae Dei genetricis ecclesiae</u>	<u>per titulum sancte Praxedis</u> usque ad <u>sanctam Mariam maiorem,</u>
	ibique **finita antiphona** a scola, subdiaconus regionarius more solito portat crucem ad altare et facit
innuit pontifex scola ut dicatur **letania**, repetentes ter vicissim.	**letaniam**, respondente scola cum acolitis,
10. Postquam autem ingreditur pontifex in ecclesia, vadit in sacrario cum diaconibus suis et ceterus clerus vadit ante altare et percomplet letania sicut alibi scriptum est.	
11. Deinde inchoat scola an[tiphonam] ad introitum,	et domnus papa cantat missam, sed non cantatur *Kyrieleison* propter letaniam.
et ipsa die non psallitur *Gloria in excelsis deo*.	

Perhaps it followed a portion of the urban tract of the route "a porta Aurelia usque ad portam Praenestinam" described in the Einsiedeln Itinerary (eighth–ninth century).[33] As was customary for Roman processions, a litany began on the approach to the stational church (OR 20.9).[34] While the pope vested for Mass, the clergy took their places at the front of the nave (*ante altare*), after which the schola (also *ante altare*) sang the introit ("Suscepimus deus," though not specifically identified).

Nothing in this description identifies February 2 as a Marian festival. Were it not for the title of the ordo and the lighted candles, one might have difficulty identifying the occasion. In fact, OR 20 could well be a description of *any* Roman collect followed by a procession to the stational church. None of the Marian chants later identified with the feast are named, and the Mass has not yet adopted a festal character: the singing of the Gloria is specifically excluded (OR 20.11).

Two manuscripts of Ordo Romanus 15 (ca. 775–80) note the presence at the start of the Hypapante procession of clergy, monks, and laity from the suburbs with a "large multitude of pilgrims come from many lands" (a phrase reminiscent of Ambrose Autpert).[35] The pope gave a candle to each of the participants, who walked in procession according to rank, the laity preceding the clergy, as an "antiphon from the antiphoner" was sung.[36] A censer and seven candles were carried before the pope, a typically Roman detail reported by both manuscript traditions of OR 15 but absent from the earlier OR 20. Lamps were to be lit in front of every house along the processional route. The terminology of OR 15 follows the Roman style, though preserved in a "gallicanized" collection of Ordines Romani from the late eighth century.

The Hypapante Procession in the Twelfth Century

By the twelfth century (and probably long before) the focus of Hypapante had been reoriented toward a Marian celebration. The right column of table 2 aligns the "purificatio sanctae Mariae" as described in the *Liber politicus* of Canon Benedict of St. Peter's (ca. 1140) with OR 20. Little appears to have changed over the course of four centuries. Details that seem to be new might not be "new" at all but mere elaborations of what had received only cursory mention (or none at all) in OR 20. The *sacrarium* of OR 20.2 is identified as the church of S. Martina.[37] Genuinely different in Benedict's account, however, is the presence of eighteen *imagines* (presumably Marian icons) brought from the diaconiae, which by this time were no longer foundations devoted exclusively to charitable works but churches akin to the tituli.[38] These icons replaced the seven regional crosses of OR 20. Now there is a single *crux stationalis*, carried before the pope.[39] "Exurge domine" is identified as a quasi-introit for entry into S. Adriano, but now the prayer is Preces populi tui, most likely to be identified with one of the prayers for

Saturday in Ember Week of December that refers to "the visitation of thy loving kindness" (pietatis tuae visitatione).[40]

Benedict supplies topographical details (underlined in the right column of table 2) about the route taken by the procession from S. Adriano, through the Forum of Nerva and up the Esquiline to S. Maria Maggiore. The laity gathered around the icons carried by the deacons, as they had done earlier around the seven regional crosses. Mentioned here for the first time in a Roman rubrical source is the antiphon "Adorna thalamum tuum," sung during the procession, which still concludes with the traditional Roman *litania*, not with a chant proper to the feast. A rubrical note in the *Liber politicus* specifies the omission of Kyrie eleison, which had already been sung during the litany on the approach to the stational church, S. Maria Maggiore.[41] Nothing is said about omission of the Gloria, so one must assume that it was sung.

While it cannot be established that the twelfth-century processional route described by Canon Benedict duplicated the one traversed four centuries earlier, the narrow, poorly maintained streets of medieval Rome offered few options for accommodating a large movement of people from one place to another.[42] Figure 1, a map of part of the Forum Romanum and the Subura region, indicates some of the sites mentioned by Benedict.[43] Modern thoroughfares are lightly traced as orientation.

After leaving S. Adriano (fig. 1, no. 3) the procession turned left and immediately left again into the Forum of Nerva (fig. 1, no. 4), also known as the Forum transitorium, and towards the Subura region to the north. The structure Benedict calls "Arcum Nerve" is probably to be identified with a quadrifrons arch at the entrance to the Forum of Nerva whose bases were discovered in a recent excavation of the area.[44] Benedict's reference to the procession's passing "per forum Trajani" (table 1, col. 2) is confusing, since this large complex (fig. 1, no. 1) was located northwest of S. Adriano and thus in a direction opposite that taken by the procession. The procession passed by the dominant structure in the Forum of Nerva, the temple of the goddess Minerva (fig. 1, no. 5), and exited through a structure known in antiquity as the arcus Aurae ("aureus" in the Middle Ages and in Benedict's description) into an apsed portico (fig. 1, no. 6) that gave access to the Subura region beyond.[45]

Continuing along the Argiletum (approximately the modern via della Madonna dei Monti) and Clivus Suburanus, it passed S. Pietro in Vincoli on the right (fig. 1, no. 7). This church was the ancient *titulus Eudoxiae*, hence Canon Benedict's reference to a route "per clivum iuxta Eudoxiam." The procession then continued "per silicem iuxta domum Orphei," the present via di S. Lucia in Selci, so called because it was (exceptionally for the Middle Ages) covered with paving stones (Lat. *silex*). This street formed part of the Clivis Suburbanus that adjoined

Figure 1. Map of the Imperial Fora and Subura.
(Adapted with the permission of the Swedish Institutes of Rome and Athens from Torgil
Magnuson, *The Urban Transformation of Medieval Rome, 312–1420*. Suecoromana: Studia
Artis Historiae Instituti Romani Regni Sueciae 7 [Stockholm, 2004]).

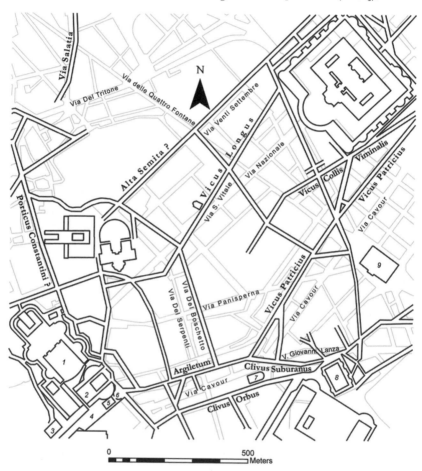

Legend
1. Forum of Trajan
2. Forum of Augustus
3. S. Adriano
4. Forum transitorium (Forum of Nerva)
5. Temple of Minerva

6. Porticus absidiata
7. S. Pietro in Vincoli
8. Porticus Liviae
9. S. Maria Maggiore

the Porticus of Livia (fig. 1, no. 8). Descending this sloping street, the procession passed by the "house" of Orpheus. The church of S. Lucia in Selci, sometimes known as S. Lucia in Orphea ("Orthea" in the Einsiedeln itinerary), was built into a large structure whose original purpose is unclear. Perhaps this is what Benedict construed as the "house of Orpheus."[46] Continuing along the Clivus Suburanus, the procession turned north at S. Prassede before ascending the Esquiline to S. Maria Maggiore (fig. 1, no. 9) for Mass.

Hypapante in Other Roman Observances of the Twelfth Century

There were other Roman observances of Hypapante in the middle of the twelfth century, contemporary with the *Liber politicus* (table 3). The *Liber censuum* (1192) of Cencius Savelli reveals that the antiphon "Lumen ad revelationem" had been added for the pope's distribution of candles to members of the papal court and certain laity "pro voluntate sua."[47] A feature of the *Liber censuum* ritual not encountered in previous Roman liturgical prescriptions for this day is the singing of Te Deum as the procession entered the church. The pope dons white vestments and a miter embroidered with gold (*aurifrisiata*) for the festive Mass. The nearly contemporary ordo of Albinus confirms Savelli's account of the collect and procession.[48]

The Lateran canons did not participate in the papal-urban procession; instead, they observed their own rite following the traditions of the canons of S. Frediano of Lucca, who had been summoned to reform the Lateran at the beginning of the twelfth century.[49] No collect ceremony precedes the blessing of candles. As the sacristan lit the candles the canons sang the antiphon "Lumen ad revelationem" with the canticle "Nunc dimittis." During the procession, which did not leave the cloister, they chanted the antiphons "Ave gratia plena" and "Adorna thalamum" *tractim et spatiose*, both to enhance the solemnity of the observance and to make sure that the music did not end before the procession did. If necessary, however, other antiphons or responsories from the *historia* of the feast could be sung. The chant for entry into the church was the antiphon "Cum inducerent." Since the canons were mainly non-Romans, they would have sung everything in Gregorian chant.

The canons of St. Peter's also had their own observance "in purificatione sancte Marie," as attested by the twelfth-thirteenth century sacramentary of the basilica (BAV, Archivio San Pietro, F 18, fols. 107–9v). This corresponds to the non-papal order of service in some manuscripts of the Ordinary of Innocent III (with the same title).[50] (See table 3.) The canons gathered at the church of S. Maria in Turre, located at the northeast corner of the atrium of Old St. Peter's. After the candles had been blessed and sprinkled with holy water, they were incensed and

Table 3. Chants of the Roman Hypapante/Purification Procession in Rubrical Sources.

Liber politicus (1140)	Ordo Lateranensis (1143)	Liber censuum (1192)	BAV, ASP F 18 (12–13 c.)	Ordinal of Innocent III (1213–16)
Ad s. Adrianum	In choro	Ad s. Martinam	S. Maria in Turre	Ad ecclesiam s. Marie aliter s. Martine
Blessing and distribution of candles		Blessing and distribution of candles to laity Ad ecclesiam s. Adriani	Blessing of candles	Blessing and distribution of candles to laity Ad s. Adrianum
	Ant. *Lumen ad revelationem* cum psalmo *Nunc dimittis*	[Ant] *Lumen ad revelationem* cum psalmo	Ant. *Lumen ad revelationem* cum psalmo *Nunc dimittis*	Ant *Lumen ad revelationem* cum psalmo *Nunc dimittis*
	Distribution of candles to canons	Distribution of candles to clergy		Distribution of candles to clergy
Ant. *Exurge domine*	Ant. *Exurge domine*	Ant. *Exurge domine*	Ant. *Exurge domine* cum psalmo *Deus auribus nostris*	Ant. *Exurge domine* Ps. *Deus auribus nostris*
Procession	Procession	Procession	Processio per paradisum	Procession
Ant. *Adorna thalamum* Pontifex cum aliis dicit psalmos	Ant. *Ave gratia plena* Ant. *Adorna thalamum* ("tractim et spatiose") aut reincipiantur aut alie antiphone vel responsoria ex hodierna historia	[No processional chants named]	*Ave M[aria gratia plena]*	Pontifex discalciatus cum omnibus psall[l]endo Ant. *Ave gratia plena* Ant. *Adorna thalamum*
	Ad portam ecclesie Ant. *Cum inducerent*	in introitu ecclesie ipsius [s. Mariae] cantat *Te deum laudamus*	Ad porta argentea Resp. *Nunc dimittis* Aliud resp. *Responsum*	Ant. *Responsum accepit*

distributed to the people during the singing of "Lumen ad revelationem" with "Nunc dimittis." The canons probably used the Roman melody, an antiphon for Lauds from the antiphoner of the basilica (BAV, Archivio S. Pietro, B 79, fol. 62v). This was followed by the traditional Roman *antiphona ad collectam*, "Exurge domine et adiuva nos." After the deacon's invitation, "procedamus cum pace," the canons processed across the atrium (*per paradisum*) to the singing of a chant for which only a partial incipit ("Ave m[...]") is provided. Most probably, this was the antiphon "Ave Maria, gratia plena," prescribed in the thirteenth-century papal sacramentary (BAV, Ottob. lat. 356, fol. 172) for the start of the procession.[51] At the Porta Argentea, the central door of Old St. Peter's, the canons sang the responsories "Nunc dimittis" and "Responsum accepit," presumably the same as the office responsories for this day in the antiphoner of the basilica (fols. 61v–62). The sacramentary does not mention "Adorna thalamum," by then an indispensable part of the musical repertoire for the feast of the Purification.

The Chants of the Hypapante Procession

OR 20 mentions merely that "antiphons" were sung by the schola and repeated by the clergy walking in front of the pope (table 2, no. 7). What were the processional "antiphonas" prescribed by OR 20, the earliest source for the Hypapante procession? If not the Marian chants (and Hypapante may not yet have been considered a Marian celebration), could they have been drawn from the traditional repertoire of Roman processional antiphons? The antiphons sung must have been well known and fairly simple, since OR 20 instructs the clergy further forward to repeat them after the schola. The block of sixteen *antifanas* in the Old Roman gradual BAV, Vat. lat. 5319 (eleventh–twelfth century) may be the repertoire intended for this and similar occasions.[52] Though no rubric defines their purpose, all of the antiphons have penitential texts ("Exaudi domine deprecationem," "Dimitte domine peccata," "Deprecamur te, Peccavimus domine," etc.) and could thus have been employed for any number of processions, including the weekday stational processions during Lent and the Major Litany.[53] Their texts fit the supplicatory mood of the February 2 procession well, and their musical style expresses perfectly the Old Roman chant dialect. The *Liber politicus* says only that the pope and his chaplains said psalms as they walked along the route, apparently taking no notice of the Marian chant(s) sung by the schola.[54] Benedict cites only a single chant, "Adorna thalamum," but this alone could hardly have sufficed for the entire distance between S. Adriano and S. Maria Maggiore.[55]

Table 3 compares rubrics and texts of chants for the Hypapante collecta and procession in five Roman sources from the twelfth and thirteenth centuries.[56] The gradual of S. Cecilia in Trastevere is the sole source of Old Roman

music for the processional chants. Neither of the other two Old Roman graduals has music designated specifically for the procession: BAV, Vat. lat. 5319 has
music only for the collecta ("Exurge domine") and Mass (fols. 30v–31v); BAV,
Archivio San Pietro, F 22 has chants for the Mass only. The canons of St. Peter's
drew on their sacramentary (BAV, ASP, F 18) for rubrics and their antiphoner
for music.

The S. Cecilia Gradual includes three processional antiphons: "Ave gratia
plena," "Adorna thalamum suum" and "Beata es virgo." The first two are translations of Greek texts; the third appears to be of Latin origin. The Greek original of
"Adorna thalamum" was part of the Palestinian monastic Office, while "Ave gratia
plena" was associated with the cathedral Office at Constantinople. This may mean
that they arrived at Rome via different routes.

The Greek original of the Roman processional chant "Ave gratia plena"
is the first-mode troparion "Χαῖρε κεχαριτωμένη." The tenth-century Typicon of
Hagia Sophia indicates that it was sung several times on Hypapante, and it is the
only chant for the feast cited by Constantine VII Porphyrogenetus (913–59) in
the *Book of Ceremonies*, where the chant is prescribed to be sung at the processional
entry of the imperial party into the narthex of Hagia Sophia.[57] The Latin translation, "Ave gratia plena," follows the Greek text closely, omitting only the conventional phrase Χριστὸς ὁ Θεὸς ἡμῶν (Christ our God) after "sol iustitie." The
translation must have been made from a Greek version that omitted this phrase.

"Adorna thalamum tuum Sion," a beautiful text that has become inextri-
cably linked to the feast, is a translation of the Greek idiomelon (a piece with
a unique melody) "Κατακόσμησον τὸν νυμφῶνά σου Σιών" (Adorn thy bridal
chamber, O Sion), sung in the Byzantine liturgy at Great Vespers of Hypapante.[58]
The hymn has been attributed to Cosmas of Maiuma (also Cosmas the Singer),
a monk of Jerusalem who was elected bishop of Maiuma in 735. His teacher,
also named Cosmas, wrote hymns as well, so there is no end of confusion about
authorship. Byzantine liturgical sources attribute the idiomelon merely to "Cosmas the monk."[59] "Κατακόσμησον" appears also in the Udzvelesi Iadgari, the
Georgian translation of the Jerusalem monastic hymnary (pre–tenth century), as a
processional hymn, thus solidifying its relationship to Jerusalem, if not to a specific
Cosmas as author.[60]

Since the texts of both chants are Eastern in origin, the Greek-speaking
Pope Sergius has sometimes been regarded a likely channel through which they
arrived at the city on the Tiber. Cosmas of Maiuma's date of birth is not known,
but since he was an adoptive brother of John Damascene (born ca. 650) and
entered the Mar Saba monastery at Jerusalem with him (ca. 700), Cosmas might
have been a mature man at the time Sergius ascended the papal throne. Arguing
against Sergius's intervention is the fact that OR 20 does not mention "Adorna

thalamon." Even if one cannot attribute its introduction to him, it must have been introduced by one of the "Greek" popes of the first half of the eighth century.

Greek clergy were enthusiastic advocates of Marian veneration in late seventh and early eighth-century Rome. A celebrated example in the visual arts is the fresco cycle sponsored by John VII (705–7) at the diaconia of S. Maria Antiqua on the Roman Forum. Identified by the *Liber pontificalis* as "natione graecus," John was, like Sergius before him, the offspring of a Syrian family that had emigrated to Sicily. John's apse decoration was replaced a few years later during the pontificate of Paul I (757–67) to make way for a revised decorative scheme. Per Jonas Nordhagen, the leading expert on the complex visual record that is S. Maria Antiqua, believed that the apse decoration of John VII portrayed the glorification of Mary.[61] Among the surviving fragments of the decorative program is a small fresco, the lower portion of which is missing, depicting the Theotokos with the child Jesus on her lap ("Madonna della nicchia"). It suggests a phrase from "Ave gratia plena" ("ipsa enim portat regem glorie, . . . adducens in manibus filium ante luciferum") and the line about Mary as "throne of the cherubim" omitted from "Adorna thalamum." Just as impressive must have been John's sumptuously decorated oratory in honor of Mary at Old St. Peter's, of which only scattered fragments now survive.[62] His final resting place was to be before the altar under a stone inscribed "Johannis Servi Sanctae Mariae."

"Adorna thalamum" translates the Greek text quite closely, omitting only one line, a reference to Mary as the "throne of the cherubim." The most striking textual variant is the replacement of νεφέλη φωτός ("cloud of light") with "new light," variously rendered as "novi luminis," "novo lumine," or "lumen luminis" (the reading of the S. Cecilia Gradual, which is at least closer grammatically to the Greek original).[63] This lack of unanimity may point to an unstable textual tradition of the original Greek text.

The (unnotated) Gradual of Mont Blandin (eighth–ninth century) transmits in alternate lines the texts of both antiphons first in transliterated Greek and then in Latin.[64] The transliteration, undoubtedly taken down from oral dictation by a scribe who did not know Greek, illustrates the familiar sound shifts that distinguish late antique and medieval pronunciation of Greek from the traditional orthography.[65] Iotazation is common: η, οι, and ει become *i*, as does υ in two of the three occurrences in "Chaere cecaritomene" ("Ave gratia plena"). The diphthong αι becomes *e*. "Cathacosmyso" usually, though not invariably, prefers *y* as the equivalent of η, ει, υ, perhaps because of its more "Greek" appearance. If a transcriber were working from a written model, it is unlikely that he would have consistently turned diphthongs into single letters.

An investigation of where the transliterated Greek text was inserted would go beyond the limits of the present essay. A number of possible combinations of events could have been in play. Did the Roman original contain the text in Greek characters (without the missing lines), which the northern French scribe of the Mont Blandin Gradual had to have read to him, apparently by two different Greek speakers? Did the model from which the gradual was copied already have alternating lines of transliterated Greek and the Latin translation? If not, how did northerners come across both the Greek text and someone to read it? Was the text sung alternately in Greek and Latin? Since the Mont Blandin antiphoner is unnotated and its format is not replicated in any surviving chant manuscript, this (together with the other questions posed) must remain unresolved.

The Music of "Adorna thalamum tuum" and "Ave gratia plena"

However the pieces happened to arrive in Rome, they were translated into Latin and set to music, probably in the early eighth century by members of the papal schola cantorum. This might place them among the last chants composed for the urban musical repertoire, whose "creative phase" supposedly ended about 715, when the chants required for the newly liturgical Thursdays of Lent were not composed anew but borrowed from other post-Pentecost Masses.

"Adorna thalamum tuum"

The ductus of the Old Roman setting of "Adorna thalamum" (example 1) manifests virtually no relationship to the surviving Byzantine melody of "Κατακόσμησον," though it can be no accident, as Christian Troelsgård has sought to demonstrate, that the melodic-poetic structure of the Greek chant is imitated in the Latin equivalent.[66] Nothing in the structure of the Latin translation would have suggested this, so one must assume that the adaptors knew the Greek melody. The translator did not, however, strive to replicate the paired syllable count of the Greek original.[67] The mode of the Byzantine piece, *echos barys*, corresponds in general terms to the F-mode of the Old Roman chant adaptation, but the musical style of "Adorna" points unmistakably to indigenous origins. (The capital letters in example 1 reflect Troelsgård's analysis of the Greek melody, not that of the Old Roman or Gregorian/Frankish versions.)

The Gregorian melody (to which the Old Roman version is compared in example 1) is an exemplary case of the "translation" of one musical idiom into another.[68] While the Old Roman "Adorna thalamum" exemplifies the meditative ductus characteristic of urban chant, the Gregorian redaction of the melody just as strongly embodies a proclamatory tone, whose every phrase manifests the distinctive manner of that musical idiom. A characteristically Italianate podatus and random movement between *F* and *a* soften the recitation effect of the Old Roman version, while the spare Gregorian version insists strongly on an embellished

Example 1. "Adorna thalamum tuum."
a. Cologny-Genève, Biblioteca Bodmeriana, C74, fol. 29. b. Rome, Biblioteca Casanatense, MS 1714 (Transcribed with permission from James M. Borders, *Early Medieval Chants from Nonantola* [Madison, WI: A–R Editions], 3:21–22).

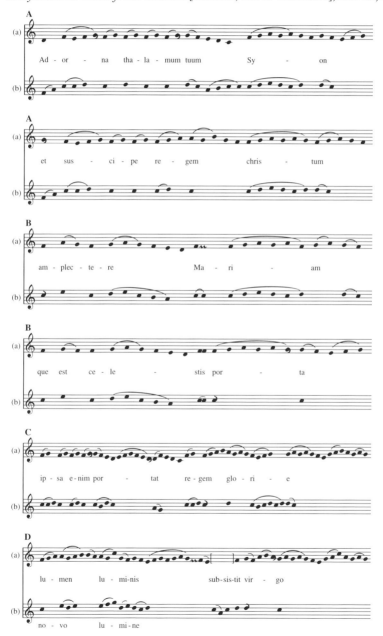

Example 1 (*continued*)

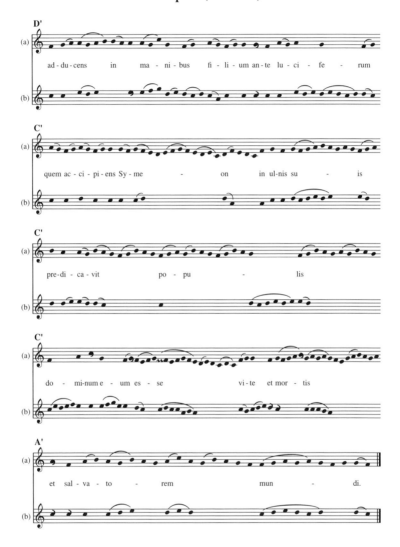

recitation on the dominant of the mode (c). The scrolling, narrow-range melody of the Old Roman version, devoid of such a focal point and moving mostly within the fourth E-a (approximately a fifth below the Gregorian tessitura), produces a more ambiguous sense of articulation. The few melismas on final syllables in the Old Roman version are truncated in the Gregorian redaction.

"Ave gratia plena"

The Old Roman version of "Ave gratia plena" (example 2) is more florid than the Gregorian, which seems to have "pruned" the longer neumes of the Roman melody, neume by neume, recasting it in an entirely different musical idiom.[69] (See especially the last two lines.) The Old Roman musical setting of "Ave gratia plena" is more elaborate than the usual Byzantine apolytikion, but comparison with a Byzantine model is in this case impossible, since a medieval melody for "Χαῖρε κεχαριτωμένη" has not been preserved. The antiphon "Beata es virgo Maria," the last processional chant in the S. Cecilia Gradual, concludes with a triple "Alleluia," unusual for a chant outside of Paschaltide. In the Gregorian tradition it serves as a responsory for the feast of the Assumption, but it is absent from the Antiphoner of St. Peter's (BAV, ASP, B 79). The Old Roman and Gregorian/Frankish versions are extraordinarily close, so much so that one might be inclined to interpret the Old Roman version of this chant as the "romanisation" of an imported melody.

Conclusions

From the foregoing there emerges a clearer, albeit not entirely unclouded, picture of the historical development of Hypapante at Rome, the feast's related procession, and the Marian chants associated with it. Beginning as a local commemoration at Jerusalem in the late fourth century and disseminated in the East, by the beginning of the seventh century Hypapante at Constantinople had taken the shape of a penitential procession followed by a liturgy at the church of the Theotokos in the Blachernae quarter. Hypapante was introduced to Rome shortly after the mid-seventh century, almost certainly due to the presence there of numerous Greek-speaking clerics and monks who had taken refuge there to escape Muslim conquests and theological controversy.

The first mention of a Roman celebration of the feast "of St. Simeon, which the Greeks call Ypapanti" with an associated procession occurs in the *Liber pontificalis*, which links Hypapante with a reorganization of Marian feasts by Pope Sergius I (687–701). The feast's description in Ordo Romanus 20 seems to represent this early stage of development. The earliest musical repertoire for this and other Roman processions may be preserved in the series of sixteen antiphons in the Old Roman gradual BAV, Vat. lat. 5319. A switch to a Marian emphasis and evidence of Byzantine influence on the celebration of Hypapante at Rome are two Greek chants that were translated into Latin in the early eighth century and given original musical settings in the Old Roman chant idiom. "Adorna thalamum tuum" and "Ave gratia plena" were incorporated in the earliest transmission of the Roman repertoire to the Carolingians, there to be recast according to the stylistic criteria of Frankish singers.

Example 2. "Ave gratia plena."

A. Cologny-Genève, Biblioteca Bodmeriana, C74, fol. 28v–29. b. Rome, Biblioteca Nazionale, MS 1343, fol. 53 (Transcribed with permission from James M. Borders, *Early Medieval Chants from Nonantola* [Madison, WI: A–R Editions], 3:21).

Example 2 (*continued*)

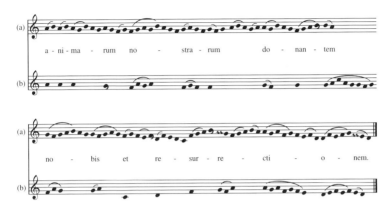

a - ni - ma - rum   no   -   stra - rum   do - nan - tem

no   -   bis   et   re - sur - re - cti   -   o - nem.

Appendix
Ordo Romanus 20
Concerning what is to be done on the Purification of St. Mary

1. That day, near daybreak, everyone proceeds from all the *diaconiae* and title churches with a litany or/and singing antiphons and carrying lighted candles in their hands; they go in groups to the church of St. Hadrian the martyr and await the pope.

2. Meanwhile, the pope proceeds to the sacristy and puts on dark vestments; the deacons likewise put on dark *planetae*.

3. Then everyone approaches the pope; they receive from him a single candle.

4. This having been done, the schola begins the antiphon "Exurge domine, adiuva nos." At the conclusion of the verse, the pope leaves the sacristy with deacons to his right and left, and the pope signals the schola to begin the Gloria.

5. Then approaching the altar, [the pope,] bowing to pray until the schola begins the *versus ad repetendum*, rises from prayer, venerates the altar, as do the deacons in turn.

6. At the conclusion of the antiphon the schola does not sing Kyrie eleison, but the pope, standing before the altar, says "Dominus vobiscum" then "Oremus," then the deacon [says] "Flectamus genua," and after a pause he again says "Levate," and the pope says the prayer.

7. Meanwhile, the seven crosses come forward, [each] carried by a crossbearer in the midst of the people. Thereafter the priests and deacons. Then the pope with the [cardinal] deacons, and two candles carried before him and a censer [carried by] a subdeacon and two crosses before him. Then the schola, singing antiphons, follows the pope.

8. When the schola finishes [an antiphon], it is repeated by the clergy who walk in front of the pope.

9. When they approach the atrium of the Church of the Holy Mother of God [S. Maria Maggiore], the pope gives a signal to begin the litany, [which is] repeated three times in alternation.

10. After the pope enters the church, he goes to the sacristy with his deacons; the rest of the clergy goes before the altar and finishes the litany, as is written elsewhere.

11. The schola begins the introit antiphon; on that day "Gloria in excelsis deo" is not sung.

Notes

1. On the history of the liturgical observance see Baumstark 1909; Franz 1909, 1:442–53; Righetti 1969, 2:115–20; Moreau 1935; Deug-Su 1974 (primarily an analysis of sermons); Stevenson 1990; Nilles 1896–97, 1:91–93; Auf der Maur 1983, 176–79; Martimort 1955, esp. 51–53.

2. The Purification is treated by Capelle (1965, 766–85) among the "fêtes mariales."

3. [Egeria] 1982, 254–56; [Egeria] 1968, 96–97.

4. *Hesychii presbyteri Sermones*, PG 93:1468. Hesychius began the sermon with the words, "This feast is called 'of the purifications'" (ἡ μὲν ἑορτὴ λέγεται καθαρσίων), thus announcing a theme that pervades the sermon.

5. Cyril of Scythopolis 1939, 236; Cyril of Scythopolis 1991, 262–68.

6. "Θυγατέρες Ἰερουσαλὴμ ἐξέλθετε εἰς ἀπάντησιν αὐτοῦ, τὰς λαμπάδας φαιδρῶς τῷ φωτὶ τῷ ἀληθινῷ ἐξάψατε"; Cyril of Jerusalem (attrib.), PG 33:1189.

7. "Μετὰ τῆς Στὼν οἱ τῶν ἐθνῶν λαοὶ φωτοφοροῦντες ὑπαντήσωμεν"; ibid.

8. "ὡς υἱοὶ φωτὸς τοὺς κηροὺς τῷ φοτὶ τῷ ἀληθινῷ Χριστῷ προσάγωμεν"; PG 33:1201.

9. Cyril of Alexandria, PG 77:1041.

10. Homily 125; Severus of Antioch (1960, 247), as cited in Stevenson 1990, 51.

11. Theophanes, *Chronographia*, anno 534; PG 108:488. The historian Nicephoros Callistos also attributed the obligation of a universal observance to Justinian (*Historia Ecclesiastica* 17.28; PG 147:292); George Cedrenos seems to link Hypapante with a disastrous earthquake that struck Antioch in the ninth year of Justinian's reign (*Historiarum Compendium*; PG 121:697–700).

12. Higgins 1952.

13. Morin 1911, 301–2 and n. 4; Klauser 1935, 17 (note to pericope 40).

14. Unfortunately, the first volume of the homiliary of the Roman priest Agimond (BAV, Vat. lat. 3835–36; ca. 700), which might have included sermons for Hypapante, has not survived.

15. Baumstark 1927, 156*.

16. Ekonomou 2007, 244–97; Llewellyn 1981; Llewellyn 1974–2003.

17. For a recent, many-faceted overview that takes account of theological controversies and the liturgy, see Ekonomou 2007, esp. 79–157.

18. Antonelli 1928; Michel 1952; Grégoire 1981; and especially Sansterre 1983, 1:31–51; Sansterre 1988.

19. Steinacker 1954; Noble 1985.

20. "Constituit autem ut diebus Adnuntiationis domini, Dormitionis et Nativitatis sanctae dei genetricis semperque virginis Marie ac sancti Symeonis, quod Ypapanti Greci appellant, letania exeat a sancto Hadriano et ad sanctam Mariam populus occurrat"; Duchesne 1886–92, 1:376 (hereafter LP); trans. Davis, 89. The LP uses the term "Ypopanti" again in the vita of Benedict III (855–58), who donated to St. Peter's a textile depicting the Annunciation, Hypopante, and Jesus's questioning of the teachers in the Temple when he was twelve years of age (LP 2:146).

21. They were later inserted in the Würzburg Gospel list (mid-seventh century); Morin 1911.

22. The wording of the text might be construed to imply that the Annunciation was still considered a feast of the Lord, not of Mary.

23. Deshusses 1992, 123–24; Dell'Oro, Rogger, 121–22. The branch of the Gregorian

Sacramentary known as the Paduense (a redaction ca. 670–80) has the title "Ypapanti ad Sanctam Mariam"; see Catella, Dell'Oro, and Martini 2005, 195.

24. Deshusses 1992, 1:123–24 (no. 27). The prayer appears in the Frankish eighth-century Gelasian sacramentaries; see Saint-Roch 1992, 735–40 and tables I–IV.

25. "Plebs universa cum sacerdotibus ac ministris hymni modula devotis per ecclesias perque congrua urbis loca procedit, datasque a pontifice cuncti cereas in manibus gestant ardentes. Et augescente bona consuetudine, id ipsum in caeteris quoque eiusdem beatae matris et perpetuae virginis festivitatibus agere didicit"; *De temporum ratione* 12 (Bede 1977, 2:323); the translation is by Faith Wallis in Bede 1999, 49. Bede certainly had access to the *Liber pontificalis.*

26. For example, Durandus 1995–2000, 3:41–42; see also De Bruyne 1922. On the implausibility of linking Hypapante with the pagan *lupercalia* (February 13–15), see Schäblin 1995. On the other hand, the connection between the pagan *robigalia* and the Major Litany, both with respect to the date (April 25) and the route of the procession, could not be more evident.

27. Chavasse 1958, 401–2. For the Gelasian text see Mohlberg 1968, 133. Chavasse was opposed by Coebergh who regarded the Gelasian as "l'oeuvre de pélerins étrangers, probablement un couple de moines-prêtres romanisants, utilisants principalement des sources romaines, mais en les arrangeant selon leur dévotion et leur gré" (Coebergh 1961, 88); see also Schmidt, 1957, 2:346–48 ("liber liturgicus qui materiam pure romanam continens, . . . liturgiam Urbis . . . proprio ingenio circumstantiis extra-romanis adaptavit").

28. *Vestimenta nigra* are specified in both Ordo 20.2 (Andrieu 1931–61, 3:235) and Ordo 50.83 (Vogel and Elze 1963–72, 2:6 [99.13]). According to the Ordinal of Gregory X (1271–76), the clerical participants in the procession walked "in nigris sive in violaciis coloribus et nudis pedibus"; white vestments are prescribed for Mass; see Van Dijk and Walker 1975, 571. A later papal ceremonial, compiled at Avignon by Cardinal Giacomo Stefaneschi in the first quarter of the fourteenth century, supplies prolific details about liturgical vestments for what seems to have become by that time a private court observance; Dykmans 1977–81, 2:354–57.

29. "Sic a multis prae ceteris anni sollemnitatibus honoratior habetur, maxime autem eo loco, quo primatum Ecclesia catholica in primo pastore sortita est. In tanta enim reverentia ab illis habetur, ut ea die cuncta civitatis turba in unum collecta, immensis cereorum luminibus coruscans, missarum sollemnia devotissime concelebrent"; Ambrose Autpert (1979, 985), as cited in Deug-Su 1974, 147. The sermon is sometimes attributed erroneously to Fulgentius of Ruspe.

30. S. Adriano, the former Curia Iulia established by Julius Caesar (AD 44) and rebuilt in 303 under Diocletian (284–305), was converted by Pope Honorius I (625–38) into a church. Since it could not have been the starting point for a Christian procession before the time of Honorius, this might narrow somewhat the chronology of the Hypapante procession at Rome. Walter Howard Frere gave precedence to the Nativity of the Virgin among the processions. Since September 8 was already the Feast of St. Hadrian, a meeting at S. Adriano before proceeding to the Marian basilica on the Esquiline would have been natural: "if it began thus, it would be found easy to extend the association to the other three festivals" (Frere 1930, 93). This interesting speculation has not been confirmed by subsequent research.

31. Andrieu 1931–61, 3:235–36 and 231; the oldest source of OR 20 (Paris, BnF, lat. MS 974) is dated "around 780–790" by Vogel 1986, 169.

32. Stäblein 1970, 509.

33. del Lungo 2004, 68, 134–35, and pl. 20; see also Pani Ermini 2001, pl. XI (itinerary VII).

34. The Romano-Germanic Pontifical (ca. 963), after first describing the "normal" conclusion of the procession, with the antiphon "Cum inducerent" and the prayer Domine Iesu Christe qui hodierna die in nostrae carnis substantia, records an alternative conclusion: "secundum Romanos autem, cum appropinquaverint atrio sanctae Mariae, faciendae sunt letaniae"; Vogel and Elze 1963–72, 2:10 (99.29).

35. "Colleguntur omnes tam clerus romanae ecclesiae quam et omnes monachi monasteriorum cum omni populo suburbano seu et copiosa multitudo peregrinorum de quacumque provintia congregati"; OR 15.79, (Andrieu 1931–61, 3:113). The manuscripts in question are Montpellier, Fac. de Médecine, cod. 412 (part of Andrieu's "collection A") and Wolfenbüttel, Herzog August Bibliothek, MS 4175. The Hypapante rubric in the St. Gall 349 manuscript of OR 15 is extremely brief, mentioning only S. Adriano and S. Maria Maggiore. Its author, according to Vogel, "had little [direct] experience of the City and its peculiarities" (Vogel 1986, 153).

36. "Venientes ad ecclesiam beati Adriani mane prima et accipiunt de manu pontificis unusquis cereum unum . . . et accendentibus cereis portantes in manibus unusquisque in ordine suo quo militat, antiphonam cantando in processione, sicut continet antiphonarius" (the reading of the Wolfenbüttel manuscript); ed. Andrieu 1931–61, 3:113. The Montpellier manuscript also implies that everyone joined in the singing: "omnes una voce canentes, unusquis in ordine suo quo militat."

37. Lombardi 1996, 275.

38. On the *imagines* see Wolf 1990, 49–50; there is a detailed analysis in de Blaauw 2002, 357–94, esp. 380. On the diaconiae see Hermes 1996, 1–120, esp. 72–73; and Bertolini (1947) 1968.

39. This cross can be seen in one of the frescos in the lower church of S. Clemente ("Transfer of the presumed body of St. Clement") and the Chapel of St. Silvester at SS. Quattro Coronati ("Baptism of Constantine" and "Constantine leading Silvester's horse").

40. Deshusses 1992, 300.

41. Benedict notes elsewhere that "Quando efficitur collecta [in Lent], ad missam non cantatur *Kyrrieleison*, quia regionarius dixit in letania"; *Lib. Pol.* 35, Fabre and Duchesne 1910, 150.

42. Victor Saxer proposes for the eighth century a processional route that differs from the route reported by Benedict, but he offers no references; see Saxer 1989, 2:964–67 (with a note on the Forum of Nerva). Saxer observes that the twelfth-century route traces that of the ninth-century Assumption procession as recorded in the biography of Pope Leo IV (847–55); LP 2:110.

43. On these and other sites see Steinby 1993–, 1:125–26 (Argiletum), 2:307–11 (Forum Nervae), 4:383–85 (Subura).

44. For an idea of what a portion of the processional route might have looked like a century earlier, see the reconstruction in Santangeli Valentini 1999, 167; see also Platner 1926, 227–29.

45. According to Richardson 1992, 168, the arch in question pierced a curved wall to the southeast of the Temple of Minerva leading to the porticus absidiata beyond. The lower story was vaulted and covered with white marble, the upper was arcaded; it filled the space behind the hemicycle of the Forum of Augustus. A drawing in the Codex Escurialensis

depicts the ruins of the Forum of Nerva with this arch in the background and with the *colonacce* still visible today; see Magnuson 2004, 34, fig. 7.

46. On the "orphea" epithet see Adinolfi 1881, 116–25.

47. Fabre and Duchesne 1910, 2:292–93.

48. Fabre and Duchesne 1910, 2:128–29.

49. *Ordo Lateranensis* 258; Fischer 1916, 128–29. Cf. Vogel and Elze 1963–72, 2:5–10 (99.13–29).

50. Van Dijk and Walker 1975, 369–70; for the papal ordinal, see ibid., 370–73 (procession from S. Adriano to S. Maria Maggiore). A similar papal ordinal has been published as *Consuetudines Liturgicae in Functionibus Anni Ecclesiastici Papalibus Observandae*; Brinktrine 1935, 40–41. The processional chants of the papal service in this Ordinal are those of the *Liber politicus* and the *Liber censuum* (see table 2).

51. Brinktrine 1935, ibid.

52. Fols. 140v–143r; for a transcription see Stäblein 1970, 560–72.

53. The latter topic is discussed in Dyer 2007.

54. That may have changed by the end of the twelfth century. According to the Ordinal of Innocent III, "pontifex discalciatus cum omnibus psal[l]endo et primicerius has antiphonas cum sotiis [*sic*] cantant ant. *Ave gratia plena*, ant. *Adorna thalamum*, ant. *Responsum accepit Symeon*;" Van Dijk and Walker 1975, 372.

55. See Benedict's "finita antiphona" near the end of the procession before the singing of the litany (*Lib. pol.* 29; Fabre and Duchesne 1910, 148B).

56. There is a non-papal ordo for the blessing of candles and procession, edited by Van Dijk in his edition of the Ordinal of Innocent III (Van Dijk and Walker 1975, 369–70). It runs the normal course of blessing, collect (with "Exurge domine"), procession "per claustrum" singing the antiphons "Ave gratia plena," "Adorna thalamum," "Responsum accepit," and entry into the church to the ringing of bells. The color of the vestments is not mentioned.

57. Mateos 1962–63, 1:223. Constantin VII Porphyrogénète 1935, 1:139 (a chant sung in procession).

58. "Χαῖρε κεχαριτωμένη" is now the dismissal chant (apolytikion) of great vespers; *Mēnaia tou holou eniautou*, 1888–1901[1902], 3:480.

59. Alexander Lingas informs me that the piece is attributed to Cosmas of Maiuma in Detorakē 1979; on Cosmas see also Suchla 2000. Cosmas's hymns are published in PG 98:513–24, 459–85, 489–512 [canon for Hypapante]; PG 98:509–14).

60. See Schneider 2004, 7–18, 28, 311 (Einleitung). My thanks to Dr. Andreas Pfisterer for drawing my attention to this publication.

61. Romanelli and Nordhagen 1964, 41 and color plate VI; Matthiae 1987–88, 1:104–16, 251–52. For an up-to-date assessment see Lucey 2007.

62. Duchesne 1886–92, 1:385; Rum 1972.

63. Wellesz's text verson has "νεοφύτου φωτὸς" and, in the first line, "θάλαμον," but no source is given; Wellesz 1947, 61.

64. *Antiphonale Missarum Sextuplex*, 36–38 (no. 29) and LXXXVIII–LXXXIX (a comparison with the "texte grec rectifié").

65. Herren 1988.

66. A comparative analysis of the Greek and Latin versions of the chant in several eastern and western musical traditions has been published by Troelsgård 1991, 13–25. I wish to express my thanks to Prof. Troelsgård for providing me with a copy of this article.

"Adorna" is also discussed in Huglo 1967, 270–71; 2005 reprint, XV. See also the study of this chant in Strunk 1977.

67. The syllable count of "Κατακόσμησον" is 12+12, 7+7, 13+13, [6+7]+[6+6], 6+7, 7+7. "Adorna" is far more irregular: 10+8, 7+7, [2 lines om.], 11+10, [7+9]+ [8+5], 7+7, 5+7.

68. The Gregorian version of "Adorna" has been borrowed (with permission) from Borders 1996, 3:21. The chant is found in other Nonantolan manuscripts (Rome, Bibl. Casanat. 1714; Bologna, Biblioteca Universitaria, MS 2824) and in Rome, Bibl. Angelica 123 (from Bologna).

69. "Ave gratia plena" is found in two Nonantolan sources: Rome, Biblioteca Nazionale Centrale Vittorio Emmanuele III, MS 1343; and Bologna, Bibl. Univ. MS 2834; the transcription is taken with permission from Borders 1996, 3:21–22. Egon Wellesz believed that "the [Gregorian] melody of *Ave gratia plena* is of Eastern origin and was originally sung to the Greek text"; Wellesz 1947, 63.

References

Primary Sources

Ambrose Autpert. 1979. *Sermo . . . in Ypapanti sanctae Mariae. Ambrosii Autperti Opera*, edited by Robert Weber. Corpus Christianorum Continuatio Mediaevalis 27B, 985–1002. Turnhout: Brepols.

Andrieu, Michel, ed. 1931–61. *Les Ordines Romani du haut moyen-âge.* 5 vols. Spicilegium Sacrum Lovaniense 11, 23–24, 28, 29. Louvain: Université Catholique de Louvain.

Bede. 1977. *De temporum ratione.* Part 6, 2 of *Bedae Venerabilis Opera: Opera Didascalia*, edited by Charles W. Jones, 2:323. Corpus Christianorum Series Latina 123B. Turnhout: Brepols.

———. 1999. *Bede: The Reckoning of Time.* Translated by Faith Wallis. Translated Texts for Historians 29. Liverpool: Liverpool University Press.

Borders, James, ed. 1996. *Early Medieval Chants from Nonantola.* 3 vols. Recent Researches in the Music of the Middle Ages and Early Renaissance 30–32. Madison, WI: A-R Editions.

Brinktrine, Joseph, ed. 1935. *Consuetudines Liturgicae in Functionibus Anni Ecclesiastici Papalibus Observandae: Sacramentario Codicis Vat. Ottobon. 356.* Opuscula et Textus Historiam Ecclesiae eiusque vitam atque doctrinam illustrantia: Series Liturgica 6. Münster: Aschendorff.

Catella, Alcestis, Ferdinandus dell'Oro, and Aldus Martini, eds. 2005. *Liber Sacramentorum Paduensis (Padova, Bibliotecs Capitolare, cod. D 47).* Biblioteca "Ephemerides Liturgicae" Subsidia, Monumenta Italiae Liturgica 3. Rome: Edizioni Liturgiche.

Cedrenos, George. *Historiarum Compendium.* PG 121:697–700.

Constantin VII Porphyrogénète. 1935. *Le livre des cérémonies.* Edited by Albert Vogt. 2 vols. Paris: Société d'édition "Les belles lettres."

Cyril of Alexandria. Homilia 12: *In occursum domini nostri Jesu Christi.* PG 77:1040–50.

Cyril of Jerusalem (attrib.). *Oratio in occursum domini nostri et salvatoris Jesu Christi.* PG 33:1187–1204.

Cyril of Skythopolis. 1939. *Kyrillos von Skythopolis.* Edited by Eduard Schwartz. Texte und Untersuchungen zur Geschichte der altchristlichen Literatur 49/2. Leipzig: Hinrichs.

———. 1991. *Cyril of Scythopolis: The Lives of the Monks of Palestine.* Translated by Richard M. Price. Cistercian Studies 114. Kalamazoo: Cistercian Publications.

Davis, Raymond, trans. 2000. *The Book of Pontiffs* (Liber Pontificalis). Rev. ed. Translated Texts for Historians 6. Liverpool: Liverpool University Press.

Deshusses, Jean, ed. 1982, 1988, 1992. *Le sacramentaire grégorien: Ses principales formes d'après les plus anciens manuscrits.* 3 vols. 2nd ed. Spicilegium Friburgense 16, 24, 28. Freiburg: Éditions Universitaires.

Duchesne, Louis, ed. 1886–92 and 1957. *Le Liber Pontificalis: Texte, introduction et commentaire.* 2 vols. Paris: Ernest Thorin. Complemented by Cyrille Vogel, *Additions et Corrections.* Paris: E. de Boccard.

Durandus, Guillelmus. 1995–2000. *Rationale Divinorum Officiorum.* Edited by Anselme Davril and T. M. Thibodeau. 3 vols. Corpus Christianorum Continuatio Medievalis 140A–140B. Turnhout: Brepols.

Dykmans, Marc, ed. 1977–81. *Le Cérémonial papal de la fin du moyen âge à la Renaissance.* Vol. 1, *Le cérémonial papal du xiiie siècle.* Vol. 2, *De Rome en Avignon ou le cérémonial de Jacques Stefaneschi.* Bibliothèque de l'Institut historique belge de Rome 24–25. Brussels: Institut historique belge de Rome.

[Egeria]. (1948) 1971. *Etherie: Journal de voyage.* Edited and translated by Hélène Pétré. Sources Chrétiennes 21. Reprint, Paris: Éditions du Cerf.

———. 1968. *Egeria: Diary of a Pilgrimage.* Translated by George E. Gingras. Ancient Christian Writers 38. New York: Newman Press.

———. 1982. *Egérie: Journal de voyage.* Edited by Pierre Maraval. Sources Chrétiennes 296. Paris: Éditions du Cerf.

Fabre, Paul, and Louis Duchesne, eds. 1910. *Le Liber Censuum de l'Église romaine.* Bibliothèque des Écoles françaises d'Athènes et de Rome, 2nd series, 6/1–2. Paris: Fontemoing. (Vol. 2 includes the *Liber politicus* of Canon Benedict of St. Peter's.)

Fischer, Ludwig, ed. 1916. *Bernhardi cardinalis et Lateranensis ecclesiae prioris Ordo officiorum ecclesiae Lateranensis.* Historische Forschungen und Quellen 2–3. Munich: Datterer.

Hesbert, René-Jean, ed. (1935) 1967. *Antiphonale Missarum Sextuplex.* Brussels: Vroment. Reprint, Rome: Herder.

Hesychius. 1978–80. *Les homélies festales d'Hésychius de Jérusalem.* Edited by Michel Aubineau. Subsidia Hagiographica 59. Brussels: Société des Bollandistes.

Klauser, Theodor. 1935. *Das römische Capitulare evangeliorum.* Liturgiegeschichtliche Quellen und Forschungen 28. Münster: Aschendorff.

Lütolf, Max. 1987. *Das Graduale von Santa Cecilia in Trastevere (Cod. Bodmer 74).* 2 vols. Cologny-Genève: Fondation Martin Bodmer.

Mateos, Juan, ed. 1962–63. *Le typicon de la Grande Église (Ms. Sainte-Croix no. 40, Xe siècle).* 2 vols. Orientalia Christiana Analecta 165–66. Rome: Pontificiale Institutum Orientalium Studiorum.

Mēnaia tou holou eniautou. 1888–1901 [1902]. 6 vols. Rome.

Migne, Jacques-Paul, ed. 1857–66. *Patrologiae cursus completus: Series Graeca.* 161 vols. Paris: Ateliers Catholiques. [PG]

Mohlberg, L. Cunibert, ed. 1968. *Liber sacramentorum Romanae aeclesiae ordinis anni circuli.* Rerum Ecclesiasticarum Documenta, Series Maior: Fontes 4. 2nd ed. Rome: Herder.

Morin, Germain. 1911. "Liturgie et basiliques de Rome au milieu du VIIe siècle d'après les listes d'Évangéliaire de Würzburg." *Revue bénédictine* 28: 296–330.

Nicephoros Callistos. *Historia ecclesiastica* 17.28. PG 147:292.

Severus of Antioch. 1960. *Les Homiliae Cathedrales de Sévère d'Antioche: Traduction syriaque de Jacques d'Édesse.* Edited and translated by Maurice Brière. Patrologia Orientalis 29. Paris: Firmin-Didot.

Stäblein, Bruno. 1970. *Die Gesänge des altrömischen Graduale Vat. lat. 5319.* Transcribed by Margareta Landwehr-Melnicki. Monumenta Monodica Medii Aevi 2. Kassel: Bärenreiter.

Tarchnischvili, Michel, ed. 1959. *Le grand lectionnaire de l'église de Jérusalem (Ve–VIIIe siècle).* 2 vols. Corpus Scriptorum Christianorum Orientalium 188–129, Scriptores Iberici 9–10. Louvain: Secrétariat du Corpus SCO.

Theophanes. *Chronographia.* PG 108:488.

Van Dijk, Stephen J. P., and Joan Hazelden Walker, eds. 1975. *The Ordinal of the Papal Court from Innocent III to Boniface VIII and Related Documents.* Spicilegium Friburgense 22. Freiburg: Universitätsverlag.

Vogel, Cyrille, and Reinhard Elze, eds. 1963–72. *Le pontifical romano-germanique du dixième siècle.* 3 vols. Studi e Testi 226–27, 269. Vatican City: Biblioteca Apostolica Vaticana.

Secondary Sources

Adinolfi, Pasquale. 1881. *Roma nell'età di mezzo.* 2 vols. Rome: Fratelli Bocca.

Antonelli, Ferdinando. 1928. "I primi monasteri di monaci orientali in Roma." *Rivista di Archeologia Cristiana* 5:105–21.

Auf der Maur, Hansjörg. 1983. *Herrenfeste in Woche und Jahr.* Vol. 1 of *Feiern im Rhythmus der Zeit.* Gottesdienst der Kirche 5. Regensburg: Friedrich Pustet.

Baumstark, Anton. 1909. "Rom oder Jerusalem? Eine Revision der Frage nach der Herkunft des Lichtmessfestes." *Theologie und Glaube* 1:89–105.

———. 1927. "Untersuchungen." In *Die älteste erreichbare Gestalt des Liber Sacramentorum anni circuli der römischen Kirche* [Padua, Bibl. Cap. D 47], edited by Cunibert Mohlberg. Liturgiewissenschaftliche Quellen und Forschungen 11–12. Münster: Aschendorff.

Bernard, Philippe. 1996. *Du chant romain au chant grégorien (IVe–XIIIe siècle).* Paris: Les Éditions du Cerf.

Bertolini, Ottorino. (1947) 1968. "Per la storia delle diaconie romane nell'alto medioevo sino alla fine del secolo VIII." *Archivio della Società romana di storia patria* 70:1–145. Reprinted in Ottavio Banti, ed. *Scritti scelti di storia medievali.* 2 vols. Livorno: Società Editrice "Il Telegrafo." 1:311–460.

Bickersteth, E. 1953. "John Chrysostom and the Early History of the Hypapante." *Atti dello VIII congresso internazionale di studi bizantini, Palermo, 3–10 aprile 1951.* 2 vols. Studi Bizantini e Neoellenici 8. Rome: Associazione Nazionale per gli Studi Bizantini. 2:401–4.

Blaauw, Sible de. 2002. "Contrasts in Processional Liturgy: A Typology of Outdoor Processions in Twelfth-Century Rome." In *Art, Cérémonial et Liturgie au Moyen Âge: Actes du colloque du 3e Cycle Romand de Lettres, Lausanne-Fribourg, 24–25 mars, 14–15 avril, 12–13 mai 2000,* edited by Nicolas Bock et al., 357–94. Rome: Viella.

Capelle, Bernard. 1965. "Les fêtes mariales." In *L'Église en prière,* edited by Aimé-Georges Martimort, 766–85. 3rd ed. Paris: Declée.

Cavallo, Guglielmo. 1982. "Cultura e libri greci in Italia fra tarda Antichità e Alto Medioevo." In *I Bizantini in Italia,* edited by Carlo Belli, Pietro Orlandini, and Giovanni Pugliese Carratelli, 500–508. Milan: Scheiwiller.

Chappet, A. 1907–53. "Cosmas de Maïouma (Saint)." In *Dictionnaire d'Archéologie Chrétienne et de Liturgie*, edited by Fernand Cabrol. 15 vols. in 30, vol. 3: cols. 2993–97. Paris: Letouzey et Ané.

Chavasse, Antoine. 1958. *Le sacramentaire gélasien (Vaticanus Reginensis 316): Sacramentaire presbytéral en usage dans les titres romains au VIIe siècle.* Bibliothèque de Théologie, series 4; Histoire de Théologie, vol. 1. Tournai-Paris: Declée.

Coebergh, Charles. 1961. "Le sacramentaire gélasien ancien: Une compilation de clercs romanisants du VIIIe siècle." *Archiv für Liturgiewissenschaft* 7: 45–88.

De Bruyne, Donatien. 1922. "L'origine des processions de la Chandeleur et des Rogations à propos d'un sermon inédit." *Revue Bénédictine* 34: 14–26.

Del Lungo, Stefano. 2004. *Roma in età carolingia e gli scritti dell'Anonimo Augiense.* Miscellanea della Società Romana di Storia Patria 48. Rome: Società Romana di Storia Patria.

Dendy, David R. 1959. *The Use of Lights in Christian Worship.* Alcuin Club Collections 41. London: SPCK.

Denysenko, Nicholas. 2007. "The *Hypapante* Feast in Fourth to Eighth Century Jerusalem." *Studia Liturgica* 37: 73–97.

Detorakē, Theocharē E. 1979. *Kosmas ho melodos, bios kai ergo* [Cosmas the melodist: Life and work]. Analecta Vladaton 28. Thessalonica: Patriarchikon Hidryma Paterikōn Meletōn.

Deug-Su, I. 1974. "La festa della purificazione in Occidente (secoli IV–VIII)." *Studi medievali*, series 3/15: 143–216.

Dyer, Joseph. 2007. "Roman Processions of the Major Litany (*litaniae maiores*) from the Sixth to the Twelfth Centuries." In *Roma Felix: Formation and Reflections of Medieval Rome*, edited by Éamonn Ó Carragáin and Carol Neuman de Vegvar, 112–37. Aldershot: Ashgate.

Dyer, Joseph. Forthcoming. "Katakosmēson ton nymphōna sou Siōn—Adorna thalamum tuum Sion: East and West in the Medieval Roman Celebration of Candlemas." In *Cantus Planus: Papers Read at the Fifteenth Meeting of the IMS Study Group—Dobogókő, 2009, August 23–29*, edited by László Dobszay. Budapest: Institute for Musicology of the Hungarian Academy of Sciences.

Ekonomou, Andrew J. 2007. *Byzantine Rome and the Greek Popes: Eastern Influences on Rome and the Papacy from Gregory the Great to Zacharias, A.D. 590–752.* Lanham, MD: Lexington Books.

Franz, Adolph. 1909. *Die kirchlichen Benediktionen im Mittelalter.* 2 vols. Freiburg im Breisgau: Herder.

Frere, Walter Howard. 1930. *The Kalendar.* Vol. 1 of *Studies in Early Roman Liturgy.* Alcuin Club Collections 28. Oxford: Oxford University Press.

Grégoire, Réginald. 1981. "Monaci e monasteri in Roma nei secoli VI–VII." *Archivio Romano di Storia Patria* 104: 5–23.

Groen, Bert. 2001. "The Festival of the Presentation of the Lord: Its Origin, Structure and Theology in the Byzantine and Roman Rites." In *Christian Feast and Festival: The Dynamics of Western Liturgy and Culture*, edited by P. Post et al., 345–82. Louvain: Peeters.

Hermes, Raimund. 1996. "Die stadtrömischen Diakonien." *Römische Quartalschrift für christliche Altertumskunde und Kirchengeschichte* 91: 1–120.

Herren, Michael W. 1988. "Evidence for 'Vulgar Greek' from Early Medieval Latin Texts and Manuscripts." In *The Sacred Nectar of the Greeks: The Study of Greek in the West in the Early Middle Ages*, edited by Michael W. Herren, 57–84. King's College London Medieval Studies 2. London: King's College.

Higgins, Martin. 1952. "Note on the Purification (and Date of Nativity) in Constantinople in 602." *Archiv für Liturgiewissenschaft* 2: 81–83.

Huglo, Michel. (1967) 2005. "Relations musicales entre Byzance et l'Occident." In *Proceedings of the XIIth International Congress of Byzantine Studies: Oxford, 5–10 September 1966*, edited by Joan M. Hussey, 267–80. Oxford: Oxford University Press. Reprinted in Michel Huglo, *Les ancien répertoires de plain-chant*, Variorum Collected Studies 804. Aldershot: Ashgate.

Llewellyn, Peter. 1974–2003. "Roma: II. Dal secolo VI al secolo X." In *Dizionario degli istituti di perfezione*, 7: col. 1896–903. Rome: Edizioni Paoline.

———. 1981. "The Names of the Roman Clergy, 401–1046." *Rivista della Storia della Chiesa in Italia* 35: 335–70.

Lombardi, Ferruccio. 1996. *Roma: Le chiese scomparse; La memoria storica della città*. Rome: Palombi.

Lucy, Stephen J. 2007. "Art and Socio-Cultural Identity in Early Medieval Rome: The Patrons of Santa Maria Antiqua." In *Romas Felix: Formation and Reflections of Medieval Rome*, edited by Éamonn Ó Carragáin and Carol Neuman de Vegvar, 139–58. Aldershot: Ashgate.

Magnuson, Torgil. 2004. *The Urban Transformation of Medieval Rome, 312-1420*. Suecoromana: Studia Artis Historiae Instituti Romani Regni Sueciae 7. Stockholm: Swedish Institute in Rome.

Martimort, Aimé-Georges. 1955. "Les diverses formes de procession dans la liturgie." *La Maison-Dieu* 43: 43–73.

Matthiae, Guglielmo. 1987–88. *Pittura Romana del Medioevo*. 2 vols. Revised by Maria Andoloro (vol. 1) and Francesco Gandolfo (vol. 2). Rome: Palombi.

Michel, Anton. 1952. "Die griechischen Klostersiedlungen zu Rom bis zur Mitte des 14. Jahrhunderts." *Ostkirchliche Studien* 1: 32–45.

Moreau, Edouard de. 1935. "L'Orient et Rome dans la fête du 2 février." *Nouvelle Revue Théologique* 6: 1–20.

Nilles, Nicolaus. 1896–97. *Kalendarium Manuale utriusque Ecclesiae Orientalis et Occidentalis*. 2 vols. Innsbruck: Rauch [Pustet].

Noble, Thomas. 1985. "The Declining Knowledge of Greek in Eighth- and Ninth-Century Rome." *Byzantinische Zeitschrift* 78: 56–62.

Pani Ermini, Letizia. 2001. "*Forma Urbis*: Lo spazio urbano tra VI e IX secolo." In *Roma nell'alto medioevo: 27 aprile–1 maggio 2000*, 2:255–344, pls. I–XVII. Settimane di studio del Centro Italiano di studi sull'alto medioevo 48. Spoleto: Centro Italiano di Studi sull'Alto medioevo.

Platner, Samuel Ball. 1929. *A Topographical Dictionary of Rome*. Completed and revised by Thomas Ashby. Oxford: Oxford University Press.

Renoux, Athanase, ed. 1969–71. *Le codex arménien Jérusalem 121*. 2 vols. Patrologia Orientalis 35/1 and 36/2. Turnhout: Brepols.

Richardson, Lawrence. 1992. *A New Topographical Dictionary of Ancient Rome*. Baltimore: The Johns Hopkins University Press.

Righetti, Mario. 1969. *Manuale di Storia Liturgica*. 3rd ed. 4 vols. Milan: Ancora.

Romanelli, Pietro and Per Jonas Nordhagen. 1964. *S. Maria Antiqua*. Rome: Istituto Poli-
grafico dello Stato.
Rum, Alberto. 1972. "Papa Giovanni VII (705–707): 'Servus sanctae Mariae.'" In *De culto
mariano saeculis VI–XI*. Acta Congressus Mariologici-Mariani Internationalis in Cro-
atia anno 1971 celebrati, 3:249–63. Rome: Pontificia Academia mariana Internationalis.
Saint-Roch, Patrick. 1992. "Le 2 février dans les Gélasiens francs." In *Memoriam Sanctorum
Venerantes: Miscellanea in onore di Monsignor Victor Saxer*, 736–40, tables I–IV. Studi
di Antichità Cristiana 48. Vatican City: Pontificio Istituto di Archeologia Christiana.
Sansterre, Jean-Marie. 1983. *Les moines grecs et orientaux à Rome aux époques byzantine et
carolingienne (milieu du VIe s.–fin du IXe s.)*. 2 vols. Académie Royale de Belgique:
Mémoires de la Classe des Lettres, 2nd ser., 66/1. Brussels: Palais des Académies.
———. 1988. "Le monachisme byzantin à Rome." In *Bisanzio, Roma e l'Italia nell'alto
medioevo*, 2:701–46. Settimane di Studio del Centro Italiano di Studi sull'Alto Medioevo 34. Spoleto: Centro Italiano di Studi sull'Alto Medioevo.
Santangeli Valentini, Riccardo. 1999. "Strade, case e orti nell'alto medioevo nell'area del
Foro di Nerva." *Mémoires de l'École Française de Rome: Moyen Âge* 111: 163–68.
Saxer, Victor. 1989. "L'utilisation par le liturgie de l'éspace urbain et suburbain: L'exemple
de Rome dans l'antiquité et le haut Moyen-Âge." In *Actes du XIe Congrès Interna-
tional d'Archéologie Chrétienne: Lyon, Vienne, Grenoble, Genève et Aoste (21–28 septembre
1986)*. 2:917–1033. Studi di Antichità Cristiana 41, Collection de l'École Française de
Rome 123. Vatican City: Pontificio Istituto di Archeologia Sacra.
Schäublin, Christoph. 1995. "Lupercalien und Lichtmess." *Hermes* 123: 117–25.
Schmidt, Hermann. 1957. *Hebdomada Sancta*. 2 vols. Rome: Herder.
Schneider, Hans-Michael. 2004. *Lobpreis im rechten Glaube: Die Theologie der Hymnus an
den Festen der Menschenwerdung der alten Jerusalemer Liturgie in Georgischen Udzvelesi
Iadgari*. Hereditas 29. Bonn: Borengässer.
Steinacker, Harold. 1954. "Die römische Kirche und die griechischen Sprachkenntnisse
des Frühmittelalters." *Mitteilungen des Instituts für Österreichische Geschichtsforschung*
62: 28–66.
Steinby, Eva Margareta, ed. 1993–. *Lexicon topographicum urbis Romae*. 6 vols. [to date].
Rome: Quasar.
Stevenson, Kenneth. 1990. "The Origins and Development of Candlemas: A Struggle for
Identity and Coherence?" In *Time and Community: In Honor of Thomas Talley*, edited
by Neil Alexander, 43–76. Washington, DC: The Pastoral Press.
Strunk, Oliver. 1977. "The Chants of the Byzantine-Greek Liturgy." In *Essays on Music in
the Byzantine World*, 297–330. New York: Norton.
Suchla, Beate Regina. 2000. "Cosmas the Singer." In *Dictionary of Early Christian Lit-
erature*, edited by Siegmar Döpp and Wilhelm Geerlings, translated by Matthew
O'Connell, 144. New York: Crossroads.
Troelsgård, Christian. 1991. "The Musical Structure of Five Byzantine Stichera and Their
Parallels among Western Antiphons." *Cahiers de l'Institut du moyen-âge grec et latin*
61: 3–48.
Vogel, Cyrille. 1986. *Medieval Liturgy: An Introduction to the Sources*. Revised and translated
by William G. Storey and Niels Krogh Rasmussen. Washington, DC: The Pastoral
Press.

Wellesz, Egon. 1947. *Eastern Elements in Western Chant: Studies in the Early History of Ecclesiastical Music.* Copenhagen: Munksgaard.

Wolf, Gerhard. 1990. *Salus Populi Romani: Die Geschichte römischer Kultbilder im Mittelalter.* Weinheim: VCH Verlagsgesellschaft.

"Laureata plebs fidelis": A Victorine Sequence from the Feast of Corpus Christi in Thirteenth-Century Liège

Barbara R. Walters

Thirteenth-century liturgy shaped public and personal lives in ways largely unimaginable to the contemporary lay and critical consciousness except, perhaps, if one might liken these ritual performances to the protocol of the modern scientific experiment. A striking difference between the contemporary laboratory experiments executed by highly educated scientists and the religious rituals of the medieval period stems from the convergence of political, theological, and moral authority then granted to the celebrant of the Mass. Membership in the Catholic Church was involuntary, and even kings looked to the papal hierarchy and its sacraments to legitimate claims to earthly power, although awe was often coupled with hostile resentment. Therefore, alterations to the daily rounds of prayers in the thirteenth century, but especially additions to the section of the liturgical year that reenacts the life of Jesus on earth, the *Temporale*, signal landmark shifts in both medieval human consciousness and the geopolitical-cultural terrain in which it was constituted.

In fact, only one such feast was added to the *Temporale* in the thirteenth century, the Feast of Corpus Christi, also known as the Feast of the Blessed Sacrament, or the *Fête Dieu*. The feast day celebrates the Real Presence, or the transubstantiation of the body and blood of Christ during the Eucharist, a theological doctrine mandated for the faithful at the Fourth Lateran Council in 1215. Miri Rubin (1991, 1) notes that the Eucharist, a liturgical ritual that turned a "fragile small wheaten disc into God," shaped the epicenter around which the entire medieval religious world system revolved.

In 1246 Bishop Robert de Thorette was first in establishing the new feast in the Diocese of Liège by a letter to all clergy, in response to the two-score efforts of a local religious woman, Juliana Mont Cornillon (1193–1258). In 1252, the Dominican cardinal legate, Hugh of Saint-Cher, extended celebration of the new feast to Germany, Dacia, Bohemia, Moravia, and Poland by a decree of indulgence for all in his jurisdiction. And, in 1263, Pope Urban IV, formerly Jacques de Pantéléon of Troyes and archbishop of Liège during the initial 1246 approbation, adopted the Feast of Corpus Christi for the universal church by a papal bull, Transiturus. He sent a copy of the bull with a letter to the deceased Juliana's friend and confidante Eve, the anchoress, at Saint-Martin in Liège.

Liturgical scholars executing research for the seventh centennial celebration of the feast in 1946, most notably Lambot and Fransen (1946) and Delaissé (1950), were unanimous in crediting Juliana with promoting the new Feast of Corpus Christi among the Dominicans in Liège. Juliana chose a young and innocent monk, John, "[q]uem licet in litterarum scientia nosceret imperitum" (although she was aware that he lacked literary knowledge) to compose the new feast (Delville 1999, 136). Juliana's vita (authored by an eyewitness, and most likely her friend Eve) reports that the young cleric "centonated" the entire office and Mass via a miraculous intervention of God, while Juliana prayed (Delville 1999, 136–41).[1] Juliana, in contrast to the young cleric John, was then aged fifty-four and widely reputed to be of capacious intellect and tenacious memory. She had learned to read and write in French and Latin as a girl and had memorized at least the psalms and St. Bernard's sermons on the Song of Songs (cf. Newman 1989, 27). This perhaps explains John's requests for assistance and corrections during the compositional process. "And when he had composed some part of the office, he took it to her and said: 'This, Madam, was sent to you from on high; view and examine it to see if there is anything to correct in the song or in the text'"[2] (Delville 1999, 138).

In 1475 a glossator inserted a note into the vita of Juliana indicating that the office was preserved at a church at Tongres and elsewhere, and that the first antiphon began with the words "Animarum cibus." Using this clue, Lambot discovered a version matching the description of the original office in a composite manuscript from the thirteenth century, which was assembled at Tongres in 1537: The Hague, Koninklijke Bibliotheek, MS 70.E.4 (Lambot and Fransen 1946, 99–101). This version of the office draws heavily on the theological understanding of the Eucharist found in the writings of Alger of Liège and Hugh of Saint-Victor. It has no musical or textual materials that overlap with the later and more famous version attributed to St. Thomas Aquinas, although it contains many of the central textual themes and musical mottos or quotes used in the later and more elegant work. The young student Aquinas may have coincided in Cologne with biblical exegete Hugh of Saint-Cher in 1252, before the latter departed for the curia and the former for Paris to complete his work toward becoming a master in theology. As a mature and distinguished theologian, Aquinas served as advisor to Urban IV between 1259 and 1268, with full access to the Curia, its library, and its other resources.

Societal Factors Surrounding the Original Office

Two factors loom large in the shifting sociopolitical landscape that gave rise to the initiation of the new Feast of Corpus Christi in Liège. First, primogeniture and the crusades resulted in a disproportion in the ratio of males to females in the general population of Europe (Duby 1978), while a special dispensation that allowed women to live religious lives outside of orders may have contributed to the spatial concentration of women in the Low Countries. These women, often called beguines, began congregating in Liège in second part of the twelfth century. Initially their lifestyle as unmarried women living outside religious orders created suspicion and prosecution based on their outward similarity to heretical groups such as Albigensians, or Cathars. However, in 1216 Cardinal Jacques de Vitry—friend of Marie d'Oignes (1177–1213) and author of her vita—gained a special exemption from Innocent III that allowed the women to live in communal houses without affiliating with a religious order (Bartoli 1999). Marie d'Oignes was a religious woman outside orders whose reputation and influence was such that St. Francis himself attempted a pilgrimage to meet her and the circle of women under her influence (King 1998, 10). Thereafter, or at least until the mid-thirteenth century, these women became religious exemplars noted for their orthodox piety and devotion to the Eucharist (Bynum 1982, 170–262). Marie d'Oignes was, in fact, credited with introducing women's issues at papal level (Wogan-Browne and Henneau 1999, 7) and with first prophesying the new Feast of Corpus Christi (Simenon 1922). This early successful petition for local empowerment provided direction when the beguines again came under suspicion during the papal inquisition founded by Gregory IX, who was elected to the papacy in 1227.

Second, during Juliana's formative years, the diocese of Liège, on the border between nascent France and Germany, was drawn into the vortex of conflict between the Ghibellines and the Guelphs, the respective parties of Emperor Frederick II and the Papacy. Until the end of the twelfth century the bishop of Liège was an integral part of the imperial *Reichskirchensystem*, a religiopolitical system that rested on mutual support and interdependence between the emperor and the bishops. The Liège bishops were prince-bishops and rulers of the territories in which their diocesan institutions were located. After the collapse of the power of the emperor early in the thirteenth century, the alliance fell apart and the prelates became de facto prince-bishops of independent territories. Starting with French-born Bishop Hugh of Pierrepont (1200–1229), the Liège prelates shifted allegiance away from the emperor and toward the Papacy, while successive popes nourished their ties to France (Kupper 1999). Between the years 1238 and 1278, Liège became a Guelph citadel (Rubin 1991, 172). French-born Pope Urban IV, native of Troyes and erstwhile archdeacon of Liège, who elevated the Feast of

Corpus Christi for the universal church in 1264, aligned with French Capetian Charles I of Anjou, brother of Louis IX, immediately after his papal election in 1261. The consequent defeat of Manfred, son of Frederick II, in Sicily in 1266 and the execution of the latter's grandson Conradin in 1268 ended the Hohenstaufen dynasty (Abulafia 1999, 508–10). The Feast of Corpus Christi was initiated in Liège shortly after the contingent and decisive moment in a historical chain of events: the excommunication of Frederick II by Innocent IV at the Council of Lyon. Juliana's supporters for the new feast can be found among the friends of the papacy; her opponents number among the supporters of Frederick II (Walters 2004, 285–301).

These politico-theological and demographic factors point to an institutional crisis and to the precarious position of the Liège women during the thirteenth century. The institutional crisis, combined with the marginal status of women, must have produced an intense internal desire for public affirmation of the central symbols of the church and the security of its hierocratic authority. The new Feast of Corpus Christi, modeled on the prophecies of Marie d'Oignes, provided a direction, an idea, for the requisite public manifestation of penitence, humility, and other virtues through the outward sign of the elevated Host and Eucharist. Its source in Juliana, who lived with and among the beguines after leaving the monastery at Mont Cornillon in 1247, enhanced its influence among the women, as well as their credibility, by promoting the new feast honoring the sacrament.

"Laureata plebs fidelis" and the Victorine Sequence

I have selected for close examination and analysis the Victorine sequence "Laureata plebs fidelis," which appears as one of two independent pieces after the office services for Animarum cibus—the Liège office for the Feast of Corpus Christi—in The Hague, MS 70.E.4 on folios 94r to 95r. I have chosen this sequence for two important reasons. First, the music-text relationships and structure comply with the musical form characteristic of the Victorine sequence, a form that facilitated oral transmission (cf. Fassler 1993). Thus, only an "insider" rather than a novice could have composed the sequence. Musicologist Peter Jeffery (1992, 54) notes: "it is hard to disagree with the notion that shared categories of perception and understanding are surely prominent among the elements that define a musical culture, that distinguish each musical culture from all others, and that determine who is a member or 'insider' to a culture, and by the same token who is an 'outsider.'" The sequence's appearance in the newly composed Corpus Christi office service lends weight to the argument that the erudite Juliana, who was also a singer, composed this version of the office rather than the voice of the Holy Spirit whispering to the young, naïve John. Mulder-Bakker (2005, 91) similarly notes: "Even if the hagiographer suggests . . . that John wrote the actual text, he allows no room for doubt that Juliana is the intellectual author."

Second, the artistry of the sequence expresses in music-text relationships a religious vision that could indeed "wring devotion from hearts of stone" (Delville 1999, 140; cf. Corrigan 2002). The artistry takes us past a mechanical sociopolitical analysis of why thirteenth-century women joined the Corpus Christi movement to the elegance, simplicity, and Christocentric purity of Juliana's vision as its charismatic centerpiece. Through the sequence we can examine the artistry and aesthetic communication itself as one rationale for those who followed.

"Laureata plebs fidelis" as Victorine Sequence

The music for "Laureata plebs fidelis," as in all Victorine sequences, is derived from a Carolingian "Alleluia" and its prosula, or the coupling of an "Alleluia" melisma with a textual insertion. In this case the "Alleluia" was most likely joined to its prosula, "Dulce lignum," in the tenth century. The textual insertion was adapted from a sixth-century poem by Venantius Fortunatus, "Pange Lingua." The melody of the prosula exactly replicates the melody of the original "Alleluia." The "Alleluia's" position in the liturgy before the Gospel reading heightened familiarity with the "Alleluia" melodies and called attention to the allegory of solo musical performance as the individual before God. The musical sourcing of "Laureata plebs fidelis" from the "Alleluia Dulce lignum" places the sequence in the same tune family as "Laudes crucis," a twelfth-century Parisian sequence composed to celebrate the finding of the True Cross. The latter was one of the most popular sequences of the medieval period and was also selected by St. Thomas for his Corpus Christi sequence, "Lauda Syon" (cf. Fassler 1993). The Aquinas sequence sets new words to the exact same music as used in "Laudes crucis," and is one of five sequences that remained in the repertory after the Council of Trent.[3]

Analysis of "Laureata plebs fidelis"

Example 1 and text 1 provide transcriptions and translations of "Laureata plebs fidelis" as found in MS 70.E.4. The text of the sequence consists of eleven strophes, with each strophe divided into two halves. Each strophe is labeled with a number, and each hemistrophe with a letter—for example, Ia and Ib. Each hemistrophe consists of two or three lines with eight (sometimes seven) syllables in trochaic meter, plus a closing line of seven syllables in trochaic meter. Within a strophe, each hemistrophe is isometric with respect to meter and to its rhyme scheme (except in the case of rhymes in 3 and 5). Each melodic line typically matches two paired hemistrophes of text and is divided into three or four segments—for example, m1a, m1b, m1c. Each melodic segment accompanies at least one line of verse but may be recalled to accompany a different line for special musical-textual effects.

The melody of the sequence is in mode 1. The modal structure is highlighted by the consistent use of the final to end each strophe, except for strophe VIII which ends on the cofinal. Each of the melody segments is characterized by modal structure so that just as each line of poetry ends with a syllable in a rhyme scheme, each of the melodic segments end on the final or cofinal of the mode. And there is a frequent and characteristic use of the podatus as a cadential formula, occurring in seven of the eleven strophes. The most important music-text relationships result from the interplay of melody and words to create a structure that organizes and amplifies the semantic content of the particular text. Thus, in utilizing the sequence form which was associated in the medieval mind with the space between human existence and the heavens above, "Laureata plebs fidelis" opened a space for the human community which shared the sacrament of the Eucharist.

In her analysis of "Laudes crucis," Fassler (1993, 65) identified four major sections that give structure to the Victorine sequence in general through semantic and syntactic connections between music and text: (1) an exordium, (2) a history of the cross through Old Testament scripture, (3) an expression of the power of the cross in contemporary life, and (4) a final prayer to Jesus. This analysis of "Laureata" follows Fassler's work and adds a diagram modeled on McGrade's analysis of the sequence in the Feast of the Dispersion of the Apostles (cf. McGrade 1996). A rustic Latin text heralds the new Feast of Corpus Christi and its celebration of the Sacrament of the Eucharist. The text is divided into five sections based on breaks in the poetic structure and meaning, intensified by the accompanying musical phrase relationships, labeled m1a, m1b, m1c, extending through m11c. The five sections include: (1) an exordium, in strophes I and II, lauding the new Corpus Christi feast; (2) an expression of the meaning of the feast as promised in the Old Testament, in strophes III, IV and V; (3) an exhortation of the Sacrament, in strophes VI and VIIa; (4) a doxology of the Sacrament, in strophes VIIb, VIII, and IX; and (5) a praise of Jesus in strophes X and XI. Note that in addition to semantic contents, strophes I and II contain two halves with three lines each; strophes III and IV, two halves with four lines each; strophe V, two halves with three lines each; strophes VI, VII, and VIII two halves with four lines; and strophes IX, X, and XI, two halves with three lines each. Diagram 1 illustrates the sectional breaks and highlights in bold those musical segments or cells that return to create the musical structure and the meaning of the sequence.

The opening melodic segment, 1a, recalls the "Alleluia dulce lignum" although "Laureata" is composed in a different church mode (mode 1 rather than mode 8), and celebrates the new Feast of Corpus Christi. Melodic segment m1b, **B**, represents the sacramental theme through its association with the text:

"sacramento Christi carnis" (the sacrament of the body of Christ). A notated B-flat cancels the tritone. Segment m1c is a cadential formula, and melodic unit m2a opens the second strophe with an exact musical quote from "Dies Irae," **DI**. Fransen (Lambot and Fransen 1946, 104–5) in his derision of "Laureata" suggested that this is mere coincidence, since it never returns. However, this claim reflects more on Fransen's limited musical vocabulary than those of the composer, since it is virtually inconceivable that the placement of this most famous exact quotation from "Dies Irae" to accompany a text concerning Christ's passion in "Laureata" could have been so placed by accident.

The second section, which begins with strophe III, expresses the relationship of the new feast to events in the Old Testament and opens with an exact quotation of the sacramental theme, m1b, or **B**. The text refers directly to the sacrament as "Hoc."[4] I have identified the melodic material in m4a, 4b, and 4c as the "sacrificial theme," **T**, through the sections' association with the text: "Et hoc quidem designavit agnus sine macula quem edendum immolavit quondam lex Mosayca" (And the lamb without blemish also signified this, the one which was once sacrificed and had to be eaten according to Mosaic law). And again we find a melodic echo of the "Alleluia dulce lignum," at m5b, **DL**. Melody segment m5 contains an exact musical quote from the opening of the "Laudes crucis" sequence, which comes directly from the opening of the "Alleluia dulce lignum." The text is: "Caro cuius tam serena nobis esca sit amena fidei mysterio" (May his flesh be pleasant food for us in the mystery of faith) and "Quam provide manna celi figuravit Israheli nobili presagio" (The manna from heaven given as a noble exemplar to Israel was a form of this food).

The shift to the next major text section at strophe VI is clearly marked by the repetition of the melody in segments m6a and m6b—the strophe opens on the leap of the fifth and is then repeated. The motion intensifies in strophe VIIa, with the return of **T**, the sacrifice theme. The text/music at "O dulce convivium" (O sweet banquet), on hemistrophe 7b, breaks the form with new music, rather than duplicating m7a, to mark the dramatic transition toward the centerpiece. The composer most likely chose the seventh strophe as an allegory for the seven sacraments. Hemistrophe 7b is therefore decoupled from 7a to become part of the doxology of the Sacrament. The transition is symbolized by the fourfold repetition of melodic units 8a and 8b across the eight lines of strophe VIII, a sign of the cross. The melodic segment is the only segment which cadences on the cofinal.

Strophe IX brings back the sacrificial theme, **T**, and heralds the climax of the piece. This climax arrives in strophe X, when the sacrificial theme, **T**, and the sacramental theme, **B**, are brought together in the longest melodic segment of the sequence with the text: "Nam effectus tue mortis nos emundat a peccatis per missae mysteria" (For the effect of your death cleanses us from our sins through the mystery of the Mass), in the first hemistrophe, 10a; and "Summe templum trinitatis sempiternam confer nobis gloriam in patria" (O temple of the most high Trinity, confer upon us everlasting glory in heaven), in 10b, the second hemistrophe.

The sequence ends with three scalar segments that together have the widest ambitus in the piece. Melodic segment 11b, which covers the octave from C (subfinal) to D, and proclaims the text: "Iesu, decus angelorum spoliator infernorum humili victoria" (Jesus, glory of angels, despoiler of hell, by humble victory). Here, B-natural is noteworthy in its absence.

Summary and Conclusions

Juliana Mont Cornillon is by far the more likely generative source for the Victorine sequence than the young and inexperienced canon John. Despite certain irregularities in Latin inflections in the text, the composition conforms to an "insider's" understanding of thirteenth-century liturgical culture, as well as to then current fashions in chant composition style (cf. Gjerdingen 1988, 269; Jeffery 1992, 54). The use of the well-known genre, the sequence, points to a scene of shared conventions framed for oral transmission.

The analysis of the composition is central to understanding Juliana's appeal to her followers in the religious community of thirteenth-century Liège. As the inquisitorial procedures against heretics became institutionalized in the papacy in the mid-thirteenth century, the process spread through Europe with its inevitable strong arm, arousing fear, anxiety, and uncertainty. In Liège local networks were further disrupted by the shift in allegiance on the part of the prince-bishops away from the emperor and toward Capetian France, as well as by internecine quarrels among the descendants of Baldwin IX. The community of women—powerless, marginal, and perhaps anxious about status—especially expressed its eagerness to resolve religiopolitical boundary ambiguity through group allegiance to a common sign, manifest as fervor for the Eucharistic host (cf. Bynum 1982, 18–19). The movement for the new feast day celebrating the sacrament served these psychic needs while providing a symbol of unity that served to consolidate the material interests of the Curia and its potential allied forces.

Without the analysis of "Laureata plebs fidelis" and close reading of her vita, Juliana might be mistaken for a follower, making sycophantic choices between pathological humility and *auto da fe*. The sequence, however, reveals a solution rich in imagination and replete with powerful inner resources—a serious, intense, and aesthetic response to the compelling needs and concerns of the Liège community of religious women. Papal recognition via a letter from Urban IV to Eve confirms Juliana's generative influence as the charismatic leader of a popular movement toward its religious center (cf. Weber 1978, 241). Writes Weber (1978,

1120) with such eloquence about the general sociological case, "Every charisma is on the road from a turbulently emotional life that knows no economic rationality to a slow death by suffocation under the weight of material interests: every hour of its existence brings it nearer to this end."

The potential amplification of Juliana's credits raises the question of the relationship between her sequence and that of St. Thomas Aquinas, *Summa* compiler of the later official Roman office. A comparison of the two sequences at the literal textual level reveals no common text phrases shared between the Juliana Mont Cornillon sequence and the official Aquinas version adopted by Urban IV in 1264. Since both "Laureata plebs fidelis" and "Lauda Syon" draw melodic material from the same source, the "Alleluia" associated with "Dulce lignum," this common source and the use of standard thirteenth-century formulae may explain traces of concords connecting the two sequences as found in shared melodic cells. Stylistically, the Aquinas sequence sets new words to old music, the "Lauda Syon" text to the music of "Laudes crucis," in contrast to Juliana who reorganizes old texts and composes new music.

Brasington (2001) makes an important, and perhaps relevant, claim in his article about a papal letter by Zacharias from the eighth century purporting to quote the poor grammar of an ignorant priest in a query regarding whether this invalidated a baptism. The letter has survived generations of transmissions with varied scribal corrections to become a staple text to students of early Latin literacy. Brasington argues that it is the spirit of its argument—the ideas, and not its functional exemplar of "bad Latin"—which has fostered the letter's preservation. A baptism, according to Zacharias, is valid even for the case in point in which the priest substituted "in nomina patria filia et spiritu scientia" for "in nomine patris filii et spiritus sancti."

The same principle may apply to the original Liège office of the Feast of Corpus Christi and its sequence, "Laureata." In spite of its irregular Latin inflections and rustic style, the original office survives as a witness to the ideas and spirit of the geopolitical terrain in which it took root and to its source in Juliana of Mont Cornillon. The office's source is often biblical and meditative as well as doctrinal, and its ideas were transmitted indirectly to Aquinas through Hugh of Saint-Cher and Pope Urban IV, who acknowledged Juliana's friend Eve in the papal bull instituting the new feast.

Contrasts at the human level explain the *rustica* versus *Imprimatur* status of "Laureata" and "Lauda Syon" after the Council of Trent; these are manifest in the extraordinary differences in power, authority, and opportunities between women and men, personified in the lives of Juliana and Aquinas. While intellectually gifted, Juliana completed her studies in the provincial monastery at Mont Cornillon under Sister Sapientia. Her exposure and sources were limited to the diocese of Liège and the library at the monastery. Aquinas, by contrast, entered the University of Naples at the age of nineteen, studied with Albert the Great in Cologne, and then pursued a master's degree in theology at the University of Paris, where he later served as regent master. He served as conventual lector in Orvieto with close ties to the papacy and access to an astonishing array of textual sources, in addition to the rich human contacts that resulted from his proximity to the papal court (Torrell 1996). Juliana died in a recluse's cell at Fosses after she and three companions fled from Mont Cornillon, and thence the shelters of several Cistercian nunneries. Within five days of her death the Cistercians moved Juliana to a section of their cemetery reserved for saints. The official process was slower. Aquinas was officially canonized in 1323, Juliana over five hundred years later, in 1869. Given all of the limitations, it is less remarkable that the office attributed to Aquinas overshadowed that of Juliana Mont Cornillon than that the latter bears mentioning in a context shared with one of the greatest minds in history.

Example 1. "Laureata plebs fidelis."
Transcription by Vincent Corrigan, published in Barbara Walters, Vincent Corrigan, and Peter Ricketts, *The Feast of Corpus Christi*. (University Park, PA: Pennsylvania State University Press), 180–81. Reproduced with permission.

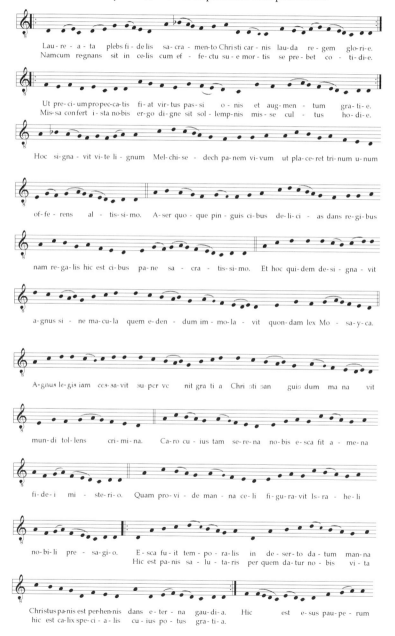

Example 1 (*continued*)

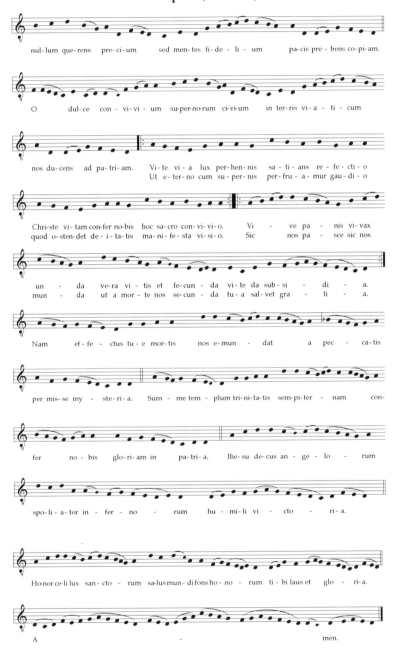

nul-lum que-rens pre-ci-um   sed men-tes fi-de-li-um   pa-cis pre-bens co-pi-am.

O   dul-ce con-vi-vi-um su-per-no-rum ci-vi-um   in ter-ris vi-a-ti-cum

nos du-cens ad pa-tri-am.   Vi-te vi-a lux per-hen-nis   sa-ti-ans re-fe-cti-o
                             Ut e-ter-no cum su-per-nis   per-fru-a-mur gau-di-o

Chri-ste vi-tam con-fer no-bis hoc sa-cro con-vi-vi-o.   Vi   -   ve pa - nis vi-vax
quod o-sten-det de-i-ta-tis ma-ni-fe-sta vi-si-o.   Sic   nos pa - sce sic nos

un - da   ve-ra vi-tis et fe-cun - da vi-te da sub-si - di - a.
mun - da   ut a mor-te nos se-cun - da tu-a sal-vet gra - ti - a.

Nam   ef-fe - ctus tu-e mor-tis   nos e-mun - dat   a pec - ca-tis

per mis-se my - ste-ri-a.   Sum - me tem - plum tri-ni-ta-tis sem-pi-ter - nam   con-

fer   no-bis   glo-ri-am in   pa-tri-a.   Ihe-su de-cus an - ge-lo - rum

spo-li-a-tor in-fer-no - rum   hu-mi-li vi - cto - ri-a.

Ho-nor ce-li lux san-cto - rum sa-lus mun-di fons ho-no - rum ti-bi laus et glo - ri-a.

A - men.

Text 1. "Laureata plebs fidelis"

Translation by Barbara R. Walters and Vincent Corrigan with thanks
to Joseph A. Komanchak for comments.

1a

Laureata plebs fidelis
Sacramento Christi carnis
Lauda regem glorie.

Faithful people,
Crowned with the sacrament of the body
of Christ,
Praise the king of glory.

1b

Nam cum regnans sit in celis
Cum effectu sue mortis
Se prebet cotidie.

Although reigning in heaven,
By the effect of his death,
He gives himself each day.

2a

Ut precium pro peccatis
Fiat virtus passionis
Et augmentum gratie.

In order that the virtue of his passion
May be the price for our sins
And increase of grace.

2b

Missa confert ista nobis
Ergo digne sit solemnis
Misse cultus hodie.

This mass confers these things upon us,
Therefore, let the celebration of the Mass
Be worthily solemn today.

3a

Hoc signavit vite lignum
Melchisedech panem vivum
Ut placaret trinum unum
Offerens altissimo

The tree of life signified this (mystery),
Melchisedech offering bread and wine
To the Most High
To please the triune God.

3b

Aser quoque pinguis cibus
Delicias dans regibus
Nam regalis hic est cibus
Pane sacratissimo.

And like Aser, giving delights to kings
In the form of rich food,
This is also royal food,
By means of the most sacred bread.

4a

Et hoc quidem designavit
Agnus sine macula
Quem edendum immolavit
Quondam lex Mosayca.

And the lamb without blemish
Also signified this,
The one that was once sacrificed and had
to be eaten
According to Mosaic law.

4b

Agnus legis iam cessavit
Supervenit gratia
Christi sanguis dum manavit
Mundi tollens crimina.

The law of the slaughtered lamb has now
ceased,
For grace has come instead
When the blood of Christ flowed,
Expiating the sins of the world.

5a
Caro cuius tam serena
Nobis esca sit amena
Fidei mysterio.

May his flesh so serene
Be pleasant food for us
In the mystery of faith.

5b
Quam provide manna celi
Figuravit Israheli
Nobili presagio.

Te manna of heaven
Given as a noble exemplar to Israel
Was a form of this food.

6a
Esca fuit temporalis
In deserto datum manna
Christus panis est perennis
Dans eterna gaudia.

Temporal food it was
That manna given in the desert
Christ is perennial bread
Giving eternal joys.

6b
Hic est panis salutaris
Per quem datur nobis vita
Hic est calix specialis
Cuius potus gratia.

Here is the bread of salvation
Through which life is given to us,
Here is the special chalice
Whose beverage is grace.

7a
Hic est esus pauperum
Nullum quaerens precium
Sed mentes fidelium
Pacis prebens copiam.

Here is the food of the poor
Which requires no price,
But granting the minds of the faithful
An abundance of peace.

7b
O dulce convivium
Supernorum civium
In terris viaticum
Nos ducens ad patriam.

O sweet banquet
Of heavenly citizens
On earth food for the journey
That leads us to our homeland.

8a
Vitae via, lux perhennis
Satians refectio
Christe, vitam confer nobis
Hoc sacro convivio.

Way of life, continual light,
Satisfying refreshment,
Christ, conferring life to us
By this sacred banquet.

8b
Ut eterno cum supernis
Perfruamur gaudio
Quod ostendit Deitatis
Manifesta visio.

That with those above
We might eternally enjoy
The happiness that
The manifest sight of God reveals.

9a
Vive panis, vivax unda
Vera vitis et fecunda
Vitae da subsidia.

Living bread, lively flow of water
True and fruitful vine
Give us succor for life.

9b
Sic nos pasce, sic nos munda
Ut a morte nos secunda
Tua salvet gratia.

Therefore nourish us, therefore cleanse us,
So that your favorable grace
May preserve us from death.

10a
Nam effectus tue mortis
Nos emundat a peccatis
Per misse mysteria.

For the effect of your death
Cleanses us from our sins
Through the mystery of the Mass.

10b
Summe templum trinitatis
Sempiternam confer nobis
Gloriam in patria.

O temple of the most high Trinity,
Confer upon us everlasting
Glory in heaven.

11a
Iesu, decus angelorum
Spoliator infernorum
Humili victoria.

Jesus, glory of angels,
Despoiler of hell,
By humble victory.

11b
Honor celi, lux sanctorum,
Salus mundi, fons bonorum,
Tibi laus et gloria. Amen.

The honor of heaven, the light of saints,
The salvation of the world, the fount of good,
To you praise and glory. Amen.

Diagram of "Laureata plebs fidelis"

"Laureata…"	"Hoc signavit…"	"Esca…"	"Hic est"	"Vite via"	"Nam effectus…"
Exordium	Old Testament	Sacrament	Doxology of the Sacrament	Praise Jesus	Amen

Strophes

I	II	III	IV	V	VI	VII	VIII	IX	X	XI
1a 1b	2a 2b	3a 3b	4a 4b	5a 5b	6a 6b	7a - 7b	8a 8a	9a 9b	10a 10b	11a 11b Amen

Melodic Units

I	II	III	IV	V	VI	VII	VIII	IX	X		XI
m1a A	**m2a D**	**m3a B**	**m4a T**	m5a TC	**m6a**	**m7a T'**	**m8a**	**m4a' T'**	**m10a T"**		m11a
m1b B	m2b	m3b	**m4b T**	**m5b "DL"**	m6a	m7b	**m8b**	**m4c TC**	**m10b T"&B**		m11b
m1c C	m2c C'	m3c	**m4c TC**	m5c C	m6b	m7c	m8a	**m3d' C'**	m1c C		m2c C'
		m3d C'	m4d C"		m6c	**m1c C**	m8b				

C = cadential formula
B = sacrament theme
D = Dies irae theme
T = sacrifice theme
TC = sacrifice theme cadence
"DL" = quote from "Dulce lignum…"

Notes

Funding for this research was provided by a Professional Staff Congress–City University of New York Research Award.

1. Jeffery (1992, 14) explains the centonization process characteristic of chant composition as one through which melodic segments were pieced together in a formulaic way.

2. "Hoc domina mea vobis mittitur de supernis; videte et examinate si quid sit in cantu vel littera corrigendum."

3. Saucier (2010, 1) has recently shown, "through a newly-identified example of contrafactum, Laureata plebs shares an identical melody and similar imagery with a sequence commemorating the liégeois martyr, St. Lambert. The music and message of Laureata plebs thus yield fresh insight in to the theology and liturgy of Corpus Christi as intimately connected to hagiography and sacrifice."

4. I.e., "Hoc est meum corpus" (This is My Body).

References

Primary Sources

MS 70.E.4 The Hague, Koninklijke Bibliotheek, MS 70.E.4

Secondary Sources

Abulafia, David. 1999. "The Kingdom of Sicily under the Hohenstaufen and Angevins." In *C. 1198–c. 1300*. Vol. 5 of *The New Cambridge Medieval History*, edited by David Abulafia, 497–521. Cambridge: Cambridge University Press.

Bartoli, Marco. 1999. "Les femmes et l'*Église au XIIIe siècle*." In *Actes du Colloque de Liège*. Vol 1 of *Fête-Dieu (1246–1996)*, edited by André Haquin, 55–79. Louvain-la-Neuve: Institut d'Études Médiévales de l'Université Catholique de Louvain.

Brasington, Bruce C. 2001. "*In nomine patria*: Transmission and Reception of an Early Papal Letter concerning Baptism." *Codices Manuscripti* 37/38: 1–5.

Bynum, Caroline Walker. 1982. *Jesus as Mother: Studies in the Spirituality of the High Middle Ages*. Berkeley: University of California Press.

Corrigan, Vincent. 2002. "Travel and Transformation: The Corpus Christi Office in Germany." Paper delivered at the 23rd Annual Medieval Forum, Plymouth State College, Plymouth, NH.

Delaissé, L. M. J. 1950. "A la recherche des origines de l'office du Corpus Christi dans les manuscrits liturgiques." *Scriptorium* 4: 220–39.

Delville, Jean-Pierre. 1999. *Vie de Sainte Julienne de Cornillon*. Vol. 2 of *Fête-Dieu (1246–1996)*. Critical edition. Louvain-la-Neuve: Institut d'*Études Médiévales de l'Université Catholique de Louvain*.

Duby, Georges. 1978. *Medieval Marriage: Two Models from Twelfth-Century France*. Baltimore: The Johns Hopkins University Press.

Fassler, Margot Elsbeth. 1993. *Gothic Song: Victorine Sequences and Augustianian Reform in Twelfth-Century Paris*. Cambridge: Cambridge University Press.

Gjerdingen, Robert O. 1988. *A Classic Turn of Phrase: Music and the Psychology of Convention*. Philadelphia: University of Pennsylvania Press.

Grundman, Herbert. 1995. *Religious Movements in the Middle Ages*, translated by Steven Rowan. Notre Dame, IN: University of Notre Dame Press.

Jeffery, Peter. 1992. *Re-Envisioning Past Musical Cultures: Ethnomusicology in the Study of Gregorian Chant*. Chicago: University of Chicago Press.

King, Margot H. 2003. "General Introduction." In *Two Lives of Marie d'Oignies*, translated by Margot H. King, 9–12. Toronto: Peregrina Publishing Co.

Kupper, Jean-Louis. 1999. "La cité de Liège au temps de Julienne de Cornillon." In *Actes du Colloque de Liège*. Vol. 2 of *Fête-Dieu (1246–1996)*, edited by André Haquin, 19–26. Louvain-la-Neuve: Institut d'*Études Médiévales de* l'Université Catholique de Louvain.

Lambot, Cyrille, and Paul-Irénée Fransen. 1946. *L'Office de la Fête-Dieu Primitive*. Maredsous: Editions de Maredsous.

McGrade, Michael. 1996. "Gottschalk of Aachen, the Investiture Controversy, and Music for 'The Feast of the *Divisio Apostolorum*.'" *Journal of the American Musicological Society* 3: 351–408.

Mulder-Bakker, Anneke B. 2005. *Lives of the Anchoresses: The Rise of the Urban Recluse in Medieval Europe*, translated by Myra Heerspink Scholz. Philadelphia: University of Pennsylvania Press.

Newman, Barbara, trans. 1989. *The Life of Juliana Mont Cornillon*. Toronto: Peregrina Publishing Co.

Quenardel, Oliver. 1997. *La Communion Eucharistique dans "Le Héraut de L'Amour Divin" de Sainte Gertrude D'Helfta*. Abbaye de Bellefontaine: Brepols.

Rubin, Miri. 1991. *Corpus Christi: The Eucharist in Late Medieval Culture*. Cambridge: Cambridge University Press.

Saucier, Catherine. 2010. "The Earliest Sequence for Corpus Christi: Conflating Sacrament and Sacrifice in Medieval Liège." Paper presented at the American Musicological Society National Meeting, Indianapolis, IN.

Simenon, G. 1922. "Les Origines de la Fête-Dieu." *Revue ecclésiastique de Liège* 13: 345–58.

Torrell, Jean-Pierre, OP. 1996. *Saint Thomas Aquinas: The Person and His Work*, Translated by Robert Royal. Vol. 1. Washington, DC: Catholic University of America Press.

Walters, Barbara. 2004. "Church-Sect Dynamics and the Feast of Corpus Christi." *Sociology of Religion* 65: 285–301.

Weber, Max. 1978. *Economy and Society*, edited by Guenther Roth and Claus Wittich, translated by Ephraim Fischoff et al. 2 vols. Berkeley: University of California Press.

Wogan-Browne, Jocelyn, and Marie-Elisabeth Henneau. 1999. "Liège, the Medieval 'Woman Question' and the Question of Medieval Women." In *New Trends in Feminine Spirituality: The Holy Women of Liège and Their Impact*, edited by Juliette Dor, Lesley Johnson, and Jocelyn Wogan-Browne, 1–32. Turnhout: Brepols.

A Newly Recognized Polyphonic Christmas Gospel, *Liber generationis*: And Another Look at the Polyphony in the Manuscript Assisi, Biblioteca del Sacro Convento, MS 695

Julia Wingo Shinnick

The manuscript Assisi, Biblioteca del Sacro Convento, MS 695 was written in Paris about 1230 for use in Reims, possibly as a liturgical ornament for the new cathedral being built to replace the edifice badly damaged by the disastrous fire of 1210.[1] The codex is a troper-proser that contains several polyphonic settings among its more than 250 liturgical, musically notated items (including 176 complete or recoverable sequences, seventy Mass Ordinary pieces, eight alleluias, and twelve *varia* items). In addition to its three polyphonic Mass Ordinary items and four polyphonic Marian sequences (one, "Ave sydus lux dierum," a double texting of the sequence "Verbum bonum"), there is an eighth polyphonic item in Assisi 695[2] that has not been previously recognized as such. This is the setting of the *Liber generationis* (the Christmas Gospel: Matthew 1:2–16), found on folios 34v through 36v of the Assisi 695 troper. The eight Assisi 695 polyphonic pieces are listed in table 1.

Table 1. The Eight Polyphonic Pieces in Assisi 695

Text incipit	Folio	Voices	MS section	Genre
Factus homo	fol. 2r	à 2	Troper	Agnus trope
Summe rex sempiterne	fol. 15v	à 3	Troper	Kyrie trope
Liber generationis	fol. 34v	à 2	Troper	Gospel
Voci vita sit unita	fol. 52v	à 2	Troper	Sanctus trope
Gaude Dei genitrix	fol. 111r	à 2	AS I	Sequence
Sicut pratum picturatur	fol. 236r	à 2	AS III	Sequence
Verbum bonum et suave	fol. 238v	à 2	AS III	Sequence
Ave sydus lux dierum	fol. 238v	à 2	AS III	Sequence

The Polyphonic Gospel, *Liber generationis*

The polyphonically notated portions of the Assisi 695 polyphonic Gospel, *Liber generationis*, are shown in facsimile in figures 1 and 2, and the entire Gospel is

Figure 1. Assisi, Biblioteca del Sacro Convento, MS 695, fol. 35.
Opening of polyphonic Gospel, *Liber generationis*. (Photograph by Pater Gerhard Ruf.
Printed by permission of the Sacro Convento, Assisi.)

Figure 2. Assisi, Biblioteca del Sacro Convento, MS 695, fol. 36v. Closing of polyphonic Gospel, *Liber generationis*. (Photograph by Pater Gerhard Ruf. Printed by permission of the Sacro Convento, Assisi.)

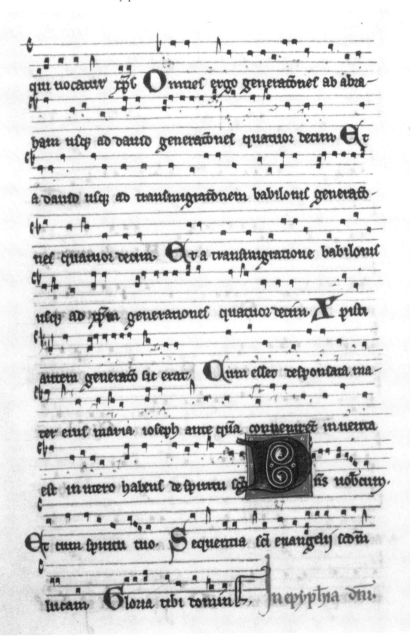

transcribed in appendix A. I initially concentrate on this piece, bringing in the other seven polyphonic pieces as they bear on my central hypothesis: that all eight polyphonic items in Assisi 695 were specifically written and/or included in this manuscript to ornament the Marian liturgy of the newly-built cathedral Notre-Dame-de-Reims.

The *Liber generationis* at Reims was associated not only with the birth of Christ but also with the Conception and Nativity of Mary; it was sung at Reims Cathedral on the feasts of St. Anne, Mother of the Virgin Mary (July 26), the Nativity of the Virgin (September 8) and the Conception of the Virgin (December 8)[3] as well as on that gospel's traditional Christmas date.[4] Given its performance tradition, the addition of a second voice to this Gospel text may indeed have been intended to honor Mary, the patron saint of the new cathedral.

Perhaps one reason the piece has not previously been recognized as polyphony is that the added voice appears only on the first four staves of folio 35r (figure 1), and on the first, second, sixth, seventh, and eighth staves of folio 36v (figure 2). Furthermore, the added voice is written in light brown ink above and below the original voice (in darker ink) and seems at first glance merely a notation of an alternate, more decorated monophonic version of the melody.

Upon closer examination, however, it becomes apparent that the added voice was intended to form polyphony with the original melody, even though only nine of the thirty-seven staves of notation for the *Liber generationis* contain the added pitches. If we take into consideration the formulaic nature of the Gospel recitation, it soon becomes clear that the notator added the pitches of the second part with great economy; as soon as the original voice begins to repeat a previous formula, the added voice disappears. When the recitation formula changes so that previous pitches for the added voice can no longer be applied, added pitches in brown ink reappear, providing the second voice for the closing of the Gospel.

The Assisi 695 melody for this Gospel is close to that in RS 224 (a fourteenth-century Reims cathedral book) and less close to the Paris version in BnF 1112 (from Notre Dame of Paris).[5] The added voice, however, is not present in RS 224, BnF 1112 or any of the other sources for this Gospel examined for this study.[6] In fact, polyphonic Epistles and Gospels became a popular phenomenon mainly in eastern Germany and Bohemia only in the fourteenth century and later.[7]

A similarity does exist, however, between the Assisi 695 Gospel setting and a two-voice setting of the Epistle for the Assumption, *In omnibus requiem quesivi* from the late eleventh-century Saint-Martial manuscript, BnF 1139 (example 1).[8] Like the Assisi 695 Gospel, the BnF 1139 Epistle does not contain notation for both voices throughout; rather, both voices are notated only in the introduction and the beginning of the first verse. After this only the florid upper voice is notated, but one can fill in the lower (reciting) voice in the remaining phrases

Example 1. "In omnibus requiem quesivi," BnF 1139, fol. 44v. Opening of verse.

by virtue of the formulaic nature of the setting and by virtue of the fact that the lower voice consists mainly of long-held notes against the florid upper part. The original voice of the Assisi 695 version of the *Liber generationis* is more active than the original voice in the polyphonic Epistle from BnF 1139, and in Assisi 695 the partially notated voice is the more florid part. Both pieces, however, follow the principle of notating only the necessary portions of the added voice.

The polyphony resulting from the addition of the second voice in the Assisi 695 *Liber generationis* is relatively simple and conceivably could have been improvised by a second performer familiar with the original part. Particularly in the first section of the Gospel setting, the added voice does not move consistently according to the rules for improvised discant or "fifthing";[9] rather, when the two voices are heard together, the effect to some extent resembles heterophony. Enough contrary motion occurs, however, especially in the second section (beginning at the words "omnes ergo"), to justify interpreting the added voice as having been intended to form polyphony with the original melody.

The level of dissonance is especially high in the first section (opening "Liber generationis" to "Omnes ergo"). It is likely that here the added voice was intended to be pitched at a different level from that at which it is apparently notated, since the later scribe's additions were restricted to the space remaining above and below the original part. This is most obvious at the end of the first system (figure 1). Here the melisma on the second syllable of the word "filii" is clearly a rise and descent of a fourth, but it takes place within the space of two staff lines rather than rising above the staff to yield a clear intervallic profile.[10]

The added voice traces an appropriate gestural component, although its pitch level remains open to interpretation. A "literal" transcription of the first system yields inappropriately discordant polyphony (example 2).[11] But "stretching" the pitches of the added line in accordance with its gestural aspect provides a more performable version (example 3).[12] To conclude the first phrase, at the word "Abraham" one may borrow the pitches from the only occasion in which the second voice completes the cadence, at the words "fratres eius." Again, the ascending and descending gesture may be expanded to yield a satisfying closure on the unison (example 4).[13] Neither the notation of the second voice nor that of the original melody was, of course, used by the performers during the actual liturgical

Example 2. "Liber generationis," Assisi 695, fol. 35. Literal transcription of opening.

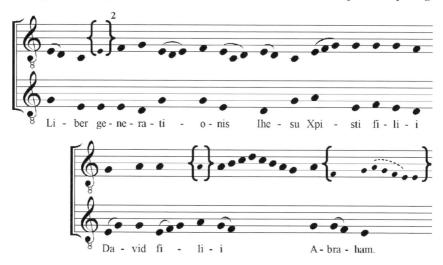

Example 3. "Liber generationis," Assisi 695, fol. 35.
Performers' transcription of opening phrase.

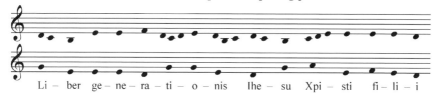

Example 4. "Liber generationis," Assisi 695, fol. 35. Cadence.

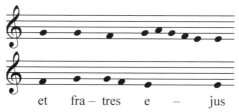

performance of the *Liber generationis*. Most likely the added voice represents the performance practice of the time at Reims Cathedral and was written down as an added reminder for the performers, who may have traditionally improvised a second voice. Whether this Gospel setting represents the performance practice of thirteenth-century Reims or a later attempt at Assisi is difficult to determine, but a Reims origin for the second voice cannot be ruled out.

The Polyphonic Proses and Mass Ordinary Pieces in Assisi 695

A total of four polyphonic proses (all Marian) appear in Assisi 695, one on the final folio of the first of Assisi 695's three prosers, and three on the final folios of the third proser.[14] A condensed listing of the manuscript's folio sequence, including its three distinct prosers, appears in figure 3.[15] Contrary to the assumption of Max Lütolf, the appearance of these proses at the end of the first and third prosers does not indicate that they are later additions to the manuscript.[16] Since all four proses have the light red and blue verse initials and two settings have the *initiales champies* common to the rest of the manuscript,[17] these pieces were very likely part of the original collection. Another argument against the polyphonic sequences as additions to Assisi 695 may be found in the fact that the final groups of monophonic proses in both the first and third prosers are Marian. This suggests that the monophonic and polyphonic pieces were grouped together because of their shared subject and function as Marian pieces. The polyphonic sequences of Assisi 695 are characteristic representatives of what Cristina Hospenthal[18] considers isolated witnesses from a predominantly non-written practice. These, like other extant polyphonic sequences from the thirteenth and fourteenth centuries, represent particular favorites or special, local compositions from a wide practice of improvised performance.

Considering the polyphonic Mass Ordinary pieces, I begin with the Kyrie trope "Summe rex sempiterne," which appears in only three manuscripts listed in *Analecta hymnica* by Blume and Bannister.[19] Besides Assisi 695, the only other manuscript source for the trope is the early fourteenth-century Dublin troper-proser Cambridge, University Library, MS Additional 710 (CUL 710). This setting is monophonic, making the Assisi 695 version the only polyphonic setting of the melody with the text "Summe rex sempiterne." The melody (Melnicki 171),[20] however, occurs in one other polyphonic setting (for two voices) with a different text, "Creator puritatis," in the eleventh (Marian) fascicle of W1. Unlike the rare "Summe rex" text, Melody 171 is widespread before the fourteenth-century, appearing in at least thirty-four manuscripts.[21]

According to Melnicki, seven other tropes (in addition to "Summe rex sempiterne") occur with the same melody, and three of these appear in manuscripts from the twelfth and thirteenth centuries. These three tropes (besides "Summe

Figure 3. Assisi 695. Folio sequence showing
placement of Marian/polyphonic items.

I.   **Troper, fols. 2r–55r.**

> fol. 2r [Polyphonic Marian Agnus interpolated here}:
> *Recipe infra ante Alleluya: **Agnus Dei: Factus homo... (à 2)**]*

A. **Kyrie section. [Ends with two Marian Kyries; last one polyphonic]:**
  fol. 15v *{Kyrie}: Summe rex sempiterne...(à 3)*
B. **Gloria section [Begins with troped Gloria rubricated for Mary]**
  fol. 17r *De Beata Virgine Maria: Gloria: Spiritus et alme...*
C. **Varia section: Epistles, Gospels, Laudes, etc.**
D. **Sanctus section.**
E. **Agnus section [Ends with three interpolated Sanctus pieces, the last, polyphonic. Following the polyphonic Sanctus, 2 more Agnus pieces and, at the
  foot of fol. 53v, the direction to the polyphonic Agnus on folio 2r]**
  fols. 52v–53v [Marian] *Sanctus: Voci vita sit unita...* (à 2)

> fol. 53v [at foot of page]: *Require supra in secundo folio libri.*
> [Marian Agnus effectively inserted here through direction to fol. 2r]

[Troper Closes with eight Marian Alleluias]

II. **First Proser, fols. 56r–111v. [Closes with 4 Marian Proses, the last polyphonic]:**
  fols. 108r–110r [Three monophonic Marian proses]
  fol. 111r *Alia de Sancta Maria: Gaude Dei genitrix...Alleluya* **(à 2)**
III. **Second Proser, fols. 112r–162r.**
IV. **Third Proser, fols. 162v–239v. [Closes with 12 Marian proses; the last 3 polyphonic]:**
  fols. 227r–235r monophonic Marian proses, plus
  fol. 236r *De Beata Virgine: [S]icut pratum picturatur...*(à 2)
  fol. 238r *De Beata Virgine Maria. Alia: Verbum bonum et suave..*(à 2).
  [with added second text]: *Ave syderus lux...*(à 2)

rex") are "Cum iubilo iubilemus," "Marie laus et amor pater," and "Creator puritatis"; all three are explicitly Marian texts.[22]

Looking at example 5, we see that the "Summe rex" text is not overtly Marian. The lack of explicit reference to the Virgin, however, is not unusual in Marian
tropes. According to Ann-Katrin Andrews Johansson in her study of Marian proper
tropes, most of these "texts are more focused on Christ and God."[23] Additionally,
in line 3a of the "Summe rex" text, the words "spiritus alme" call to mind the widespread Marian Gloria trope "Spiritus et alme." Indeed, "Summe rex" concludes on
folio 16v of Assisi 695, and the next entry in the troper is a Gloria with the trope
"Spiritus et alme" (fol. 17r), rubricated "De beata Virgine Maria."[24] This, considered
along with the fact that the Kyrie preceding "Summe rex" is a Marian Kyrie, and
along with the overwhelmingly Marian use of Melody 171 in other thirteenth-
century manuscripts such as BnF 1112, W1, ARS 135, SS XIV, and Vat 2049, provides a convincing argument for classifying the Assisi 695 setting as a Marian one.[25]

Example 5. Kyrie, "Summe rex sempiterne," AS, fols. 15v–16v. Text and translation.

1a.	Summe rex, sempiterne dator vite, eleyson. Kyrie eleyson.	Highest king, giver of eternal life, have mercy. Lord have mercy.
1b.	Rex iusticie, pater pie, eleyson. Kyrie eleyson.	King of righteousness, holy Father, have mercy. Lord have mercy.
1c.	Creator creature universe, eleyson. (fol. 16r) Kyrie eleyson.	Creator of all creation, have mercy. Lord have mercy.
2a.	Summe superni regis nate, eleyson. Xpiste eleyson.	Highest born of the heavenly king, have mercy. Christ have mercy.
2b.	Salvator mortis nostre tua morte, eleyson. Xpiste eleyson.	Savior of our death by your death, have mercy. Christ have mercy.
2c.	Pax* patri pari potestate, eleyson. Xpiste eleyson.	Equal to the Father with equal power, have mercy. Christ have mercy.
3a.	(fol. 16v) Summe spiritus alme, eleyson. Kyrie eleyson.	Highest bountiful Spirit, have mercy. Lord have mercy.
3b.	Procedens ab utroque paraclyte, eleyson. Kyrie eleyson.	Proceeding from both and each, Paraclete, have mercy. Lord have mercy.
3c.	Triune et une, Deus immense, e[leyson.}	Three and one, boundless God, have mercy.
3d.	In fine venture iudex in carne, e[leyson.}	You who are to come at the end in the flesh as judge, have mercy.
3e.	Paterna pietate nos tuere, eleyson.	With paternal love watch over us, have mercy.

*Line 2c: "Pax" in AS is probably a scribal error for "Par" (as in Cu 710).

Example 6. Sanctus, "Voci vita sit unita," AS, fol. 52v–53v. Text and translation.

Sanctus, sanctus, {sanctus, Dominus deus sabaoth. Pleni sunt celi et terra gloria tua, Osanna in excelsis. Benedictus qui venit in nomine domini.}

1a. Voci vita	1b. Dum (fol. 53r) sacratur
sit unita	quo dampnatur
legis amicitia,	peccati malitia,
2a. Caro panis, sanguis vinum	2b. Quod delevit serpentinum
dum fiunt veraciter,	virus efficaciter.
3a. Hoc est corpus Xpisti verum	3b. Quod contrivit hostem ferum
natum matre virgine,	salvato sic homine.
4a. Hoc in cruce	4b. Hoc surrexit
sexta luce	et revexit
passum vicit infera.	carnem (fol. 53v) super sydera.
5a. Hic est cibus,	5b. Unde chorus
hic est potus	hic devotus
dans manna vivificum;	concinat plausificum:

Osanna in excelsis.
Holy, holy, holy, Lord God almighty, Heaven and earth are full of your glory.
Osanna in the highest. Blessed is he who comes in the name of the Lord.
1a. May life be united with voice through the friendship of the law,
1b. While the act of consecration takes place by means of which the evil of sin is condemned,
2a. While the flesh, the blood, are truly made bread, wine
2b. Which [mystery] has justly destroyed the serpent's poison.
3a. This is the true body of Christ, born as body of the virgin mother,
3b. Which [body] has trod upon the bestial enemy with mankind delivered accordingly.
4a. This [body], having suffered on the Cross at the sixth light, conquered the infernal regions.
4b. This [body] rose up and revived the flesh above the stars.
5a. This is food, this is drink, bestowing life-giving manna;
5b. Wherefore let this devoted chorus sing harmoniously the approbation:
Osanna in the highest.

Like the polyphonic "Kyrie: Summe rex," the polyphonic Sanctus trope "Voci vita sit unita" (example 6) does not at first glance seem to be a strongly Marian text.[26] But Gunilla Iversen notes a connection to another Marian Sanctus trope in the words "manna vivificum" (line 5a, 3) which recall both the phrase "spiritale manna" in the explicitly Marian Sanctus trope "Mariam concrepet," and the phrase "vitale manna" in another Sanctus trope written to the same melody as "Mariam concrepet."[27] These indirect Marian associations, considered together with the direct reference to the Virgin in line 3a, 2 ("natum matre virgine") of "Voci vita" and the appearance of the trope in the eleventh fascicle of W1, firmly establish it as Marian.[28]

The Agnus trope "Factus homo" (example 7), like the Hosanna trope "Voci vita," has as its central image the Incarnation. But the text of "Factus homo" is explicitly Marian; the name Mary (in "de virgine carne Maria") occurs in the first

Example 7. Agnus, "Factus homo," AS, fol. 2r. Text and translation.

{A}gnus Dei {qui tollis peccata mundi,}	Lamb of God, who takes away the sins of the world,
1. Factus homo, sumpta de virgine carne Maria,	1. Made man, the flesh having been assumed from Mary, a virgin,
{miserere nobis. Agnus Dei, qui tollis peccata mundi}	{have mercy on us. Lamb of God, who takes away the sins of the world,}
2. Quem genuit mater sine patre, pater sine matre,	2. Whom the mother bore without a Father, the Father without a mother,
{miserere nobis. Agnus Dei qui tollis peccata mundi}	{have mercy on us. Lamb of God, who takes away the sins of the world,}
3. Virginis auxilio, propulsis hostibus, omnem dona nobis pacem.	3. With the aid of the Virgin, with the enemies driven out, give us complete peace.

of the three text lines, and both of the other lines refer to her also: "mater sine patre" (line 2) and "virginis auxilio" (line 3).[29] The polyphonic Agnus has been inserted on folio 2, and, as noted in figure 3, a careful marginal note on that folio directs one to place the piece "infra ante Alleluya" (below, before the Alleluya).

On folio 53v, at the end of the Agnus section where there was insufficient room for the polyphonic Marian Agnus, another marginal note directs one to "Seek above on the second folio of the book" (Require supra in secundo folio libri) for the piece which should have been placed here. Thus the Marian polyphonic Agnus effectively closes the Agnus section of the troper, conforming to the general pattern of placing Marian pieces at the ends of sections of the troper.

Sources for the text of "Factus homo" total four, of which all except Assisi 695 are English manuscripts.[30] In the fifteenth-century manuscript Ob L5, a rubric assigns this troped Agnus to "principal duplex feasts of Blessed Mary with verses" and adds "on other feasts and commemorations it is sung without verses."[31] In W1 the troped Agnus appears in the Marian eleventh fascicle. All three polyphonic Mass Ordinary pieces in Assisi 695 are thus linked to the Marian tradition, and two of the three (Kyrie and Agnus) effectively appear as the last items in their respective sections of the Troper.

Conclusions: A Prototype for the Polyphonic Mass Cycle?

A question that naturally arises in a situation like that of Assisi 695, where a manuscript contains three special polyphonic Mass Ordinary pieces linked to the same saint, is whether or not a case can be made for the three pieces as a proto-Mass cycle: a Kyrie, Sanctus, and Agnus intended to be performed as a group. Codicological considerations of placement have suggested such a grouping, and additional observations on inks and styles of initials can provide further evidence in support of this hypothesis. The addition of the Sanctus trope "Voci vita" could have been made shortly after the manuscript was completed, although the lack of an *initiale champie* for any of the Sanctus or Agnus entries after the incomplete Agnus on folio 52v leaves the time of addition uncertain. The Agnus trope "Factus homo" (fol. 2r) clearly belongs to the same group as the pieces on folios 52v through 53v because of the similarity of its verse initials and ink and because it was apparently written immediately after the pieces on folio 53v, as the marginal notes suggest.

Further codicological evidence also supports the hypothesis that "Factus homo" and "Voci vita" are additions to Assisi 695. The lack of an *initiale champie* for "Factus homo" as well as for all of the other Sanctus and Agnus pieces found on folios 52v through 53v (except the first, incomplete Agnus on fol. 52v, which has an *initiale champie*) implies that all of these pieces were added after the illuminator had finished his work. Furthermore, the use of a lighter, brown ink and dark red ornamental verse initials (instead of the alternating light red and blue initials in the remainder of the manuscript) for these folios (52v–53v, excluding the incomplete, untroped Agnus at the top of fol. 53v) also marks these pieces as additions. Lütolf, however, states, "the difference in the flow of the handwriting [on these folios as opposed to the rest of the manuscript] is only trifling";[32] hence, these additions could date from a time quite soon after the completion of the bulk of the manuscript. I suggest that these six pieces (the Sanctus "Voci vita" on fols. 52v–53v; the Agnus "Factus homo" on fol. 2r; the Agnus "Mortis dira" on fol. 53v; the one untroped Agnus on fol. 53v; and the two untroped Sanctus pieces on fol. 52v) were added not long after the manuscript was completed, and that these additions occurred at Reims after Assisi 695 was first taken there from Paris.

The cathedral of Reims, like many others of its era, is dedicated to the Virgin Mary, but the placement of the Coronation of the Virgin as the subject of the sculptures featured on the central portal of the west facade provides an especially significant tribute to the "Queen of Heaven." In light of this particular Marian emphasis, it is not difficult to conclude that the three polyphonic Mass Ordinary pieces and the four polyphonic Marian sequences in Assisi 695 may well have been used together as a group on feasts of the Virgin at Reims, along with the polyphonic Gospel *Liber generationis* on the feasts of the Nativity and Conception of the Virgin, the patron saint of Notre-Dame-de-Reims. The three polyphonic Mass Ordinary items might also have been used at Christmas at Reims, in keeping with the conflation of Christ and the Virgin in the Incarnation and the major role of the Virgin in the salvation cycle as a link between the feasts of the Temporale and Sanctorale. More specifically, one can imagine that the polyphonic Sanctus and Agnus pieces were added for the dedication of the choir and sung at Mass together with the Kyrie "Summe rex," the polyphonic *Liber generationis* and one of the polyphonic Marian proses when the chapter of canons took possession of that area on September 7, 1241, the eve of the Feast of the Nativity of the Virgin, and the symbolic "birth" of the new Reims Cathedral, Notre-Dame-de-Reims.

Notes

1. During the first two decades (1211–31) of the construction of the Gothic cathedral Notre-Dame-de-Reims, a desire may have arisen to adorn the new building not only with sculpture, painting, stained glass, and stonework but also with beautiful liturgical music. The construction of a new cathedral had been prompted on May 6, 1210, by a fire that destroyed a part of the town, severely damaging the basilica church originally dedicated in the year 862 in the presence of Charles the Bald and subsequently enlarged and reconstructed twice (once ca. 970 and again beginning in 1157). According to Leclerq (1948, 14:2262), we know from Aubry de Trois-Fontaines, a chronicler of the time, that during the first twenty years the work had been pursued with prodigious activity. In fact, on September 7, 1241, the chapter took possession of the choir. When these events are considered in light of the fact that Laon Cathedral (begun ca. 1160 and completed in 1235) would have been in use and in its last stages of construction during the first two decades of the work on Reims Cathedral, it is not difficult to imagine that the Reims chapter might have wanted to emulate or best their neighbors. Such emulation could well have extended to the festal liturgies celebrated in Laon Cathedral and to the books containing those liturgies.

2. Throughout this study I refer to this manuscript as either AS 695, Assisi 695, or AS.

3. See Shinnick (1997, 32–34) for a discussion of manuscript evidence for the celebration of the Feast of the Conception of the Virgin in Reims as early as the twelfth century.

4. Chevalier 1900, 195, 205, 248, 249, 250, 255, 264. The Reims ordinals call for the *Liber generationis* for all of these feasts, listing its incipit both in the descriptive section and in the tables of Gospel and Epistle readings.

5. See Shinnick (1997, 199) for a comparison of the *Liber generationis* melody in Assisi 695 with those in eight other manuscripts.

6. The manuscripts whose settings of the *Liber generationis* were compared to that of Assisi 695 are: RS 224, BnF 1112, BL 17341, LoA, Wo F160, BnF 904, SS XIV, BnF 1139, and Li 2(17). A list of all manuscripts mentioned in this study appears in the list of references.

7. Göllner 1969. Göllner's transcriptions of three- and four-voice settings of the Christmas Gospel from eighteen different manuscripts from the fourteenth through the sixteenth centuries bear little resemblance to the two-voice version in Assisi 695. The five fourteenth-century settings of the *Liber generationis* in Göllner's collection are all for three voices and consist of two general types: (1) settings in which the three voices alternate one by one on short segments of a phrase and join in full three-voice polyphony only at the ends of phrases, and (2) settings in which all three voices participate continuously in the note-against-note (and ligature-against-ligature) fashion of discant.

8. The Epistle for the Assumption is a reading from the apocryphal book Ecclesiasticus (The Wisdom of Jesus, Son of Sirach) 24:11–20.

9. For details of the technique of improvised discant, see Fuller 1978.

10. My thanks to Cynthia Cyrus for these observations distinguishing the gestural and pitch components of the added voice.

11. The notes enclosed in braces in example 2 are taken from other corresponding sections of the AS 695 added voice.

12. Appendix B presents both a literal transcription and a suggested performers' transcription of the first phrase. The notes enclosed in braces in example 3 correspond to analogous notes in other matching sections of the AS added voice.

13. Because the notation for the added voice in the first section of the setting extends to a cadence point only at the words "Iudam et fratres eius," I have used this formula at the other fifteen cadence points in the first section of the transcription in appendix A. After the change in recitation formula (at the words "Omnes ergo"), the last cadences are at the (inverted) fifth (the pitch *a* in the tenor above the pitch *e* in the added voice). The setting of the original voice in the Assisi 695 Gospel corresponds to the largest of the three groups of monophonic *Liber generationis* settings noted by Huglo and McKinnon 2001, 10:169. See also Shinnick, (1997, chap. 3), for a discussion of monophonic settings of the *Liber generationis* compared to the Assisi 695 setting.

14. "Gaude dei genetrix," on fol. 111r–v, a contrafact of a first-epoch sequence, also occurs in CA 32, ARS 135, and CUL 710. "Sicut pratum," a late sequence, appears on fols. 236r–238v of AS and also in CA 32. Li 2(17) contains only the text of "Sicut pratum," and BnF 3156 contains only a monophonic version of the sequence, added to the manuscript at a later date. "Verbum bonum," a late sequence, on fols. 238v–239v of AS, is very widespread, with eleven polyphonic sources. "Ave sydus lux," a double texting with "Verbum bonum," appears only in AS and CA 32. All four AS sequences are for two voices, and all four are cast in tetrardus mode.

15. See appendix C for a complete manuscript inventory of Assisi 695.

16. Lütolf 1970, 206.

17. The *initiale champie* for "Gaude Dei" has been cut from the manuscript, and since "Verbum bonum" and "Ave sydus" are a double texting, they share one *initiale champie*, the letter *V*.

18. Hospenthal 1990. All of the sequences considered by Hospenthal have Marian texts (except *Magnus Deus*, for the feast of St. Stephen, December 26), a fact reflecting the rise of the cult of Mary that began in the twelfth century. Hospenthal remarks that "actual concordances [for the polyphonic sequences] do not exist" and "the individual pieces are isolated for the most part." She sees the mode of composition of these pieces as one "close to an *ad hoc* practice as it is described by John of Afflighem" and describes these polyphonic sequences as having the following characteristics: two voices, wide agreement in the range of both voices, syllabic settings, short phrases, and a predominance of contrary motion in mostly step-wise progression.

19. Blume and Bannister 1905, 91–92, no. 28.

20. Landwehr-Melnicki 1955, 113–14.

21. The manuscripts surveyed for the present study fall into ten categories: (1) England/Sarum, (2) east Francia, (3) Italy, (4) Paris Mendicants, (5) Paris (Notre Dame and/or Saint-Victor), (6) north and northeast France, (7) Normandy/French Sicily/northwest France, (8) central France, (9) south France and (10) other.

22. Landwehr-Melnicki 1955, 113–14. The texts of the four later tropes are not listed in *Analecta hymnica*, and the manuscripts in which they appear were not available for examination; it is not clear whether or not the later tropes to Melnicki 171 are also Marian texts.

23. Johansson 1998, 46.

24. It is significant that by appearing first in the Gloria section, the Marian Gloria "Spiritus et alme" breaks with the manuscript pattern of placing Marian pieces at the end of sections (figure 3). The Kyrie and Gloria are the only two Mass Ordinary items that occur successively in the Mass, unseparated by any other prayers or chants. These two chants might naturally have been perceived as a pair; hence their placement in Assisi 695.

25. See Shinnick (1997, chap. 3) for more discussion of the liturgical assignments for Melody 171 in these other manuscripts.

26. In *Analecta Hymnica, Voci vita* is edited as a prose for the Feast of Corpus Christi.

27. Iversen 1990, 207–8.

28. The eleventh fascicle of W1 has long been acknowledged as a Marian collection. See Roesner 1974.

29. Johansson (1998, 46) points out that although some proper tropes "have the form of a prayer or address directed to the Virgin, these are mostly found to the Assumption and Nativity feasts in Italy," and "most of the tropes mention the Virgin in the third person."

30. Blume and Bannister, 1905, 377, no. 393; and Hiley 1986, 115. The four sources are: Assisi 695; ARS 135 (Paris, Bibliothèque de l'Arsenal, MS 135), a late thirteenth-century London manuscript of Sarum use; Ob L5 (Oxford, Bodleian Library, Lat. lit. b. 5), a fifteenth-century gradual of York use from East Drayton (Notts); and Cjc 102 (Cambridge, St. John's College, MS 102, D. 27), a fourteenth/fifteenth-century Benedictine ordinal and customary from St. Mary's, York.

31. "In festis principalibus duplicibus Beatae Mariae cum versibus: In aliis festis et commemorationibus sine versibus cantetur."

32. Lütolf 1970, 209.

References

Manuscripts

ARS 135   Paris, Bibliothèque de l'Arsenal, MS 135; missal-proser-Kyriale. Sarum. Second half of 13th c.

AS   Assisi, Biblioteca del Sacro Convento, MS 695; troper-proser. Paris/Reims. 1230s.

BL 17341   London, British Library, MS Add. 17341; Evangeliary. Paris, Sainte-Chapelle. Last quarter of 13th c.

BnF 904   Paris, Bibliothèque nationale de France, MS lat. 904; Gradual with proser. Rouen (Cathedral). 13th c.

BnF 1112   Paris, Bibliothèque nationale de France, MS lat. 1112; missal with Kyriale and proser. Paris (Notre-Dame). 1220s.

BnF 1139   Paris, Bibliothèque nationale de France, MS lat. 1139; proser with five sequence collections. Saint-Martial. Late 11th–early 13th c.

BnF 3156   Paris, Bibliothèque nationale de France, MS lat. 3156; manuscript of Latin prose with several musical additions. Paris. 13th c. Musical items added later.

CA 32   Cambrai, Bibliothèque Municipale, MS C. 32; Psalter-hymner-proser. Maubeuge. Late 13th c.
Cjc 102   Cambridge, St. John's College, MS (102) D 27; Ordinal and customary. St. Mary's, York (Benedictine). 14th /15th c.
CUL 710   Cambridge, University Library, MS Add. 710; Ordinal-Kyriale-troper-proser. Dublin (Sarum use). Early 14th c.
Li 2(17)   Limoges, Bibliothèque Municipale, MS 2 (17); Gradual. Fontévrault (Benedictine). Ca. 1260–80.
LoA   London, British Library, MS Egerton 2615; Circumcision Office with supplement of polyphonic pieces; Beauvais lessons, Daniel play. Beauvais. 1227–34.
Ob L5   Oxford, Bodleian Library, MS Lat. lit. b.5; Gradual. East Drayton (York use). 15th c.
RS 224   Reims, Bibliothèque Municipale, MS 224; Missal. Reims (cathedral). Second half of 14th c.
SS XIV   Rome, Santa Sabina, Biblioteca della Curia generalizia dei Domenicana, MS XIV, lit. 1; Dominican exemplar. Paris (Dominican). 1259–62.
Vat 2049   Vatican City, Biblioteca apostolica vaticana, MS lat. 2049; missal. Paris (Franciscan). Second half of 13th c.
W1   Wolfenbüttel, Herzog August Bibliothek, cod. guelf. 628 Helmstad. (Heinemann no. 677); a principal source for Notre-Dame polyphony. Scotland (St. Andrews). Ca. 1230.
Wo F160   Worcester, Cathedral Chapter Library, MS F. 160; music for complete liturgy. Worcester (Benedictine). Ca. 1230.

Printed Sources

Blume, Clemens, and Henry Marriott Bannister. 1905. *Tropen zum Ordinarium Missae. Vol. 1 of Tropi, Graduales Tropen des Missale im Mittelalter.* Analecta Hymnica medii aevi 47. Leipzig: O. R. Reisland.

Chevalier, Ulysse. 1900. *Sacramentaire et martyrologe de l'abbaye de Saint-Rémy: Martyrologe, Calendrier, Ordinaires et Prosaire de la Métropole de Reims (VIIe–XIIIe siecle) Publiés d'après les manuscrits de Paris, Londres, Reims et Assise.* Bibliothèque liturgique 7. Paris: Alphonse Picard, Libraire.

Fuller, Sarah. 1978. "Discant and the Theory of Fifthing." *Acta Musicologica* 50: 241–75.

Göllner, Theodor. 1969. *Die Mehrstimmigen Liturgischen Lesungen.* 2 vols. Tutzing: Hans Schneider.

Hiley, David. 1986. "Ordinary of Mass Chants in English, North French and Sicilian Manuscripts." *Journal of the Plainsong and Mediaeval Music Society* 9: 1–128.

Hospenthal, Cristina. 1990. "Zur mehrstimmigen Sequenz des 13. und 14. Jahrhunderts in Frankreich." In *Atti del XIV Congresso della Società Internazionale di Musicologia: Trasmissione e recezione delle forme di cultura musicale,* edited by Angelo Pompilio et al., 637–46. Turin: Edizioni di Torino.

Huglo, Michel and James McKinnon. 2001. "Gospel." In *The New Grove Dictionary of Music and Musicians,* edited by Stanley Sadie, 10:168–72. 2nd ed. 29 vols. New York: Macmillan.

Iversen, Gunilla, ed. 1990. *Tropes du Sanctus.* Corpus Troporum VII. Acta Universitatis Stockholmiensis. Studia Latina Stockholmiensia 34. Stockholm: Almqvist and Wiksell.

Johansson, Ann-Katrin Andrews, ed. 1998. *Tropes for the Proper of the Mass.* Vol. 4: *The Feasts of the Blessed Virgin Mary.* Corpus Troporum IX. Acta Universitatis Stockholmiensis. Studia Latina Stockholmiensia 21. Stockholm: Almqvist and Wiksell.

Landwehr-Melnicki, Margareta. 1955. *Das einstimmige Kyrie des lateinischen Mittelalters.* Regensburg: Gustav Bosse.

Leclerq, Henri. 1948. "Reims." In *Dictionnaire d'archéologie chrétienne et de liturgie,* edited by Fernand Cabrol, 14:2262. Paris: Letouzey et Ane.

Lütolf, Max. 1970. *Die mehrstimmigen Ordinarium missae-Sätze vom ausgehenden 11. bis zur Wende des 13. zum 14. Jahrhundert.* 2 vols. Bern: Paul Haupt.

Roesner, Edward H. 1974. "The Manuscript Wolfenbüttel, Herzog-August-Bibliothek, 628 Helmstadiensis: A Study of Its Origins and of Its Eleventh Fascicle." PhD diss., New York University.

Shinnick, Emilie Julia Wingo. 1997. "The Manuscript Assisi, Biblioteca del Sacro Convento, ms. 695: A Codicological and Repertorial Study." PhD diss., University of Texas at Austin.

Thannabaur, Peter Josef. 1962. *Das einstimmige Sanctus der römiscshen Messe in der handschriftlichen Überlieferung des 11. bis 16. Jahrhunderts.* Munich: Walter Ricke.

Appendix A. "Liber generationis" (AS, fols. 34v–36v).

1. As in AS, fol. 36v (opening of Epiphany Gospel, *Factum est autem*)
2. Notes printed with small noteheads and enclosed in braces are taken from other corresponding parts of the AS added voice. Notes in braces in the lower voice likewise come from corresponding sections of the setting.

Appendix A (*continued*)

A - bra - ham au - tem ge - nu - it Y - sa - ac.

I - sa - ac au - tem ge - nu - it Ia - cob.

Ia - cob au - tem ge - nu - it Iu - dam et fra - tres e - ius.
Pha - res au - tem ge - nu - it Es - rom.
A - ram au - tem ge - nu - it A - mi - na - dab.
Na - a - son au - tem ge - nu - it Sal - mon.
Bo - oth au - tem ge - nu - it O - beth ex Ruth.

Iu - das au - tem ge - nu - it
Es - rom au - tem ge - nu - it
A - mi - na - dab au - tem ge - nu - it
Sal - mon au - tem ge - nu - it
O - beth au - tem ge - nu - it

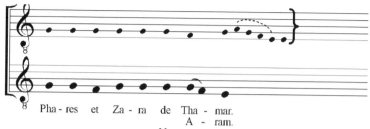

Pha - res et Za - ra de Tha - mar.
A - ram.
Na - a - son.
Bo - oz de Ra - tha.
Ies - se.

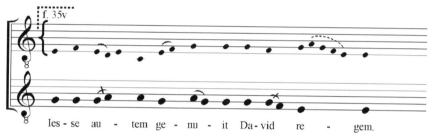

Ies - se au - tem ge - nu - it Da - vid re - gem.

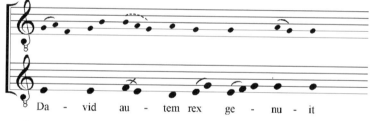

Da - vid au - tem rex ge - nu - it

Sa - lo - mo - nem ex e - a que fu - it U - ri - e.

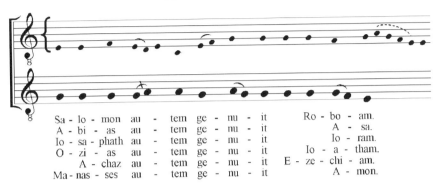

Sa - lo - mon	au	-	tem	ge	-	nu	-	it	Ro - bo - am.
A - bi - as	au	-	tem	ge	-	nu	-	it	A - sa.
Io - sa - phath	au	-	tem	ge	-	nu	-	it	Io - ram.
O - zi - as	au	-	tem	ge	-	nu	-	it	Io - a - tham.
A - chaz	au	-	tem	ge	-	nu	-	it	E - ze - chi - am.
Ma - nas - ses	au	-	tem	ge	-	nu	-	it	A - mon.

Ro - bo - am	au	-	tem	ge	-	nu	-	it
A - sa	au	-	tem	ge	-	nu	-	it
Io - ram	au	-	tem	ge	-	nu	-	it
Io - a - tham	au	-	tem	ge	-	nu	-	it
E - ze - chi - as	au	-	tem	ge	-	nu	-	it
A - mon	au	-	tem	ge	-	nu	-	it

A - bi	-	am.
Io - sa - phath.
O - zi	-	am.
A - chaz.
Ma - nas - sen.
Io - si	-	am.

Appendix A (*continued*)

fol. 36r

Io - si - as au - tem ge - nu - it Ie - cho - ni - am et fra - tres

e - ius in trans - mi - gra - ti - o - ne Ba - bi - lo - nis.

Et post trans - mi - gra - ti - o - nem Ba - bi - lo - nis Ie - cho - ni - as

ge - nu - it Sa - la - thi - el.

Appendix A (*continued*)

Sa - la - thi - el   au – tem ge - nu - it   Zo - ro - ba - bel.
A - bi - uth   au – tem ge - nu - it   E - le - a - chim.
{A} - zor   au – tem ge - nu - it   Sa - doch.
A - chim   au – tem ge - nu - it   E - li - ud.
E - le - a - zar   au – tem ge - nu - it   Ma - than.[3]

Zo - ro - ba - bel   au – tem ge - nu - it   A - bi - ud.
E - le - a - chim   au – tem ge - nu - it   A - zor.
Sa - doch   au – tem ge - nu - it   A - chim.
E - li - ud   au – tem ge - nu - it   E - le - a - zar.
Na - than   au – tem ge - nu - it   Ia - cob.

Ia - cob au – tem ge - nu - it   Io - seph vi - rum Ma - ri – e,

fol. 36v

De qua na - tus est Ihe - sus   qui   vo - ca - tur Xpi – stus.

3. Scribal error for *Nathan*.

Appendix A (*continued*)

Appendix A (*continued*)

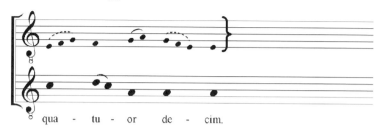

qua - tu - or de - cim.

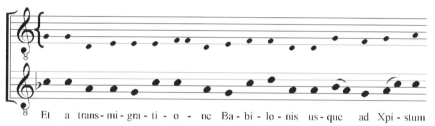

Et a trans - mi - gra - ti - o - ne Ba - bi - lo - nis us - que ad Xpi - stum

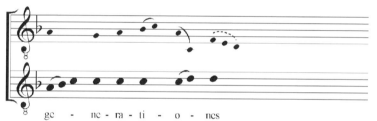

ge - ne - ra - ti - o - nes

qua - tu - or de - cim.

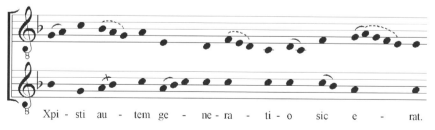

Xpi - sti au - tem ge - ne - ra - ti - o sic e - rat.

Cum es - set de - spon - sa - ta   ma - ter e - ius Ma - ri - a

Io - seph   an - te quam con - ve - ni - rent in - ven - ta

est in u - te - ro ha - bens de Spi - ri - tu san - cto.

Appendix B. "Liber generationis" (AS, fol. 34v). First Polyphonic Phrase, Literal and Performers' Transcriptions, Compared.

Li – ber ge – ne – ra – ti – o – nis Ihe – su Xpi – sti fi – li – i

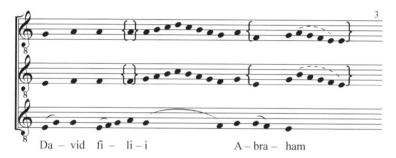

Da – vid fi – li – i A – bra – ham

1. The added voice is transcribed on the upper staff as literally as possible.
2. The notes on the center staff represent a possible performer's transcription.
3. Braces indicate notes taken from other corresponding sections of the AS added voice.

Appendix C. Assisi. Biblioteca del Sacro Convento, MS 695:
Inventory of Contents

Key
{ } = missing from manuscript, i.e., not written in
[ ] = cut out of manuscript
( ) = editorial comments
Italics = rubrics.
<u>*Italics and underlined*</u> = marginalia
* = a piece with custodes
(*) = a piece partially provided with custodes
Alleluya = Alleluya cue preceding a sequence
A = Upper case *A*, possibly indicating a sequence special to Reims liturgy
A = Illuminated *A* of Alleluya cue, possibly indicating a sequence special to Reims

fol. 1r   Iste liber est domini Mathei sancte Marie in Porticu diac. card.
          (Written two times, in two different hands.)
fol. 1v
fol. 2r   *Recipe infra ante Alleluya:* Agnus Dei: Factus homo sumpta de virgine . . .
          (polyphonic à 2)
fol. 2v   Sacrarii Socii conventus: sed hoc in Archivo custoditur. Ab hoc perpulchro
          antiphonario et graduali imagines cuncta ablata sunt: Proh pudor!
          Questo libro contendo de Santi Francesis . . .
          (Remarks made by an unknown, on the question of provenance and date.)
fol. 3r   {Kyrie}: [Te Xpiste rex s]upplices exoramus . . .
fol. 3v   {Kyrie}: [Pater creator omnium] ac pie rex . . .
fol. 4r
fol. 4v   {Kyrie}: [Theorica]m practicamque vitam . . .
fol. 5r   [Kyrie: Saba]oth iudex discheos . . .
fol. 5v
fol. 6r   {Kyrie}: Cunctipotens genitor . . .
fol. 6v   {Kyrie}: Orbis factor . . .
fol. 7r   Kyrie: Deus sempiterne vita . . .
fol. 7v   {Kyrie}: [Summe De]us qui cuncta . . .
          (also see fol. 12v)
fol. 8r   {Kyrie}: [Clemens rect]or eterne pater . . .
fol. 8v
fol. 9r   Kyrie: Fons bonitatis . . .
fol. 9v   {Kyrie}: [Rex v]irginum amator . . .
fol. 10r
fol. 10v {Kyrie}: Kyrion o theos pater . . .
          ("Cyrion" in the manuscript)
fol. 11r {Kyrie}: [Alpha et Ω] princeps et origo . . .
fol. 11v {Kyrie}: [O Deus] immense rex . . .
fol. 12r
fol. 12v {Kyrie}: [Summ]e Deus qui cuncta . . . (see also fol. 7v)

fol. 13r	{Kyrie}: [Pater cunct]a qui gubernas . . .
	{Kyrie}: [O R]ex Clemens . . .
fol. 13v	
fol. 14r	Kyrie: (three without tropes)
fol. 14v	Kyrie: (five without tropes)
fol. 15r	Kyrie: (two without tropes)
	Kyrie: Deus pater auctor Marie . . .
fol. 15v	{Kyrie}: Summe rex sempiterne . . . (Polyphonic à 3)
fol. 16r	
fol. 16v	
fol. 17r	*De Beata Virgine Maria*: Gloria: Spiritus et alma
fol. 17v	Gloria: (one without tropes)
fol. 18r	Gloria: (one without tropes)
fol. 18v	
fol. 19r	Gloria: Regnum tuum soli{d}um . . .
fol. 19v	
fol. 20r	Gloria: Cuius reboat in omni . . .
fol. 20v	
fol. 21r	
fol. 21v	
fol. 22r	*[Nativi]tate Domini epistola*: [Laudes Deo dic]am per secula . . .
fol. 22v	
fol. 23r	
fol. 23v	*Sancti Stephani epistola*: Lectio actuum apostolorum. In diebus illis: Stephanus, plenus gratia . . .
fol. 24r	
fol. 24v	
fol. 25r	*De Sancto Stephano epistola*: Lectio actuum apostolorum.
	Vernant fortia iam quorum trophea in celi regia. In diebus illis: Stephanus, plenus gratia . . .
fol. 25v	
fol. 26r	
fol. 26v	
fol. 27r	*Iohannes Evangelista*: Ad laudem regis glorie vox . . .
fol. 27v	
fol. 28r	
fol. 28v	*Sanctorum Innocentium*: Laus honor virtus Deo nostro . . .
fol. 29r	
fol. 29v	
fol. 30r	
fol. 30v	
fol. 31r	(Vacant)
fol. 31v	*Benedictio Cerei [Paschalis]:* [E]xultet iam amgelica turba . . .
fol. 32r	*Prefatio*: Vere quia dignum . . .
fol. 32v	

fol. 33r
fol. 33v
fol. 34r
fol. 34v   *In Nativitate Domini*: [Ini]tium sancti evangelii secundum Matheum. Gloria tibi Domine . . .
fol. 35r   *Evangelium*: Liber generationis Ihesu Xpisti . . .
fol. 35v
fol. 36r
fol. 36v   *In Epyphania Domini*: Dominus vobiscum et cum spiritu tuo. Sequentia sancti evangelii secundum Lucam. Gloria tibi Domine . . .
fol. 37r   *Evangelium*: [Factum est] autem cum [baptizaretur omnis] populus . . .
fol. 37v
fol. 38r
fol. 38v   *Secundum usum Parisiensis ecclesiae. Versus ad sacrandum crisma*: O redemptor sume carmen . . .
fol. 39r
fol. 39v   *Idem est alio cantu*: O redemptor sume carmen . . .
fol. 40r   *Fortunati versus*: Salve festa dies . . .
fol. 40v
fol. 41r   *Laudes*: [Xpistus v]incit, Xpistus regnat . . .
fol. 41v
fol. 42r
fol. 42v
fol. 43r
fol. 43v   (Vacant)
fol. 44r   Sanctus: Sancte ingenite genitor . . .
fol. 44v   Sanctus: Perpetuo numin[e] . . .
            Sanctus: (one without tropes)
fol. 45r   Sanctus: (two without tropes)
            Sanctus: Summe pater deitatis amor . . .
fol. 45v   Sanctus: Genitor omnium . . .
fol. 46r   Sanctus: Rex sine principio . . .
fol. 46v   Sanctus: Principium sine principio . . .
fol. 47r   Sanctus: Fons vivus vite . . .
fol. 47v   Sanctus: Deus pater cuius presentia . . .
            Sanctus: Sanctorum exultatio . . .
fol. 48r   Sanctus: (two without tropes)
fol. 48v   Sanctus: (one without tropes)
            Sanctus: Trinitas unitas deitas . . .
fol. 49r
fol. 49v   Sanctus (one without tropes)
fol. 50r   Agnus: Vulnere quo[rum laedi]mur . . .
            Agnus: Fons indeficiens pietatis . . .
fol. 50v   Agnus: [Rex] eterne Domine . . .
            Agnus: Deus deorum creator . . .

fol. 51r   Agnus: Lux lucis . . .
            Agnus: (one without tropes)
fol. 51v   Agnus: (one without tropes)
            Agnus: Quem Iohannes in deserto . . .
fol. 52r   Agnus: (four without tropes)
fol. 52v   Agnus: (one without tropes)
            Sanctus: (two without tropes)
            Sanctus: Voci vita sit unita . . . (Polyphonic à 2)
fol. 53r
fol. 53v   (below): *Require supra in secundo folio libri*
            Agnus: (one without tropes)
            Agnus: Mortis dira . . .
fol. 54r   Alleluia: Hodie Maria Virgo . . .
            Alleluia: Per te Dei genitus . . .
            Alleluia: Post partum virgo . . .
fol. 54v   Alleluia: Gaude Virgo . . .
            Alleluia: Dulcis virgo . . .
            Alleluia: Virga Iesse . . .
fol. 55r   Alleluia: Adsumpta est Maria . . .
            Alleluia: Pulcra es amica . . .
fol. 55v   (Vacant)
fol. 56r   *[Dominica prima]:* [Salus eterna] indeficiens mundi vita . . .
fol. 56v   *[Dominica secunda]:* [R]egnantem sempiterne . . .
fol. 57r   *Dominica tercia*: [Qui regis scep]tra forti dextra . . .
            Dominica quarta Adventus: Iubilemus omnes una . . .
fol. 57v   *Ad primam missam*: Salus eterna. *ut supra.* (cue only)
            vel Alleluya: [Natus ante] secula Dei filius . . .
fol. 58r
fol. 58v   *Ad secundum missam*: Regnantem etc. (cue only)
            vel Alleluya: Salve porta perpetue . . .
fol. 59r
fol. 59v   *In Die Natalis Domini ad missam. Prosa*: Xpisti hodierna . . .
fol. 60r
fol. 60v   *In Galli cantu. Prosa*: Nato canunt omnia* . . .
fol. 61r   *Ad missam*: Alleluya: [Eya simu]l recolamus laudibus* . . .
fol. 61v
fol. 62r   *Ad magnam missam*: Letabundus exultet . . .
fol. 62v
fol. 63r   *Alia de eodem*: Celeste organum hodie sonuit . . .
fol. 63v
fol. 64r   *De Sancto Stephano*: [Magnus Deus in uni]versa terra . . .
fol. 64v   *Sancti Iohannis Evangeliste*: Organicis canamus Domino . . .
fol. 65r
fol. 65v   *vel*: Alleluya: Nostram musicam . . .
fol. 66r   *Sanctorum Innocentium*: [Cel]sa pueri concrepent melodia . . .

fol. 66v

fol. 67r

fol. 67v   *In Die Epyphanie*: Epyphaniam Domino canamus* . . .

fol. 68r

fol. 68v   *vel*: Alleluya: Festa Xpisti omnis* . . .

fol. 69r

fol. 69v   *In Purificatione Beate Marie Virginis*: [Hac clara die tu]rma festiva dat* . . .

fol. 70r   *In Annuntiatione Beate Marie*: Ave Maria gratia plena . . .

fol. 70v

fol. 71r   *In Die Pasche ad missam*: [F]ulgens preclara rutilans(*) . . .

fol. 71v

fol. 72r

fol. 72v   *Istud residuum non dicitur nisi in die Penthecoste*: Paraclyti sancti . . .

fol. 73r   Alleluya: Pangite celsa voce . . .

fol. 73v   Alleluya: Laudes salvatori voce modulemur . . .

fol. 74r

fol. 74v

fol. 75r

fol. 75v   Alleluya: Alme mundi Ihesu tua fidelia . . .

fol. 76r   *In Pascha*: [Victime Paschali] laudes immolant . . .

fol. 76v   *In [Inventione Sancte Crucis]:* Laudes crucis attolla[mus] . . . (See also fol. 82 v)

fol. 77r

fol. 77v

fol. 78r

fol. 78v   *In Die ascensionis*: [R]ex omnipotens die hodierna* . . .

fol. 79r

fol. 79v   *In Die Penthecostes*: Fulgens preclara (incipit only)
           [S]ancti spiritus adsit . . .

fol. 80r

fol. 80v

fol. 81r   Alma chorus domini . . .

fol. 81v   *De Sancte Trinitate*: [Benedicta semper] sancta sit . . .

fol. 82r

fol. 82v   *De Inventione Sancte Crucis*: Laudes crucis attollamus . . . (See also fol. 76 v)

fol. 83r

fol. 83v

fol. 84r

fol. 84v   *De Sancta Cruce*: Salve crux sancta . . .
           Apostolorum Petri et Pauli: Laude iocunda melos* . . .

fol. 85r   *Divisio*: Sacra Paule ingere dogmata* . . .

fol. 85v

fol. 86r   *Benedicti Abbatis*: Laudum carmina creata* . . .

fol. 86v   *Beate Marie Magdalenis*: Mane prima sabbati . . .

fol. 87r

fol. 87v   *Alia*: *A*lleluya: Laus tibi Xpiste* . . .

Appendix C (*continued*)

Appendix C (*continued*)

fol. 108r *Sanctorum Petri et Pauli Apostolorum*: Due vere sunt olive . . .
            De Sancto Petro Apostolo: Petrus splendor . . .
fol. 108v *De Sancta Maria*: Ave maris stella* . . .
fol. 109r
fol. 109v *Alia*: Missus Gabriel de celis* . . .
fol. 110r
fol. 110v *Alia*: [V]irgini Marie laudes . . .
fol. 111r *Alia de Sancta Maria*: Gaude Dei genitrix . . . Alleluya (Polyphonic à 2)
fol. 111v
fol. 112r [*In Adventu Domini*]: [Splendor patris] et figura se conformans . . .
fol. 112v
fol. 113r *In Natali Domini. Prosa*: In excelsis canitur . . .
fol. 113v
fol. 114r *Alia*: [L]ux est orta gentibus . . .
fol. 114v
fol. 115r *Alia*: In natale salvatoris* . . .
fol. 115v
fol. 116r *Alia*: Nato nobis salvatore . . .
fol. 116v *Alia*: [Iu]bilemus salvatori quem* . . .
fol. 117r
fol. 117v *De Sancto Stephano Protomartyre*: [Heri mundus] exultavit . . .
fol. 118r
fol. 118v
fol. 119r *Sancti Iohannis Evangeliste*: Gratulemur ad festivum . . .
fol. 119v
fol. 120r *De Beato Thoma Martyre*: Sponsa virum lugeo . . .
fol. 120v
fol. 121r *Sancte Genovefe Virgine*: Genovefe sollempnitas* . . .
fol. 121v
fol. 122r *In Die Epyphanie*: Virgo mater salvatoris* . . .
fol. 122v
fol. 123r
fol. 123v *Sancte Agnetis Virginis*: Animemur ad agonem* . . .
fol. 124r
fol. 124v *Sancti Vincente Martyris*: [E]cce dies preoptata* . . .
fol. 125r
fol. 125v
fol. 126r *In Conversione Sancti Pauli Apostoli*: Corde voce pulsa celos . . .
fol. 126v
fol. 127r *In Purificatione Beate Marie*: [T]emplum cordis adornemus . . .
fol. 127v
fol. 128r
fol. 128v *In Annuntiatione Beate Marie*: [S]alve mater salvatoris vas electum* . . .
fol. 129r
fol. 129v

fol. 130r *Alia*: Paranymphus salutat* . . .

fol. 130v *In Die Pascha*: [Z]ima vetus expurgetur* . . .

fol. 131r

fol. 131v

fol. 132r *Per octavis*: Salve dies dierum . . .

fol. 132v

fol. 133r *In septimana Pasche*: Ecce dies celebris . . .

fol. 133v

fol. 134r *Alia*: Lux illuxit dominica . . .

fol. 134v *In octavis*: Mundi renovatio . . .

fol. 135r

fol. 135v *In Die Penthecostes*: [L]ux iocunda lux insignis . . .

fol. 136r

fol. 136v *De eodem*: Simplex in essentia . . .

fol. 137r

fol. 137v *De Sancta Trinitate*: Profitentes unitatem . . .

fol. 138r

fol. 138v

fol. 139r *Sanctorum Nerei et Achillei Martyrum*: Celebramus victoriam* . . .

fol. 139v *In Susceptione Reliquiarum Sancti Victoris*: Ex radice caritatis* . . .

fol. 140r

fol. 140v

fol. 141r *Sancti Iohannis Baptiste*: Ad honorem tuum* . . .

fol. 141v

fol. 142r *Isti duo versus qui secuntur non dicuntur nisi in decollatione*, Capitali iustus* . . .

fol. 142v *De Sancto Petro Apostolo*: Gaude Roma caput* . . .

fol. 143r

fol. 143v

fol. 144r *De Sancto Petro Apostolo*: Roma Petro glorietur* . . .

fol. 144v

fol. 145r

fol. 145v *De Sancto Victore*: Ecce dies triumphalis . . .

fol. 146r

fol. 146v

fol. 147r

fol. 147v *Sancti Laurentii Martyris*: [P]runis datum admiremur . . .

fol. 148r

fol. 148v

fol. 149r *In Assumptione Beate Marie Virginis*: [Ave vir]go singularis mater* . . .

fol. 149v

fol. 150r

fol. 150v *In octavis*: O Maria stella maris* . . .

fol. 151r

fol. 151v *De Sancto Bartholomeo Apostolo*: Laudemus omnes* . . .

Hiatus in the manuscript. The contents of nine missing folios, listed here in the Roman numerals given in the original index, can be ascertained from the index as follows:

fol. XCVII   *De Sancto Germano*: Ecce dies . . .
fol. XCVIII   *In Decollatione (Sancte Iohannis)*: Precursorem . . .
fol. C   *In Nativitate Beate Virginis*: Ave Mater . . .
fol. CI   *In Exaltatione Crucis*: Salve crux . . .
fol. CII   *Sancti Michaelis*: Laus erumpat . . .
fol. CIII   *De Sancto Dyonise*: Gaude . . .
fol. CV   *De quolibet Sancto*: Superne . . .

fol. 152r
fol. 152v *De Sancto Marcello Episcopo*: Gaude superna civitas* . . .
fol. 153r
fol. 153v
fol. 154r *Sancti Andree Apostoli*: Exultemus et letemur . . .
fol. 154v
fol. 155r *De apostolis. Prosa*: Cor angustum dilatemus* . . .
fol. 155v
fol. 156r
fol. 156v *Omnium apostolorum*: Stola regni* . . .
fol. 157r
fol. 157v
fol. 158r *De apostolis*: Celi solem* . . .
fol. 158v *In dedicatione ecclesie*: Rex Salomon fecit templum* . . .
fol. 159r
fol. 159v *Alia*: Quam dilecta tabernacula* . . .
fol. 160r
fol. 160v *De Beata Virgine*: Iesse virgam humidavit* . . .
fol. 161r *Sancti Victoris Martyris hymnus*: <u>Ihesu tuorum militum</u>* . . .
fol. 161v *In laudibus hymnus*: <u>Aurora diem nuntiat</u> . . .
        De Sancta Cruce {hymnus}: <u>Ave crux lignum</u> . . . (without music).
fol. 162r *In laudibus hymnus*: <u>Eterni patris unicum</u> . . . (without music).
        Sancti Augustini Episcopi et Confessoris {hymnus}: <u>Clarum pater Augustine</u> . . . (without music).
        Sancte Marie Magdalene hymnus: <u>Lauda mater ecclesia lauda</u> . . .
fol. 162v *In laudibus hymnus*: Eterni patris unice . . .
        De Nativitate Domini. Prosa.
        (The prose actually begins on fol. 163 r, but the rubric is on fol. 162 v.)
fol. 163r *De Nativitate Domini. Prosa*: [A]nte thorum virginalem . . .
fol. 163v
fol. 164r
fol. 164v *Alia de eodem*: Novum canticum cantemus . . .
fol. 165r
fol. 165v *Alia*: In sapientia disponens omnia . . .
fol. 166r

Appendix C (*continued*)

fol. 188r *Alia*: Quicumque vult salvus . . .(music is incomplete)
fol. 188v
fol. 189r *De Sancto Spiritu*: Veni sanctam pneuma* . . .
fol. 189v *Alia de eodem*: Stans a longe publicanus*..
fol. 190r *In Nativitate Sancti Iohannis Baptiste*: [P]recursoris et baptiste* . . .
fol. 190v
fol. 191r
fol. 191v
fol. 192r *Alia de Sancto Iohanne*: Inter natos mulierum . . .
fol. 192v
fol. 193r
fol. 193v *Sancti Iacobi Apostoli*: Pangat chorus in hac die . . .
fol. 194r
fol. 194v *Sancti Xpistofori Episcopi*: Xpisti calix quam preclarus . . .
fol. 195r
fol. 195v
fol. 196r *Sancti Germani Episcopi*: [L]ux illuxit triumphalis . . .
fol. 196v
fol. 197r *In Inventione Sancti Stephani Sociorumque Eius*: O athleta gloriose . . .
fol. 197v
fol. 198r
fol. 198v
fol. 199r *Sancti Laurentii Martyris*: Martyris eximii levite* . . .
fol. 199v
fol. 200r *In Annuntiatione Beate Marie*: [V]irgo gaude speciosa* . . .
fol. 200v
fol. 201r *Maglorii Episcopi et Confessoris*: Ad honorem patris* . . .
fol. 201v *Quintini Martyris*: [P]er unius casum . . .
fol. 202r
fol. 202v
fol. 203r *Sancti Martini Episcopi et Confessoris*: Gaude Syon que diem . . .
fol. 203v
fol. 204r *Alia*: Rex Xpiste Martini decus . . .
fol. 204v
fol. 205r
fol. 205v *Sancti Gendulphi Episcopi et Confessoris*: Ecce magno sacerdoti . . .
fol. 206r
fol. 206v
fol. 207r
fol. 207v *Sancte Katherine Virginis et Martyris*: [V]ox sonora nostri chori* . . .
fol. 208r
fol. 208v *Alia*: Iocundare plebs fidelis* . . .
fol. 209r
fol. 209v
fol. 210r

Appendix C (*continued*)

Prope est ruina: The Transformation of a Medieval Tenor

Alice V. Clark

The motet in fourteenth-century France is perhaps the ultimate insider art, a complex genre produced mostly within a relatively small community attached to individuals near the center of French royal power. Modern scholars have sought entry into that inner circle, in part by searching for intertextual connections between motets and other musical and literary works.[1] In this essay I will explore the relationship between two motets that share tenor material: the anonymous "Super cathedram Moysi / Presidentes in thronis seculi / Ruina," found in the interpolated *Roman de Fauvel*, and "Tant doucement m'ont attrait / Eins que ma dame d'onnour / Ruina," by Guillaume de Machaut. This is a particularly interesting pair because Machaut does not at first glance appear to react to the earlier work at all save by using its tenor, but closer examination can show a pattern of modeling through opposition, replacing the image of Fauvel with that of Faux Semblant, the world of French politics with that of *fin'amors*.

This kind of reinterpretation, reminiscent of Harold Bloom's notion of "misreading,"[2] is similar to that found in two other cases where Machaut borrows a tenor, and it may represent an approach unique to him. In both "Quant vraie amour enflamee / O series summe rata! / T. Super omnes speciosa" (M17) and "Christe, qui lux es et dies / Veni creator spiritus / T. Tribulatio proxima est et non est qui adjuvet" (M21), Machaut uses the tenor of an earlier motet as the source for his own work, but in both of those pieces, as in the case under consideration here, Machaut creates a motet without immediately apparent connections to that source, in terms either of subject matter or structural issues, the two areas where intertextual relationships between motets are most likely to be found. There are reasons, however, to see these works as responses to the earlier motets that provide their tenors, creating a kind of relationship all the more interesting for being hidden.[3] In his "Ruina" motet, Machaut hides any obvious connection between his motet and its source by writing in French rather than Latin, with an amatory rather than an admonitory subject, but

Table 1. Fourteenth-Century Motets Sharing Tenor Material.

Tenor	Motet 1	Motet 2	Notes
Alma redemptoris mater	V11	H4	identical melody
Dolor meus	H17	H19	identical melody[1]
Gaude . . . / Super omnes . . .	V7	M17	V7 includes M17[2]
Neuma quinti toni	F33(129)	Sanders	identical melody[3]
Ruina	F4(4)	M13	one change
Tribulatio . . . / Et non est . . .	M8	M21	M21 includes M8[4]
Tristis est anima mea	F25(71)	H15	different melodies

Note: Motets with *F* numbers come from the *Roman de Fauvel* and are edited in Schrade 1956; *V* numbers refer to motets attributed to Philippe de Vitry edited in the same volume. *H* numbers are given to motets in Harrison 1968; *M* numbers refer to the motets of Guillaume de Machaut, edited in Ludwig (1926–54) and in Schrade ([1956] 1977). "Sanders" refers to the motet "Floret cum vana gloria / Florens vigor ulciscendo / T. Neuma quinti toni," edited in Sanders 1975, 37–42.

1. The tenor of H19 gives the melody twice, at two different pitch levels a fifth apart.

2. The overlapping section is identical in the two motets, though at different pitch levels (V7 begins and ends on F, M17 on C). The intervallic content is the same.

3. V6 uses the same tenor text, but with a different melody, and this would seem to suggest no intertextual connection with the two *Fauvel* motets. In fact, the melodic difference may well support the notion that Philippe de Vitry may not be the composer of F33(129), though some modern scholars attribute it to him on stylistic grounds or through its citation in the *Ars Nova* treatises.

4. The section in common has the same pitches, though there is a difference in signature, and therefore in intervallic content, between the two tenors.

he provides musical clues that encourage us to look more closely for possible intertextual links.

Seven pairs of motets from fourteenth-century France have common tenor material, usually shared identically (see table 1). The two motets on "Tristis est anima mea" appear in manuscripts copied a half-century apart, so there is little reason to believe the composer of the later motet knew the earlier one, and the difference in tenor melodies is not surprising. Most often, though, where two motets have a common tenor, the shared melody is identical. Given the variation of chant readings from one place to another, this would seem to suggest either that the composers of the two motets came from or were active in the same geographic center, or that the composer of the later motet took the tenor of the earlier motet as its source. In either case, the common melodic material encourages us to look for further connections: if the motets are written by the same person, or by composers active in the same place, it seems likely that the later motet has some relationship to the earlier one.

The "Ruina" tenor is a special case in two ways: first, because it appears not to have a chant source, and, second, because there is a single small variant between the melodies found in the two motets under consideration here. Although I have located several hitherto unidentified tenors for fourteenth-century motets,[4] I have not found this one, nor has anyone else to my knowledge. At this time it is hard to avoid the conclusion that no source exists, meaning that the composer of the earlier motet must have written the melody—a rare occurrence but not unprecedented—and that Machaut could therefore have only gotten it from the *Fauvel* motet. The variant, to be discussed more fully below, could simply be a matter of miscopying, but I believe it may in fact be a purposeful alteration that serves as a symptom of a conscious act of general reinterpretation whereby Machaut responds to the earlier motet by creating something demonstrably different.

"Super cathedram Moysi / Presidentes in thronis seculi / T. Ruina" (F4[4]) is best known from the deluxe manuscript of the *Roman de Fauvel* (Paris, Bibliothèque nationale de France, MS fonds français 146, compiled ca. 1316–17), though it also appears in the related Brussels rotulus (Brussels, Bibliothèque Royale, MS 19606). Six motets appear in both Pn 146 and the Brussels rotulus, leading Edward H. Roesner to suggest that the *Fauvel* music "may have circulated more widely [than simply in Pn 146]—albeit not for very long."[5] The wider circulation of this motet is confirmed by its other source, an English fragment that preserves part of its triplum and tenor, and the two theoretical treatises that cite it.[6] Another sign of the popularity of this motet is the use of the first two lines of its motetus, "Presidentes in thronis seculi / sunt hodie dolus et rapina," as the framing refrain for strophe 26 of the *Fastrasie* of Watriquet de Couvin.[7]

The motet appears near the beginning of the *Roman de Fauvel*, as the first three-part motet and the last of four motets that together introduce the opening of the story. Fauvel is an ass—literally—whom Fortune has elevated to power over all stations of French society, sacred and secular; everyone flatters and pets Fauvel, from kings to peasants, poor clerks to the pope. The very name of Fauvel betrays his evil nature: Gervais de Bus, the author of the narrative, gives us two different etymologies, one meaning "veiled falseness" (*faus + vel*, or *fauseté velee*), and the other derived from the first letters of six vices that are said to descend from him (*Flaterie, Avarice, Vilanie, Varieté, Envie, Laschetê*).[8] At the end of the story, Fauvel and his bride, Vain Glory, give birth daily to *Fauveaux nouveaux*. While these "new Fauvels" have infected every nation, they are a particular menace to *le jardin de douce France* (the garden of sweet France). The author nevertheless holds out hope that God, through the Virgin Mary (the *lis de virginitê*),

will someday save the *lis de France*—that is, the fleur-de-lis that is the symbol of
France (lines 3220–80).

This motet accompanies a description of Fauvel's influence on clerics, mentioning specifically the Dominicans and Franciscans, among others (lines 60–68).[9]
The upper-voice texts of the motet, both in Latin, are *admonitiones* suitable for
this point in Fauvel's story. The triplum opens with a clear reference to a speech of
Jesus as given in the Gospel of Matthew: "The scribes and the Pharisees [changed
to the 'new flock of priests' in the motet] sit on Moses' seat; so practice and observe
whatever they tell you, but not what they do; for they preach, but do not practice"
(Matt. 23:2–3, RSV). This passage is cited in two texts that may have been known
to the creator of the motet and are certainly relevant to the tone of clerical criticism: a poem by Walter Map against wayward priests and a bull of Boniface VIII
concerning quarrels between the mendicants and parish clergy.[10] Two other literary uses of this text will be discussed below. Just as the motet's triplum criticizes
those in authority in the church, so the motetus criticizes secular authority: "The
rulers on the thrones of this world today are Deceit and Plunder." The last line of
this text—"calamity is near!"—has the sound of a proverbial statement, though
no source for it has been found.[11] If one were located, it might make it possible to
locate a source for the tenor as well, but at this time both remain unique.

The musical style of the motet is typical of the genre as practiced in the late
thirteenth and early fourteenth centuries, with minimal rhythmic stratification
between a relatively slowly moving tenor and more rapidly moving upper voices.
The notational style of the *Fauvel* version is similarly backward looking for the
fourteenth century, using undifferentiated semibreves in place of semibreves and
minims; the version in the Brussels rotulus is in a later notational style, but with
the same rhythmic meaning.[12] The motet's tenor *talea* effectively divides in half,
creating two statements of the quasi-modal pattern *long-breve-breve-maxima* (the
second time the maxima is replaced by a long followed by a long rest), and this
rhythmic pattern is often reflected in the motetus as well. The tenor melody is
stated twice, each time divided into five taleae, with no diminution. This structure,
however, is not reflected in the upper voices, as is often the case in fourteenth-
century motets. Units of eight longs (the length of the talea) do predominate,
especially in the motetus, but longer units in the motetus and shorter ones in the
triplum are interspersed with these, giving the piece an irregularity more in keeping with the thirteenth-century motet than that of the fourteenth century.

There is, however, one moment when tenor and upper-voice forms coincide: the beginning of the second statement of the tenor melody (therefore the
midpoint of the motet, at mm. 40–42) is marked by a note one full breve in length
in both motetus and tenor, while the triplum has a semibreve followed by a rest of
two semibreves. This moment is the only time after the first phrase of the motet

Figure 1. Length of musical-textual units (in longs). Not to scale.

Triplum	7		6	8		8		6		6	‖		8		4		8		4		6		8
Motetus	8			10		8			8			8	‖			10			8			8			11	
Tenor		8		8		8		8			8	‖		8			8			8			8			8

when both upper voices end a phrase together, and the fact that they hold the same rhyming vowel (*is* in the triplum, *i* in the motetus) reinforces the strength of this phrase end. The moment is also marked in the textual structure, as the midpoint of the motetus text and the moment when the triplum moves from six-line to five-line stanzas. This emphasis on the motet's midpoint stands out in the context of an otherwise irregular work.

Machaut's motet "Tant doucement m'ont attrait / Eins que ma dame d'onnour / T. Ruina" (M13) is almost certainly later, since the *Fauvel* motet had to have existed by the time of the compilation of that manuscript around 1316–17, while no work of Machaut's can be securely dated before 1324.[13] Where "Super cathedram Moysi / Presidentes in thronis seculi / T. Ruina" emphasizes the sins of sacred and secular authority, both all too anxious to curry favor with Fauvel, Machaut's motet is a French-texted lover's complaint. Bel Accueil (Fair Welcome) and his cronies attracted the Lover at first, promising the Lady's mercy, but she has knowingly ignored him. The allegorical characters are traitors, but the Lover himself remains true. The triplum describes the actions of the allegorical figures while the motetus focuses on the Lady, whose own look and sweet laugh attracted and sustained the Lover; now she knows of his love and yet withholds herself. The bottom line of the complaint, figuratively and literally, is a ruin as complete and final for the Lover in personal terms as is that foretold by the *Fauvel* motet on the political level.

Scholars have often made connections between motets in terms of easily quantifiable criteria, especially structural issues such as number of taleae, talea length, and so on.[14] These aspects are concrete enough to be easily recognized today, and recent work suggests they do indeed form an important way for medieval composers to create relationships between motets. In this case, however, those features seem not to be related, or at least not in a straightforward manner: the *Fauvel* motet has two statements of the tenor melody, Machaut's one; the earlier motet has five taleae of eight longs each where the later one has four taleae of fourteen longs; and so on. The triplum texts of both motets have bipartite stanzas with repeating elements, while both motetus texts use a single rhyme pair in

Example 1a. 4F(4) and M13 tenor melodies.

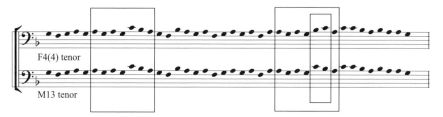

Example 1b. M13 tenor.

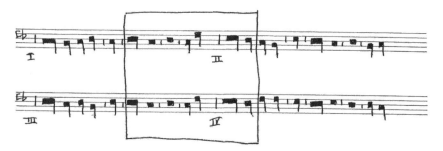

alternation, but these poetic structures are fairly common, so it is hard to claim this similarity as a sign of influence. Moreover, the text structures are modified slightly in the *Fauvel* motet to emphasize the midpoint, where the tenor melody repeats, while the midpoint of Machaut's motet is unmarked.

As mentioned above, there is one small variant between the tenor melodies of these two motets, a variant turning on the ordering of a single pair of notes (see the small box within example 1a.). Since motets sharing tenors nearly always use identical melodies, it is tempting to suggest that this variant makes a relationship between these two motets impossible, but given the lack of another source for the melody, we must at least allow for the possibility that Machaut may have instigated this change—if so, to what end? Machaut's melody makes apparent and extends to nearly twice its original length a seemingly unimportant internal repetition (boxed in the example). Moreover, the talea rhythm he gives to the melody audibly emphasizes the similarity thus created, including a striking ascending fourth at the end of taleae 1 and 3 (see example 1b). The singer or listener is therefore given an impression (though, as it happens, a false one) of a repetition of the tenor melody. This pseudo-repetition in the tenor is also marked by melodic repetition in the upper voices, especially in the motetus, surrounding the transition to the second and fourth taleae (see examples 2a and 2b). Exact melodic repetition is relatively rare in this repertory, though Machaut uses it in several motets to underline structural events.[15] Although Machaut's motet really

Example 2a. M13, transition between taleae 1–2.

Example 2b. M13, transition between taleae 3–4.

only has one tenor statement, this subtle change in tenor melody and the parallels in the upper voices at the same point may serve as a gesture to the tenor repetition of the *Fauvel* motet, as well as a demonstration that Machaut saw something in the melody the earlier composer perhaps did not. This idea of false impressions will return below.

Machaut extends his talea structure to the upper voices, with an exactness not often seen and not at all present in the earlier motet on this tenor melody. After two variants in the first talea, both motetus and triplum rhythms repeat exactly until breve 20 of the final talea (m. 105), where the slight alteration may serve a closural function. The pervasive use of this kind of talea reflection in the upper voices is a technique generally associated with works produced from the middle of the fourteenth century and beyond, so its use here can serve, like the use of hocket and imperfect rather than perfect tempus and modus, to emphasize the up-to-date qualities of Machaut's work, since these aspects of *ars nova* rhythmic practice were apparently unavailable to the composer of the earlier motet. None of the techniques Machaut uses here are unusual for him, but together they serve to emphasize the stylistic differences between the musical world of the *Fauvel* motet and his own.

All this suggests more differences between the two motets than similarities. Machaut's apparent borrowing of the *Fauvel* motet's tenor, however, encourages us to look for further connections. The differences outlined above may be seen not as a matter of chance, but rather as an attempt on Machaut's part to distance his motet from the earlier work, in terms of its musical style and its subject matter, while at the same time connecting the clerical satire of the *Fauvel* motet to his own lover's complaint by means of a tenor that declares both to be forms of ruin.

With this possibility in mind, I would like to return to Jesus's speech against the scribes and Pharisees. The Gospel passage underpinning the triplum text of the *Fauvel* motet, where it serves to criticize clerics who say one thing and do another, is also cited in two of the seminal works of amatory literature in the Middle Ages: Andreas Capellanus's *Art of Courtly Love*, and Faux Semblant's speech in Jean de Meun's part of the *Roman de la Rose*. The *Rose* must have been known to Machaut, and it is quite possible he knew Andreas's work as well. In both cases the speaker uses Jesus's diatribe to emphasize the importance of subterfuge in the pursuit of love. This process of saying one thing and meaning another, which can be seen as hypocritical, becomes something positive, and indeed necessary, in the Lover's quest.

The noble would-be lover in the eighth dialogue of *The Art of Courtly Love* says that while it is a good thing for a clerk to avoid love, he has no special responsibility to do so:

> But if with his tongue he rightly discharges this office, he is freed from
> the burden, for any other sins he may commit are no more severely
> punished in him than in any layman, since he is naturally driven to

> them by the incentive of the flesh just like all the rest of mankind. This
> is what the authority of the Gospel proclaims; for the Lord, seeing His
> clergy, in accordance with the frailty of human nature, about to fall
> into various excesses, said in the Gospel, "The scribes and the Pharisees
> have sitten on the chair of Moses. All things whatsoever they shall say
> to you, observe and do: but according to their works do ye not," just
> as though he said, "You must believe what the clergy say, because they
> are God's deputies; but because they are subject to the temptation of
> the flesh like other men, you must not regard their works if they hap-
> pen to go astray in anything." Therefore it is enough for me if, when I
> stand by the altar, I devote myself to proclaiming the word of God to
> my people.[16]

He is therefore safe from censure as long as he proclaims how others should act;
he need not show them in his own actions as well. Indeed, Andreas goes on to
argue that a clerk makes a better lover than a layman, because he is more cautious.

Faux Semblant (False Seeming) uses the Gospel passage as part of his long
harangue about the mendicant orders:

> In order that you may recognize the criminals who do not stop deceiv-
> ing people, I will now tell you the words that we read of Saint Mat-
> thew, that is to say the evangelist, in the twenty-third chapter: "Upon
> the chair of Moses" (the gloss explains that this is the Old Testament),
> "the scribes and pharisees have sat." These are the accursed false people
> that the letter calls hypocrites. "Do what they say, but not what they
> do. They are not slow to speak well, but they have no desire to do so.
> To gullible people they attach heavy loads that cannot be carried; they
> place them on their shoulders, but they dare not move them with their
> finger."[17]

This seems like a strange thing to find in a *summa* of romantic practice, and Faux
Semblant's speech has occasioned a good deal of scholarly discussion. During his
speech he refers to current events, notably Guillaume de Saint-Amour's attack on
the mendicants for begging rather than working for their bread—remember that
the papal bull that uses this biblical passage also dealt with the mendicants—and
Faux Semblant emphasizes that he can most easily be found among the religious,
where he can hide by saying one thing and doing another. Despite this implicit
criticism of clerical hypocrisy, however, it is important to remember that the allegorical figure appears in this story as an ally of Love. Faux Semblant's role here is
in part to demonstrate that would-be lovers must present an attractive appearance,
even if they hide some aspects of reality in order to do so: "the advent of Faux
Semblant reduces all the noble qualities of Amant and Rose to surface appearances that hide or mask deceit and cover vices or defect."[18] For Sarah Kay (1995,

29–30) he becomes a symbol of the unreliability of language that permeates Jean de Meun's part of the *Rose* story, while Susan Stackel argues that deceit is necessary in order to pluck the Rose, noting that "the lover succeeds in approaching the rose only on the occasions that Faux Semblant with all his tricks and turns is somehow present."[19] As such, Faux Semblant becomes both a character that modern readers have difficulty integrating into the *Rose* quest and a character of critical importance to that quest.

Perhaps some of these ideas of the necessity of deceit and the distinction between surface appearances and inner reality were in Machaut's mind as he transformed a satirical motet into an amorous one, and they can serve as a sort of pivot between the two works. In this light it may be helpful to notice that the triplum narrator is initially attracted not only by Bel Accueil but also Samblans d'Amours—not Love itself but the *appearance* of love. Similarly, just after the midpoint the poet refers to Samblans d'Attraire—appearance of attraction—rather than the Sweet Attraction (Dous Attrait) of the opening. In the last stanza, he complains that these characters have worked against him, "com faus traitour prouvé" (like false proven traitors). The distinction between the appearance of good on the one hand and treacherous actions on the other is not only reminiscent of the Gospel diatribe but it is the very nature of Faux Semblant, who uses the Gospel text to his own ends.

Machaut may, however, be criticizing Faux Semblant's role in the Lover's quest by associating the *Rose* character with Fauvel through the means of the common tenor. The *ruina* associated with Fauvel in the earlier motet now belongs to Faux Semblant, linking the two allegorical characters by their deceit, here seen as not necessary but harmful. In turn, the "sweet garden of France" endangered by Fauvel is linked to the garden in which the Lover's Rose resides.[20]

The concern for appearance as opposed to reality that comes from Faux Semblant also recalls Machaut's likely alteration of his tenor source, where through melodic and rhythmic manipulation he gives us the illusion of a structural repetition, a feature highlighted in the earlier motet that in fact does not take place in the later one. Musically as well, then, Machaut seems to warn us that all is not as it seems, and we should not always trust what we see or hear.

Faux Semblant, only alluded to here, is directly evoked in another of Machaut's motets, "Amours qui a le pouoir / Faus Samblant m'a deceü / T. Vidi Dominum facie ad faciem" (M15). Kevin Brownlee sees this motet as embodying in the first instance an "opposition between Amours and Faux Semblant,"[21] the two characters evoked at the beginning of the triplum and motetus, respectively, and secondly an opposition between "the fallen linguistic world of appearances"[22] and the only real truth, the Word of God as represented in the motet's tenor. This motet demonstrates that Machaut was interested in Faux Semblant and his relationship with Love, and that Machaut can take a critical stance toward appearances. The notion that Faux Semblant is also present but hidden within Machaut's "Ruina" motet is in keeping with his nature: as he tells us, he can be found in the cloister, in the world of the scribes and Pharisees, and, we might add, in the world of Fauvel and the garden of the Rose.

Machaut therefore borrows a tenor, but he puts that tenor into a different context, using it to put a spotlight on the distinctions between appearance and reality. Fauvel's story shows us what is wrong with the government of France; Faux Semblant's perhaps what is wrong with *fin'amors*. By connecting these two ideas, Machaut shows us that seeming opposites are actually related, and that ruin is all around us.

Notes

The present essay originated as a paper given to a graduate conference in medieval studies at Princeton University; it also informed part of the first paper I gave at the International Congress on Medieval Studies at Kalamazoo, in 1994. It seemed appropriate to offer in Ingrid's memory the fruit of such early graduate work, as a tribute to her concern for fostering young scholars. This written version was submitted in 2002; some of this material was also used in Clark 2003.

1. As Daniel Leech-Wilkinson has put it, "the greater part of the surviving isorhythmic repertory from before about 1365—the approximate date of the Ivrea codex—was the work of a relatively small group of composers who knew one another's output, very possibly working together as part of a continuous tradition in the same area" (1982–83, 20). Considerations of intertextuality in the medieval motet are too numerous to list here, but see especially the work of Margaret Bent, Kevin Brownlee, Sylvia Huot, and Jacques Boogaart.

2. The basic statement of this concept is Bloom 1973. The classic statement of musical borrowing as competition as much as homage is perhaps Brown 1982. That study, focused on the later fifteenth and sixteenth century, should be read in combination with Meconi 1994.

3. I have examined the M8 / M21 pairing in Clark (2005) and the V7 / M17 pairing in Clark (2003).

4. See Clark 1999.

5. Roesner, Avril, and Regalado 1990, 25.

6. The fragment is found in Oxford, Bodleian Library, MS Bodley 271, binding fragments, folio A, described in Wathey 1993, 66–68. The theoretical citations are in the Erfurt anonymous (or Wolf anonymous 3), which gives it as an example of perfect modus, and the anonymous *dictus* Theodoricus de Campo, which cites it for its breves altered by duplex longs. See Wolf 1908, 37, and Sweeney 1971, 39–40.

7. This connection was first noticed by Dahnk 1935, 11. Watriquet's *Fastrasie* is edited in Scheler 1868, 295–309; stanza 26, covering lines 329–39, is on p. 307. All thirty stanzas are based on refrains, but this is the only one using Latin material.

8. See Långfors 1914–19, lines 240–60. Subsequent references to this work will be made in the text.

9. The reference to the mendicants (Jacobins and Cordeliers) comes immediately following the motet, so that the narrative glosses the motet, or vice versa.

10. The Map verses, from *Sermo Goliae ad praelatos*, are lines 25–28:

> Vae! qui super Moysi cathedram sedetis!
> lex a vobis dicitur, quam vos non impletis
> ejus in ecclesia speciem tenetis,
> cujus proculdubio vitam non habetis.

See Wright 1841, 43. Boniface's bull, revoked by Benedict XI and renewed by Clement V, is *Super cathedram praeeminentiae pastoralis*; see Dahnk (1935, 12), citing *Corpus Juris Canonici*, ed. E. Friedberg (Leipzig, 1881), 2: col. 1162.

11. It is, however, reminiscent of the opening of a poem by Hildebert of Lavardin, bishop of Le Mans (1056–1113):

> Par tibi, Roma, nihil, cum sis prope tota ruina;
> quam magni fueris integra fracta doces.

See Krautheimer 2000, 200. Krautheimer translates the above lines as follows: "Rome, without compare, though all but shattered; your very ruins tell of greatness once enjoyed." Whether the author of the motetus text is referring to this poem, and what such a reference might mean for the motet, is unknown at this time. If the author is alluding to Hildebert's text, the motet could be seen as an oblique reference to the ruin of Rome, interpreted either as the seat of popes or the seat of empire (or both), through the activities of Fauvel. Hildebert argues that ancient Rome fell in part because it was pagan—in other words, it worshipped false gods—and it is possible that Fauvel could be seen as a successor to those gods, a more recent figure who has led the new Rome astray. Full consideration of this possible allusion and its implications is beyond the scope of this study.

12. This notational issue is discussed in the introduction to Roesner, Avril, and Regalado 1990.

13. This is M18, "Bone pastor Guillerme / Bone pastor / T. Bone pastor," written for Guillaume de Trie, archbishop of Reims 1324–34. The most recent discussion of this motet and its possible dating and context can be found in Robertson 2002, 53–68. Lawrence Earp suggests that this motet was likely not Machaut's first, even if it is the first that can be dated with any certainty, and he points out that there were opportunities for contact between Machaut and Philippe de Vitry, among others, earlier in the decade. See Earp 1995, 9–11.

14. Classic studies of this type include Leech-Wilkinson (1982–83), and unpublished work by Margaret Bent and David Howlett on the so-called musician motets.

15. See Clark 2004.

16. Andreas Capellanus 1941, 125.

17. Lines 11599–619. See Guillaume de Lorris and Jean de Meun 1974, and Guillaume de Lorris and Jean de Meun 1971.

18. Kelly 1995, 65.

19. "Access to Bel Accueil is gained only through the treachery of Faux Semblant and Atenance Contrainte"; Stackel 1991, 58.

20. Anne Walters Robertson's magisterial study, reconsidering Machaut's motets 1–20 as a spiritual journey, appeared after this essay was written. In her reading, this motet reflects a moment of inconstancy, where the wanderer looks back to a time of earlier happiness, when he saw Lady Wisdom, but is frustrated by his inability to recreate that experience. His accusations of treachery, then, are actually unfounded, though they appear to be

true. The discrepancies between word and action, illusion and reality that are manifested at this moment of Robertson's spiritual journey are to my mind compatible with the more secular reading given here. See Robertson 2002, especially 159–61.

21. Brownlee 1991, 5.
22. Brownlee 1991, 12.

References

Andreas Capellanus. 1941. *The Art of Courtly Love*. Translated by John Jay Parry. New York: Frederick Ungar Publishing Co.

Bloom, Harold. 1973. *The Anxiety of Influence: A Theory of Poetry*. London: Oxford University Press.

Brown, Howard Mayer. 1982. "Emulation, Competition, and Homage: Imitation and Theories of Imitation in the Renaissance." *Journal of the American Musicological Society* 35: 1–48.

Brownlee, Kevin. 1991. "Machaut's Motet 15 and the *Roman de la rose*: The Literary Context of *Amours qui a le pouoir / Faus Samblant m'a deceü / Vidi Dominum*." *Early Music History* 10: 1–14.

Clark, Alice V. 1999. "New Tenor Sources for Fourteenth-Century Motets." *Plainsong and Medieval Music* 8/2: 107–31.

———. 2003. "Machaut's Tenor Borrowings." Paper given at the Symposium on Late Medieval and Early Renaissance Music, Kloster Neustift/Novacella, Italy.

———. 2004. "Listening to Machaut's Motets." *Journal of Musicology* 21/4: 487–513.

———. 2005. "Machaut Reading Machaut: Self-Borrowing and Reinterpretation in M8 and M21." In *Citation and Authority in Medieval and Renaissance Musical Culture: Learning from the Learned* (Festschrift for Margaret Bent), edited by Suzannah Clark and Elizabeth Eva Leach, 94–101. Studies in Medieval and Renaissance Music 4. Woodbridge, Suffolk: The Boydell Press.

Dahnk, Emilie. 1935. *L'Hérésie de Fauvel*. Englesdorf-Leipzig: E. & E. Vogel.

Earp, Lawrence. 1995. *Guillaume de Machaut: A Guide to Research*. Garland Composer Resource Manuals 36. New York: Garland.

Guillaume de Lorris and Jean de Meun. 1971. *The Romance of the Rose*. Translated by Charles Dahlberg. Princeton: Princeton University Press.

———. 1974. *Le roman de la rose*. Edited by Daniel Poirion. Paris: Garnier-Flammarion.

Harrison, Frank Ll., ed. 1968. *Motets of French Provenance*. Polyphonic Music of the Fourteenth Century 5. Monaco: Éditions de l'Oiseau-Lyre.

Kay, Sarah. 1995. *The Romance of the Rose*. Critical Guides to French Texts 110. London: Grant & Cutler Ltd.

Kelly, Douglas. 1995. *Internal Difference and Meanings in the Roman de la Rose*. Madison: University of Wisconsin Press.

Krautheimer, Richard. 2000. *Rome: Profile of a City, 312–1308*, with a new forward by Marvin Trachtenberg. Princeton: Princeton University Press.

Långfors, Arthur, ed. 1914–19. *Le Roman de Fauvel par Gervais du Bus*. Société des Anciens Textes Français. Paris: Librairie de Firmin Didot et Cie.

Leech-Wilkinson, Daniel. 1982–83. "Related Motets from Fourteenth-Century France." *Proceedings of the Royal Musical Association* 109: 1–22.

Ludwig, Friedrich, ed. 1926–54. *Guillaume de Machaut: Musikalische Werke.* Leipzig and Wiesbaden: Breitkopf & Härtel.

Meconi, Honey. 1994. "Does *Imitatio* Exist?" *Journal of Musicology* 12: 152–78.

Robertson, Anne Walters. 2002. *Guillaume de Machaut and Reims: Context and Meaning in his Musical Works.* Cambridge: Cambridge University Press.

Roesner, Edward H., François Avril, and Nancy Freeman Regalado. 1990. Introduction to *Le Roman de Fauvel in the Edition of Mesire Chaillou de Pesstain: A Reproduction in Facsimile of the Complete Manuscript Paris, Bibliothèque Nationale, Fonds Français 146.* New York: Broude Brothers.

Sanders, Ernest H. 1975. "The Early Motets of Philippe de Vitry." *Journal of the American Musicological Society* 28: 24–45.

Scheler, August, ed. 1868. *Dits de Watriquet de Couvin.* Brussels: Comptoir universel d'imprimerie et de librairie, Victor Devaus et Cie.

Schrade, Leo, ed. (1956) 1977. *Guillaume de Machaut: Oeuvres complètes* 2 vols. Polyphonic Music of the Fourteenth Century 2–3. Reprint in 5 vols., Monaco: Éditions de l'Oiseau-Lyre.

———, ed. 1956. *The Roman de Fauvel; The Works of Philippe de Vitry; French Cycles of the Ordinarium Missae.* Polyphonic Music of the Fourteenth Century 1. Monaco: Éditions de l'Oiseau-Lyre.

Stackel, Susan. 1991. *False Roses: Structures of Duality and Deceit in Jean de Meun's Roman de la Rose.* Stanford French and Italian Studies. Saratoga, CA: ANMA Libri.

Sweeney, Cecily, ed. 1971. *De musica mensurabili (MS. Rome, Biblioteca Vaticana, Barberini 307).* Corpus Scriptorum de Musica 13. N.p.: American Institute of Musicology.

Wathey, Andrew. 1993. *Manuscripts of Polyphonic Music: The British Isles, 1100–1400.* RISM B IV, 1–2, Suppl. 1. Munich: Henle.

Wolf, Johannes. 1908. "Ein anonymer Musiktraktat aus der ersten Zeit der 'Ars Nova.'" *Kirchenmusikalisches Jahrbuch* 21: 34–38.

Wright, Thomas, ed. 1841. *The Latin Poems Commonly Attributed to Walter Mapes.* Camden Society 16. London: Camden Society.

Ideological Clashes in a
Cinquecento Edition of Plainchant

Richard J. Agee

Although most Europeans probably heard more plainchant than any other type of music during the course of the late Middle Ages and Renaissance, the study of chant for the cinquecento period has only recently begun to evoke serious scholarly attention once again. For instance, the late Laurence Feininger's huge collection of fourteenth- to seventeenth-century manuscripts and printed editions of the church liturgy, now at the library of the Castello del Buonconsiglio at Trent, has served as an inspiration and resource to scholars of plainchant, as the numerous publications and completed theses from Italy in the last decades can attest (see, for instance, Curti and Leonardelli, 1985; Leonardelli, 1988; Gozzi, 1994; Dal Prà, 1995; Curti and Gozzi, 1995; Indino, 1998; Cattin, Curti, and Gozzi, 1999; and Baroffio, Curti, and Gozzi, 2000). At the University of Michigan, "Renaissance Liturgical Imprints: A Census" or RELICS, a computer database first established by David Crawford and James Borders, has proved extremely useful for the study of chant during the Renaissance (Crawford et al., n.d.; hereafter cited as REL-ICS). Further, Theodore Karp has compared readings for plainchant melodies from many different editions printed from 1580 until the late nineteenth century. Despite the inflated historical reputation of the gradual printed in Rome by the Medici Press in 1614–15, the so-called *Editio Medicaea*, Karp found very little evidence of its influence on subsequent editions and, indeed, few clear and direct relationships among the many readings he examined (see Karp 1999a, 1999b, and 2005). This paper will touch upon the role of Palestrina in chant reform, will visit a scandalous lawsuit, and then conclude with a comparison of a small chant book to three others, in the hope that detailed analyses of chant editions from Italy during the early years of the Catholic Reformation might reveal distinct connections among the sources.

Held intermittently from 1545 until 1563, the Council of Trent included many participants who hoped to reform the liturgy by cutting back on the florid growth of the later Middle Ages, and arrive at a uniform liturgical practice.

Although the council approved the elimination of nearly all of the late medieval musical growth unanchored to biblical texts, such as all but four of the sequences and all of the tropes in the Mass, ultimately the disparate and irreconcilable opinions expressed during the council effectively prevented any further reform of Catholic plainchant. Nevertheless, in the next few years two printed liturgical monuments to reform appeared under Pius V (r. 1566–72): the new *Breviarium Romanum* in 1568, and in 1570 the reformed *Missale Romanum* (Sodi and Triacca 1998; Sodi and Triacca 1999; Dyer 2001, 545). While these books figured as remarkable landmarks in the standardization of the Catholic liturgy, they dealt with only its words and not its music—obviously the music presented many more problems than simply the words alone (Molitor 1901–2, 1:1–21). Pope Pius's successor, Gregory XIII (r. 1572–85), hoped to continue the spirit of his predecessor by reforming and standardizing the musical practice of chant as well. In 1577 he commissioned the most well-known composer in Rome at the time, Giovanni Pierluigi da Palestrina, and the composer Annibale Zoilo to edit the music of the Catholic liturgy and create a reformed gradual, antiphoner, and psalter (Respighi [1900], 28–33; Molitor 1901–2, 1:47–56, 297–98; Haberl 1902, 4–5; Ruini 1985, 66–67; Lincoln 2001, 862; Lockwood, O'Regan, and Owens 2001, 941).

Apparently the intervention of an obscure Spanish composer—Don Fernando de las Infantas—served in halting the impending revision of Roman plainchant. Upon learning of Gregory XIII's appointment of Palestrina and Zoilo to carry out the reform, Infantas dashed off a furious memorandum from Rome to Philip II, king of Spain, and condemned any alterations to music he thought both written by and named after Pope Gregory I. Philip II also may have balked at the economic burden of compelling all Spanish churches to purchase the new liturgical books. At any rate, in 1578 Philip seems to have pressured Pope Gregory XIII, who clearly wished to curry the favor of a devout and wealthy Spain, to withdraw his support from Palestrina and Zoilo (Molitor 1899, 367–73; Haberl 1900, 168–72; Respighi [1900?], 38–51, 121–34; Molitor 1901–2, 1:37–41, 236–93, 296–97, 302–5, 2:86–122, 238–58; Haberl 1902, 5–7; Mitjana 1918, 45–55; Sesini 1933, 88–91; Ruini 1985, 67).

Still, the continuing influence of Palestrina in this saga remains of paramount importance. A century ago a controversy raged in European musicological circles over whether Palestrina's aborted efforts at reform of plainchant in the 1570s had indeed carried over to the *Editio Medicaea* of the Roman Gradual in 1614–15. The widespread conclusion at that time, notwithstanding Haberl's views to the contrary, was that it did not—in other words, that the year 1578 had spelled the end of Palestrina's efforts toward chant reform (Haberl 1894; Molitor 1899; Haberl 1900; Respighi [1900?]; Molitor 1901–2, passim; Haberl 1902, 1–42).

Yet at least some of the reformed melodies of Palestrina and Zoilo may have survived, at least for a few decades. In a strange quirk of fate, evidence for the existence of these melodies surfaced in a series of trials held from 1596 until 1602 that involved Palestrina's son Iginio, who had attempted to sell forgeries of reformed chant books as his deceased father's work. Iginio himself claimed to have seen his father's manuscript of the reformed gradual in the mid-1580s (Molitor 1901–2, 2:7), while Palestrina's copyist claimed that he had seen the composer's manuscript of the reformed chant melodies and had also copied similar melodies by Zoilo (Molitor 1901–2, 2:26–27); the composer Giovanni Maria Nanino testified that he had visited Zoilo's widow in Loreto in May of 1596 and at that time had seen the composer's manuscript of reformed melodies that included a *Graduale Dominicale*, a *Proprium Sanctorum*, and an *Antiphonarium* (Molitor 1901–2, 2:35); and another witness testified that he had heard that the manuscript of Palestrina's chant reform did exist and that these melodies were currently being used by a monk at San Marcello (Molitor 1901–2, 2:7). However, after all the witnesses had been deposed, a final report on the affair to Pope Clement VIII concluded that Iginio's *Antiphonarium* and *Proprium Sanctorum* were blatant forgeries, and only the *Graduale Dominicale* could possibly be considered the work of Palestrina (Baini [1828] 1966, 1:117; Molitor 1901–2, 2:45–53, 222–29). Although Iginio's chant books were confiscated in 1602 and placed in the archive of the Mons Pietatis, neither Haberl nor Molitor were able to locate them over a century ago (Haberl 1894, 9; Respighi [1900?], 83–89; Molitor 1901–2, 2:57).

Now let us return to 1578, the year in which Gregory XIII apparently withdrew his support for chant reform. Some unpublished documents in the Venetian State Archive and the Imperial Chancellery in Vienna suggest that Palestrina's attempts at having his reformed melodies published may not have ended with the withdrawal of papal approval. In 1582 Angelo Gardano arranged for an agent of his in Rome to negotiate a contract with Palestrina, although exactly to what end is not specified. Then, in the following year, Gardano petitioned the Imperial Court in Vienna for a printing privilege of ten-year duration. In his supplication, Gardano indicated his wish to protect the rights of publication within the Empire for books of plainchant edited by Palestrina and Zoilo, fully five years after support apparently had been withdrawn by the same pope who was still pontifex maximus (Agee 1998, 67–69). Perhaps Palestrina and Zoilo had already completed enough work on the project—and thought there would be a large enough market for the liturgical books—that they were considering issuing plainchant editions outside of the official Roman court channels.

Thus it seems extremely likely that many of Palestrina's reforms of chant were indeed carried forward—not to the much later *Editio Medicaea* of 1614, as Haberl had speculated (Haberl 1894), but instead to the Gardano chant books published in Venice during the late 1580s and early 1590s. Maybe Palestrina or Zoilo went directly to Gardano in Venice, or perhaps Gardano approached them— this is something that we may never know. Nor may we ever learn if the melodies from the Gardano chant books were actually based on the chant reforms of Palestrina and Zoilo, since the composers might have found it necessary to hide their participation in a project that the pope seems to have terminated under pressure from Spain. Nevertheless, it is clear that efforts toward editions of reformed plainchant continued in Venice throughout the decade of the 1580s and into the 1590s.

Further evidence of continued activity in this regard can be seen in the biography of Andrea Gabrieli. Since the preface to Gardano's *Graduale Romanum* refers to Andrea Gabrieli as a major contributor (Catholic Church 1591, 2r; Molitor 1901–2, 2:260–61; Ruini 1985, 67–68; Gozzi 1995, 402–4; Indino 1998, 20–21; Indino 1999, 207–8), and since Gabrieli had died in August of 1585 (Morell 1983, 110), clearly there seems to have been editorial activity on a plainchant edition in Venetian circles at least six years before the publication of this gradual in 1591. Consequently we can assume that Palestrina and Zoilo may indeed have ceased their activity on a revision of Roman plainchant sometime between about 1583, the date of Gardano's petition for an imperial privilege on Palestrina's plainchant editions, and about 1585, the year of Andrea Gabrieli's death. Chant reform, having been aborted in the Eternal City, had moved from Rome to Venice. The Venetian printer Angelo Gardano issued a diminutive reformed Franciscan Gradual and Antiphoner (Catholic Church 1587), which was edited by Ludovico Balbi, followed four years later by the elephantine reformed *Graduale Romanum* (Catholic Church 1591), which was edited by composers active in the *Veneto*—Andrea Gabrieli, Balbi, and Orazio Vecchi.

A few errors should be pointed out that continue to be promulgated in the literature over the identities, dates, and editors of the Gardano *Graduale, et Antiphonarium* and the Gardano *Graduale Romanum* (Indino 1998, 9; Indino 1999, 208n8). First, many scholars have simply conflated or confused the two publications or their editors (Gibelli 1969, 430; Fellerer 1976a, 9; Meier 1976, 48; Rostirolla 1980, 61; Baroffio 1995, 13; Morelli and Gibelli 1999, 90; Rostirolla 2001, 528). Others have indicated that the *Graduale Romanum* must have been edited by Giovanni Gabrieli rather than Andrea (Mischiati 1966, 1348; Martin 1980, 584; Martin 2001, 366), an error traceable as far back as Caffi's mid-nineteenth-century volume on music at St. Mark's (Caffi [1854–55] 1972–73, 1:176; Kenton 1967, 65; Gozzi 1995, 404). In an article on the Gardano *Graduale Romanum*, Gozzi seemed to have known of the minuscule 1587 Franciscan *Graduale, et Antiphonarium* only through its undated title on the 1591 Gardano booklist. He speculated, ironically, that the Franciscan *Graduale, et Antiphonarium* probably consisted of well over two hundred pages in folio (Gozzi 1995, 402).

Another long-standing error can be traced back to a misreading of Molitor, who apparently knew the 1591 Gardano *Graduale Romanum* only from an exemplar lacking a title page. Given the death of Andrea Gabrieli in the middle of the previous decade, he dated the volume "nach 1585," later read by some as 1585. Thus the ghost of the "*Graduale Romanum* published by Gardano in 1585" has continued to haunt us (Molitor 1901–2, 2:173; Fellerer 1976a, 9; Fellerer 1976b, 119).

Certainly by the 1580s the spirit of the Renaissance had made its impact not only in the secular but also in the sacred sphere. The cardinals' commission on music, appointed as a result of the Council of Trent, had insisted on the intelligibility of words in polyphonic sacred music, a notion largely derived from the influence of Renaissance humanists (Fellerer 1953; Lockwood 1970, 74–100, 127–35; Fellerer 1976a, 2:7–9; Dyer 2001, 545–46). The reformers of plainchant in the post-Tridentine period also wished to employ their new humanistic sympathies in the restoration of these melodies. Taken as a whole, the number of these reforms seems dizzying. They included (1) the introduction of accentual declamation, (2) the abbreviation of melismas to improve declamation and text intelligibility, (3) a transformation of the traditional medieval Latin texts to reflect the influence of classical Latin, (4) the widespread application of the B♭, (5) word painting to highlight the text, (6) simplification of chant notation and application of mensural notation forms, and (7) modal clarification through the alteration of opening and cadential pitches (Molitor 1901, xi; Molitor 1901–2, 1:183–215; Meier 1969, 106–7; Gozzi 1995, 404–14; Indino 1998, 47–49; Levy, Emerson et al. 2001, 851). No doubt these were the sort of sweeping revisions to plainchant that Fernando de las Infantas found so objectionable. Nevertheless, compared with the extensive reforms just cited that can be seen throughout the *Editio Medicaea* of 1614–15 and later publications, the *Gardano* chant books exhibit a relatively light editorial hand.

The tiny 1587 Gardano *Graduale, et Antiphonarium* (RELICS 2650, at US BE), with examples labelled GA1587 in table 1 and figure 1 below, shall serve as the central focus of this paper. It was one of the very first reformed chant books published after the Council of Trent that included the reformed texts of both the 1568 *Breviarium romanum* and 1570 *Missale romanum* as well as significant melodic reform. This modest publication, edited by Balbi, consists of only thirty folios, and may be seen as a prefatory study to the major edition of the 1591 Gardano Gradual, which also listed Balbi among its editors. The dedication to this edition provides us with a number of classical allusions typical of the Renaissance, with references to both Mars and Hercules. One advantage in choosing the *Graduale, et Antiphonarium* of 1587 as the central focus here is that it provides a clear basis for restricting what would otherwise prove to be an intimidating number of liturgical pieces for analysis. While the *Graduale*'s office chants may be peculiar to Franciscan practices at the *Santo* in Padua (where Balbi was employed at the time), the vast majority of chants for the Mass contained in the edition can easily be located in the standard Solesmes editions of the gradual.

As the basis for comparison with the Mass pieces in the *Graduale, et Antiphonarium*, three other publications have been chosen. The first, labelled G1580 (the Liechtenstein Gradual, RELICS 890, at US CHH), adheres to the new texts of the reformed missal of 1570 yet shows little evidence of editorial tampering with the traditional melodies as transmitted from the Middle Ages. The multiple-impression process, with red lines and black neumes, allows the traditional neumatic shapes to survive with little difficulty. Unfortunately, the edition is marred by many errors in placement of clefs and alignment of the neumes with the staff lines (Catholic Church 1580; Baini [1828] 1966, 1:99–100). The edition labeled G1591 is the Gardano *Graduale Romanum* (RELICS 746, at US CU). While adhering to the new texts of the reformed missal, the melodies themselves, as with GA1587, have also undergone a transformation. Given Angelo Gardano's virtually exclusive experience with the single-impression process, here, as in GA1587, the traditional neumes have been simplified to allow single pieces of type to carry both notes and staff lines. The consequence is that many of the neumes have been broken into their constituent pitches, destroying the traditional neumatic flow but increasing the level of pitch accuracy so compromised in the multiple-impression G1580 (Catholic Church 1591). The last edition, labeled G1615, is the second volume of the *Editio Medicaea*, edited by Anerio and Soriano, also based on the reformed missal but with melodies edited by an even stronger hand than in the Gardano publications (Ruini 1985; Indino 1998, 47; RELICS 2684; Baroffio and Kim, 2001). Once again we find the multiple-impression printing process, with lines and pitches printed separately. Thus, although somewhat modernized, the *Editio Medicaea* can be seen to be more traditional in notation than the more radical approach taken in the Gardano books (Baroffio and Sodi 2001; Baroffio and Kim, 2001).

Forty-three melodies, or 81 percent of the total fifty-three Mass pieces from GA1587, are common to all four of these editions, and an attempt has been made to quantify the editorial changes from edition to edition through a modal analysis. Modal classification was used to place the melodies into groups, and the initial phrase and cadential pitches were examined to determine what modal alterations the editors carried out on the traditional melodic forms. In cinquecento Italy two conflicting theoretical systems of cadential classification emerged, as Meier and Powers have pointed out. On the one hand, Pietro Aaron advocated myriad acceptable cadential pitches, similar to the actual practice of plainchant. On the other hand, Zarlino restricts his description of possible cadence pitches to a rigorous systematization of species fourths and fifths that seems to have little precedent in practical terms—apparently theory rather than practice helped to shape this new configuration (Meier 1988, 105–22; Powers 2001, 805–6, 812–14; see also Aaron [1525] 1979, chaps. 9–12; and Zarlino [1573] 1966, pt. 4, chaps. 18–29).

The editors of the three reformed editions cited here were influenced enormously but in varied ways by the theorists and by practice. An analysis of the initial phrase pitches and the modal cadences found in GA1587 and in the corresponding pieces of the three graduals may be found in table 1.

Notice that for the initial phrase pitches of the Dorian mode 1 pieces, the Gardano books correspond closely to the traditional G1580, whereas the *Editio Medicaea* (G1615) removes any suspicion of plagality by entirely eliminating any phrase openings below the final. For the cadential pitches, the solutions adopted by the reformers prove less radical, with various moderate attempts to strengthen the final, the fifth above, or the mediating third. The results for the Hypodorian mode 2 are similar—the Gardano books follow the traditional pattern of opening phrase pitches, but G1615 eliminates any opening pitch but the final. The small changes in the cadences here demonstrate a concern with ambitus, since all of the reform books eliminate the high B and thus preserve the implied range as plagal in nature.

The initial phrase pitches of Phrygian mode 3 present a similar pattern: the Gardano books alter the initial phrase pitch on A to the G that mediates the species of fifth, while G1615 alters all but one of the initial phrase pitches to the final. The cadential pitches show significant variation. GA1587 and G1591 reinforce the species of fifth or mediating third and downplay the traditional upper c' *repercussio*. In contrast, the editors of the *Editio Medicaea* seem more concerned about the ambitus and radically reduce the number of cadences below the E final that might suggest a plagal mode. Hypophrygian mode 4 reflects a similar concern about plagality in its initial phrase pitches—G1615 demonstrates a slight preference for avoiding the lower C. In terms of cadence pitches, the Gardano reform books bear more similarity to the traditional melodic modal structures while G1615 once again reinforces the ambitus of the plagal mode by cadencing not eleven but fifteen times on tones below the final E.

In Lydian mode 5, the Gardano books add opening phrase pitches on the fourth below the final to emphasize the species of fourth, consistent with Zarlino's theories, although the *Editio Medicaea* radically moves all opening phrase pitches to the fourth below the final F. In terms of cadential pitches, all three reform books strengthen the fifth and third above the final, and given that mode 5 is authentic, cadences below the final appear somewhat less frequently. In the plagal Hypolydian mode 6, the Gardano books retain the traditional modal profile of initial phrase pitches, while G1615 apparently eliminates a cadence on the lower

D to highlight the species of fourth in the mode. The cadences of the Gardano books retain a similar profile to the medieval melodic shapes, but the *Editio Medicaea* adds three entirely unprecedented cadences to reinforce the mediating third above the final A at the expense of the cadences on D below the final and even of the final itself.

Only a single piece utilizes Mixolydian mode 7, and there are no changes in the opening phrase pitches or the cadential parameters from one book to the next. However, in plagal Hypomixolydian mode 8, the *Editio Medicaea* alters the opening notes of the chant phrases to reinforce the final and species of fourth by eliminating any opening pitches but those on G and D; G1615 also adds cadences on D and d' to highlight the species of fourth and fifth above and below G.

Figure 1 presents the gradual *Os iusti meditabitur* in versions from all four editions. Text accent and intelligibility, so dear to the humanists, clearly play a major role in the editing of these melodies. The number of pitches in the opening phrase "Os iusti" have been halved in the three reform books, thus making the text somewhat more comprehensible. GA1587 preserves the general medieval profile of the following phrase on "meditabitur," but in G1591 and G1615 the melody and its relationship to the word have been altered to stress the accented syllable *ta* rather than preserving the traditional melisma on *bi*. The same is true of all three later books at "sapientiam," with the shortening of the melisma on *am* that places more emphasis on the accented third syllable, relegating the last unaccented syllable to the final pitch or pitches of the phrase. A shortening of the melismas on unaccented syllables also holds true for the following words in the reform graduals: "eius," "iudicium," "eius" again, "supplantabuntur," and once again, "eius."

In modal terms, at nearly every cadence at least one of the melodies carries a variant pitch from the others, and on occasion three differing cadential pitches occur among the four chant books. Balbi, in GA1587, seems intent on stressing the species of fifth and mediating third of a melody in first mode—he ends the word "sapientiam" on the modal *repercussio* A, concludes the following "eius" on the modal final D, and once again inserts the modal final for the last syllable of "supplantabuntur." In contrast, when Balbi teamed up with the other editors of G1591, the cadences generally tend to reflect much more closely the traditional cadence points, whether they reinforced the mode or not—perhaps this would imply an earlier redaction by a more conservative Gabrieli. By the time Anerio and Soriano edited the *Editio Medicaea*, the reinforcement of the mode is once more based on the species of fourth, fifth, and mediating third, with an emphasis on the modal final D, as at "sapientiam" and "ipsius," the mediating third, as at the first "eius," and the fifth above the final A, as at "loquetur."

These musical redactions of the melodies, however, pose a strange contradiction and disjunction when compared to the textual reforms of the liturgy. Pope

Clement VII had instructed Cardinal Quiñonez to create a reformed breviary, and although in its greatly shortened form the new Breviary of 1535 proved quite popular among the common clergy, Clement's Tridentine successors withdrew their favor from the edition. Ultimately it was under the post-Tridentine Pius V that the new breviary and missal were published—not with an abbreviation of the texts but a restoration based on old Roman manuscripts carried out in the spirit of antique purity (Baini [1828] 1966, 1:78; Respighi [1900?], 11–15; Gozzi 1994, 1:45–48; Baroffio, Curti, and Gozzi 2000, 66–68). After the Council of Trent, as we have seen, the musical reformers began where Quiñonez had left off in his editing of text with a shortening of melodies and a simplification of notation. The products of this reform were the Gardano chant books, the *Editio Medicaea*, and numerous editions of plainchant issued in subsequent centuries. Only with the Gothic revival of the nineteenth century and the activities at Solesmes and elsewhere did editors of plainchant turn once again to the old Roman books and the spirit of antique purity that had been embodied in the reforms of Pius V (Bergeron 1998, passim).

This paper concludes with references to the ideological clashes mirrored in Balbi's edition of the 1587 Gardano *Graduale, et Antiphonarium*. Certainly any such attempt to publish an edition of plainchant can be considered an act of deference to the Middle Ages. At the same time, the shortening of melismas, improved accentual declamation, attempts at modal corrections, and the neoclassical allusions of the edition's preface mirror the humanistic reforms of the Renaissance. Yet the title page moves beyond the Renaissance by acknowledging the reformed missal and breviary that resulted from the Council of Trent and the Catholic Reformation. Consequently it is the confluence and conflict of medieval, Renaissance, and Catholic Reformation ideals in this tiny Franciscan *Graduale, et Antiphonarium* that both leads us back to the centuries whose musical culture it preserves and to the centuries that follow in its illumination of the ever-changing practices of plainchant.

Table 1. Modal Analyses

Number of Mass pieces in GA1587: 53. Number of Mass pieces from GA1587 included below: 43. Those excluded are apparently chants associated with local liturgy that cannot be found in other common sources (9) or are cast into a different mode than in other chant books (1): 10. Brackets indicate transposition.

DORIAN MODE 1 (12 pieces)

Opening pitches	G1580	GA1587	G1591	G1615
a	1	1	—	1
g f	1	1	1	—
e	—	—	—	—
d	6	7	6	11
c	4	3	4	—
Cadential pitches	**G1580**	**GA1587**	**G1591**	**G1615**
c'	1	1	1	—
b	—	—	—	—
a	18	20	17	20
g	6	4	6	3
f	12	15	13	12
e	3	4	5	3
d	35	35	34	37
c	5	1	4	5

HYPODORIAN MODE 2 (4 pieces)

Opening pitches	G1580	GA1587	G1591	G1615
d	3	3	3	4
c	1	1	1	—
Cadential pitches	**G1580**	**GA1587**	**G1591**	**G1615**
b	1	—	—	—
a	—	1	2	3
g	1	5	3	4
f	5	5	3	4
e	5	16	15	14
d	13	16	15	14
c	4	3	4	3
[B♭]	2	1	1	2

PHRYGIAN MODE 3 (4 pieces)

Opening pitches	G1580	GA1587	G1591	G1615
a	1	—	—	—
g f	2	1	2	1
e	1	1	1	4
Cadential pitches	**G1580**	**GA1587**	**G1591**	**G1615**
c'	5	2	2	5
b	3	4	3	3
a	4	6	5	5
g	5	6	7	3
f	1	1	2	4
e	5	4	3	6
d	4	4	5	2
c	1	1	1	—

HYPOPHRYGIAN MODE 4 (6 pieces)

Opening pitches	G1580	GA1587	G1591	G1615
e	1	1	1	2
d	—	1	1	1
c	2	1	1	—
Cadential pitches	**G1580**	**GA1587**	**G1591**	**G1615**
a	1	2	1	1
g	2	3	3	5
f	3	5	4	3
e	15	12	13	8
d	9	9	7	10
c	2	2	4	5

Table 1 (*continued*)

LYDIAN MODE 5 (6 pieces)

	G1580	GA1587	G1591	G1615
Opening pitches				
f	5	4	4	—
e	—	1	1	—
d	1	1	1	—
c	—	1	1	6
Cadential pitches				
d'	14	17	17	16
c'	—	1	1	1
b	8	9	9	10
a	2	2	1	2
g/f	23	19	20	20
e	2	3	2	—
d	4	2	3	—
c	—	—	—	4

HYPOLYDIAN MODE 6 (4 pieces)

	G1580	GA1587	G1591	G1615
Opening pitches				
f	1	1	1	2
e	—	—	—	—
d	1	1	1	—
c	2	2	2	2
Cadential pitches				
a	1	1	1	3
g/f	19	18	19	14
e	—	—	—	4
d	3	3	2	1
c	3	4	4	4

MIXOLYDIAN MODE 7 (1 piece)

	G1580	GA1587	G1591	G1615
Opening pitches				
g	1	1	1	1
Cadential pitches				
d'	1	1	1	1
c'	1	1	1	1
b	1	1	1	1
a	—	—	—	—
g	2	2	2	2

HYPOMIXOLYDIAN MODE 8 (6 pieces)

	G1580	GA1587	G1591	G1615
Opening pitches				
g'	3	4	3	5
f	1	1	1	—
e	1	1	1	—
d	1	1	1	1
Cadential pitches				
d'	4	5	5	1
c'	2	1	1	5
b	2	2	2	2
a	22	22	23	21
g/f	6	6	6	3
e	—	—	—	1
d	1	1	—	3

Figure 1. Gradual, "Os iusti meditabitur," Dorian mode 1.

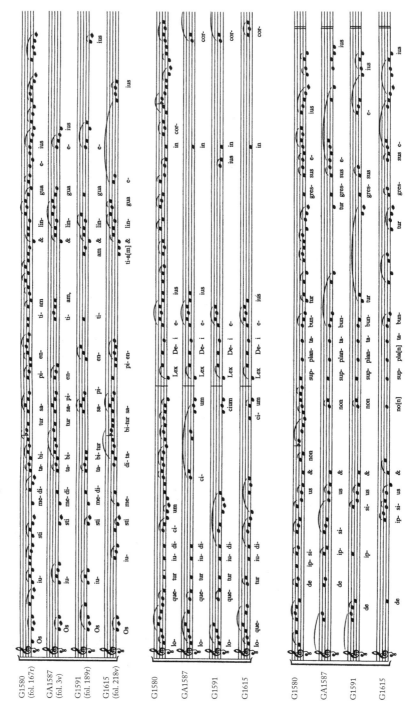

References

Aaron, Pietro. (1525) 1979. *Trattato della natura et cognitione di tutti gli tuoni di canto figurato non da altrui piu scritti.* Reprint, New York: Broude Brothers.

Agee, Richard J. 1998. *The Gardano Music Printing Firms, 1569–1611.* Rochester, NY: University of Rochester Press.

Baini, Giuseppe. (1828) 1966. *Memorie storico-critiche della vita e delle opere di Giovanni Pierluigi da Palestrina.* 2 vols. Reprint, Hildesheim: Olms.

Baroffio, Bonifacio G. 1995. "Il Concilio di Trento e la musica." In *Musica e liturgia nella riforma tridentina*, edited by Danilo Curti and Marco Gozzi, 9–17. Trento: Provincia Autonoma di Trento, Servizio Beni Librari e Archivistici.

Baroffio, Bonifacio G., Danilo Curti, and Marco Gozzi, eds. 2000. *Jubilate Deo: Miniature e melodie gregoriane; Testimonianze della Biblioteca L. Feininger.* Trento: Provincia Autonoma di Trento, Servizio Beni Librari e Archivistici.

Baroffio, Bonifacio G., and Eun Ju Kim, eds. 2001. *Graduale de sanctis: Iuxta ritum Sacrosanctae Romanae Ecclesiae; Editio Princeps (1614–1615).* Facsimile edition. Monumenta Studia Instrumenta Liturgica 11. Città del Vaticano: Libreria Editrice Vaticana.

Baroffio, Bonifacio G., and Manlio Sodi, eds. 2001. *Graduale de tempore: Iuxta ritum Sacrosanctae Romanae Ecclesiae; Editio Princeps (1614).* Facsimile edition. Monumenta Studia Instrumenta Liturgica 10. Città del Vaticano: Libreria Editrice Vaticana.

Bergeron, Katherine. 1998. *Decadent Enchantments: The Revival of Gregorian Chant at Solesmes.* Berkeley: University of California Press.

Caffi, Francesco. (1854–55) 1972–73. *Storia della musica sacra nella già Cappella ducale di San Marco in Venezia dal 1318 al 1797.* 2 vols. Bibliotheca Musica Bononiensis, sez. III, n. 50. Reprint, Bologna: Forni.

Catholic Church. 1580. *Graduale Sacrosancte Romane Ecclesie integrum & completum tam de Tempore quam de Sanctis Juxta ritum Missalis noui ex decreto Sacrosancti Concilij Tridentini restituti.* Venice: Ex officina Petri Liechtenstein, Latine, Lucidus Lapis, Patricij Agrippinensis. Exemplar in RELICS 890, at US CHH.

———. 1587. *Graduale, et Antiphonarium omnium dierum festorum ordinis minorum, Iuxta ritum Missalis & Breviarij Novi.* Venetiis: Apud Angelum Gardanum. Exemplar in RELICS 2650, at US BE.

———. 1591. *Graduale Romanum: Iuxta ritum Missalis Noui, ex Decreto Sacrosancti Concilij Tridentini restituti....* Venice: Apud Angelum Gardanum. Exemplar in RELICS 746, at US CU.

Cattin, Giulio, Danilo Curti, and Marco Gozzi, eds. 1999. *Il canto piano nell'era della stampa: Atti del Convegno internazionale di studi sul canto liturgico nei secoli XV–XVIII; Trento Castello del Buonconsiglio, Venezia, Fondazione Ugo e Olga Levi, 9–11 ottobre 1998.* Trent: Provincia autonoma di Trento, Servizi beni librari e archivistici.

Crawford, David, James Borders, Barbara Haggh-Huglo, and David Rutherford, eds. N.d. *Renaissance Liturgical Imprints: A Census (RELICS)*, accessed May 31, 2007, http://www-personal.umich.edu/~davidcr/.

Curti, Danilo and Marco Gozzi, eds. 1995. *Musica e liturgia nella riforma tridentina.* Trento: Provincia Autonoma di Trento, Servizio Beni Librari e Archivistici.

Curti, Danilo, and Fabrizio Leonardelli, eds. 1985. *La Biblioteca Musicale Laurence K. J. Feininger: Trento, Castello del Buonconsiglio, 6 sett.–25 ott. 1985: Catalogo.* Trent: Provincia Autonoma di Trento, Servizio Beni Culturale.

Dal Prà, Laura. 1995. *Un museo nel Castello del Buonconsiglio: Acquisizioni, contributi, restauri: Catalogo.* Trento: Provincia Autonoma di Trento, Servizio Beni Culturali: Castello del Buonconsiglio, Monumenti e Collezioni Provinciali.

Dyer, Joseph. 2001. "Roman Catholic Church Music." In *The New Grove Dictionary of Music and Musicians,* edited by Stanley Sadie, 21:544–70. 2nd ed. 29 vols. London: Macmillan.

Fellerer, Karl Gustav. 1953. "Church Music and the Council of Trent." *Musical Quarterly* 39: 576–94.

———. 1976a. "Das Konzil von Trient und die Kirchenmusik." In *Geschichte der katholischen Kirchenmusik,* 2:7–9. 2 vols. Kassel: Bärenreiter, 1972, 1976.

———. 1976b. "Der Cantus Gregorianus im 17. Jahrhundert." In *Geschichte der katholischen Kirchenmusik,* 2:119–21. 2 vols. Kassel: Bärenreiter, 1972, 1976.

Gibelli, Vittorio. 1969. "Balbi, Ludovico." In *Die Musik in Geschichte und Gegenwart,* edited by Friedrich Blume, 15:430–31. 17 vols. Kassel: Bärenreiter.

Gozzi, Marco. 1994. *Le fonti liturgiche a stampa della Biblioteca Musicale L. Feininger presso il Castello del Buonconsiglio.* 2 vols. Trento: Provincia Autonoma di Trento, Servizio Beni Culturali, Servizio Beni Librari e Archivistici.

———. 1995. "Il Graduale di Angelo Gardano (1591)." In Dal Prà 1995, 399–414.

Haberl, Fr. X. 1894. "Giovanni Pierluigi da Palestrina und das offizielle Graduale Romanum der Editio Medicaea von 1614." *Musica sacra,* Ausserordentliche Beilage zu Nr. 2: 1–14.

———. 1900. Review of *Giovanni Pier Luigi da Palestrina e l'emendazione del Graduale Romano,* by Carlo Respighi; and of *Zur Vorgeschichte der Medicaea,* by P. Raphael Molitor. *Kirchenmusikalishes Jahrbuch* 15: 165–79.

———. 1902. *Storia e pregio dei libri corali ufficiali.* Rome/Ratisbon: Pustet.

Indino, Annarita. 1998. "Il *Graduale* stampato da Angelo Gardano nel 1591." Tesi di Laurea, Università degli Studi di Lecce.

———. 1999. "Il Graduale stampato da Angelo Gardano (1591)." In Cattin, Curti, and Gozzi, 1999, 207–21.

Karp, Theodore. 1999a. "On the Transmission of Some Mass Chants, c. 1575–1775." In Cattin, Curti, and Gozzi, 1999, 81–97.

———. 1999b. "Some Chants for the Mass Proper, ca. 1575–1800." Paper presented at the Annual Meeting of the American Musicological Society, Kansas City, Missouri.

———. 2005. *An Introduction to the Post-Tridentine Mass Proper.* 2 vols. Musicological Studies and Documents 54, 1–2. Middleton, WI: American Institute of Musicology.

Kenton, Egon. 1967. *Life and Works of Giovanni Gabrieli.* Musicological Studies and Documents 16. N.p.: American Institute of Musicology.

Leonardelli, Fabrizio. 1988. *Catalogo delle opere a stampa della Biblioteca musicale Laurence K. J. Feininger: Musica e liturgia nelle pubblicazioni tra XV e XX secolo.* 2 vols. Catalogo Bibliografico Trentino, Monografie, 4. Trento: Provincia Autonoma di Trento.

Levy, Kenneth, John A. Emerson et al. 2001. "Plainchant [plainsong]." In *The New Grove Dictionary of Music and Musicians,* edited by Stanley Sadie, 19:825–86. 2nd ed. 29 vols. London: Macmillan.

Lincoln, Harry B. 2001. "Zoilo, Annibale. Works: Sacred." *The New Grove Dictionary of Music and Musicians,* edited by Stanley Sadie, 27:862–63. 2nd ed. 29 vols. London: Macmillan.

Lockwood, Lewis. 1970. *The Counter-Reformation and the Masses of Vincenzo Ruffo*. Studi di Musica Veneta 2. Venice: Fondazione Giorgio Cini, Centro di Cultura e Civiltà.

Lockwood, Lewis, Noel O'Regan, and Jessie Ann Owens. 2001. "Palestrina [Prenestino, etc.], Giovanni Pierluigi da ['Gianetto']." In *The New Grove Dictionary of Music and Musicians*, edited by Stanley Sadie, 18:937–57. 2nd ed. 29 vols. London: Macmillan.

Martin, Willliam R. 1980. "Vecchi, Orazio [Horatio] (Tiberio)." In *The New Grove Dictionary of Music and Musicians*, edited by Stanley Sadie, 19:584–86. 20 vols. London: Macmillan.

———. 2001. "Vecchi, Orazio [Horatio] (Tiberio)." In *The New Grove Dictionary of Music and Musicians*, edited by Stanley Sadie, 26:366–68. 2nd ed. 29 vols. London: Macmillan.

Meier, Bernhard. 1969. "Modale Korrektur und Wortausdeutung im Choral der Editio Medicaea." *Kirchenmusikalisches Jahrbuch* 53:101–32.

———. 1976. "Choralreform und Chorallehre im 16. Jahrhundert." In *Geschichte der katholischen Kirchenmusik*, edited by Karl Gustav Fellerer, 2:45–53. 2 vols. Kassel: Bärenreiter, 1972, 1976.

———. 1988. *The Modes of Classical Vocal Polyphony Described According to the Sources: With Revisions by the Author*. Translated by Ellen S. Beebe. New York: Broude Brothers Ltd.

Mischiati, Oscar. 1966. "Vecchi, Orazio Tiberio." In *Die Musik in Geschichte und Gegenwart*, edited by Friedrich Blume, 13:1346–54. 17 vols. Kassel: Bärenreiter.

Mitjana, Rafael. 1918. *Don Fernando de las Infantas, teólogo y músico*. Madrid: Junta para Ampliación de Estudios e Investigaciones Científicas/Centro de Estudios Históricos.

Molitor, P. Raphael. 1899. "Zur Vorgeschichte der Medicea." *Römische Quartalschrift für christliche Altertumskunde und Kirchengeschichte* 4:367–74.

———. 1901. *Reform-Choral: Historisch-kritische Studie*. Freiburg im Breisgau: Herdersche Verlagshandlung.

———. 1901–2. *Die nach-tridentinische Choral-Reform zu Rom: Ein Beitrag zur Musikgeschichte des XVI. und XVII. Jahrhunderts*. 2 vols. Leipzig: Leuckart.

Morell, Martin. 1983. "New Evidence for the Biographies of Andrea and Giovanni Gabrieli." *Early Music History* 3: 101–22.

Morelli, Giorgio, and Vittorio Gibelli. 1999. "Balbi, Lodovico." In *Die Musik in Geschichte und Gegenwart*, edited by Ludwig Finscher, 2:89–90. 2nd ed. 21 vols. Kassel: Bärenreiter.

Powers, Harold S. 2001. "Mode." In *The New Grove Dictionary of Music and Musicians*, edited by Stanley Sadie, 16:775–860. 2nd ed. 29 vols. London: Macmillan.

Respighi, Carlo. [1900?]. *Nuovo studio su Giovanni Pier Luigi da Palestrina e l'emendazione del Graduale Romano*. Rome: Società di San Giovanni Evangelista/Desclée, Lefebvre.

Rostirolla, Giancarlo. 1980. "Balbi, Lodovico." In *The New Grove Dictionary of Music and Musicians*, edited by Stanley Sadie, 2:60–62. 20 vols. London: Macmillan.

———. 2001. "Balbi, Lodovico [Ludovico]." In *The New Grove Dictionary of Music and Musicians*, edited by Stanley Sadie, 2:528–29. 2nd ed. 29 vols. London: Macmillan.

Ruini, Cesarino. 1985. "Editoria e musica liturgica: Appunti su alcune vicende del Graduale e dell'Antifonario tra il XVI e XVII secolo." In Curti and Leonardelli 1985, 62–71.

Sesini, Ugo. 1933. *Decadenza e restaurazione del canto liturgico*. Milan: Casa Editrice d'Arte e Liturgia B. Angelico.

Sodi, Manlio, and Achille Maria Triacca, eds. 1998. *Missale Romanum: Editio Princeps (1570)*. Città del Vaticano: Libreria Editrice Vaticana.

———, eds. 1999. *Breviarium Romanum: Editio Princeps (1568)*. Città del Vaticano: Libreria Editrice Vaticana.

Zarlino, Gioseffo. (1573) 1966. *Istitutioni harmoniche*. Reprint, Ridgewood, NJ: Gregg Press.

Interpreting the Repertory

Music on the Run in Italian *Novelle*: Plagues, Devotional Movements, and Intimate Gatherings Away from Home

Cathy Ann Elias

The notated music that has come down to us offers only limited guidance for reconstructing historically correct performances of secular music before 1600. Specific combinations of voices and instruments are rarely indicated, leaving open a variety of possibilities. A piece texted in all voices in one source may appear in another with no text at all. What were the performance conventions, how did they change over time, and what was the role of instruments? All of these questions bring up another aspect of music making—improvisation. Recently Timothy J. McGee, reiterating Nino Pirrotta's point that our view of music making before 1600 is distorted because we have not taken into account the prominent role of improvisation in musical life, offers proposals for performing improvised music.[1] He outlines the three common practices: "Instrumentalists improvised music for dancing and processing, singers improvised melodies to accompany their poetry, and on some occasions the poetry too was improvised" (McGee 2003, 31).

Italian literary sources containing musical descriptions are a valuable source for understanding performance practice. I shall give specific examples of music making found in several of them. These sources provide details about the performance of specific pieces, about the diverse instrumental combinations used in these idealized settings, and often support conjectures made by McGee concerning improvisation.

One genre in particular, collections of Italian *novelle* in the *cornice/giornate* format or a variant of it, provides us with many descriptions of the musical entertainment of Italians away from home. *Novelle* are framed with a travel story, and this framing story, the *cornice*, always includes descriptions of musical performances. With very few exceptions, the travelers are of the noblest character and well educated, but, as we move from the trecento to the cinquecento, the stories they tell become more lewd, while descriptions of their daily music making remain pure and idyllic.

The cornice/giornate format originates with Giovanni Boccaccio's (1313–75) *Decameron* and has a long history.[2] To frame his novelle Boccaccio describes the flight of a group of upper-class virtuous young people from Florence and the 1348 plague. They pass their days in the hills outside Florence singing, dancing, and telling stories. Boccaccio writes the texts for the songs they sing and provides descriptions of their performances. Giovanni Sercambi (1347–1424), in his *Novelliere*, refashions the *Decameron*. In his cornice a group of clergy and laymen, including children, decide to leave Lucca in 1374 to escape the plague. Sercambi reinterprets parts of the Bianchi movement—to which he was an eyewitness.[3] Unlike the Bianchi, Sercambi's fictional pious group travels around northern Italy eating delicious meals, singing *ballate* and *canti morali*, reciting poetry, telling stories, playing games, and dancing. Many of the texts they sing have extant music.

The cinquecento writer Giovanni Francesco Straparola (ca. 1480–1557?) also imitates the format of the *Decameron* in *Le piacevoli notti*. His cornice unfolds as follows: Ottaviano Maria Sforza, bishop-elect of Lodi, and his daughter Lucretia escape from the turmoil of the Milanese court and travel to Lodi. Experiencing more problems there, they decide to go to Venice, and become guests of Ferier Beltramo. Not wanting to impose, they travel to the island of Murano, where they find a beautiful palace. They decide to remain there for a number of days to avoid the debauchery of city life in Venice during carnival. Lucretia invites ten young ladies, two matrons, and several accomplished gentlemen, including Pietro Bembo and the talented viol players Antonio Molino and Benedetto Trivigiano. They pass the nights singing, dancing, and telling stories.

Two other cinquecento writers provide descriptions of trips made for rest and vacation. Tomaso Costo's (ca. 1560–ca. 1630) cornice in *Il Fuggilozio* takes place in Posilipo near Naples in the summer home of Prior Ravaschiero, a rich Genovese man, who unfortunately has gout. He retreats there to uplift his spirits. A group of his friends, all male, decide to visit him to try and cheer him up. Seeing that he is in pain, they decide to remain for seven days in hopes of uplifting his spirits. His friends are well educated, come from good families, and are talented musicians. They bring their musical instruments and give themselves new names, as one commonly did in the Academies.

In his *Dodici giornate* in *Salò e sua riviera*, Silvano Cattaneo (1514?–1553/64) recounts a trip around Lake Garda made by Count Fortunato Martinengo with the author and some students who are on vacation from the University of Padua. Musical performances are an important part of their entertainment. They often sing *sonetti* and *canzoni* with the accompaniment of instruments.

Several other works in a similar literary format were supposedly written for instructional purposes of one sort or another. Pietro Fortini (ca. 1500–62), in *Le giornate delle novelle dei novizi* and *Le piacevoli et amorose notti dei novizi*, instructs youths who are inexperienced and embarrassed by their lack of verbal cleverness and social grace in courtly manners. Fortini came from a *popolare* family and was associated with the Sienese *Congrega de'Rozzi* (Society of the Uncouth). His group includes five charming well-bred ladies and two lovely youths who play musical games, sing sweet songs, and improvise poetry to instrumental accompaniment, but these eloquent people, in their idyllic setting, tell the most bawdy and obscene stories.

Pietro Aretino (1492–1556), on the other hand, mocks courtly love in his *Sei giornate*. He did not try to reenvision an upper class courtly scenario but rather insults it and everyone associated with it. While his contemporaries recreated ideal social settings, he chose to focus on decadence. *Sei giornate* is divided into two parts: *Ragionamento della Nanna e della Antonia* and *Dialogo nel quale Nanna insegna a la Pippa*. In the first part Nanna tells Antonia about the life of nuns, wives, and whores; and in the second part Nanna teaches her daughter Pippa the fine art of prostitution. Scattered throughout this work are descriptions of musical performances, some based on courtly poetry, others simply lewd.[4]

Musical descriptions from these works shed new light on or substantiate current speculations concerning musical entertainment before 1600 in Italy. By comparing and contrasting the information from a variety of these sources, we can appreciate the diverse musical practices from the trecento through the cinquecento. I will begin with two trecento writers, Boccaccio and Sercambi.

If one only studies the musical performances in Boccaccio's *Decameron*, one would draw narrow conclusions about the performance practice of the ballata. In the *Decameron* Boccaccio includes the texts of the songs the group sang; all of them are ballate. At the end of seven of the ten evenings, a single person sings a ballata. No musical settings for these texts have been discovered. This is not surprising because Boccaccio composed the poetry for the *Decameron*; he did not choose preexisting texts with musical settings as Sercambi did. Howard Mayer Brown provides a musical setting of a ballata contemporary with the *Decameron*, "Io vo' ben a chi vuol bene a me" by Gherardello da Firenze, to suggest what type of music the group might have sung, but quickly concludes, based on the difficulty of performing in the florid style of the ballata, that Boccaccio's well-to-do group must have sung simpler songs, more closely related to *laude* (Brown 1977, 329). McGee points out that the style and performance circumstances of the lauda and ballata are very different. He is convinced that well-trained amateurs were not only capable of singing their contemporaries' ballate, both monophonic and polyphonic, but also of improvising them, and he provides a model for improvisation (McGee 2003, 62).

Sercambi's literary output, a generation later, seems to substantiate McGee's conclusions. Sercambi includes descriptions of musical performances and the texts of the songs in *Il Novelliere*. Music survives for eleven of the texts, seven two-voice madrigals, three two-voice ballate, and one monophonic ballata. Sercambi describes a performance of the monophonic ballata "Io vo' ben a chi vuol bene a me" that Brown singles out as being too difficult for Boccaccio's group. Several singers, girls and boys, sing the ballata: "the *preposto* commanded the dancers to dance, and having done it, she commanded that the singers sing a cazonetta; and after that, the group should go to dinner. And, having given the order, the dances began; the instruments continued to sound until the dances stopped, and having stopped, the boys and girls sang in this way a cansona: 'Io vo'ben a chi vuol bene a me.'"[5] Since Sercambi indicates that this ballata was appropriate for children to sing, one might conclude that members of Boccaccio's group should have been able to perform it too. For other musical pieces Sercambi indicates throughout *Il Novelliere* that several people are to sing each part, not just one, as in the *Decameron*. For example, the leader of the group indicates that men and women are to sing together a two-voice madrigal by Donato: "The group and the *preposto* having listened to the delightful story, and men and woman singers started to sing pleasing and honest songs in this fashion: 'Come da lupo pecorella presa.'"[6] A survey of Sercambi's texts with extant music suggests that polyphonic music was the norm and the group performed all songs, including the monophonic ballata, with several singers to a part. It seems unlikely that there was an abrupt shift from monophonic to polyphonic singing among amateur singers one generation apart.[7]

    McGee also points out that it would be reasonable to assume that people sang different styles of music, and did not necessarily use a single model when improvising (McGee 2003, 36–37). Sercambi's group sang music in different styles: ballate, *moralità*, and laude. The laude are sung in Latin but the short verses with many repeating lines indicate that these are very simple musical pieces. On the other hand, the preposto praises Sercambi's group for picking up phrases in other languages, suggesting that well-bred people also might have been exposed to songs in different languages and possibly different musical styles: "The two-voice canzonette sung by the women brought much delight to the brigade; and the preposto, very happy that his brigade through their walk has nimbly learned grammar, German, French, and other languages."[8] At another point the preposto suggests that a canzonetta should be sung for the common folk: "but to give pleasure to the common folk he ordered the singers to sing a canzonetta. They quickly sang '*Ciascun faccia per sé*.'"[9] The preposto immediately comments on the performance: "the notable canzonetta of the singers was no less pleasing than that of the religiosi."[10]

    Niccolò da Perugia set this ballata text by Soldanieri for two voices, and the music survives in several sources including the Squarcialupi Codex (Elias 2002,

100). Sercambi seems to suggest that music such as this piece in the florid style was not considered as sophisticated and difficult to sing as scholars have thought, and also that it was accessible to and enjoyed by common folk. The *preposto* indicates that this song was as pleasing as the ones sung by the *religiosi*, a part of Sercambi's traveling group, who performed *moralità*. On some occasions the *religiosi* used known melodies for their *canti morali*: "the religiosi began to sing, with those melodies that were requested in this way: 'Tu, ignorante, sequi le ricchesse.' The preposto, having heard the sweet melodies . . ."[11] Were some of the melodies used to sing *canti morali* in the florid style? Rossi points out that the music for "Ciascun faccia per sé" by Niccolò, sung for the common folk above, was also used for singing laude texts. There is an incipit referring to this text with the rubric *cantasi come* "Ciascun faccia per sé" in *Canzonette antiche* (Sercambi 1974, 3:64n4).

Literary sources continue to yield interesting information in the cinquecento. In *Le piacevoli notti*, Straparola describes the singing that took place each night: seven occasions include instrumental accompaniment, and the remaining six were apparently a cappella performances. Flutes, lutes, *lironi*, a lira, and a viola were used to accompany singers. Music survives for several of these texts in the form of madrigals by Giovanni Nasco ("Ardo tremando," night seven, and "Se'l tempo invola," night twelve) and Vincenzi Ruffo ("Questa fera gentile," night eight). Straparola's descriptions indicate that instrumental accompaniment was common in madrigal performances.[12] For example, on the eighth night, five women sing Ruffo's madrigal "Questa fera gentile" to the accompaniment of instruments: "the Signora wanted all five of them together with their instruments to sing a canzone. Whereupon the damsels, with joyful faces, and looking as fair as angels, began in this fashion their cantilena: '*Questa fera gentile*.'"[13] This madrigal is for five voices, and the lower parts are in the male range. Since the women would have needed the aid of an instrument capable of playing bass parts to perform all five voices, perhaps they used *lironi*. In another performance, Straparola suggests that this is the case: "the signora wanted all five of them [all women] with their lironi to sing a *canzonetta*."[14]

As I mentioned above, Pietro Aretino mocks courtly love in his *Sei giornate: Ragionamento della Nanna e della Antonia* and *Dialogo nella Nanna insegna a la Pippa*. Topics include the art of being a good prostitute, and uses of music for such purposes. Scattered throughout this work are descriptions of musical performances, some based on courtly poetry and some based simply on lewd texts. For example, on the first day of part one, Nanna describes performers gathered around a book singing "Divini occhi sereni" accompanied with a silver lute: "there were four who were looking at a book, and one, with a silver lute tuned to their voices, sang '*Divini occhi serene*.'"[15] Several composers have set this text. Most likely Aretino is referring to the famous one by Philippe Verdelot.

A more interesting performance occurs on the third day, in the garden under a fig tree. Balia and Comare, in the presence of Nanna and Pippa, discuss how Comare enjoyed leading a poor man on until he made a complete fool of himself. Among the many things he did to try to win her love was to hire musicians who sang with and without instruments to her in the mornings.[16] He also took part in some of the performances. One morning, she describes him singing "Alma mia fiamma e donna" while accompanying himself with the lute (Aretino 1969, 327). "Alma mia fiamma e donna" is a unique setting of a four-voice madrigal. The text is by Aretino and the music is by Tommaso Bargonio. Antonfrancesco Doni (1513–74), in his *Dialogo della musica* (1554), includes the music for "Alma mia fiamma e donna," and the interlocutors discuss the merits of the piece before performing it (Doni 1965, 72–82). Unlike the solo performance of this polyphonic work described by Aretino, Doni's characters perform this madrigal a cappella. Later that day, Aretino mentions that a large group of people all around the book sang "Poi che il mondo non crede."[17] These descriptions by Aretino are unusual because in these literary sources there is rarely any mention of musicians performing from written music. Almost always they perform preexistent music from memory.

Pietro Fortini, in the cornice of *Le giornate delle novelle dei novizi*, describes five witty ladies who come together with two elegant youths in a garden to pass the time telling stories and singing. On day four, for example, Ipolito sings while accompanying himself with a keyboard instrument: "they were treated to a pleasant sound that Ipolito sweetly extracted from the *gravicembalo* to the sound of which with a pleasant face he added some verses."[18] At the end of day four, Emilia sings a series of verses suggesting some type of improvisatory performance or the use of a simple formula for singing strophic verses: "with happy countenance rose, and without further ado picked up a sweet-sounding lute that she had near, and tuned it softly, playing it, joining to it her angelic and divine voice, and piously began to sing thus: '*Fortuna infin non posso*.'"[19] On day six Constansio picks up a lute and sings verses about how deeply he feels in love. The company asks him to sing more and he does. Then he sings a third song to Ipolito, who responds by picking up a lute and singing back to him. Constansio responds by singing back in answer, and they continue singing verses in this fashion for a long time (Fortini 1988, 607–704). Again, this is an example of an improvisatory performance possibly using a formulaic musical pattern capable of playing chordal accompaniment similar to the Petrucci models designed to recite poetry. Fortini shows a preference for this type of performance. There are many similar examples of musical entertainment in his *Le piacevoli e amorose notti dei novizi*.

In his *Dodici giornate*, Cattaneo describes performances of sonnets most likely improvised, and accompanied by the lute. Reinforcing this notion is the fact that we know of no polyphonic settings of these texts, judging by the *Nuovo Vogel* index (although it does not include anthologies). "Messer Luigi took a lute and having tuned it . . . began singing the sonnet that follows, not without the gracious harmony of his instrument: *'Non per cantar d'augelli in verdi fronte.'*"[20] McGee hypothesizes that there was a long stable tradition of improvisational practices, and points out that only during the sixteenth century is there iconographic evidence of the use of what would be Petrucci-style models: "if the nature of the music for improvisation has changed in the late fifteenth century from lightly accompanied melody to the three- or four-part polyphonic texture of the *frottola*, rather than depicting a solo singer with his lira da braccio, the later images should contain either a group of instruments or a single instrument that is more easily adapted to multiple polyphonic lines such as a keyboard instrument or lute" (McGee 2003, 50). The literary sources reinforce the evidence from iconography, substantiating McGee's conclusions. Many of the performances in the works of Fortini and Cattaneo explicitly mention the use of the lute and keyboard to accompany the singer who is improvising verses, while these instruments are absent from earlier descriptions of improvised music.

In *Il Fuggilozio*, Costo describes many vocal performances, most of which include instruments. He also provides us with a variety of ways to perform these pieces and introduces us to local musical traditions. For example, on the second day, several men sing a villanella: "In the meantime a beautiful boat went by, and in it, among many gentlemen there were some musicians who walked about singing a villanelle."[21] Later in that day the members of the group discuss how one should compose a good villanella text (Costo 1989, 166–67). After the discussion, Costo mentions one by the noted musician Fabrizio Dentice: "the Sig. Giulio Carafa, a gentleman no less literate than valiant, did not, at times, refuse to put his hands to them [write poems for villanelle], and I remember that he wrote one that starts '*Io conosco il mio errore*' . . . which, Fabrizio Dentice, the famous musician, set to music, and it is often sung by very noble company."[22] Then they sing another villanella to accompaniment of instruments: "and so Studioso, Svegliato, and Accorto, having tuned the instruments, started to sing the villanella just discussed, after which they sang also the following one, '*Crudelissimo amore.*'"[23] In the following description, Costo suggests that all of them had learned this "new and beautiful" madrigal: "The viols were brought forth, and because everyone knew the madrigal referred to above as a new and beautiful thing, they decided to sing it also, and it was this: '*Chi vuol veder col sol due chiare stele.*'"[24]

On the third day, Costo provides us with a description of a boat passing by filled with important noble citizens, whom he names, and many female and male musicians—including "le Moschelle e Fumia" (Vittoria Moschella and Eufemia Jozella, known as Fumia), two of the most famous female singers of the day, who play and sing diverse beautiful things (Costo 1989, 265–66). A little later, Il Modesto sings and accompanies himself with the lyre: "And thus, asked by the Prior and by the others, he sang it by himself, with the sound of the lyre, and it was this one: '*Beate membra, ch'a sì nobil Alma.*'"[25] On the fourth day everyone discusses philosophy and they are reminded of a sonnet set to music as a madrigal, and they sing it with the accompaniment of instruments, "because the philosophical question raised by Sollecito reminded them of a nice sonnet made by one of them relating to this matter, and set to music as a madrigal, and having tuned the instruments, they sang it, and it was the following: '*Se come vuol colui che di natura.*'"[26] On the fifth day they decide to sing a madrigal with viols: "When the discussion was finished, things were arranged for the music, and after they tuned the viols, they did as before, and they sang the following madrigal: '*L'esempio d'ogni strazio è nel mio cuore.*'"[27]

One might hazard a guess that part of being a well-bred amateur musician would be the ability to perform from memory. The descriptions by each of the writers above, with the exception of a few examples from Aretino, indicate that amateurs in these delightful social settings performed music from memory. Costo's descriptions suggest that the majority of music they performed was not improvised and they knew the pieces well. When reminded of a piece in their discussions, often they would stop and perform it, indicating that they had a "standard repertory." As with all previous writers, instruments were an integral part of vocal performances in Costo too.

This brief selection of musical descriptions of performances from the trecento through the cinquecento gives us a glimpse of what selected writers— Boccaccio, Sercambi, Straparola, Fortini, Cattaneo, Aretino, and Costo—thought were ideal performances of music by their fictional well-bred amateurs. Informal music making by amateurs was an important and perhaps even the most common way that secular music was performed during this extended period, and literary works are one major source for descriptions of such events.

The texts suggest a continuous tradition of both performance of written pieces and improvisation by amateurs in informal settings, where the combination of instruments and voices was determined by what was available, rather than being the result of careful planning. The authors indicate that it was more common to include instruments when performing vocal music, especially madrigals, than to leave them out. The well-bred citizens in the stories felt free to use whatever musical forces were available for their amateur performances. A variety of performance possibilities would be a necessity for a casual evening among a group of friends: specific instrumentation would require people with specific talents and, thus, special planning. The descriptions in these works suggest a more informal arrangement and atmosphere.

As musical styles change, performance practices may change too, but the use of instruments and the freedom to substitute them for voices seems to remain through these literary sources. Aretino, Straparola, and Costo provide a rich variety of examples illustrating the way in which madrigals were performed: (1) they were sung a cappella, (2) instruments doubled the vocal parts, (3) performers sang some of the parts using instruments for the remaining ones, and (4) performers sang the top voice, playing the other parts with an instrument. They were performing preexisting pieces rather than improvising. With the exception of some instances in Aretino, the performances are from memory. Just as people gather informally together today singing and accompanying themselves from memory, for instance, with a guitar, a similar practice seems to have been common in earlier times.

The ability to improvise in a given style could well be the result of having mastered a certain repertory and a collection of techniques. As McGee has shown, once one learned how to sing florid trecento ballate, even improvising new ones would not be that difficult. The growing interest in declamation and accentuation in setting and reciting texts to music, and the continuing concern for conveying the meaning of texts, converged in the last quarter of the cinquecento in the solo performance of madrigals. Aretino gives us an early glimpse of this type of performance that would become so popular later.

Fortini presents us with examples of improvisational games, consisting of long dialogues sung to improvised music or possibly formulaic patterns, such as the Petrucci-type models. The instruments used are keyboards or lutes, capable of producing the necessary chordal structures representing a later style of improvisation. Other writers such as Aretino and Costo present more descriptions of solo singing with accompaniment, foreshadowing the importance of the virtuoso singing of the early Baroque. At the same time, the names of well-known musicians appear as participants in idealized settings, perhaps indicating that truly exceptional performance required skills that went beyond those of talented amateurs. This preliminary study shows that works of imaginary fiction are an important complement to traditional sources for performance practice and remain a rich area for further exploration.

Notes

I would like to thank Bonnie J. Blackburn and Jan W. Herlinger for their comments and suggestions.

1. See McGee (2003) for a survey of the literature on improvisational practices.

2. Citations for the summaries of literary works without direct quotes are found in the references.

3. For a discussion of the Bianchi, see Bornstein 1993.

4. Both Cattaneo and Aretino deviate from the cornice/novelle tradition. They provide only what in the other works is the framing story, omitting novelle.

5. "il quale proposto comandò a' dansatori che una dansa facessero, e fatta, li cantatori una cansonetta cantassero, e ditta, la brigata a cenare andassero. E fatto il comandamento, le danse prese, li stromenti sonando tanto che le danse restarono, e restate, i cantarelli e cantarelle con voci puerili cantarono in questo modo una cansona: 'Io vo'ben a chi vuol bene a me'" (Sercambi 1974, 2:355).

6. "La brigata e'l preposto udita la dilettevole novella, e' cantatori e le cantarelle comincionno a cantare cansonette piacevoli e oneste in questo modo: 'Come da lupo pecorella presa'" (Sercambi 1974, 1:326).

7. For a detailed discussion of the musical performances in Sercambi's *Il Novelliere* and *Croniche*, see Elias 2002. Part of the discussion on Sercambi is from this article.

8. "La divisa canzonetta cantata per le cantarelle diè molto diletto alla brigata; e il proposto, molto contento che la sua brigata per lo caminare agiatamente avea imparato gramatica, lingua tedesca, franciosa e altre lingue" (Sercambi 1974, 3:204).

9. "ma per dare a' grossi alcuno piacer comando che i cantatori dicano qualche cansonetta. Loro presti dissero: 'Ciascun faccia per sé'" (Sercambi 1974, 3:64).

10. "la notabile cansonetta de' cantatori, non meno piaciuta che quella de' religiosi" (Sercambi, 1974, 3:65).

11. "li religiosi comincionno a dire, con quelle melodie in canto che si richiede in questo modo: '*Tu, ignorante, segui le ricchesse.*' Lo proposto udite le dolce melodie . . ." (Sercambi 1974, 2:362–63).

12. This section relies on the author's article, "Musical Performance in 16th-Century Italian Literature"; see Elias 1989.

13. "la Signora volse che tutte cinque insieme col lor stromenti cantassero una canzone. Le quali con lieti visi e angelichi sembianti in tal maniera incominciorono la lor cantilena: 'Questa fera gentile'" (Straparola 2000, 2:519).

14. "volse la Signora che tutte cinque con i lor lironi cantassero una canzonetta" (Straparola 2000, 2:567).

15. "erano quattro che guardavano sopra un libro; e uno, con un liuto argentino accordato con le voci loro, cantava 'Divini occhi sereni'" (Aretino 1969, 45–46).

16. "I primi musici d'Italia; e con gli stormenti e senze, cantò molte cosette nuove" (Aretino 1969, 327).

17. "Cantarono al libro, con un monte di gente intorno" (Aretino 1969, 327).

18. "trattenuti da un piacevol suono quale Ipolito dolcemente cavava de la dolceza d'un gravicembalo, e al suono di quello con lieta fronte alcuna rima spiegata" (Fortini 1988, 1:391).

19. "con bel sembiante si levò in piè e senza altro dire prese un soavissimo leúto che quinci vicino aveva, e dolcemente acordatolo, sonando unì la sua angelica e divina voce, e pietosamente cosí a cantare incominciò: 'Fortuna, infin non posso'" (Fortini 1988, 1:496).

20. "Messer Luigi preso un liuto, e accordatolo … diede principio cantando al Sonetto, che segue, non, senza la graziosa armonia del suo stromento: 'Non per cantar d'augelli in verdi fronte'" (Cattaneo 1970, 110).

21. "Passò in questo una bellissima filuca nella quale fra molti gentiluomini erano alcuni musici che andavano cantando una villanella" (Costo 1989, 163).

22. "il Sig. Giulio Carrafa, Cavaliero non men letterato che valoroso, non s'è alle volte sdegnato di porvi mano, e fra l'altre mi ricordo ch'ei ne fece una che incomincia 'Io conosco il mio errore, / E so che l'empio Amore', alla quale Fabrizio Dentice, musico famosissimo, pose l'aria come si dice, onde s'è piú volte cantata in brigate nobilissime" (Costo 1989, 167). There is a setting by Giulio Oristagno in his "Il Primo Libro di Madrigali a cinque voci" (Venice, Angelo Gardano 1588): see Vogel, Einstein, Lesure, and Sartori 2001.

23. "e cosí lo Studioso, lo Svegliato, e l'Accorto, accordati gli stromenti, si posero a cantare la predetta, dopo la quale cantarono anche la sequente: 'Crudelissimo Amore'" (Costo 1989, 167).

24. "furono arrecate le viole, e perché tutti sapevano il madrigale accennato di sopra, come cosa nuova e bella si risolsero di cantarlo anch'essi, e fu questo: 'Chi vuol veder col sol due chiare stelle'" (Costo 1989, 563).

25. "E cosí, pregatone dal Priore e dagli altri, lo cantò a suon di lira egli solo e fu questo: 'Beate membra, ch'a sì nobil Alma'" (Costo 1989, 267).

26. "perché a proposito della filosofica questione dal Sollecito accennata si ricordarono d'un bel sonetto da un d'essi fatto in tal materia ed accomodato con l'aria ad uso di madrigale accordàti ch'ebbono gli strumenti, lo cantarono e fu il seguente: 'Se come vuol colui che di natura'" (Costo 1989, 354).

27. "Ora finito che si fu di ragionare, si diede ordine alla musica e messes'in punto le viole, fu, secondo l'altre volte, cantono il seguente madrigale: 'L'esempio d'ogni strazio è nel mio cuore'" (Costo 1989, 412).

References

Aretino, Pietro. 1969. *Sei giornate: Ragionamento della Nanna e della Antonia (1534); Dialogo nel quale la Nanna insegna a la Pippa (1536)*. Edited by Giovanni Aquilecchia. Scrittori d'Italiana 245. Bari: Guis. Laterza & Figli.

Boccaccio, Giovanni. 1974. *Decameron, Edizione diplomatico-interpretativa dell'autografo Hamilton 90*. Edited by Charles S. Singleton. Baltimore: John Hopkins University Press.

Bornstein, Daniel E. 1993. *The Bianchi of 1399, Popular Devotion in Late Medieval Italy*. Ithaca: Cornell University Press.

Brown, Howard Mayer. 1977. "Fantasia on a theme by Boccaccio." *Early Music* 5: 324–39.

Cattaneo, Silvan, and Bongianni Grattarolo. 1970. *Salò e sua riviera*. Historiae urbium et regionum Italiae rariores 78. Bologna: Forni Editore.

Il Codice Squarcialupi: MS Mediceo Palatino 87, Biblioteca Medicea Laurenziana di Firenze. 1992. Edited by F. Alberto Gallo. Firenze: Giunti Barbèra.

Costo, Tomaso. 1989. *Il Fuggilozio*. Edited by Corrado Calenda. I Novellieri Italiani 36. Roma: Salerno Editrice.

Doni, Antonfrancesco. 1965. *Dialogo della musica*. Edited by G. Francesco Malipiero. Arranged by Virginio Fagotto. Collana di musiche veneziane inedite o rare 7. Venezia: Fondazione Giorgio Cini; Vienna, Universal Edition.

Elias, Cathy Ann. 1989. "Musical Performance in 16th-Century Italian Literature: Straparola's *Le piacevoli notti.*" *Early Music* 17: 161–73.

———. 2002. "Sercambi's *Novelliere* and *Croniche* as Evidence for Musical Entertainment
in the Fourteenth Century." In *The Italian Novella*, edited by Gloria Allaire, 81–103.
New York: Routledge.

Fortini, Pietro. 1988. *Le giornate delle novelle dei novizi.* Edited by Adriana Mauriello. 2 vols.
I Novellieri Italiani 28. Roma: Salerno Editrice.

———. 1995. *Le piacevoli e amorose notti dei novizi.* Edited by Adriana Mauriello. 2 vols. I
Novellieri Italiani 28. Roma: Salerno Editrice.

McGee, Timothy J. 2003. "*Cantare all'improvviso*: Improvising to Poetry in Late Medieval
Italy." In *Improvisation in the Arts of the Medieval Ages and Renaissance.* Early Drama,
Art, and Music Monograph Series. Kalamazoo, MI: Medieval Institute Publications.

Sercambi, Giovanni. 1974. *Il novelliere.* Edited by Luciano Rossi. 3 vols. I Novellieri Italiani
9. Roma: Salerno Editrice.

Straparola, Giovan Francesco. 2000. *Le piacevoli notti.* Edited by Donato Pirovano. 2 vols. I
Novellieri Italiani 29. Roma: Salerno Editrice.

Vogel, Emil, Alfred Einstein, Françoi Lesure, and Claudio Sartori. 1977. *Bibliografia della
musica italiana vocale profana pubblicata dal 1500 al 1700.* New ed. 3 vols. Pomezia,
Italy: Staderini-Minkoff.

Dancing in the Street: Fourteenth-Century Representations of Music and Justice

Eleonora M. Beck

In a famous demonstration of civic pride, Duccio's *Maestà* was carried in a public procession from the artist's workshop to the Cathedral of Siena. Agnolo di Tura recounts: "And the Sienese bore the said painting to the cathedral on Wednesday, the ninth day of June [1311], with great devotions and processions; with the bishop of Siena, Messer Roger of Casole with all the cathedral clergy, and with all the religious of Siena, and the lords [of the signory] with the city officials, podestà and captain, and all of the most worthy citizens in order, lighted lamps in their hands. And thus afterward the women and children went in a procession through Siena around the Campo, all the bells sounding a Gloria."[1] Music accompanied the festivities: a Gloria from the Mass resonated through the city, and records note payments for trumpeters, flautists, and timpanists who played on this occasion (Larner 1971, 71). Together, painting and music promoted the achievements of the "Nove," the governing body of Siena from 1287–1355, credited with achieving economic prosperity and peace in the city that could boast, at the time, the largest public square in central Tuscany, the largest hospital, the largest altarpiece (Duccio's *Maestà*), and the groundwork for the largest cathedral on the peninsula (Borsook 1980, 35).

Ambrogio Lorenzetti's fresco *Effects of Good Government in the City* in the Palazzo Pubblico celebrates peaceful and prosperous Siena under the rule of the "Nove" (fig. 1). Ten dancers (one of whom sings and plays a tambourine) appear prominently in the central piazza. Larger than any other figures in the fresco, they seem oblivious to the actions around them. What is the significance of the implied music in this fresco? What role does music play in a just society? It is the purpose of this paper to explore fourteenth-century conventions of musical representation and examine the connections between the depiction of music in fresco painting and the inclusion of songs into narrative texts. In addition to Lorenzetti's fresco, this paper will examine representations of music in Giotto's Scrovegni Chapel, the *cornice* of Boccaccio's *Decameron*, and early fourteenth-century French narratives,

173

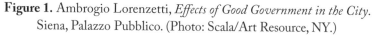

Figure 1. Ambrogio Lorenzetti, *Effects of Good Government in the City.* Siena, Palazzo Pubblico. (Photo: Scala/Art Resource, NY.)

including the *Roman de Fauvel* and Oresme's treatise *De Moneta*. It will be shown that representations of music making (1) traditionally decorate landscapes and literary narratives designed for the inclusion of music; (2) represent the harmonious life citizens experienced as a result of the "Nove's" commitment to justice and the common good; and (3) function in a similar way as *exempla* in sermons, and as such are introduced into the narrative to illustrate a particular concept (in this case justice). Indeed, musical scenes were used as propaganda for the good life promulgated by local governments. Not only was the enjoyment of music part of a peaceful community celebration but it was—in and of itself—illustrative of the consequences of justice in good government.

Painted on the east wall of the "Sala dei Nove," the *Effects of Good Government in the City and Country*, or *Buon Governo*, forms part of a series that includes the *Allegory of Good Government* (on the north wall) and the *Effects of Bad Government on the City*, or *Mal Governo*, on the west wall. The south wall contains large windows that overlook the central piazza of Siena. Lorenzetti signed his name on the mural in large letters: Ambrosius Laurentii de Senis hic pixit utrunque

(Ambrogio Lorenzetti of Siena painted both) and received a substantial sum for his work, about 103 florins, between April 1338 and May 1339. The titles were bestowed upon Lorenzetti's picture only in the late eighteenth century; prior to that time they were generally described as *Peace and War*.[2]

The *Effects of Good Government* captures a view of the city from the windows of the Palazzo Pubblico. In addition to the splendid palazzi, the artist has painted the newly built *duomo* and its striped bell tower in the upper left-hand corner of the scene. Another church with its decorative rose window appears between the towers towards the middle of the picture. Two roads converge in the piazza, dividing the space into three areas. This space is demarcated by the walls of the city on the right and the striped tower and dome of Siena's cathedral on the left. The red and white brick houses and narrow towers define the upper half of the image, emphasizing the expansiveness of the city by leading the viewer's eye upwards. At the same time, the space of the lower half of the picture is occupied by the piazza, which anchors the image and creates more room for the movements of the figures.

Lorenzetti populates this landscape with individuals contributing to the good of the whole city or the "Ben Comun."[3] Looking from left to right we see the nobles leaving the picture towards the left, then the group of five men and two children playing a game; the eye then wanders back into the open space of a wide street (where the picture has been damaged or vandalized). There we follow the movement of the two men on horseback about to disappear behind the building in the foreground, where we observe cobblers at work, a teacher lecturing, merchants selling their wares, men tending mules loaded with wood and other goods, and, finally, the shepherds about to exit through the city gates. Overhead, men build a tower.[4] In the midst of this action stand ten dancers highly unified in appearance and purpose. One dancer plays a tambourine while the others wind their way around her forming a spiral, firmly grounding all of them in the center of the picture. (This is in stark contrast to the exiting nobles on the left and the movement of merchants through the city gates on the right.) Although difficult to determine with complete certainty, the dance is traditionally believed to be a *carole* (Brainard 2001, 884).[5]

Scholars have interpreted the dance and implied music as representing justice and the common good. With regard to the *Effects of Good Government* dancers, Uta Feldges-Henning (1972, 155) writes: "Where justice reigns, music can be performed freely." Anna Eörsi (1978) argues that the dancers are a reflection of "peace originating in good government." Eörsi believes that the dancers are women and can be construed as an allusion to the nine Muses, who, according to Pythagorean doctrine, are the goddesses of harmony and of society. In effect they embody the Platonic notion of the harmony of the spheres as revealed in the harmony of music.

The image of justice, a female figure holding scales, has two primary sources in the medieval period. The first is a secular one, originating in the courts of law in Rome and appearing in coinage of the period.[6] Here justice relates to the rights of citizens and the law that protects those rights. The second source originates in Christian doctrine. Christian art appropriated justice as a divine virtue and aligned it with other virtues and vices. The *Psychomachia* of Prudentius of the early fifth century seems to be the first instance of the allegory of the battle for man's soul between the cardinal and theological virtues—respectively, fortitude, justice, prudence, and temperance; and hope, faith and charity.[7] With the establishment of new localized governments in the thirteenth century, the image of justice was resurrected to promote new autonomous city governments. Indeed, by the end of the trecento practically all piazzas, churches, public palaces, or chambers included a representation of justice. Even tombs displayed justice, probably reflecting past civic duty.

Aquinas contributed significantly to bringing the secular and sacred branches of justice together. His thoughts on the subject are scattered throughout the *Summa Theologica* and occupy an entire question in II-II of the *Summa*. Question 58 considers the nature of justice and its relation to the other virtues.[8] For Aquinas, and his guide Aristotle, justice is an activity: "Justice is a habit according to which a person is said to be active by choosing that which is right" (Porter 1990, 20–21). Citing Cicero, Aquinas stresses that justice must be understood as an activity that relates individuals to one another: "there is Cicero holding that the purpose of justice is to hold men together in companiable living in common. This implies a social relationship. Therefore justice is occupied only with our dealings with others" (22–23). When addressing the question "Is Justice a General Virtue?" in article 5, Aquinas extends the arms of justice to include the common good: "Accordingly the value in each and every virtue, whether it composes a man in himself or whether it disposes him in relation to others, may be referred to the common good, to which justice orders us. In this way the acts of all the virtues can belong to justice in that it orders a man to the common good. It is in this sense that justice is called a general virtue" (32–33).

This passage is most relevant to the two uses of music and justice discussed in this paper. Music in the frescoes by Lorenzetti and Giotto (as we will see) relate to justice by way of the common good, which is the relationship between individuals in a community. The playing of music in both settings is conducted in groups, and justice is defined as relating to the actions between individuals. Since justice is predicated on action, Lorenzetti's representation of music making suggests that the playing of music is a just act in concurrence with the common good. Aquinas's only consideration with respect to the performance of music is that it be done in a temperate manner, never overstepping what is rational.[9]

Oppositely, injustice suggests the choice to commit an unjust act. Here Aquinas makes an interesting distinction between someone who willfully knows he is committing an unjust act and one who commits an act out of passion. The latter is not deemed an unjust act (Aquinas 1975, trans. Gilby, question 59, 58–59). In fact he agrees with Aristotle, who believes that "it is not easy for anyone to do something unjust by choice, and as something agreeable in itself, not for some other reason" (59). In Lorenzetti's image of *Mal Governo*, injustice is represented by the willful abduction and assault of the dancing women. Justice and injustice are mirror images for Lorenzetti and Aquinas, whose *Summa* reads: "Theft and robbery are vices opposed to justice in so far as one person commits an injustice against another" (Aquinas 1975, trans. Lefébure, question 66.4, 73). Relating Aquinas to Lorenzetti's musical performance, we know that where justice exists, music is performed; in a state dominated by tyrannical rulers, music does not exist.

I suggest that the dancers depicted in the Lorenzetti fresco are a self-contained musical group and as such can easily be extracted from the picture without altering the basic narrative composition of the picture. This is evidenced by the fact that modern scholars have routinely cited the dancers independently from the original fresco and employed them as decorations. For instance, a reproduction of the figures accompanies the entry "Dance (3)" in the *New Grove Dictionary of Music and Musicians* (Brainard 2001, 884). Similarly, the figures are found in Curt Sachs's *World History of the Dance* (1937, 143), as well as in Melusine Wood's *Some Historical Dances* (1952, 16). Indeed, reversing this viewpoint, one could argue that the dancers exhibit a quality suggesting that they were added or superimposed onto the picture or piazza, which is clearly delineated by the buildings and activities in the Lorenzetti fresco. The painter has produced a space into which he can introduce the self-contained group of dancers.

In the case of the *Effects of Good Government*, the space demarcated by the piazza is occupied by the placid, concordant movements of the dancers. Conversely, in the equivalent space of the *Mal Governo* (fig. 2) on the opposite wall, terror and chaos reign; villains abduct the noblewoman—formerly on horseback—and injure or perhaps even kill one of the dancers. Music does not exist under "bad" government, just as it does not exist in Dante's *Inferno*. Functioning like an illumination in a medieval manuscript, the introduction of the dancing women illuminates the meaning of the entire fresco. Music embodies harmony, and, in this context, harmony achieved under just rule. Music's absence implied chaos.

An antecedent example of the interplay between music and justice appears in Giotto's frescoes in the Scrovegni Chapel of Padua (fig. 3, ca. 1305–7).[10] Accompanying the famous series of scenes dedicated to the story of Joachim and Anna, the life of the Virgin, the life of Christ, the Passion, and the Last Judgment, Giotto painted fourteen personifications of virtues and vices in imitation polished

Figure 2. Ambrogio Lorenzetti, *Mal Governo*. Siena, Palazzo Pubblico.
(Photo: Scala/Art Resource, NY.)

marble niches below the lowest register of frescoes on the sidewalls of the chapel. Placed almost at eye level, these figures represent present and everyday life. The virtues appear on the walls beneath heaven and the *Last Judgment*, while the vices are on the side beneath hell. The images are paired so that the virtues and vices are placed directly across the chapel from one another. Reading from the entrance towards the altar one finds *Hope/Despair*, *Charity/Envy*, *Faith/Idolatry*, *Temperance/Anger*, *Fortitude/Inconstancy*, and *Prudence/Folly*. The pair of *Justice* and *Injustice* are the largest and are situated at the middle of the nave, seated on thrones.

This placement is not the only difference between the portrayal of *Justice/Injustice* and the other pairs of virtues and vices. Citing Vasari, Zdekauer (1913, 400–401) notes that Giotto raised *Justice* to a level never before seen. He instilled in her a new civic sense and placed her on the earth and in life. Most notably, *Justice* and *Injustice* are the only pair to be complemented by tiny scenes. Underneath the figure of *Justice*, Giotto created a relief-like space in which he placed three dancing women. One holds a tambourine while the other two strike poses. The three figures, in turn, are framed by two sets of men on horseback who move toward them. Reminiscent of pastoral scenes described in fourteenth-century madrigal texts—where young men venture into the country to meet beautiful maidens—Giotto's image captures the blissful life one can enjoy when justice prevails in society.[11]

Figure 3. *Justice* and *Injustice*, Padua, Scrovegni Chapel. (Photo: Scala/Art Resource, NY; and Cameraphoto Arte, Venice/Art Resource, NY.)

Beneath *Injustice* this idyllic world is destroyed. The dancers appear to be attacked by robbers; the men are pushed off their horses. There is no music. The juxtaposition of these opposing images creates a kind of "before and after effect" similar to the one previously alluded to in Lorenzetti's *Effects of Good and Bad Government*. As in the interpolation of an illumination or literary snippet, the introduction of the dancers seems to explain and amplify the scene above. Music illuminates the concept of justice in the trecento, whereas the lack of it represents the presence of injustice and the inevitable consequences of betrayal and anarchy. Furthermore, the pairing of music and justice may provide a clue to unraveling the meaning of the musical angels that surround the figure of Christ in Giotto's accompanying *Last Judgment* in the Scrovegni Chapel. Jonathan Riess (1984, 72) fleshes out the parallels between Christ-Judge and the figure of Justice and cites Kantorowicz, who writes: "Interrelations between Christ and Justice [in political and juristic writings] were so numerous that the transition was often impercep-tible" (Riess 1984, 73).

    Two other important frescoes in the trecento—Bonamico Buffalmacco's *Triumph of Death* and Andrea da Bonaiuto's *Allegory of the Dominican Order*—also display self-contained musical scenes with women seemingly interpolated into the narrative of the picture.[12] In the Buffalmacco image, ten aristocrats sit in a well-defined garden. One of them, a woman, plays a psaltery, while a man plays a fiddle. The tapestry-like backdrop of trees and foliage separates the garden from the chaos of the accompanying scene. The implied music itself seems to entrance the aristocrats, distracting them from the demonic figure of death that hovers just to the left. Similarly, music occupies a well-defined space in the Bonaiuto fresco. Seven dancers and a tambourine player are placed in relief-like manner beneath a platform on which are seated four figures representing the pleasures enjoyed by members of the aristocracy during their leisure time: music, falconry, hunting, and contemplation. As in the case of the Lorenzetti fresco, the dancers seem oblivious to their surroundings, occupying a space defined by the aristocrats above and the heretics below. The dancers could easily be separated from their original context without losing their cohesion as a community of performers. Even in their four-three-one aggregation they seem to mimic musical "gruppetti."

The representation of a musical group introduced into a preformulated visual backdrop suggests a connection to the exemplum, a short moralizing narrative included in thirteenth- and fourteenth-century sermons to illustrate abstract themes.[13] The great vogue of the exemplum in the thirteenth century was fueled by the friars' increased commitment to preaching in the vernacular. Stories could be either sacred or secular, historical or fictional. They provided moral lessons or amusement, and underscored the sermon deliverers' own interpretations of the principal narrative. Like songbooks, exempla were gathered in large collections and arranged in alphabetical order, by a common theme, or according to the virtues and the vices.

Comparing a musical representation to an exemplum is crucial to understanding music's role in the fourteenth-century narratives. Like an exemplum, a musical scene 1) provides an interlude in the action and introduces a particular mood in the landscape; 2) captures the essence of the message of the narrative (i.e., under *Justice* there is peace and prosperity) and serves as a complementary metaphor for the lesson being taught; 3) can be appended to a narrative; and 4) can stand alone as a complete, self-sustaining compositional unit. The comparison to the exemplum also substantiates the subtle but important distinction between music as symbol and music as example. Music is not iconographically symbolic of justice, as scales are. Rather, the performance of music illuminates the ideal of prosperous life under the rule of just government.

That representations of music and dance traditionally appear in visual narratives has important implications for consideration in fourteenth-century literary contexts.[14] The most salient example is Boccaccio's *Decameron*, the tale of ten nobles who leave Florence in 1348 to escape the ravages of the Black Death. During their two-week excursion, they entertain themselves daily by telling stories, eating delectable foods, and wandering through lush gardens. Within this narrative, Boccaccio systematically includes the text of a ballata at the end of each day—there are ten ballatas in all. After dinner the tables are cleared and each member of the company is instructed to sing a tune to the accompaniment of lute and vielle while others join in a dance. For instance, at the conclusion of the first day we read:

> instruments were sent for, and the queen decreed that a dance should begin, which Lauretta was to lead whilst Emilia was to sing a song, accompanied on the lute by Dioneo. No sooner did she hear the queen's command than Lauretta promptly began to dance and she was joined by the others, whilst Emilia sang the following song in amorous tones:
>> In mine own beauty take I such delight
>> That to no other alive could I
>> My fond affections plight. (Boccaccio 1972, 112–13)

Music scholars have heretofore examined musical references in the *Decameron* for clues relating to trecento performance practice.[15] Another reason to study musical references in the *Decameron* is that by viewing the music as illuminating the concept of justice, the meaning and reason for the inclusion are unveiled. Boccaccio's methodical inclusion of a musical performance at the end of each day is exemplary of good, just government and underscores the importance of music and dance in the daily routine of the group's newly-constructed society.[16] Music and dance, performed within the confines of community, reflect and promote peace in Boccaccio's world. The dance advances the sense of allegiance among friends. Ultimately, music contributes to their physical well-being, quelling the onset of the plague.

But what are the implications of the connection of music and good government for notated musical interpolations in the fourteenth century? For a consideration of this we need to turn our attention to the French repertory. Beginning with poetry written in northern France in the early thirteenth century, the custom of interspersing romances and other narratives with texts of songs, excerpts from them, or even shorter refrains, became widespread (Coldwell 1981). With its refrain snippets, eighteen rondeaux, seven chansons de toile, and eighteen chansons by troubadours and trouvères mentioned by name—including two by the châtelain de Couci and three by Gace Brulé—Jean Renart's narrative *Guillaume de Dole* (ca. 1228) may have begun this trend. Further examples include the *Roman de la Violette* (ca. 1230), and, most significantly in the history of music, the *Roman de Fauvel* (1309–13).

The *Roman de Fauvel* stands as the greatest testament to the practice of musical insertions in the late Middle Ages. One of twelve extant manuscripts of the *Roman* (Paris, Bibliothèque nationale de France, MS f. fr. 146) displays over one hundred and sixty interpolations on its pages. A typical medieval satire, the *Roman* describes political and social corruption in France as symbolized by an ass or a horse by the name of Fauvel. A note on folio 23v confirms that Chaillou de Pesstain, a member of the French court, made both musical and textual additions: "Hereafter follows what sir Chailloud de Pesstain has added to this book besides the above-mentioned lines which are sung."[17] The pieces cover a wide range of styles, from Latin motets and conductus to vernacular ballades and rondeaux. Practically all of the music can be found in other earlier sources, and only a few pieces may have been written specifically for the edition of the *Roman*.

The musical additions in the *Roman* have been hitherto viewed as relating to the narrative they accompany, in many instances highlighting the plight of corrupt French officials who try to manipulate their fate. Edward Roesner explains in his foreword to the facsimile edition: "the musical pieces in Chailloud's edition of *Fauvel* have generally been selected and placed so as to amplify or complement the content of the roman verses that they accompany or gloss." He concludes, "thus, the satire on the Roman curia ascribed in one manuscript to Philip the Chancellor, 'Que me vertam nescia,' fits neatly with the *Roman* verses around it, which deal with the clergy's adulation of Fauvel" (Roesner 1990, 15).

I argue that musical pieces introduced in the *Roman* address a specific civic concern, namely, just rule. Indeed, music contributes directly to what the editors of the *Roman* facsimile edition call a "royal admonitio, a lavish and entertaining moral satire on the themes of good government and corruption" (Roesner 1990, 50). Several musical insertions speak to the need for justice. For instance, we find the following conductus by Walter of Châtillon:

> Over almost every court
> preside the indifferent,
> in whose power lies
> the process of justice and
> judgment. (Rosenberg 1991, 35)

A lai text by Philip the Chancellor entitled "Veritas, equitas, largitas" (fols. 22rc–23ra) lists a stream of past virtues and present vices characterizing ruling men:

Truth,
equity,
[and] generosity,
have fallen;
deceit,
depravity,
[and] niggardliness
flourish;
urbanity
has vanished.

The third stanza contains a striking reference to harmony:

Law, reason,
[and] discretion,
the protectors
of harmony,
[and] compassion
[and] redress,
the defenders
of distress,
are proscribed and exiled.

There are two mentions of justice in later stanzas:

Fraud, cheating,
 [and] corruption
in the guise of justice
ambition,
[and] treason
disguised by ash
[and] sackcloth
revel in the reward
due virtue.

and

The passion of treacherous
malice hides
behind the mask of zeal
[and] the crime of false
accusation
behind the figure of justice.
(Rosenberg 1991, 80–82)

The association of music with civic affairs in the *Roman* has its political underpinnings in French theoretical writing of the first decade of the fourteenth century. Johannes de Grocheo's *De musica* (ca. 1300) provides an important source for the uses of music in Paris at the turn of the century.[18] Grocheo's treatise is laden with references to a public audience, frequently returning to the notion of a Parisian intellectual community of musicians. For instance, three different kinds of music are designated "according to how the men in Paris use it and just as it is necessary for the use of its citizens."[19] Grocheo assigns the first category of music: "We say that one category is that of civil or simple music, which they call vulgar music."[20] Christopher Page translates *musica civilis* as "the music of those governed by civil law."[21] Though not naming the virtue directly, the governor of civil law is clearly the figure of justice.

The sense of *musica civilis* certainly pervades the musical insertions in the *Roman de Fauvel*. Several of the types of music included fall under Grocheo's first category, including the monophonic conductus and the lai under the category *cantus gestualis*. The second category, *cantilena*, comprises the *rotunda vel rotundellus* and *ductia*, described by Page as consisting of the rondeau and carole, respectively. It is striking that Grocheo places dance songs (whether instrumental or vocal) in the public category. Not only do these pieces provide entertainment, their performance is exemplary of community activities.

In this paper's final example we find that musical forms themselves were adopted as metaphors for good government. A French treatise dedicated to coinage provides a fascinating source relating musical structure to just rule. In chapter 25 of Nicole Oresme's *De Moneta* ("That a tyrant cannot be lasting"), written in the middle of the fourteenth century, the author discusses the short tenure of the tyrant who raises money by alterations of monetary values. Echoing a philosophy of successful government discussed previously with respect to the "Ben Comun" of Lorenzetti's *Good Government*, Oresme explains: "You must know, therefore, that the difference between kingdom and tyranny is that a tyrant loves and pursues his own good more than the common advantage of his subjects, and aims at keeping his people in slavery; a king, on the contrary, prefers the public good to his own and loves above all things, after God and his own soul, the good and public freedom of his subjects" (42). Oresme continues by making an allusion to the human body, reminiscent of Boethius: "The state or kingdom, then, is like a human body, and so Aristotle will have it in Book V of the *Politics*. As, therefore, the body is disordered when the humours flow too freely into one member of it, so that one member is often thus inflamed and overgrown while the others are withered and shrunken and the body's due proportions are destroyed and its life shortened; so also is a commonwealth or a kingdom when riches are unduly attracted by one part of it" (43).

The author next introduces an example or exemplum about music to highlight the concept of good government, comparing the state to a harmonious body consisting of concordant parts: "Again, as in a chorus, a unison has no power to please, and excessive or improper dissonance destroys and spoils the whole harmony, but a proportional and measured difference of tone is needed to produce the sweet melody of a joyous chorus; so also, generally, equality of possessions of power in all sections of the community is inconvenient and inconsistent, but too great a disparity destroys and spoils the harmony of the state, as appears from Aristotle in *Politics*, Book V" (44). In the following passage Oresme extends the comparison to the tenor and the princely ruler: "But especially if the prince is too great, and is out of tune with the rest of the commonwealth, the sweet melody of the kingdom's constitution will be disturbed" (44). Oresme's philosophy of government applies to the distribution and conception of voices in the motet repertory that appears in *Fauvel*. Indeed, Oresme's optimal distribution of material wealth—not in equality, but then again not in complete authority—is reminiscent of the salient characteristic of fourteenth-century motets: the hegemony of the tenor voice in a piece for two or more voices. Like Oresme's conception of good government, the tenor of a motet acts as the foundation of the piece, supporting the melody through its many twists and turns, while at the same time not overpowering it by becoming equally complex. In Oresme's recipe for good government—as in the Lorenzetti, Giotto, Boccaccio, and French examples—justice, and with it music, must prevail.

Notes

1. Translated by Bowsky 1981, 284.

2. Ca. 1450, Lorenzo Ghiberti (Morisani 1947, 38) describes the murals as follows: "In the palazzo of Siena is painted in his hand *Peace and War*, the one that pertained to peace and the way that merchants and their wares are secure under the greatest security, and the way they leave them in the woods, and the way they return to claim them" (Author's translation).

3. The Aristotelian notion of common good, or "Ben Comun", was adopted by scholastics in the thirteenth and fourteenth centuries. For more on the medieval political institutions, see Lynam 1953 and Ullman 1961. In the accompanying mural, the *Allegory of Good Government*, Lorenzetti painted the figure of "Ben Comun" as a bearded old man holding a shield. A detailed discussion of this figure appears in Rubenstein 1958. For a discussion of Italian public art in the late Middle Ages, see Riess 1981 and Southard 1979.

4. Uta Feldges-Henning (1972, 151) has proposed that some of the activities represent the "ars mechanica" as defined by Hugh of St. Victor in the second book of his *Didascalicon*. The activities he lists include working with wool, armor, navigation, agriculture, theater, and medicine.

5. For a general discussion of dance in the Middle Ages, see McGee 1989. Stevens (1986, 159–98) describes the dance-song in detail. For the social uses of the carole in France, see Page 1990, 110–33.

6. The most comprehensive essay on the history of the image of justice is Zdekauer 1913. Zdekauer has traced the first appearance of justice as a seated figure to Roman coinage under the dominion of Augustus.

7. For further discussion, see Katzenellenbogen 1939.

8. On Aquinas, see Porter 1990.

9. On temperance and music in Boccaccio's *Decameron*, see Beck 1997.

10. The exact dates of the frescoes' composition are not known and evidence provided by later viewers suggest that the work was painted between 1303 and 1306 (Basile 1993, 9). See also Stubblebine 1995, xi–xii.

11. Basile (1993, 319) explains that the scenes "depict the serene unfolding of life governed by Justice and brutality and violence provoked by Injustice."

12. For the meaning of music in these frescoes, see Beck 1998.

13. A comprehensive discussion of the exemplum appears in Welter 1973. The model of the exemplum has also been used to examine literary conventions in Boccaccio's *Decameron*; see Delcorno 1985, 191–92. In art history, see Hans Belting's discussion of the exemplum in fourteenth-century painting (1985).

14. It was traditional for writers of the period to interrupt their narratives with complete poems, for instance, in Dante's *Vita Nuova*. The earliest ballata texts in Italian sources were additions to a collection of notarial acts entitled the *Memoriali di Bologna*. Compiled between 1266 and 1435, the *Memoriali* contain over one hundred poems placed in the margins and spaces between entries. See Levi 1912–13, 280. Giovanni Gherardi da Prato's *Paradiso degli Alberti* contains several poetic additions, among them a complete ballata text by Francesco Landini, "Or su gentili spirti ad amar pronti."

15. Brown 1977 and Yudkin 1981.

16. The *problem* and significance of the ballatas' inclusion is discussed in Manciardi and Massera 1901, 102–14 and Beck 1998, 139.

17. On the embellishment and expanded version of Gervias de Bus *Roman de Fauvel*, see Morin 1992 and Reaney 1986.

18. On Grocheo and the ars antiqua motet see Page 1993, 65–111.

19. Rohloff 1972, 124; translation in Grocheo 1973, 11.

20. Rohloff 1972, 124; translation in Grocheo 1973, 12. See also Page's table of Grocheo's types of music 1993, 73. For Page (1993, 77), the phrase *prout ad usum vel convictum civium* reflects Grocheo's "concern for the way music ensures peace, prosperity, and good government in the community (civitas)."

21. Page 1993, 77. On music and the invention of the state, see Page 1990, 171–73. For a postmodern reading of Grocheo, see Peraino 2001.

References

Aquinas, Thomas. 1975. *Summa Theologica*. Translated by Thomas Gilby. Great Britain: Eyre and Spottiswoode.

Aquinas, Thomas. 1975. *Summa Theologica*. Translated by Marcus Lefébure, OP. Cambridge, UK: Cambridge University Press.

Basile, Giuseppe. 1993. *Giotto: The Arena Chapel Frescoes*. New York: Thames and Hudson.

Beck, Eleonora M. 1997. "Music in the Cornice of Boccaccio's *Decameron*." *Medievalia et Humanistica* 24: 33–49.

———. 1998. *Singing in the Garden: Music and Culture in the Tuscany Trecento*. Lucca: Libreria Italiana Musicale.

Belting, Hans. 1985. "The New Role of Narrative in Public Painting of the Trecento: Historia and Allegory." *Studies in the History of Art* 16: 151–68.

Boccaccio, Giovanni. 1972. *The Decameron*. Translated by G. H. McWilliam. Harmondsworth: Penguin.

Borsook, Eve. 1980. *The Mural Painters of Tuscany from Cimabue to Andrea del Sarto*. Oxford: Clarendon Press.

Bowsky, William. 1981. *A Medieval Italian Commune: Siena under the Nine, 1287–1355*. Berkeley and Los Angeles: University of California Press.

Brainard, Ingrid. 2001. "Dance (3)." In *The New Grove Dictionary of Music and Musicians*, edited by Stanley Sadie, 6:883-888. 2nd ed. 29 vols. New York: New Grove Dictionaries.

Brown, Howard Mayer. 1977. "Fantasia on a Theme by Boccaccio." *Early Music* 5: 324–39.

Coldwell, Maria. 1981. "Guillaume de Dole and Medieval Romances with Musical Interpolations." *Musica Disciplina* 35: 55–86.

Delcorno, Carlo. 1985. "Studi sugli exempla e il *Decameron* II—Modelli exemplari in tre novelle (I 1, III 8, II 2)." *Studi sul Boccaccio* 15:191–92.

Eörsi, Anna. 1978. "Donne danzanti sull'affresco: Efficacia del Buon Govern in città di Ambrogio Lorenzetti." *Acta historiae artium Academiae Scientiarum Hungaricae* 24: 85–89.

Feldges-Henning, Uta. 1972. "The Pictorial Program of the Sala della Pace: A New Interpretation." *Journal of the Warburg and Courtauld Institutes* 35: 145–62.

Grocheo, Johannes de. 1973. *Concerning Music (De Musica)*. Translated by Albert Seay. Colorado College Music Press Translations, no. 1. Colorado Springs: Colorado College Music Press.

Kantorowicz, Ernest. 1957. *The King's Two Bodies: A Study in Medieval Political Theology*. Princeton: Princeton University Press.

Katzenellenbogen, Adolf. 1939. *Allegories of the Virtues and the Vices in Mediaeval Art from Early Christian Times to the Thirteenth Century*. Translated by Alan Crick. London: Warburg Institute.

Larner, John. 1971. *Culture and Society in Italy 1290–1420*. Studies in Cultural History. New York: Scribner.

Levi, Ezio. 1912–13. "Cantilene e ballate dei sec. XII e XIV." *Studi Medievali* 4: 279–334.

Lynam, Gerald J. 1953. *The Good Political Ruler According to St. Thomas Aquinas*. Philosophical Series 144, Abstract 1. Washington DC: Catholic University of America Press.

Manciardi, Luigi, and Aldo Massera. 1901. "Le dieci ballate del *Decameron*." *Miscellanea Storica della Valdelsa* 9/2: 102–14.

McGee, Timothy. 1989. *Medieval Instrumental Dances*. Bloomington: Indiana University Press.

Morin, Joseph. 1992. "The Genesis of Manuscript Paris, Bibliothèque Nationale Fonds Français 146, with Particular Emphasis on the Roman de Fauvel." PhD diss., New York University.

Morisani, Ottavio, ed. 1947. *I Commentari di Lorenzo Ghiberti*. Naples: R. Ricciardi.

Oresme, Nicholas. 1956. *De Moneta of Nicholas Oresme and English Mint Documents*. Translated by Charles Johnson. London: Thomas Nelson and Sons.

Page, Christopher. 1990. *The Owl and the Nightingale*. Berkeley: University of California Press.

————. 1993. *Discarding Images: Reflections on Music and Culture in Medieval France*. Oxford: Clarendon Press.

Peraino, Judith. 2001. "Re-Placing Medieval Music." *Journal of the American Musicological Society* 54/2: 209–64.

Porter, Jean. 1990. *The Recovery of Virtue: The Relevance of Aquinas for Christian Ethics*. Louisville, KY: Westminster/John Knox Press.

Reaney, Gilbert. 1986. "The Chronology and Structure of the Roman de Fauvel." In *Le Musique et le Rite Sacre et Profane: Actes du XIIIe Congrès de la Société Internationale de Musicologie, Strasbourg, 29 Août–3 Septembre 1982*, ed. Marc Honegger, Christian Meyer, and Paul Prévost, 85–104. Strasbourg: University of Strasbourg.

Riess, Jonathan. 1981. *Political Ideals in Medieval Italian Art: The Frescoes in the Palazzo dei Priori, Perugia (1297)*. Ann Arbor: UMI Research Press.

————. 1984. "Justice and the Common Good in Giotto's Arena Chapel Frescoes." *Arte Cristiana* 72: 69–80.

Roesner, Edward, François Avril, and Nancy Freeman Regalado. 1990. *Le Roman de Fauvel: In the Edition of Mesire Chaillou de Pestain: A Reproduction in Fascimile of the Complete Manuscript Paris Bibliothèque Nationale, Fonds Français 146*. New York: Broude Brothers.

Rohloff, Ernst. 1972. *Die Quellenhandschriften zum Musiktraktat des Johannes de Grocheo*. Leipzig: Deutscher Verlag für Musik.

Rosenberg, Samuel, and Hans Tischler, eds. 1991. *The Monophonic Songs in the Roman de Fauvel*. Lincoln: University of Nebraska Press.

Rubenstein, Nicolai. 1958. "Political Ideas in Sienese Art: The Frescoes by Ambrogio Lorenzetti and Taddeo di Bartolo in the Palazzo Pubblico." *Journal of the Warburg and Courtauld Institutes* 21: 179–207.

Sachs, Curt. 1937. *World History of the Dance*. Translated by Bessie Schönberg. New York: W.W. Norton.

Southard, Edna. 1979. *The Frescoes in Siena's Palazzo Pubblico, 1289–1539: Studies in Imagery and Relations to other Communal Palaces in Tuscany*. New York: Garland.

Stevens, John. 1986. *Words and Music in the Middle Ages*. Cambridge: Cambridge University Press.

Stubblebine, James. 1995. *Giotto: The Arena Chapel Frescoes*. New York and London: W.W. Norton.

Ullman, Walter. 1961. *Principles of Government and Politics in the Middle Ages*. New York: Barnes and Noble.

Welter, Jean Thiébaut. 1973. *L'Exemplum dans la Littérature Religieuse et Didactique du Moyen Âge*. Geneva: Slatkine Reprints.

Wood, Melusine. 1952. *Some Historical Dances (Twelfth to Nineteenth Century): Their Manner of Performance and Their Place in the Social Life of the Time*. London: Wyman and Sons.

Yudkin, Jeremy. 1981. "The Ballate of the *Decameron* in the Musical Context of the Trecento." *Stanford Italian Review* 1: 49–58.

Zdekauer, Ludovico. 1913. "Iusticia: Immagine e idea." *Bollettino Senese di Storia Patria* 20: 383–425.

Apres vos fais: Machaut Reception as Seen through the Chantilly Codex (F-CH 564)

Elizabeth Randell Upton

Guillaume de Machaut (ca. 1300–1377) is the best known of all fourteenth-century composers, in part due to the excellent survival of his compositions. According to the famous inscription in Machaut MS A, Machaut himself supervised the copying of a manuscript containing his collected works, both poetical and musical; five other large copies of Machaut's complete works made in the fourteenth century also survive to the present.[1] Machaut's exceptionally prominent profile in his own time and ours derives in part from royal patronage: he was secretary to John of Luxembourg, king of Bohemia, and when John's daughter Bonne married the son of the king of France, Machaut acquired her patronage as well. Bonne's children (including the future King Charles V and his brothers Jean Duke of Berry and Philippe Duke of Burgundy) must have grown up knowing Machaut's works, and as adults their remembered fondness translated itself into continued prominence for the artist. The existence of so many deluxe manuscript copies of Machaut's works suggests a fashion among European royalty and nobility.

Machaut's reputation among his patrons was evident both during his life and posthumously. But what can be told at this great distance in time of the reception of his music? Was it heard? By whom, where, and for how long? Anne Robertson has shown that Machaut's famous "Messe de Notre Dame" could have been famous in its own time as well; it would have been performed at Reims Cathedral on Saturdays throughout the year, even following the composer's death, as per the terms of Machaut's will (Robertson 1992). And the fact that Machaut's songs continued to be copied in anthology manuscripts after his death testifies to their continuing value, at least to readers if not performers.[2] But there is no way of knowing how long Machaut's chansons could have remained current in performers' mouths and listeners' ears. Or is there?

Friedrich Ludwig (1926–29) first noticed the existence of ballades based on quotations from Machaut's works, a phenomenon explored more fully by Ursula Günther (1972).[3] This suggests that Machaut's songs continued to be performed and were familiar to audiences, at least audiences of musical connoisseurs. Unlike the long notes of a snippet of chant used as a motet tenor, quotations of songs in other songs are clearly meant to be heard and identified. The quotations involve both words and music, cementing the intentionality of the quotation. The materials quoted tend to be the most memorable parts of a ballade—the opening verse and the refrain—and placing the quoted music in the same prominent positions means the audience was meant to hear and recognize the borrowed material. Quotation of this sort is meaningful if the listeners can remember and identify the music being quoted, and so testifies to the continued performances of Machaut's songs.

Of all the anthologies that transmit any of Machaut's chansons, only one source provides correct attribution to the composer. This is the Chantilly Codex, F-CH 564, hereinafter *Ch*, the central source for late fourteenth-century French song.[4] Besides three ballades by Machaut, this manuscript also transmits the two ballades identified by Ludwig that quote Machaut's words and music, and the famous double-ballade lament for Machaut's death, "Armes Amours Dames Chevaliers," attributed to F. Andrieu with words by Eustache Deschamps. The presence of these various items suggests that it is worth examining this particular manuscript as it relates to Machaut reception in the first few decades after the composer's death. As a full description of the manuscript has not been published since Gordon Greene's edition of 1981/82, it may be worth summarizing here the details of this source based on my own examination and researches.[5]

Probably copied shortly after 1400, *Ch* is a large collection—ninety-nine songs in four gatherings, organized by number of voices, and a final gathering containing thirteen motets—and it was originally meant to be even larger, for at least one gathering of six bifolios (twenty-four pages) has been missing since the fifteenth century. Yet its music is not arranged by composer, by genre, or chronologically, as is, for example, the more helpfully organized Florentine anthology, the Squarcialupi Codex.[6] The uncrowded page layout and the elegance of both the music and text hands make clear that *Ch* was to be a luxurious presentation volume, yet the book was never finished—text and music copying were completed but the pages were not decorated, spaces left at the beginning of each voice part never received their illuminated initials, and the ample margins likewise remained blank. Nor, it seems, was the manuscript bound as a volume until after 1861, when Henri d'Orléans, the Duke of Aumale (1822–97), purchased it and brought it to Chantilly from Florence.[7] Clues we wish we had concerning the identity of the intended original owner, such as coats of arms or any dedications, were either never entered or were lost with the missing first gathering some time in the fifteenth century. The single indication of ownership before the nineteenth century raises more questions than it answers: a note dated 1461 on the back of the fifteenth-century index to the manuscript identifies Francesco d'Alto biancho degli Alberti as the owner. The Alberti were in exile from Florence during the years that the music of the Chantilly Codex was being written, collected, and copied; and there is no way of telling when or where they gained possession of the manuscript.[8]

The place of origin of *Ch* has never been identified, even after more than a century of research and speculation. Most scholars have looked to the musical repertory for clues to the manuscript's origin, but such clues as there are conflict with each other. *Ch* has long been notable for the many historical figures mentioned in its songs, either named outright or through allusion. These figures include (in descending order of rank) Pope Clement the Seventh (1378–94); King John I of Aragon (1350–95) and his sister, Eleanor of Aragon, queen of Castille (1358–82); Jean, duc de Berry (1340–1406); Gaston "Phébus," Count of Foix and Béarn (1343–91); and Guillaume de Machaut (ca. 1300–1377). Some of these people did know each other—several were relatives, by birth or marriage—but we cannot tie compositions honoring this group to any single court.[9]

Ch is unusual among fourteenth- and early fifteenth-century manuscripts for the number of composer attributions it supplies. Thirty-four composers' names appear, but almost a third of the pieces are anonymous and unattributable through extant concordances. Those composers who can be identified have careers ranging in time from midcentury through the 1390s, and in space from northern France to Iberia and Italy. Additionally, several of the composers' names are clearly aliases, including Trebor (which is Robert spelled backwards) and S. Uciredor (Rodericus in reverse, producing the unexpected pun: "murderer"). Indeed, Solage, who with ten compositions is the best-represented composer in the manuscript, cannot be identified because his name too is an alias, from the Latin *solacium* (Old French *solaz*, Italian *sollazzo*), meaning pleasure, entertainment, pastime.

Although most of the songs have French texts, and a few are in Latin, the manuscript itself was probably made in Italy or at least by an Italian scribe. The music is copied on Italian six-line staves, instead of the French five-lined ones. The only exceptions are the two Baude Cordier works, and these are clearly later additions, tipped into the manuscript on single sheets. It is ironic that these two pieces, notated respectively in the form of a heart and a circle, are the most frequently reproduced pages from this manuscript, considering they were not originally part of the manuscript at all. The first published hypothesis as to the source's origin—that our manuscript was an Italian copy of a now-lost French original—was proposed by the Duke of Aumale, who wanted to see his possession as deriving from the royal milieu of his own medieval ancestors.[10] Positing a lost "original" manuscript is unduly complicated; more likely is that copies of individual songs were collected until enough music for an entire volume was assembled, at which point the present manuscript was copied.[11]

Another Italian element shapes what is probably the most well-known aspect of this manuscript: its notation. Many of the songs are notated with a variety of new note shapes invented to represent further divisions of the minim, the smallest note value in use throughout the fourteenth century. Some of these shapes have been shown to have come from Italian notation, prompting some scholars to see the advanced notation present in *Ch* and other late fourteenth-century sources as having arisen from a conflation of French and Italian notational theory and practice. In addition to the new note shapes and new note values, a number of compositions in *Ch* play with mathematical proportions, putting into practice what had previously been a topic of music theory; new mensuration signs and instructions in the form of canons are deployed to indicate the proportions and their use.

The notation and other musical theoretical aspects of the *Ch* compositions received the lion's share of twentieth-century scholarly attention, but the poetic texts are no less interesting; and I would go so far as to say that the works in the manuscript may have been chosen for inclusion as much for their literary interest as for their musical value.[12] Far from the monolithic "love song" profile of so many medieval song collections, *Ch* is notable for the variety of its lyrics. Interesting literary aspects of the texts include poems using *Roman de la Rose*-style allegorical personifications, both elaborating on some actual characters from the *Roman* and inventing new ones in the same manner; poems based on word games such as acrostics or puns; poems that are dream visions; and others that are elaborate descriptions of heraldic images—some still unidentified—and settings of mottoes. In fourteen songs the poet compares his love, devotion, struggle, or suffering to that experienced by mythological characters such as Phœbus Apollo, Jupiter, Venus, Narcissus and Echo, Zephirus, and Orpheus; or biblical figures, including Jacob and Rachel, David and Absalom, Samson and Delilah, and Jonas; or heroes and heroines of history and romance such as Charlemagne, Roland, Hector, Alexander, Helen and Paris, Guenevere and Lancelot, and Tristan and Isolde. Of particular interest to musicologists, thirteen songs concern music and music making itself, including one text—Guido's "Or voit tout en aventure" (*Ch* 28)—that ironically deplores the new notation and figures of the theorist Marchettus of Padua, "that are completely contrary to good, perfect art," as defined by Philippe de Vitry, even as the musical setting makes use of them.[13]

Among all these interesting, atypical, and more modern compositions appear three older ballades by Guillaume de Machaut: Ballade 18, "De petit peu" [*Ch* 14]; Ballade 23, "De Fortune me doy pleindre et loer" [*Ch* 78]; and Ballade 34, the double ballade "Quant Theseus/Ne quier veoir" [*Ch* 88]. The presence of these three older works in *Ch* can help us to evaluate Machaut's reputation among connoisseurs of music some twenty years after his death.

First I will discuss *Ch* as it relates to the other anthology manuscripts that contain songs by Machaut. It is telling that all three ballades have other concordances outside the main Machaut codices; they are among that small group of Machaut's chansons that, for whatever reason, circulated independently of the complete work manuscripts. No other single surviving source transmits all three of *Ch*'s Machaut ballades, but two manuscripts—the Trémoille manuscript and the Reina Codex—each contain two of these three. The now-lost Trémoille manuscript, which, according to a library inventory of 1404 belonged to Philip the Bold of Burgundy, was mostly a book of motets, but it also contained thirty-five chansons, including the largest collection of Machaut chansons outside of his own manuscripts: eight ballades and one rondeau.[14] Only a single bifolio of the manuscript survives today, but that bifolio includes the manuscript's index which shows that "De petit peu" and "De fortune," two of *Ch*'s three Machaut ballades, appeared on the same page. The Reina Codex contains seven Machaut ballades, including "De Fortune" and the double ballade "Quant Theseus/Ne quier voir."[15] Of the other manuscripts transmitting Machaut works, *Ch* shares one of its three Machaut ballades with each; the few exceptions concern fragments.[16] The most frequently transmitted of *Ch*'s Machaut ballades, judging from surviving copies, was "De petit peu"; Chantilly shares it with four other sources.[17] That all three of *Ch*'s Machaut works appear in other Italian sources suggests that these ballades were circulating in Italy, and strengthens the hypothesis that *Ch* too is an Italian manuscript.

Ch is the only anthology with correct attributions to Machaut: two of its three Machaut ballades are attributed to the composer.[18] While it is true that the lost Strasbourg source had three works attributed to "Wilhelmi di Maschandio," the name was added later, probably in the late fifteenth century, to works not actually by Machaut; the three genuine Machaut works in Strasbourg remained unattributed. It is puzzling that the third *Ch* Machaut ballade, "De Fortune," did not receive an attribution as did the other two. While not credited, "De Fortune" is given pride of place in the manuscript: it is copied on the first page of a new gathering, the only gathering devoted to four-part songs (*Chans a .iiii. vois*, as *Ch*'s fifteenth-century index put it). Perhaps *Ch*'s compiler was marking the significance of this ballade by its prominent placement.

Another difference between Chantilly and the anthologies concerns the transmission of poetic texts. Of the anthologies, only *ModA* resembles Chantilly in consistently including the full texts of *formes fixes* chansons. The Reina Codex (*PR*) customarily omits second and third strophes, while the Panciatichi Codex (*FP*) and *Pit* include only text incipits, and those only in the cantus part. It is intriguing to speculate on why *ModA* and *Ch* include full texts—were they prepared for owners who could read and understand the French poems? Were the songs familiar or unfamiliar to the readers? And why might the other Italian anthologies omit the poetry? Were the compilers and/or intended owners more interested in the music? Could they understand the language? These are questions for further research on manuscript culture in the period, questions beyond the scope of this paper.

One might conclude that the presence of merely three works by Machaut, out of 112 in *Ch* as it survives today, suggests that Machaut and his music were no longer very interesting to the compiler of *Ch*, but that conclusion would be wrong. That they were included at all should be read as demonstrating continued interest. It is impossible to determine whether these three ballades were the only Machaut works the compiler could find, or whether they were chosen from among others that were circulating, or whether more Machaut works might have appeared in the missing first gathering; but the placement of "De Fortune" and the attributions of the other two Machaut ballades argues for some appreciation on the compiler's part for the value of the older composer's work.

The presence of three compositions in this source, each related to Machaut and his work in a different way, also argues for an appreciation of Machaut both by the composers who followed him and by the compiler of the Chantilly Codex. I will now discuss these three compositions in turn, with an eye to reading their significance for our understanding of Machaut's posthumous reputation among composers, patrons, and listeners at court.

The first is F. Andrieu's setting of Eustache Deschamps's deploration for the death of Machaut in 1377, *Ch* 84, "Armes, amours / O flour des flours."[19] This work speaks directly to the question of Machaut's posthumous reputation.[20] In the opening stanza of the first ballade, set as Cantus I, the poet calls upon a huge crowd of courtly society to mourn Machaut, while in the opening stanza of the second ballade, set as Cantus II, Deschamps addresses the dead Machaut directly, asking him: "O Guillaume, earthly god of harmony! After your deeds, who will win the prize over all poets? Surely, I do not know him."

> *Ch* 84 "Armes, amours/ O flour" (F. Andrieu)[21]
> [Cantus 1]
>
> [A]rmes amours dames chevalerie
> clers musicans [et] fayseurs en françoys,
> Tous soffistes to[u]te poetrie
> tous cheus q[ui] ont melodieuses vois,
> Ceus q[ui] cantent en orgue aucu[n]es foys
> [et] q[ui] ont ch[ie]r le doulz art de musique
> demenes duel ploures car cest bien drois:
> La mort machau le noble rethouryque.
>
> Onques damo[u]s ne parla en follie,

ains a este en tous ces dis courtouis.
Aussi a mols a pleut sa cha[n]terie.
as grans seigne[ur]s aus contes aus lo[n?]gus[22]
he horphe[us] asses lamenter ce dois
[et] regreter dun regi.et [=regret] autentiq[ue]
arthe[us] aussy alphe[us] to[u] trois ◌ʒ
La mort [machau le noble rethouryque.]

Pries por li si ques nulls ne soublier
ce vo[us] require le vayli de valois.
Car y nest amor duy nul en vie[23]
tel com il fu ne ne sera tes moys ◌ʒ
complains s[er]a de co[n]tes [et] roys
Jusquo lonc tamps per sa bone practique
vestes vo[us] de noir plores tous champenois ◌ʒ
La mort [et c] ◌ʒ

[Weapons, loves, ladies, chivalry, / Clerks, musicians, and writers
in French, / All sophists, all poetry, / All those who have melodious
voices, / Those who sing to the organ on occasion / And who hold dear
the gentle art of music, / Give way to grief, lament, for it is only right,
/ *The death of Machaut, the noble rhetorician.*

Never of love did he speak foolishly, / But has been courteous in all
his poems. / Thus has his singing always greatly pleased / Great lords,
counts, and burghers. / O Orpheus! Much must thou lament / And
grieve with a real grief! / Arethusa too, Alpheus, all three, for / *The
death of Machaut, the noble rhetorician.*

Pray for him so that he will never be forgotten, / This asks of you
the Bailiff of Valois, / No one like him is alive, nor will there be such a
man as he was ever again. / There will be plaints of counts and kings /
For many years, for his goodly craft. / Don garments of black, weep, all
Champenois, for / *The death of Machaut, the noble rhetorician.*]

[Cantus II]

[O] fflour des flours de touto melodie
tres doulz maistres qui cant fuestes adrois ◌ʒ
Guillaume mondains diex darmonnie
apres vos fais qui obetndra le choys ◌ʒ
Sur tous fayseurs certes ne le cognoys
vo nom sera precieuse relique ◌ʒ
Car lon ploura en france en artois
La mort Machaut le noble retorique ◌ʒ

Le fo[n]s chierie [et] la fonatyne helie
dont vo[us] estes le ruissel [et] le dois ◌ʒ
Ou poetes mirent leur estudie
co[n]vie[n]t carro[n]t do[n]t ie suy molt esbais

las cest po[ur] vo[us]qui mo[r]t gisies tous frois.
Ay mi dolent depit faillant replique ᴂ
Ploures arples [et] cors saracynois:
la mort Machaut [et c] ᴂ

Ploures rebele viele [et] ciphonie.
Psalterio[n] to[us] instrume[n]s courtois.
Guisternes fleustes herpes [et] chelemie
[et] traversaynes [et] vo[us] imples de vois ᴂ
Timpane ossy metes en or se doys
tous instrumens q[ui] estes tout antique[ues]
faites devoir ploures ge[n]til galoys ᴂ
La mort [et c] ᴂ

[O flower of the flower of all melody / Gentle master who was so
adroit! / O William, worldly god of harmony! / After your deeds, who
will win the prize / Over all poets? Surely, I do not know him. / Your
name will be a precious relic, / For it will be lamented in France and in
Artois, / *The death of Machaut, the noble rhetorician.*

The fount of Dirce, the fountain of Helie, / Of which you are the
stream and the course, / In which the poets have put their study, / Must
now be muted, which distresses me greatly. / Alas! It is for you, who lie
cold and dead, / That I have grievous pain, lacking reply, / Weep, harps
and Saracen horns, for / *The death of Machaut, the noble rhetorician.*

Weep, rebec (?), viol and sinfonie, / Psaltery, all courtly instruments,
/ Gitterns, flutes, harps and shawms, / traverso flutes, and you, full-
voiced, / tympanum, as well!—you must set to work; / All instruments
of ancient times, / Do your duty, noble Gauls, weep for / *The death of
Machaut, the noble rhetorician.*]

Despite the personal relationship between Deschamps and Machaut, the
poems do not exhibit the intimate feelings of the younger poet but rather adopt
an intentionally elevated tone to lament Machaut's death in what would have been
seen as an appropriately classicized high style.[24] The poems mention Machaut by
name, a rarity in a time enchanted with oblique references to dedicatees via heraldic clues or nicknames. Of the entire surviving late fourteenth-century repertory,
only four chansons—all ballades—identify their dedicatee directly by name; all
four are transmitted by *Ch.*[25] The musical setting of Deschamps's lyrics is unique
to *Ch.*

The composer set Deschamps's two ballades to music in the style of a motet,
with a more simple rhythmic style than that of contemporary chansons. Andrieu's
composition is for four voices: Deschamps's two ballades are sung simultaneously
in the same range, supported by a tenor and contratenor. The two cantus parts come
together to sing their shared refrain ("La mort Machaut, le noble rethouryque")

Example 1. *Ch* 84, "Armes, Amours/O Flour des Flours." Refrain.

homorhythmically. Several musical features mark this work as motet-like in style. The overall texture features a more slowly moving tenor underpinning more active upper voices. The text-bearing voices sing their words syllabically in short, almost choppy phrases with only a few short melismas. Finally, the tenor line is patterned rhythmically and melodically, at the beginning if not throughout the work: in its first phrase, the tenor has a seven-pitch scalar pattern that is repeated twice; the rhythmic pattern is a palindrome.

Besides the laments for Machaut, two other works in *Ch* can be connected to Eustache Deschamps: the two *fumeur* pieces, *Ch* 47, "Puisque je sui fumeux" (2^1 B) by Hasprois; and *Ch* 98, "Fumeux fume par fumée" (3^1 R) by Solage.[26]

The second item related to a work by Machaut is the ballade "Phiton, Phiton, beste tres venimeuse," by Magister Franciscus (*Ch* 18). This ballade has been

identified as honoring Gaston III, Count of Foix, who was known by the allegorical title "Fébus."[27] The text has been read as a political allegory, with handsome
Fébus representing Count Gaston and the horrible monster Python representing Gaston's enemy Jean I d'Armagnac, whom Gaston finally defeated in 1362
(Tucoo-Chala 1976, 41–42 and 224). The connection with Machaut is obvious
in the music: Magister Franciscus begins his song by taking all three voices of his
composition directly from the opening three and a half measures of Machaut's
ballade 38, "Phyton, le mervilleus serpent." After this quoted opening, the rest of
the song is completely different from Machaut's ballade.

The new work contrasts with its model in their texts as well. Once again,
Franciscus takes his opening gesture—the image of the legendary monster—from
Machaut but then goes on to write a very different kind of song. Machaut's ballade
is an allegory of love: "Python, the wondrous serpent slain by Apollo's arrow, was
a full league in length as Ovid has described him. But never was a serpent seen,
so cruel, so wicked or so proud as the one who denies me when I ask for my lady's
favour." Machaut's serpent has seven heads—Refus, Desdaing, Despit, Honte,
Paour, Durté, and Dangier: all standard symbols for the trials and obstacles that
keep a lover from his lady—and they wound the lover, who doubts that he can
stand so much torment any more. In Franciscus's ballade the monster is real, not
used as an allegorical figure; the ballade tells the story of Python's defeat, vilifying
him at great length. The poetry for "Phiton Phiton" is addressed directly to the
monster himself.

Franciscus's ballade has much longer and more melismatic musical lines
than Machaut's ballade does, and Franciscus's form is the more modern ternary
one, with the refrain set as a separate musical section, as opposed to the bipartite
form of Machaut's time. In Machaut's ballade the refrain is an integrated part of
the second section. Both ballades feature musical rhyme between sections, but
that technique is used differently in the two works. Machaut's two sections share
more than half of their musical material (11+1 breves, out of sections 22+1 and
21+1 breves in length), while Magister Franciscus's use of musical rhyme is much
shorter: only 8+1 breves are repeated in the refrain from the end of section A,
producing a very different kind of ballade.

There has been some discussion, based on chronologies of style for Machaut's music, regarding which of these two ballades is the original and which the
copy. If Franciscus's work is indeed a political allegory written for the benefit of
the Count of Foix, then Machaut's ballade must have been primary.[28] It is much
less likely that anyone would base a love complaint on a political allegory than
that someone would base an occasional work praising a nobleman on a love
song, provided that the love song was well known to the audience. The character
of Fébus is not very prominent in Machaut's lyric, but the reference would have

been significant enough to a poet and composer looking for a way to honor a nobleman with that nickname. Such a reference would also flatter a dedicatee, given Machaut's renown and his connections with the French royal family.

There is one unusual point to the transmission history of these two ballades. Machaut's ballade was copied once outside of the Machaut manuscripts: it appears in the index of the lost source Trémoille. In fact, the incipit "Phiton le merveilleus" appears in the index twice, the only incipit so repeated. The simplest explanation is that Machaut's ballade was copied twice. But it is tantalizingly possible that a scribe who knew both works was referring to two ballades by the same incipit: Machaut's original ballade and Franciscus's ballade modeled on it. A scribe who had the shared openings in mind could forget that the poetry was not identical.

The third *Ch* ballade, the 3-voice "Ma dama m'a congie donné" (#6), is modeled more closely on Machaut's 2-voice ballade "Se je me pleing, je n'en puis mais" (#15), reworking both text and music. The new poem takes Machaut's refrain for its first line, and Machaut's first line for its refrain.

Ballade 15, Guillame de Machaut[29]

Se ie me pleing ie nen puis mais·
que onques nulls si maleureuse
Ne fu ne ne cera iamais
Com ie sui ne si dolereus·
Car quant ie cuidoie secours
auoir de ma dame et et damours·
Pour mon temps quay en li use·
Ma dame ma congie donne

Et au donner ma dit que vrais
li sui· et loyaus damoureus
Et que[n] rie[n]s ne me sui meffais
V[er]s li dont m[ou]t sui merueilleus
Car ie uay espoir ne recours
Cuer· penser· ne desir ailleurs
Mais seuleme[n]t de volente
Ma dame ma congie donne

Si naray iamais b[ie]n ne pais
ne vie[n]s do[n]t mes cuers soit ioie[us]
Ne pl[us] ne feray ch[an]s ne lais
Qu[an]t amours nest v[er]s moy pite[us]
Aincois voeil definer mes iours
Et mes chans auec mes doleurs
Plus q[ue] par faire loyaute
Ma dame [et] cetera·

Compare *Ch*'s ballade (#6):

> *Ch* 6, Anonymous[30]
>
> [M]a dama m'a congie donne
> Sen sui pres mis en desespoyr ∽
> Quant son cuer abandonne
> a autrui amer dont pooir ∽
> N'arai iamais de ioye avoir
> puis quensi de li suy fourtrais
> Si ie me plaing ie n'en puis mais ∽
>
> Fortune m'a guerre donne
> contre bien mal par son voloir.
> qui m'a de ma dame iete
> [et] de tout mis en nochalor
> nulls ne puet trouver ne savoir
> qu'envers li ioye en riens me fais.
> Se ie me plaing. [et c] ∽
>
> Bien part a mi coment greve
> mesdisans mont pite mouvoir
> le font per humilite
> [et] diex li fera par chevoir
> que l'ai s[er]vi san dechevoir.
> Amors iugies selonc mes fais ∽
> Se ie me plaing [et c] ∽

The anonymous composer took Machaut's music for the first line and refrain and added a new third voice; the musical settings of the other lines are not similar. The reworking would have been recognized by anyone who knew the original ballade: not only are the first line and the refrain the most memorable parts of a ballade text but Machaut's original composition, particularly the refrain, is distinctive, with its melodic descent of a full octave in the cantus.

Machaut's ballade tells the unhappy story of a lover who, after devoting enough time to his lady, had expectations of her returning his affections, but was dismissed by her. "If I complain, I cannot help it," he begins, and the first stanza tells the sad tale. The refrain is the punch line: "my lady granted me leave to depart"—very politely, to be sure, but clearly a final decision. In the second stanza the lady makes it worse for the lover, praising him for his loyalty and telling him he did not do anything wrong. The modern equivalent would be for the lady to tell her lover, "it's not you, it's me." The lover gets the message and realizes he has no hope of changing her mind. In the third and final stanza the lover laments his sad state: things will never go well for him and he will never have peace; nothing will make his heart joyful. Because Love has no pity for him, he will make no more songs or lays; he wants to end his days, and his songs, with his sorrow, because his lady dismissed him.

Example 2. Machaut, Ballade 15 and *Ch* 6, "Ma dama ma congié donné."

Guillaume de Machaut, ballade 15 "Se je me pleing," opening

Guillaume de Machaut, ballade 15 "Se je me pleing," refrain

Example 2 (*continued*)

Ch 6, "Ma dama ma congié donné," opening

Example 2 (*continued*)

Ch 6, "Ma dama ma congié donné," refrain

The composer of the anonymous Chantilly ballade negates Machaut's lover's sad threat by not only making a new song but in a sense rewriting the same song over again. The second poem picks up where the first one ended, with the lover in despair because of his lady's dismissal. In this poem, however, the lover has had some time to get used to the shock and responds by blaming others for his pain: his lady's heart abandoned him for another lover, he can never have joy because she deceived him. In the second stanza the lover blames Fortune, who rewarded his good deeds with ill, turning his lady away from him. In the third stanza he blames malicious gossipers (*mesdisans*) for interfering, but then he comes up with a plan: Pity will move his lady by a display of his humility, and God himself will make her perceive that he, the lover, has served her without deception. We do pity him, because everyone knows this sort of thing never works. Demonstrating his humility will more likely cause his lady to perceive him as pathetic, further convincing her she made the right decision, or, as the lover might put it, further hardening her heart against him. Still, he ends his ballade hopefully, with the request that Love should judge him according to his deeds.

Why would anyone have written the second poem? The story is elaborated with a few new details, but nothing about the lover's unfortunate situation is changed in the least. The listeners can be touched once again by the poor lover's unhappiness, perhaps reliving their own sorrows in love. The second ballade does end with the lover in a hopeful mood, but anyone past the age of first love would know that he is doomed nonetheless, with no chance whatsoever of winning his lady. It is "another somebody done somebody wrong song," one of the most popular song topoi in all of recorded history.[31] As musicologists we tend to focus on the unusual works, the singular ones, the ones with historical or extra-musical significance because they stand out for us from a sea of similarly themed love songs. But much as everyone enjoys novelty from time to time, when it comes to songs what most people really want is another one, a new song, yes, but one that is just like the other songs they already love. The anonymous composer of *Ch* 6 must have understood this particularly well, for he included his model, a song he already liked, in his new work.

Only one other Machaut ballade was rewritten in this way (original refrain becomes new first line, original first line becomes new refrain) to produce a new ballade.[32] "Dame qui fust si tres bien assenée," the second ballade to have been based on a Machaut ballade, is unique to the Reina Codex (*PR*), but the second ballade's model, Machaut's "De Fortune," does appear in *Ch*.[33] A further connection between the two reworked ballades, "Ma dama m'a congie donné" and "Dame qui fust si tres bien assenée," comes from Matteo da Perugia, who, in his ballade "Se je me pleing de Fortune," not only quotes the opening words of Machaut's Ballade 15 (the model for *Ch* 6 "Ma dama") but also cites the text and music of both cantus and tenor of Machaut's Ballade 23, the model for Reina's "Dame qui fust."[34] The implications of these observations are beyond the scope of this essay, but at the very least this convergence suggests a connection between veneration of Machaut, interest in musical quotation, and Italy.

While only three works have been found that clearly quote both text and music from works by Machaut—"Phiton, Phiton" and "Ma dama" from *Ch*, and "Dame qui fust" from Reina—their existence argues for a continued familiarity with Machaut's works on the part of composers and listeners. The process of modeling a new work on an existing one is known from the troubadours and trouvères. In polyphony, direct musical quotation was previously extremely rare, limited primarily to the use of Gregorian chant for the tenor of a motet, and textual quotation was limited to the use of mottoes or proverbs in the thirteenth-century *motet enté*. Machaut himself quotes poetry from Adam de la Halle, but never bases a new song on a preexisting musical model. That Machaut's works were the first ones chosen as models for quotation by late fourteenth-century composers is a mark of respect towards the older composer, just as significant as the sentiments of

Deschamps's lament. And more examples of Machaut's musical influence are being discovered: Ursula Günther speculated that the late fourteenth-century fashion for polymetric rondeaux, musical settings that use more than one mensuration at the same time, may ultimately derive from Machaut's Rondeau 19, "Quant ma dame," in which the composer demonstrates the necessary mathematical proportions between the voices (Günther 1990). These polymetric experiments appear almost exclusively in the Chantilly and Modena codices.

In determining the scope and nature of Machaut's musical influence, it seems that we must be dealing with two different groups of people, and that Machaut and his works meant very different things to these groups. The citation of Machaut's work represented by Magister Franciscus's "Phiton, Phiton" suggests that the audience for this ballade must have been people who were somewhat familiar with a broad range of Machaut's music. Quoting the opening of Machaut's ballade would give such an audience enough to remind them of the earlier work and then dazzle them with the new material. The significance of using Machaut's work (as opposed to that of some other composer) is not so easily assessed. Most likely, since the song honors Gaston Fébus of Foix by comparing him to Apollo, and compares his latest political struggles to Apollo's battle with a fabled beast out of Ovid, any other obvious allusion must have also been meant to confer status on the new ballade. Using Machaut's work as a point of departure may thus have brought some amount of pedigree, adding another level of praise or flattery to the count (it would be flattering to Machaut as well, suggesting that he is a contemporary Ovid). I do not believe that the Machaut work was used merely to remind the audience of the story; the second poet could have dropped Ovid's name just as easily as Machaut did.

To the second group of creator(s) and audience belong the two ballades that exist only to rework those of Machaut. Their existence also makes us presume the audience's familiarity with at least some of Machaut's works in order for the new pieces to be appreciated and their composer(s) congratulated for their cleverness. By borrowing the first line and refrain—the alpha and omega of a ballade—for the new work, these ballades suggest two simultaneous attitudes towards Machaut on the part of their composers. Clearly Machaut has become an authority, worthy of study, of commentary, of emulation. The listeners are meant to recognize the quotation, meant to be reminded of the older song, meant to be flattered by their conoisseurship. But this familiarity also suggests not just that Machaut was an important composer but also that he was still a popular (in the sense of being a favorite) one whose works a courtier could reasonably be expected to recognize. And the existence of *Ch* 6, a song that reworks a Machaut ballade in order to produce another song just like it but new, testifies to an audience for courtly song that really liked Machaut's music for its own sake.

Notes

1. *F-Pn* fr. 1584 (Machaut MS A) bears the inscription "Vesci l'ordenance que G. de Machaut wet qu'il ait en son livre." The Machaut manuscripts are each described in great detail in Earp 1995.

2. Twelve ballades and three rondeaux were copied variously in twelve anthology manuscripts. Manuscript anthologies containing Machaut songs are described, with bibliography, in Earp 1992, 121–28. The manuscripts described in Earp are: Cambrai, Bibliothèque Municipale, MS B.1328 (*CaB*); Ivrea, Biblioteca Capitolare, MS 115 (*Iv*); Paris, Bibliothèque nationale de France, MS nouv. acq. fr. 23190 (*Trém*); Chantilly, Musee Conde MS 564 (formerly 1047) (*Ch*); Florence, Biblioteca Nazionale Centrale, MS Panciatichiano 26 (*FP*); Oxford, Bodleian Library, MS Canonici Pat. lat. 229 (*PadA*) and Padua, Biblioteca Universitaria, MS 1475 (*PadA*); Paris, Bibliothèque nationale de France, MS nouv. acq. fr. 6771 ("Codex Reina," *PR*); Paris, Bibliothèque nationale de France, MS it. 568 (*Pit*); Florence, Biblioteca Medicea-Laurenziana, Archivio capitolare di San Lorenzo, MS 2211 (*SL*); Biblioteca Estense e Universitaria, MS a.M.5.24 (olim lat. 568) (*ModA*); Faenza, Biblioteca Comunale, MS 117 (*Fa*); Ghent, Rijksarchief, Varia D.3360; Utrecht, Universiteitsbibliotheek, MS 6 E 37 II; Fribourg, Bibliothèque Cantonale et Universitaire, MS Z 260; Nuremberg, Stadtbibliothek, Fragm. lat. 9 and 9a; Prague, Národní knihovna (formerly Universitní knihovna), MS XI.E.9; and Strasbourg, Bibliotheque Municipale, MS 222 (C.22) (*Str*). See also Günther (1980) 2001. A chart of these chansons and their manuscripts is given in Arlt 2001.

3. The webs of musical quotation in this period have been explored more recently by Anne Stone and Yolanda Plumley.

4. Published descriptions of this manuscript include Reaney 1969, 128–60; Günther (1980) 2001; and Upton 2001, chap. 2, "The History of the Physical Object," in which I describe and discuss the physical aspects of the manuscript.

5. Greene's edition of the *Ch* chansons was published as volumes 17 and 18 of Polyphonic Music of the Fourteenth Century. A facsimile of the complete manuscript has been edited by Yolanda Plumley and Anne Stone. See Plumley and Stone 2008. A volume of essays on the Chantilly Codex, also edited by Yoland Plumley and Anne Stone, was published in 2009 (Plumley and Stone 2009).

6. Florence, Biblioteca Laurenziana, MS Mediceo-Palatino 87. A color facsimile is available in Gallo (1992), with codicological studies by John Nádas, Kurt von Fischer, Luciano Bellosi, Margherita Ferro Luraghi, Nino Pirrotta, Giuseppe Tavani, Giulio Cattin, and Agostino Ziino.

7. I discuss the acquisition of the Chantilly Codex by the Duke of Aumale (a son of Louis Philippe, the last king of France), based on archival documents I found in the Musée Condé, in Upton 2003.

8. Günther (1984, esp. 98–107) speculated on the possible involvement of the Alberti with the creation and early history of *Ch*. I discuss the Alberti in general and Francesco d'Alto biancho degli Alberti in particular, concluding that it is impossible for Francesco to have been the intended owner of the original corpus of the manuscript in Upton 2001, 89–100.

9. This has not stopped scholars from trying to associate the manuscript and its collection with a single court—for example, that of Foix, or, more recently, Aragon. For a discussion (and dismissal) of several such hypotheses, see Upton 2001, 159–84. For a discussion

of the relationships between the dedicatees of *Ch* musical works, with a genealogical table, see Upton 2001, 194–297.

10. The duke's perspective on his manuscript is discussed in Upton 2001, 23–32, and in Upton 2003.

11. This reasoning follows that articulated in Hamm 1962.

12. An inventory of the contents of *Ch* that notes the subject matter of the musical works is available in Upton 2001, 339–51.

13. Anne Stone (1994, 169–82) discusses this ballade, recognizing the irony and significantly revising Ursula Günther's earlier interpretation of the work, with important implications for our understanding of style change in the late fourteenth century.

14. Paris, Bibliothèque nationale de France, MS nouv. acq. fr. 23190 (*Trém*). For a description of this manuscript, with a list of its Machaut works, see Earp 1995, 122–23.

15. Paris, Bibliothèque nationale de France, MS nouv. acq. fr. 6771 (Codex Reina). For a description of this manuscript, with a list of its Machaut works, see Earp 1995, 124–25.

16. Padua fragment A has the "Ite missa est" of the Mass, and Rondeau 7, "Ma fin est mon commencement"; the Fribourg leaf has a Machaut motet; the Maggs rotulus contains a Machaut lai; and the Prague source has only two Machaut chansons—one rondeau and one ballade.

17. Modena (*ModA*), Panciatichi (*FP*), the Paris Italian source (*Pit*), and the Cambrai fragment B (*CaB*). Additionally, the Strasbourg manuscript, destroyed by fire in 1870, contained a version of "De fortune" with a contrafact text.

18. Attributions to Machaut outside of the Machaut manuscripts are extremely rare: besides the two Chantilly ballades the only work so marked is a motet, "Li enseignement / De touz / Ecce," attributed to "Guillermus de Mascandio" in the Fribourg leaf (Fribourg, Bibliothèque Cantonale et Universitaire, MS Z 260), a work not otherwise believed to be by Machaut (Earp 1995, 127).

19. F. Andrieu has not yet been definitively identified. Gilbert Reaney (2001) suspects that he may be the same composer as Magister Franciscus, composer of two other works in *Ch*; that suspicion is based on stylistic comparison and is not supported by any documentation. "F" could also stand for a title, such as Frater.

20. Leach (2009) discusses this work, especially as it relates to concepts of fame and reputation in the late Middle Ages; I am grateful to Dr. Leach for sending me a copy of her article in advance of publication.

21. This is a diplomatic transcription of the unique copy of this work, found on fol. 52r of the Chantilly codex. I resolve abbreviations within square brackets, but otherwise do not amend the words the scribe wrote. Uppercase letters in the manuscript are decorated, even in the tightly copied text residuum. In copying this work the scribe of *Ch* uses three punctuation signs to signal the ends of poetic verses: one with two dots connected with tracery in the shape of a letter s, one with three dots connected with tracery to form a trident lying on its side, and a simple period. The s sign is used primarily in the stanza underlaid with Cantus I's music; the trident is used in the text residuum and the stanza underlaid with Cantus II's music. I include periods where they occur; I represent the s sign in my transcription by a comma and the trident by ∞.

Howard B. Garey produced a normalized edition of the poetry for Ensemble Project Ars Nova's recording, "Ars Magis Subtiliter" (New Albion Records, NA 021, 1989). In Deschamps's complete works (Queux de Saint-Hilaire and Raynaud 1878–1903), the two ballades of Ch 84 are numbered CXXIII and CXXIV.

22. Howard B. Garey substitutes "bourgeois" for this incomprehensible word; I have followed his suggestion in my translation.

23. Garey amends this line to read "Car il n'en est au jor d'uy nul en vie," and I have followed his suggestion in my translation.

24. Deschamps is identified as Machaut's nephew in the anonymous *Regles de la seconde rhétorique*, but current literary scholarship doubts any blood relationship. In medieval terms "nephew" can also mean "heir," and Deschamps himself speaks of Machaut as a mentor. See Laurie 1998, 2–3; see also Page (1977) on the relationship between the two men. The first stanza of this poem is discussed in Jewers 1998, 163–79, especially 165.

25. The other three are *Ch* 11, "Fuions de ci" by Jacob Senleches, lamenting the death in 1382 of Eleanor of Aragon, queen of Castille; *Ch* 50, "S'aincy estoit" by Solage, praising Jean duc de Berry; and *Ch* 71, "Par les bons Gedeon" by Philipoctus da Caserta (unattributed in *Ch*), praising Pope Clement VII. All four works are discussed in Upton 2001, 185–215.

26. On the Fumeur pieces, see Unruh 1983.

27. Count Gaston seems to have taken the nickname "Fébus" in 1358; he first signed his name "Fébus" on April 16th, 1360. His battle cry, "Fébus avant!," is heard in the refrain of another ballade in the Chantilly Codex, *Ch* 55 "Se Galaas et le puissant Artus" by Johannes Cunelier; the battle cry dates to Gaston's successful campaign to East Prussia, also in 1360; see Tucoo-Chala 1976, 28–31 and 224. On the association of *Ch* 18 with Count Gaston, see Upton 2001, 239–44.

28. See Earp 1995, 354. The standard interpretation is that Franciscus was quoting Machaut's work. Hirschberg (1971, 166–70), however, proposed the idea that Franciscus's ballade is the original from which Machaut quotes.

29. This transcription follows the poem as presented in the manuscript Paris, Bibliothèque Nationale, MS fonds fr. 1586 ["Machaut C"], fols. 164r–v. The paintings in this manuscript have been dated by François Avril on art-historical grounds to 1350–56; the manuscript is seen as the earliest extant copy of Machaut's collected works. On the dating, see Avril 1982, 118–24. On Machaut C and the other Machaut manuscripts, see Earp 1995). An edition of the poem into normalized medieval French, with translation, both by Jennifer Garnham, may be found online at http://www.lib.latrobe.edu.au/MMDB/composer/H0031015.htm.

My transcription reproduces spelling and capitalization as on the page. I spell out abbreviations in square brackets. The scribe used one punctuation mark, a small diamond-shaped dot, and I have represented this sign with a small square mark. The first stanza is underlaid to the cantus part (the page turn comes between "on" and "ques" in line 2 and "ie" and "sui" in line 4), the second and third stanzas are copied as poetry in a text residuum.

30. In copying this work the scribe used dots (represented here as periods) and the S-shaped mark, represented here by ꝝ. I have added apostrophes, but changed nothing else of the scribe's orthography. Realized abbreviations are in square brackets. For a printed edition of this ballade and other fourteenth-century texts, see also Greene 1981–89.

31. "(Hey Won't You Play) Another Somebody Done Somebody Wrong Song," words and music by Chips Moman and Larry Butler, was a #1 Billboard hit for B. J. Thomas in 1975. The lyrics are particularly self-aware: the singer wants to hear a sad song because he himself is already sad. Hearing a sad song will make it possible for him to cry, while having the comfort of (virtual) company of others also disappointed in love. The refrain reads: "Hey, wontcha play / another somebody done somebody wrong song / And make me feel at home / while I miss my baby, while I miss my baby."

32. These two reworkings are the earliest known examples of this technique. Günther (1972) discusses these and other fourteenth-century examples of musical quotation.

33. "De Fortune" appears in *Ch*, Reina, and *Trém* as well as in the Machaut sources. "Ma dama m'a congie donné," the *Ch* reworking, has one concordance—it is listed in the Trémoille index—but its model "Se je me pleing" appears only in the Machaut sources. The music of "Ma dama" appears only in the Machaut sources; the poetry (without musical notation) is transmitted additionally by two text-only manuscripts. See Earp 1995, 374.

34. Lucy Cross discovered the Machaut quotations in Matteo's ballade. See Günther (1980). The revised entry on Matteo in *Grove Music Online* (Günther and Stone, 2001) retains the observation about the connection between Matteo's ballade and Machaut's works, but omits crediting the discovery to Cross. Earp (1995, 310) retains the citation in his entry on "De Fortune."

References

Andrieu, F. 1989. "Armes, amours." Edited and translated by Howard B. Garey. In "Ars Magis Subtiliter," Ensemble Project Ars Nova, liner notes. San Francisco: New Albion Records, NA 021.

Arlt, Wulf. 2001. "Machaut, Guillaume de, 9. Reception." *Grove Music Online*, ed. Laura Macy. Accessed September 29, 2005. http://www.grovemusic.com.

Avril, François. 1982. "Les manuscrits enluminés de Guillaume de Machaut: Essai de chronologie." In *Guillaume de Machaut: Poète et compositeur; Colloque-table ronde organisé par l'Université de Reims (19–22 avril 1978)*. Actes et Colloques 23. Paris: Klincksieck.

Earp, Lawrence. 1995. *Guillaume de Machaut: A Guide to Research*. New York: Garland.

Gallo, F. Alberto, ed. 1992. *Il codice Squarcialupi: Ms. Mediceo Palatino 87, Biblioteca laurenziana di Firenze*. Florence: Giunti Barbèra.

Greene, Gordon K., ed. 1981–89. *French Secular Music*. Polyphonic Music of the Fourteenth Century 18–22. Monaco: Editions de l'Oiseau-Lyre.

Günther, Ursula. 1972. "Zitate in französischen Liedsätzen der Ars nova und Ars subtilior." *Musica Disciplina* 26: 53–68.

———. 1980. "Matteo de Perusio." In *The New Grove Dictionary of Music and Musicians*, edited by Stanley Sadie, 11:830. 20 vols. London: Macmillan.

———. (1980) 2001. "Sources, MS, VII: French Polyphony 1300–1420, 3. Principal Individual Sources." In *The New Grove Dictionary of Music and Musicians*, edited by Stanley Sadie, 17:661–65. 20 vols. London: Macmillan Publishers, 1980. Revised ed. available online at *Grove Music Online/Oxford Music Online*, ed. Laura Macy. Accessed June 27, 2003. http://www.grovemusic.com.

———. 1984. "Unusual Phenomena in the Transmission of Late Fourteenth-Century Polyphonic Music." *Musica Disciplina* 38: 87–118.

———. 1990. "Polymetric Rondeaux from Machaut to Dufay: Some Style-Analytical Observations." In *Studies in Musical Sources and Style: Essays in Honor of Jan LaRue*, edited by Eugene K. Wolf and Edward H. Roesner, 75–108. Madison, WI: A-R Editions.

Günther, Ursula, and Anne Stone. 2001. "Matteo da Perugia [Matheus de Perusio, de Perusiis, Perusinis]." In *Grove Music Online/Oxford Music Online*, edited by Laura Macy. Accessed June 27, 2003. http://www.grovemusic.com.

Hamm, Charles. 1962. "Manuscript Structure in the Dufay Era." *Acta musicologica* 34: 166–84.

Hirschberg, Jehoash. 1971. "The Music of the Late Fourteenth Century." PhD diss., University of Pennsylvania.

Jewers, Catherine A. 1998. "*L'Art de musique et le gai sentement*: Guillaume de Machaut, Eustache Deschamps and the Medieval Poetic Tradition." In *Eustache Deschamps, French Courtier-Poet: His Work and His World*, edited by Deborah M. Sinnreich-Levi, 163–79. New York: AMS Press.

Laurie, Ian S. 1998. "Eustache Deschamps: 1340(?)–1404." In *Eustache Deschamps, French Courtier-Poet: His Work and His World*, edited by Deborah M. Sinnreich-Levi, 1–72. New York: AMS Press.

Leach, Elizabeth Eva. 2009. "Dead Famous: Mourning, Machaut, Music and Renown in the Chantilly Manuscript." In *A Late Medieval Songbook and Its Context: New Perspectives on the Chantilly Codex (Bibliothéque du Château de Chantilly, Ms. 564)*, edited by Anne Stone and Yolanda Plumley. Turnhout: Brepols.

Ludwig, Friedrich, and Heinrich Besseler, eds. 1926–29. *Guillaume de Machaut: Musikalische Werke*. Leipzig: Breitkopf & Härtel.

Page. Christopher. 1977. "Machaut's 'Pupil' Deschamps on the Performance of Music." *Early Music* 5: 484–91.

Plumley Yolanda, and Anne Stone, eds. 2008. *Codex Chantilly, Bibliothéque du Château de Chantilly, Ms. 564: Fac-similé and Introduction*. Turnhout: Brepols.

———. 2009. *A Late Medieval Songbook and Its Context: New Perspectives on the Chantilly Codex (Bibliothéque du Château de Chantilly, Ms. 564)*. Turnhout: Brepols.

Queux de Saint-Hilaire, Auguste Henry Édouard, and Gaston Raynaud, eds. 1878–1903. *OEuvres complètes de Eustache Deschamps*. 11 vols. Société des anciens textes français. Paris: Firmin Didot & Cie.

Reaney, Gilbert, ed. 1969. *Manuscripts of Polyphonic Music (c.1320–1400)*. RISM B IV, 2. Munich: Henle.

———. 2001. "Andrieu, F.," *Grove Music Online*, ed. Laura Macy. Accessed September 29, 2005. http://www.grovemusic.com.

Robertson, Anne Walters, 1992. "The Mass of Guillaume de Machaut in the Cathedral of Reims." In *Plainsong in the Age of Polyphony*, edited by Thomas F. Kelly, 100–139. Cambridge, MA: Harvard University Press.

Schrade, Leo, ed. 1977. *Guillaume de Machaut: Oeuvres Complètes*. Vol. 4, *Les Ballades*. Monaco: Éditions de L'Oiseau-Lyre. Originally published in vol. 3 of Polyphonic Music of the Fourteenth Century.

Stone, Anne. 1994. "Writing Rhythm in Late Medieval Italy: Notation and Musical Style in the Manuscript Modena, Biblioteca Estense, Alpha.M.5.24." PhD diss., Harvard University.

Tucoo-Chala, Pierre. 1976. *Gaston Fébus: Un Grand Prince d'Occident au XIVe siècle*. Pau: Marrimpouey.

Upton, Elizabeth Randell. 2001. "The Chantilly Codex (F-CH 564): The Manuscript, Its Music, Its Scholarly Reception." PhD diss., University of North Carolina at Chapel Hill.

———. 2003. "Inventing the Chantilly Codex." *Studi Musicali* 31: 181–231.

Unruh, Patricia. 1983. "'Fumeur' Poetry and the Music of the Chantilly Codex: A Study of Its Meaning and Background." MA thesis, University of British Columbia.

Reading (into?) Renaissance Dance: *Misura* in the Service of Dramaturgy

Nona Monahin

Fifteenth-century Italian *balli* are social dances in which programmatic or dramatic elements are often discernable and at times even explicitly referred to in the original sources.[1] This essay examines the concept of *misura* as it applies to such balli, and shows how the choice of misura may be connected to the dramaturgy of the dance. It also presents a reading of a ballo in which a programmatic content is not immediately apparent but which, on closer examination, may be found to contain a hidden satirical subtext that appears to reinforce established codes of societal behavior.[2]

The dance sources examined for this study include the earliest known Italian dance treatise, believed to date from the mid-fifteenth century, *De arte saltandj et choreas ducendj* of Domenico da Piacenza,[3] renowned dancing master to the Sforza and Este households[4]; and two slightly later treatises by Domenico's former students: *De pratica seu arte tripudii* by Guglielmo Ebreo of Pesaro (later known as Giovanni Ambrosio), who became an esteemed dancing master in his own right,[5] and the *Libro dell'arte del danzare* by the courtier Antonio Cornazano, who presented his treatise to Ippolita Sforza on the occasion of her betrothal.[6] These works contain choreographic descriptions of many *bassadanze* and balli, and provide accompanying music for the latter in the form of monophonic melodies in mensural notation. It should be noted that Domenico, and undoubtedly also Guglielmo, composed the music for his own ballo choreographies.[7]

In fifteenth-century Italy the word ballo, as well as being a general term for dance, could denote a particular dance type practiced by members of the nobility.[8] Such balli were social dances choreographed for a specified number of participants (usually a small number, such as one male-female couple, or three dancers, or three or four couples). They frequently incorporated dramatic elements—usually along the lines of flirtation between the men and the women—thereby providing enjoyment and amusement not only for the dancers but also for the onlookers since, in the society of the Italian Renaissance nobility, social dances were often designed to be observed as well as danced.[9]

Musically the most conspicuous characteristic of these balli was that most of them were sectional, featuring the use of different meters and tempos within the same dance, based on a system of four different misure. The four misure described in the fifteenth-century dance treatises are, in increasing order of speed: *bassadanza*, *quadernaria*, *saltarello*, and *piva*. It may be noted that all except the *quadernaria* existed in fifteenth-century Italy as discrete dances in addition to appearing as sections of a ballo. Each misura was associated with a specific mensuration, relative tempo, and characteristic dance steps—although it was regarded as a commendable skill on the part of the dancer to be able to adapt the steps of one misura to the music of a different one.[10]

Domenico states that each subsequent misura is one-sixth "narrower" (*piu strecta*) than the preceding one, which results in a ratio of 6 : 5 : 4 : 3 corresponding to *bassadanza* : *quadernaria* : *saltarello* : *piva*.[11] Cornazano's discussion of the misure confirms these figures. Whether or not to interpret the ratios literally has been the subject of much discussion among dance history scholars today,[12] and it is not my intention to delve into the topic here—except to say that the lengthy and careful detail with which both Domenico and Cornazano explain how to fit the steps of one misura into another, and the complaints that Domenico makes regarding musicians who do not keep a constant tempo and thereby inadvertently end up switching to a different misura, seem to suggest that at least these two authors wanted their instructions to be taken literally.[13] Although Guglielmo does not discuss the relative *tempi* of the misure, he prescribes exercises that dancers can practice together with musicians in order to acquire a feel for the different misure, and, furthermore, notes that a dancer who understands the misure, "were he to take the pulse of someone who is sick or feverish, would know as well as a doctor at what rate the pulse was beating" (Guglielmo, *De pratica*, bk. 1, 11v.; trans. Sparti 1999, 103). This seems related to a comment by the fifteenth-century physician Michaele Savanarola (Sherr 1997, 331) who stated that a doctor could learn the speed of the pulse from a good musician, and indicates that these dancing masters should be added to the list of fifteenth-century writers who discuss matters of tempo and proportions in music.

Fifteenth-century balli employed a variety of dance steps which, unfortunately, are described only very vaguely in the dance sources.[14] The authors of the treatises do, however, tell us the relative duration of most of the steps by stating their relation to one tempo of the music (which usually, as may be expected, equals one breve). Thus we learn from Domenico and Cornazano that one tempo of *bassadanza* misura can accommodate either two *sempii* (two single steps), or one *doppio* (one double step), or one *ripresa*, or one *riverenza*, and so on.

I will now look briefly at the *doppio* (double step) since it occurs frequently in all four misure. The most basic form of the *doppio* consists of three changes of weight (i.e., three walking steps made with alternating feet). The timing of these three changes of weight would vary according to the misura in which they are performed. In addition to differences in timing, various embellishments could be added which highlighted the different character of each misura. Cornazano, for instance, explains that in the *bassadanza* misura the *doppio* includes a rise on the second step followed by a lowering of the heels on the third; this produces an up-and-down wave-like motion and, appropriately, Cornazano calls the rising action *ondeggiare* (to wave, to billow).[15] Domenico's comment (*De arte saltandi*, chap. 3, lines 46–52) that a dancer should move smoothly, "like a gondola . . . propelled . . . through waves [that] rise slowly and fall quickly," appears to relate to the same movement. For the *quadernaria misura* Domenico adds a *frappamento* (beat or stamp) to the *doppio*, while in the *saltarello* misura the *doppio* is combined with a *salteto* (small leap or jump). The basic step of the *piva misura* is described by Domenico as being a fast *doppio*.[16] Table 1 lists the most common characteristics of the four misure as they are described by the dancing masters. The four misure could be mixed and matched to form different balli. But how were they mixed and matched? In many of these balli the misura changes are frequent, with a misura sometimes lasting only a few bars (*tempi*) before changing to a different one. As I hope to show, the choice of misura is often connected to the dramaturgy of the ballo.

First, however, I must stress that these balli are not pantomimes; that is, they do not have fully developed storylines or narratives. Yet neither are they all totally "abstract," for Cornazano informs us that *ballitti* (a term he uses interchangeably with balli) are "compositions of several *misure*," with each such dance "ordered with some fundamental intent, such as is apparent in the *Mercantia* and *Sobria* [two of Domenico's balli] which are the opposites in meaning."[17] These two dances are, in fact, the most explicitly programmatic of all the balli, and Cornazano proceeds to explain that in *Mercantia* one woman dances in turn with four men, "like someone who trades lovers," while in *Sobria* the "modest lady" of the title spurns all suitors and dances only with her original partner. These two dances also include directions for the dancers regarding hand gestures and facial expressions.[18]

Other balli are not so explicit. Drama is sometimes suggested by the titles, as for example in a ballo called *Geloxia* (jealousy) where, appropriately, much changing of partners takes place, or in a ballo called *La Malgratiosa* (ungracious lady) where the female dancer keeps turning away from her male partner whenever he approaches her.[19] Several scholars have discussed some of the different means by which the dancing masters achieved such instances of dramatic expression, including the choice of dancers' paths (are the partners approaching one another or moving away?), the directions of individual steps (forward, back, sideways, or

Table 1. The Most Common Characteristics of the Four Misure

Misura	Relationship between the four misure as described by Domenico*	1 *tempo* (breve) of music —with subdivisions into semibreves and minims —in each misura**	Most characteristic step done to 1 *tempo* of music of given misura
Bassadanza	The "widest" (slowest) of the four misure	□ = (musical notation)	1 *doppio*, performed with wave-like *ondeggiare* motion (rising and lowering)
Quadernaria	1/6 "narrower" than *bassadanza* misura***	□ = (musical notation)	1 *doppio* with a *frappamento* (beat, stamp) added
Saltarello	2/6 "narrower" than *bassadanza* misura	□ = (musical notation)	1 *doppio* with a *salteto* (hop or leap) added
Piva	3/6 "narrower" than *bassadanza* misura (i.e., twice as fast as bassadanza misura)	□ = (musical notation) or (musical notation)	1 fast *doppio*

* Domenico is using the terms "wide" and "narrow" (Domenico, *De arte saltandi*, lines 201–25, in Smith 1995, 19–20) in reference to a graph he supplies in which the relative speeds of the misure are represented as distance. Thus, for example, the *piva* has a distance equal to half the distance of the *bassadanza*, because in the time of one *tempo* of *bassadanza* one can perform two *tempi* of *piva*.

** In the third column I have followed Domenico's example and attempted to represent graphically the relative differences in length of the breve (and its subdivisions) in each misura.

*** Another possible interpretation of the relationship of *bassadanza* misura to *quadernaria* misura is 4 : 3 rather than 6 : 5. This, however, does not result in a major change, because the *quadernaria* will still be faster than the *bassadanza* and slower than the *saltarello*. See Nevile 2004, 109–118, 158–160, for an excellent discussion of the relationship between the four misure.

turning), combined with an appropriate choice of misura (are the dancers moving quickly or slowly, gracefully or boisterously?).[20]

As can be seen from the above examples, flirtation between men and women is a recurring theme of many of these balli. One outcome of practicing dances that are based on the interaction between the sexes is the reinforcement of the accepted codes of societal behavior regarding gender roles. Whether this is a conscious (didactic maybe?) effort on the dancing master's part or an unconscious result of adhering to those same codes while choreographing the dances, the end result is the same.

In the dance sources of the fifteenth and sixteenth centuries, dancing styles are clearly divided along gender lines: all of the dancing masters make it clear that the movements of the women, on the whole, were meant to be smaller, gentler, more graceful, and more restrained than those of the men—who could display a more athletic style—even though much of the step vocabulary was shared by both sexes.[21]

In some choreographies not only do the gender-differentiated qualities of the movements but the actual design of the dance as a whole serve to reinforce the accepted codes of behavior. Let us look briefly at Domenico's ballo called *Leoncello Vecchio* for two dancers (man and woman).[22] In this dance, after a brief opening figure during which the couple enters together, the man dances away from the woman three times, each time using a different step sequence. All three times the woman follows, repeating the same movements that her partner had just performed. No doubt she can build on this design with her acting skills, as Ingrid Brainard (1990, 92) has suggested: "The image of flight and pursuit . . . gives the lady every opportunity to follow her partner with eagerness, with impatience, with annoyance or reluctance; she can imitate his manner directly, she can ridicule it by exaggeration, or she can show . . . how much more elegant her dancing is than his." Nevertheless, I believe the message would not be lost on the participants (the dancers and the onlookers) that it is the man who sets the tone, who makes the choices; the woman merely follows and copies. No matter how she chooses to render the actions, they were still predetermined by the man, and the couple's reconciliation takes place only after the woman has successfully completed the series of actions (trials?) chosen for her by the man.

Regarding the choice of misure in this dance, I find it interesting that Domenico has utilized the contrast between the rather pedestrian duple meter of the *quadernaria* and the slower tempo and more lilting (perhaps also more "perfect"?) triple meter of the *bassadanza* (compound duple in modern transcription) to make the conflict and resolution between the partners more effective, and also to add a touch of humor. The opening figure and most of the "flight and pursuit" sequence are danced in *quadernaria*, but for the man's final "flight"—that is, at the point where he is about to reconcile, to stop fleeing from his lady—the misura changes to *bassadanza*. This time, when the lady approaches him, he does not flee but takes her hand, and the couple proceeds together until almost the end of the ballo.[23] But the dance does not end in such triple-meter unanimity: for the final two *tempi* the misura suddenly reverts back to *quadernaria*, during which the man makes a *movimento*—a brief movement or gesture, unfortunately not described in the dance sources but interpreted by many dance historians as an improvised foot motion (perhaps a stamp)—to which the woman responds with another one; the "quarrel," apparently, is not over.[24]

Abrupt changes of misura to underscore conflict can also be found in Domenico's ballo called *Vercepe*, for three men and two women (*De arte saltandi*, lines 653–730). *Vercepe* could be taken for a completely "abstract" dance, were it not for Cornazano's comment that it "resembles a skirmish" (*Libro*, lines 619–20). Several writers have commented on the frequent and sudden changes in direction, accompanied by changes of misura, which in this dance evoke the chaotic nature of a skirmish; Barbara Sparti has pointed out the appropriateness of assigning the *bassadanza* misura to the women and the more boisterous *saltarello* to the men during the final part of this ballo, to emphasize what she has called a "skirmish between the sexes" (Sparti 1984, 180).

Since so many of these dances seem to reinforce the stereotypical gender roles of Renaissance court culture, I was surprised that in *Pizochara*—a ballo for four couples that is found next to *Vercepe* in Domenico's treatise—these roles appeared to be reversed.[25] The form of the dance is shown in table 2. From this table it can be seen that in the beginning the men and women dance together in couples, moving to the lively *piva misura*. After this the music slows down to *bassadanza* misura; here, the men do a *riverentia* (bow), and everyone does a *represa* (a step to the side). Next, still in *bassadanza* misura, the men dance by themselves, one behind the other, weaving (winding) their way through a stationary line of women, using walking-like steps: two *sempii* (single steps) followed by eleven *doppii* (double steps). This section ends with another *represa* to the side by everyone. Following this, the misura changes to the sprightlier *saltarello*, and now the women dance alone, weaving *their* way through the now stationary line of men. Finally, everyone dances together in couples again, to the same lively *piva misura* that opened the dance. The whole dance is then repeated.

While the overall structure of this dance is very clearly described by the choreographer, when it comes to the actual steps there is some room for variation since, as mentioned earlier, all of the fifteenth-century dance sources are vague in their descriptions of the steps. As a result, different reconstructions of the same choreography may vary in details on the level of step interpretation.[26] In this particular dance there are also a few minor ambiguities in the musical notation.[27]

Table 2. *Pizochara* by Domenico da Piacanza. Ballo for 4 Couples.

Misura	*Tempi*	Dancers	Dance steps	Comments
Piva	12	Couples	Fast *doppii*	Hand in hand, one couple behind another.
	4	Men	Fast *doppii*	Circle around their partner.
	4	Women	Fast *doppii*	Circle around their partner.
Bassadanza	1	Men	Riverentia	Reverence to partner.
	1	Couples	*Ripresa* to the right	Slow step to the right, hand in hand with partner.
	12	Men	2 *sempii*, 11 *doppii*	Fairly sedate, undulating steps, weaving through stationary line of women.
	1	Couples	*Ripresa* to the left	Slow step to the left, hand in hand with partner.
Saltarello	9	Women	*Doppii* with salteto	Doubles done with a hop or leap, weaving through stationary line of men.
Piva	16	Couples	Fast *doppii*	Start hand in hand, one couple behind the other. First couple separates, other couples dance forward (i.e., through gap created by first couple separating). New first couple separates, remaining couples dance forward, etc.

The entire dance is then repeated.

Despite these ambiguities and possible small differences, what remains clear and unchanged is that there is a definite contrast between the men's winding passage and the women's winding passage, and that what the women do is livelier, bouncier, and faster than what the men do.

While there is nothing unusual per se in women dancing the *saltarello* or men dancing the *bassadanza*, what is intriguing in this dance is the particular juxtaposition of these two sections: first, a relatively long passage for the men alone, danced to the *bassadanza* misura using mainly *doppii* steps (which, as described earlier, were walking steps, embellished in the *bassadanza* misura by the rather graceful wave-like rising and lowering motion called *ondeggiare*); next, the same figure repeated by the women but danced to the faster *saltarello* misura with its sprightlier movements. Clearly, the contrast between the men and the women is the focus of this section and, given the relative length and central position of this section, of the whole dance. What is striking here is that this juxtaposition implies a reversal of the standard gender roles that one sees in Renaissance dance, and yet

Nona Monahin

Example 1. *Pizochara.* Domenico da Piacanza.

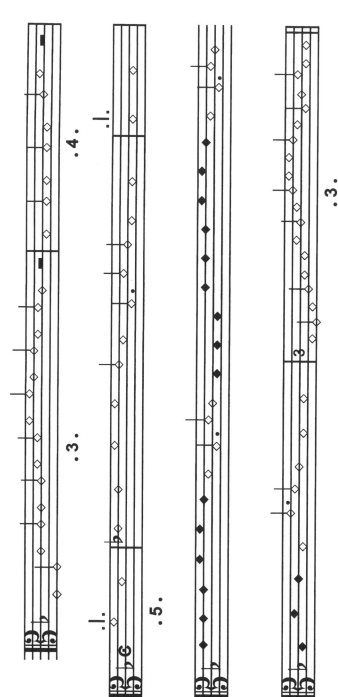

Note: The numeral 5 is probably an error. The numeral 2 would work well with the choregraphy.

Figure 1. A *pizzochera* (member of a religious society for women).
From: *Vecellio's Renaissance Costume Book: All the 500 Woodcut Illustrations from the Famous Sixteenth-Century Compendium of World Costume by Cesare Vecellio* [1598] (New York: Dover Publications, 1977), 34.

the *Pizochara* does not appear to have any obvious programmatic content to which such a "gender-role reversal" could relate.

Could the dance's title provide us with a clue to the mystery? As seen earlier, in some of the balli (e.g., *Sobria, Mercantia, Geloxia, Malgratiosa*) the title did indeed seem to correlate with the theme played out in dance's choreography. On the other hand, it was quite possible that the title *Pizochara* could have referred to a preexisting song which may have inspired Domenico's composition.[28] In any case, what was the meaning of the term *pizochara*? Aware of the risk of trying to "read" more into the dance than was intended, I decided to investigate further.

Figure 1 shows a sixteenth-century representation of a *pizzochera* [*sic*] and depicts a pious-looking old woman—stooped posture, covered head, candle and rosary in hand.[29] This old woman certainly does not appear capable of hopping her way through a *saltarello* misura! On the other hand, a sixteenth-century comedy by Grazzini called *La Pinzochera* (which is the more common Renaissance spelling of this word) portrays the title character as a procuress in charge of several young prostitutes.[30] A seventeenth-century Italian-English dictionary (Florio 1611, 382) describes a *pinzzochera* [*sic*] as "a woman that voweth chastitie without entring [*sic*] into any religious house. Also a dissembling or Saint-seeming woman"; while a present-day Italian dictionary defines a *pinzochera* as someone belonging to "a fourteenth-century movement of Franciscan tertiaries who refused obedience to ecclesiastical authorities."[31] A more common present-day definition is "bigot," especially in the sense of an apparently devout but actually falsely pious person.[32] Religious women, disobedient women, hypocrites, prostitutes—what could these different images have to do with a social dance performed by refined, noble ladies and their partners?[33]

When one examines the social and historical context of the *pinzochere*, clues emerge that point to a potential satirical subtext of Domenico's dance. Several scholars have recently investigated the history of the *pinzochere*, who can be seen as the Italian counterpart to the beguines of Northern Europe.[34] *Pinzochere* were religious laywomen of diverse backgrounds who came from all classes and walks of life. They did not take solemn vows and did not live in convents—which were controlled by male ecclesiastical authorities and often enclosed. Some *pinzochere* lived alone (and were referred to as "nuns of the home"), but mostly such women lived together in self-governed communities where they provided for their own livelihoods by caring for the sick, working as midwives, educating children, and even running hostels for pilgrims (Gill 1992). Such communities offered unattached women an alternative lifestyle that could provide them with a modicum of intellectual autonomy and economic independence.

In Renaissance society, where women were defined on the basis of their relationship to men, such independent, enterprising, and self-sufficient women were often viewed with suspicion and mistrust. Ecclesiastical authorities frequently attempted to pressure communities of *pinzochere* to convert to official convents and accept enclosure, and by the end of the sixteenth century most communities of uncloistered religious women in Italy had been outlawed (Gill 1992).

Unattached women were often suspected of immoral behavior; throughout the Renaissance period *pinzochere* were frequently the objects of satire, and were commonly portrayed as hypocrites who professed religious devotion as a cover-up for more lascivious practices. Examples of this may be found in the works of Boccaccio, in the play by Grazzini mentioned earlier, as well as in other sixteenth-century comedies, and in a Florentine carnival song.[35] What is significant about the above-mentioned satires is that when the *pinzochere* are associated with sexuality, they are presented in active, assertive roles with emphasis on their advanced age and experience in worldly matters.

Given this context, I feel that the choice of misure and the resultant gender-role reversal in Domenico's *Pizochara* is significant. The dance's title (regardless of its origin) is bound to create a certain set of expectations in the culturally informed participants—those watching or those learning the dance for the first time. They are led to expect something unusual, especially from the women, and perhaps also something a bit "risqué," all, to be sure, within accepted limits. And, it seems, the choreographer does not disappoint them.

It may further be noted that the winding path of both the men and the women (see table 2) is described in the choreography as "a guisa de una bissa," which means "in the manner of a snake." While this is the standard way of describing such a winding figure in the Renaissance dance sources, in this context it can take on further significance: the image of the biblical snake and sexual temptation comes to mind. Moreover, in his *Il Corbaccio*, Boccaccio describes the falsely pious widow (clearly a *pinzochera* character) who goes to church to seduce young men, as a snake that lies hidden in the grass waiting to catch her prey, while casting her eyes around at the "brave, valiant, and wise" young men who assemble there (Boccaccio 1972, 282–85; Boccaccio 1975, 58–61). In the *Pizochara* dance, we have the men dancing the sedate (and, as labeled by the dancing masters, "dignified")[36] *bassadanza* just before the women pounce, as it were, with their *saltarello*—although I am not suggesting that any direct reference to Boccaccio was intended.

It may be asked, why then did Domenico give the "snaking" path to the men as well as the women. Regardless of whether or not the snake image was intended, I think that by giving both sets of dancers the same path, Domenico creates balance in this section and also draws attention to the contrast between the men and the women, since, by repeating the same figure but with differences, those differences are highlighted. Furthermore, the women's hops or leaps in the *saltarello* were probably quite small, in keeping with courtly decorum, but they can appear more prominent if they are preceded by the men's *bassadanza*, which contains no such hops or leaps at all.[37]

The dance's final *piva* may be just a harmless closing section, neatly balancing the *piva* at the beginning of the dance. Yet, given the established context, the choreography is open to a more satirical reading. Once again I refer to table 2. It can be seen that the first couple separates by having the partners step sideways away from each other, and the other couples dance forward through the gap thus created; then the new first couple separates and the remaining couples dance forward, and so on. This is all done to the *piva* misura, which has the fastest tempo of all four of the possible misure. Could it look like gates opening up and couples escaping? Various possible allusions come to mind—*pinzochere* running off with the men, *pinzochere* acting as matchmakers by helping lovers elope, *pinzochere* as "free spirits" ...

The choice of *piva* misura for the opening and closing—in other words, for the framing—of this dance may have further significance. Although many balli begin with a lively misura (possibly during which the dancers hasten into the dancing area), the majority of those use *saltarello* rather than *piva* for this purpose.[38] The *piva* was associated with the "lower classes," and both Domenico (*De arte saltandi*, lines 217–18) and Cornazano (Libro, lines 424–30) comment on the *piva*'s lowly origin. Domenico (*De arte saltandi*, line 202), in fact, begins his discussion of the *piva* misura by saying, "I am called *piva* and am the saddest of the misure because I am used by the villagers in the country." (This in contrast to his introduction to the *bassadanza* which he calls the "queen of the *misure*.") Perhaps participants who were prepared (by the dance's title) to expect something potentially subversive would have derived some additional amusement from seeing the dancers enter with what could be viewed as a "lower class" dance.

The *Pizochara*, like most of the balli, should in no way be viewed as a straightforward pantomimic representation; there is no "story line." If the dance is indeed meant to be satirical, the social satire remains on the level of an implied subtext. The refined, dancing, courtly ladies probably do not *represent pinzochere*.[39] All of the dancers' movements are part of their standard court dance vocabulary; it is only through the arrangement of the material—in particular through the choice, gender-based assigning, and juxtaposition of the misure—that Domenico suggests the satirical subtext underlying his dance. In this way, without ever stepping outside the confines of Renaissance courtly decorum, the dancers could poke a little fun at figures outside their own social world, thus ultimately reinforcing their own established codes of behavior.

In conclusion, I would like to make a few comments regarding the implication of the ballo's dramatic content for performers—musicians as well as dancers—of these works today. It is clear that the dancers need to enhance the drama with their acting ability. In some balli Domenico gives very explicit acting directions, such as this example from his ballo called *Sobria*, where the men are hatching a plot to persuade the woman to dance with them: "he signals to his companion and points to the woman . . . the woman senses the movement of the men and turns around scowling."[40] Although the *Pizochara* lacks such explicit acting directions, it may contain hints that some acting may be appropriate. On two occasions the dancers perform a *represa* (a slow sustained sideways step) hand in hand with their partners. Since on both occasions this step is done to the women's side, it could appear as if the women are actually pulling their partners towards them— a surprising moment, full of comic potential. That these moments were indeed intended to be "something special" seems to be borne out by the music. On both occasions the music that accompanies such a *represa* consists of a semibreve that has a sign of congruence above it[41] and is set apart from the rest of the music by means of bar lines. In the *Sobria* example just cited, similar semibreves with signs of congruence accompany the explicit pantomimic gestures described above. Perhaps such places are an opportunity for the musicians as well as the dancers to engage in some improvisation to enhance the drama.

What about the choice of musical instruments? It is generally assumed by many scholars today that the monophonic tunes of the balli served as a framework (either as melody lines or as tenors) on which additional instruments would improvise, and Domenico himself makes it clear that at the very least two instruments, playing tenor and soprano, would accompany a ballo.[42] Since so little is known about how the music for these balli was performed, I think it is instructive to see what Guglielmo (writing under the name Ambrosio) says about the dancer's response to different instruments:

> Get four or five instruments to play, such as shawms, organs, lute, harp, pipe and tabor, or whatever other instrument there is. Have them play one by one, and have them play a *ballo*, and [get] each one to play that [same] *ballo*, each one playing by itself. The [dancer] must dance to that air ["aira"] that the instruments play. For even though they are playing one [and the same] *ballo*, each one will play with his own air. [And] although they are playing the same *ballo*, the shawms will play in one air, the organ in one air, the harp in another air, the [pipe and] tabor in another air, but all will play one and the same *ballo*. Remember that the dancer must dance with that air and with that measure and with that rhythm that the said players are playing; that is, dancing each one on his own. *And if the dancer always dances with one air, even though he dances with measure and in time but does not follow the air of the said players, his dancing will be imperfect and show little skill.*[43] [emphasis added]

Ambrosio names quite an array of instruments here—to fit both "loud" and "soft" ensembles—and, although what he is describing is merely an exercise and does not tell us how instruments were used in an actual performance situation, I think it is significant that he places so much emphasis on the dancer's response to the timbre of an instrument. It indicates, at the very least, that the dancers were expected to be very sensitive to the nuances in the music and to adjust the quality of their movements accordingly. But, if many of the dances have a dramatic content, then I think it would stand to reason that the musicians, too, would need to be familiar with the choreography and seek ways in which they might enhance the drama—in addition to improvisation and embellishment, perhaps also by such means as the choice of instruments (within the more flexible "soft" ensembles, for example) and, within such an ensemble, by alternating the instruments so as to feature now one, now the other—in order to guide the musically-sensitive dancers towards the intended dramatic interpretation.

Notes

1. For more on the ballo, see the entries on "Ballo" in Sutton 1998 and Brainard 2001a; see also Brainard 1970 and Sparti 1986.

2. The portions of this essay that discuss the *ballo* called *Pizochara* are based on Monahin (1993) and are reproduced here with permission of the publishers.

3. Domenico da Piacenza, *De arte saltandj et choreas ducendj / De la arte di ballare et danzare*, Paris, Bibliothèque nationale de France, MS fonds it. 972. English translations: Smith 1995, 1:8–67; Brainard, unpublished translation. I am grateful to Ingrid Brainard for making available to me her unpublished translation of Domenico's treatise. Transcription: Wilson 2006. For biographical data on Domenico and opinions on the date of his treatise see Brainard 1998a, Brainard 1998b, and Smith 1995, 4–7.

4. The duties of a dancing master often extended beyond choreography and could include teaching the children of the nobility to dance (with lessons beginning at a very early age), training the boys in fencing and horseback riding, choreographing dances for various festivities, and, as in the case of Domenico da Piacenza, composing the music for their own choreographies (see below). For more on dancing masters see Brainard 1979.

5. Guglielmo Ebreo, *De pratica seu arte tripudii*, Paris, Bibliothèque nationale de France, MS fonds it. 973. English translation: Sparti (1993) 1999. For biographical data on Guglielmo Ebreo, see Sparti (1993) 1999, 23–45.

6. Antonio Cornazano, *Libro dell'arte del danzare*, Rome, Bibl. Apostol. Vaticana, Cod. Capponiano Nr. 203. English translations: Inglehearn and Forsyth 1981; Smith 1995, 68–107. For biographical data on Cornazano see Smith 1995, 68–76.

7. Domenico da Piacenza, *De arte saltandi*, lines 369–71. Guglielmo Ebreo gives instructions on how to compose a ballo, both choreography and music: *De pratica*, 12v; Sparti (1993) 1999, 63, 104.

8. Cornazano, in reference to the dances in his treatise, states that these "balli and bassedanze . . . are beyond the mundane, made for elegant halls, and only to be danced by very proper ladies—not by those of the lower classes" (Cornazano, *Libro*, lines 509–13; trans. Smith 1995, 93).

9. In his rule for composing a ballo, Guglielmo Ebreo states that it "should bestow delight and pleasure on the onlookers and on those who take delight in this art . . . for dancing is considered more beautiful the more it pleases the multitude of spectators" (Guglielmo, *De pratica*, 12v; trans. Sparti [1993] 1999, 105).

10. Domenico (*De arte saltandi*, lines 250–368) discusses in detail how the steps of one misura may fit into another.

11. Florio (1611, 540) gives the following translation for *stretto*: "straight, narrow, strickt, close. Also made narrow, strained, shrunke up . . ."

12. For a summary of such debates, see Sparti (1993) 1999, 65n11; see also Nevile 1993 and Nevile 2004, 115–18, 138–60.

13. Domenico, *De arte saltandi*, chap. 11; Cornazano, *Libro*, lines 174–330. It should be borne in mind that the dancing masters were well-educated members of the courtly society, and would have been trained in music. As already noted, Cornazano himself was a courtier, while Domenico and undoubtedly also Guglielmo composed the music for their own ballo choreographies (see n. 7, above.)

14. In today's terminology the word "step," in addition to its general meaning of a movement from one foot to the other, can mean a series of foot motions that combine to

form a recognizable choreographic unit. It is in this second sense that I use the term "step" here.

15. Cornazano, *Libro*, lines 120–27. Translation of the term *ondeggiare* in John Florio, *Queen Anna's New World of Words, or Dictionaire of the Italian and English Tongues* (London: Melch, Bradwood, 1611), 341. Consulted via Early English Books Online, http://eebo.chadwyck.com/home.

16. Domenico, *De arte saltandi*, chap. 13, lines 264–65 (re *piva*); chap. 14, lines 301–2 (re *quadernaria*), lines 314–15 (re *saltarello*).

17. Cornazano, *Libro*, lines 331–43; trans. Smith 1995, 89–90.

18. In *Sobria*, for example, "he signals to his companion and points to the woman," and "the woman senses the movement of the men and turns around scowling" (Domenico, *De arte saltandi*, lines 1143–44 and 1147–48; trans. Smith 1995, 57).

19. Domenico, *De arte saltandi*, lines 562–601 (*Geloxia*), and Guglielmo, *Trattato della danza*, lines 3304–24 (*La Malgratiosa*); Smith 1995, 2:194

20. In particular, see Brainard 1990; see also Sparti 1984.

21. See, for example, the chapter entitled "Capitulum Regulare Mulierum" in Guglielmo Ebreo, *De pratica*, Paris, Bibliothèque nationale de France, MS fonds it. 973; and (under the name Giovanni Ambrogio) Paris, Bibliothèque nationale de France, MS fonds it. 476; Cornazano, *Libro*, various references; Thoinot Arbeau, *Orchesography* (Arbeau 1589; Arbeau 1967), various references, especially advice to man dancing *galliard* with a partner; Fabritio Caroso, *Nobiltà di dame* (Caroso 1600; Caroso 1986), in which several dances have less vigorous variations for the woman; likewise Cesare Negri, *Le gratie d'amore* (Negri 1602; Negri 1969).

22. Domenico, *De arte saltandi*, lines 449–73. The title may be a reference to Leonello d'Este. This dance is subtitled *Vecchio* to distinguish it from the newer *Lioncello nuovo*.

23. Note that this is not the same as the familiar *tanz-nachtanz* situation, in which a slower dance in duple meter is followed by a faster one in triple meter, because here the triple-meter *bassadanza* misura is slower than the duple *quadernaria*. In order for the juxtaposition to have resembled a *tanz-nachtanz* pattern, I believe the choreographer might have chosen a *saltarello* or a *piva* as the second *misura*.

24. For a discussion on *movimento* see Brainard 1981, 41–43; Sparti (1993) 1999, 223.

25. Domenico, *De arte saltandi*, lines 603–51. Transcriptions of the *Pizochara* music in Smith 1995, 1:248–50; Nevile 2004, 176–77; and Wilson 2006, 22. Reconstruction of the choreography in Nevile 2004, 178–81. Another version of the music for this dance (spelled *Pizocara*) appears in Giovanni Ambrosio (Guglielmo's name after his conversion to Christianity), *De Pratica*, BnF, fonds it. 476. For facsimile and transcription of the *Pizocara* melody from this manuscript see Sparti (1993) 1999, 192. The *Trattato della danza*, Siena, Biblioteca Comunale, codex L. V. 29—one of many versions of Guglielmo's *De pratica*—contains another description of this dance (now spelled *Pinzochera*), with minor changes and without music.

26. See, for example, Brainard (1981, 15–53), for reconstructions and detailed discussion of fifteenth-century dance steps; Smith (1987, 104), for reconstructions (in labanotation) of *doppio*, *saltarello*, and other fifteenth-century steps; Sparti (1993) 1999, glossary, 217–28.

27. For example: the numeral 5 in the short section corresponding to the *riverentia* and the first *represa* is most likely a scribal error; a 2 would work, indicating that this

section is to be played twice, thus giving the *riverentia* and the first *represa* two semibreves each (as is the case with the second *represa*). However, other solutions are possible; for example: it could be that the *riverentia* and the first *represa* have only one semibreve each, while the second *represa* has two (though of the same pitch)—perhaps a second *riverentia* was intended, but inadvertently omitted, just before the second *represa*. The version of the music in Ambrosio (see n. 25, above) has no numeral in the place in question, but his choreographic directions also differ somewhat.

28. It should be noted, however, that Domenico's treatise (*De arte saltandi*, lines 369–73) acknowledges the reworking of another tune (*La Figlia di Guglielmino*) into a *ballo*, but states that the remaining tunes were composed by Domenico.

29. Cesare Vecellio, *Habiti Antichi, et Moderni di Tutto il Mondo* (Venice, 1589). Reprinted in part as *Vecellio's Renaissance Costume Book* (see Vecellio [1589] 1977). The *pizzochera* illustration is on page 34 of this Dover edition.

30. Grazzini 1582; see Grazzini 1953, 243–318; see also Rodini 1970.

31. Zingarelli 1973. "Tertiary," or "of the Third Order," refers to laypersons affiliated with a religious order. See also Cross 1957, 1348.

32. Most present-day dictionaries that I consulted simply give "bigot" as the translation. Two of the meanings given by Zingarelli (1973) are "bigotta" and "bacchettona," both of which carry the suggestion of hypocrisy; cf. definitions in *The Cambridge Italian Dictionary*, 1962. Although present-day dictionaries usually give both the masculine and feminine forms of the noun ("pinzochero"/"pinzochera"), the only reference to the masculine form that I found in the Renaissance sources used for this study is in Florio's dictionary, where a "pinzocchero" is defined as a "dissembling hypocrite" (Florio 1611, 382).

33. The dancing masters emphasize that these dances were intended for the nobility, and their dance treatises are dedicated to members of the nobility. See Monahin 1993.

34. Gill 1992; Gill 1994; Guarnieri 1980; see also Herlihy 1990, 66–70 and 162–66; Herlihy and Klapisch-Zuber 1985, 226; King 1991, 103–17. My discussion of the sociohistorical background of the *pinzochere* is based on the above works. I am grateful to Katherine Gill for making available to me a prepublication version of her article.

35. Boccaccio's *Decameron* contains snide and suggestive remarks about *pinzochere* (Boccaccio 1927, 352). Although Boccaccio does not use the term "pinzochara" in his *Corbaccio* (Boccaccio 1975), it is clear that the "lascivious widow" of the story is in fact a *pinzochara*. See Guarnieri 1980, 1722, and Rodini 1970, 126; compare also the bawdy carnival song, "Canzona delle pinzochere andate a Roma" ("Song of pinzochere who have been to Rome") in Singleton 1936, 121–23. For more on the Florentine carnival songs see Galluci 1966 and D'Accone 2001. The existence of a carnival song about *pinzochere*, and a dance with gender-role reversal called *pizochara*, is intriguing, especially since carnival songs were at times performed by men dressed as women. So far, however, I have not been able to locate the music to this song, so I could not determine if there may be a connection.

36. Domenico calls the bassadanza the "queen of the misure" (Domenico, *De arte saltandi*, line 202).

37. At the risk of "reading into" the dance even more, I will add that by giving the men and the women the same serpentine path, the choreographer may be able to evoke subtly the image of the snake without associating it specifically with the women who are dancing (since they are not the only ones doing the "snaking"). This, however, must remain as speculation.

38. I examined thirty balli that have such an introductory entrance figure. Twenty-six of these use the *saltarello* misura for this figure.

39. In *Mercantia*, however, the lady does portray a less than acceptable woman. However, as Cornazano explained (*Libro*, lines 331–43), this dance was meant to be seen as a counterpart to *Sobria*, which illustrates the correct behavior. Besides, the character portrayal in *Mercantia* is achieved by harmless means such as merely dancing with several partners, not by performing any inappropriate movements.

40. Domenico, *De arte saltandi*, lines 1143–44 and 1147–48; trans. Smith 1995, 57.

41. "The term is used today to describe the mark written like a fermata or *segno* with a wide range of different meanings in sources from about 1300 to 1650. They can denote the point where a canonic voice enters (or ends), the point where other voices enter, the point from which the music of a secular song repeats, some kind of a fermata, a point of embellishment, and much else" (Fallows 2001).

42. For example, Domenico, *De arte saltandi*, lines 172–74.

43. Giovanni Ambrosio, *De Pratica* (BnF, fonds ital. 476), 25v. Guglielmo Ebreo took the name Giovanni Ambrosio after his conversion to Christianity. Ambrosio's version of *De Pratica* contains all the material of the original, plus some additions, including this "test of a good dancer." Translation in Sparti (1993) 1999, 235.

References

Primary Sources

Arbeau, Thoinot. 1589. *Orchésographie*. Langres: Jehan des Prez.

Boccaccio, Giovanni. [1350–53.] *Il Decameron*.

———. [ca.1355]. *Il Corbaccio*.

Cornazano, Antonio. n.d. *Libro dell'arte del danzare*. Rome, Bibl. Apostol. Vaticana, Cod. Capponiano Nr. 203.

Caroso, Fabritio. 1600. *Nobiltà di Dame*. Venice: Il Muschio.

Domenico da Piacenza. n.d. *De arte saltandi et choreas ducendi / De la arte di ballare et danzare*. Paris, Bibliothèque nationale de France, MS fonds it. 972.

Florio, John. 1611. *Queen Anna's New World of Words, or Dictionaire of the Italian and English Tongues*. London: Melch. Bradwood.

Giovanni Ambrosio. n.d. *De Pratica*. Paris, Bibliothèque nationale de France, MS fonds it. 476.

Grazzini, Antonfrancesco. 1582. "La Pinzochera."

Guglielmo Ebreo. n.d. *De pratica seu arte tripudii*. Paris, Bibliothèque nationale de France, MS fonds it. 973.

———. n.d. *Trattato della danza* [alternate title for *De pratica seu arte tripudii*.] Siena, Biblioteca Comunale, codex L.V. 29.

———. *See also* Giovanni Ambrosio.

Negri, Cesare. 1602. *Le Gratie d'Amore*. Milan: Pontio and Piccaglia.

Vecellio, Cesare. 1589. *Habiti Antichi, et Moderni di Tutto il Mondo*. Venice: Giovanni Bernardo Sessa.

Secondary Sources

Arbeau, Thoinot. 1967. *Orchesography*. Translated by Mary Stewart Evans. With a new introduction and notes by Julia Sutton. New York: Dover.

Boccaccio, Giovanni. 1927. *Il Decameron*. Edited by A. F. Massèra. Bari: Gius. Laterza & Figli.

———. 1972. "Il Corbaccio." In Giovanni Boccaccio, *Opere Minori in Volgare*, ed. Mario Marti, vol. 4. Milan: Rizzoli.

———. 1975. *The Corbaccio*. Translated by Anthony K. Cassell. Urbana: University of Illinois Press.

Brainard, Ingrid. 1970. "*Bassedanse, Bassadanza* and *Ballo* in the 15th Century." In *Dance History Research: Perspectives from Related Arts and Disciplines; Proceedings*, ed. Joann W Kealiinohomoku, 64–79. New York: CORD.

———. 1979. "The Role of the Dancing Master in Fifteenth-Century Courtly Society." *Fifteenth-Century Studies* 2: 21–44.

———. 1981. *The Art of Courtly Dancing in the Early Renaissance*. West Newton, Massachusetts: I. Brainard.

———. 1990. "Pattern, Imagery and Drama in the Choreographic Work of Domenico da Piacenza." *Guglielmo Ebreo a Pesaro a la Danza nelle corti Italiane del XV secolo*, ed. Maurizio Padovan, 85–96. Pisa: Pacini.

———. 1998a. "Ballo." In *International Encyclopedia of Dance*, edited by Selma Jeanne Cohen. New York: Oxford University Press.

———. 1998b. "Domenico da Piacenza." In *International Encyclopedia of Dance*, edited by Selma Jeanne Cohen. New York: Oxford University Press.

———. 2001a. "Ballo." In *The New Grove Dictionary of Music and Musicians*, edited by Stanley Sadie, 2:605–7. 2nd ed. 29 vols. London: Macmillan.

———. 2001b. "Domenico da Piacenza." In *The New Grove Dictionary of Music and Musicians*, edited by Stanley Sadie, 7:440–41. 2nd ed. 29 vols. London: Macmillan.

———, trans. Unpublished. *De arte saltandi et choreas ducendi / De la arte di ballare et danzare*, Domenico da Piacenza. BnF, fonds it. 972.

The Cambridge Italian Dictionary. 1962. Edited by Barbara Reynolds. Cambridge: Cambridge University Press.

Caroso, Fabritio. 1986. *Nobiltà di Dame*. Translated by Julia Sutton. New York: Oxford University Press.

Cross, F. L. ed. 1957. *The Oxford Dictionary of the Christian Church*. London: Oxford University Press.

D'Accone, Frank A. 2001. "Canti Carnascialeschi." In *The New Grove Dictionary of Music and Musicians*, edited by Stanley Sadie, 5:47–49. 2nd ed. 29 vols. London: Macmillan.

Early English Books Online (EEBO). Ann Arbor, MI: UMI, 1999–. http://eebo.chadwyck.com/home. Contains digital version of Florio 1611.

Fallows, David. 2001. "Signum concordantiae." *Grove Music Online*, ed. Laura Macy. Accessed 30 January 2008. http://www.grovemusic.com.

Gallucci, Joseph James, Jr. 1966. "Festival Music in Florence, ca.1480–ca.1520: Canti Carnascialeschi, Trionfi, and Related Forms." PhD diss., Harvard University.

Gill, Katherine. 1992. "Open Monasteries for Women in Late Medieval and Early Modern Italy: Two Roman Examples." In *The Crannied Wall: Women, Religion, and the Arts in Early Modern Europe*, edited by Craig A. Monson, 15–47. Ann Arbor: University of Michigan Press.

———. 1994. "Penitents, Pinzochere, and Mantellate: Varieties of Women's Religious Communities in Central Italy, ca. 1300–1520." PhD diss., Princeton University.

Grazzini, Antonfrancesco. 1953. "*La Pinzochera*." In *Teatro*, edited by Giovanni Grazzini, 243–318. Bari: Gius. Laterza & Figli.

Guarnieri, Romana. 1980. "Pinzochere." In *Dizionario degli Istituti di Perfezione*, ed. Guerrino Pelliccia and Giancarlo Rocca, 6:1722–49. Rome: Edizioni Paoline.

Herlihy, David. 1990. *Opera Muliebria: Women and Work in Medieval Europe*. New York: McGraw-Hill.

Herlihy, David, and Christiane Klapisch-Zuber. 1985. *Tuscans and Their Families: A Study of the Florentine Catasto of 1427*. New Haven: Yale University Press.

Inglehearn, Madeleine, and Peggy Forsyth, trans. 1981. *The Book on the Art of Dancing*. [Translation of Cornazano, *Libro dell'arte del danzare*.] London: Dance Books Ltd.

King, Margaret L. 1991. *Women of the Renaissance*. Chicago: University of Chicago Press.

Monahin, Nona. 1993. "Leaping Nuns? Social Satire in a Fifteenth-Century Court Dance." In *Proceedings of the Society of Dance History Scholars: Sixteenth Annual Conference, Joint Conference with the Congress on Research in Dance*, 171–79. University of California, Riverside: SDHS.

Negri, Cesare. 1969. *Le gratie d'amore*. Facsimile reprint, New York: Broude Bros.

———. 1985. *Le gratie d'amore*. Translated by Gustavia Yvonne Kendall. PhD diss., Stanford University.

Nevile, Jennifer. 1993. "The Performance of Fifteenth-Century Italian *Balli*: Evidence from the Pythagorean Ratios." *Performance Practice Review* 6: 116–28.

———. 2004. *The Eloquent Body: Dance and Humanist Culture in Fifteenth-Century Italy*. Bloomington: Indiana University Press.

Rodini, Robert J. 1970. *Antonfransesco Grazzini: Poet, Dramatist, and Novelliere 1503–1584*. Madison: University of Wisconsin Press.

Sherr, Richard. 1997. "Tempo to 1500." In *Companion to Medieval and Renaissance Music*, edited by Tess Knighton and David Fallows, 327–36. Berkeley and Los Angeles: University of California Press.

Singleton, Charles S., ed. 1936. *Canti Carnascialeschi del Rinascimento*. Bari: Gius. Laterza & Figli.

Smith, A. William. 1987. "Belriguardo (Vecchio): A Critical Discussion." In *Proceedings of the Tenth Annual Conference of the Society of Dance History Scholars*, 86–105. Riverside: SDHS.

———. 1995. *Fifteenth-Century Dance and Music: Twelve Transcribed Italian Treatises and Collections in the Tradition of Domenico da Piacenza*. 2 vols. Stuyvesant, NY: Pendragon Press.

Sparti, Barbara. 1984. "Music and Choreography in the Reconstruction of 15th-Century Balli: Another Look at Domenico's Vergepe." *Fifteenth-Century Studies* 10: 177–194.

———. 1986. "The 15th-century *Balli* Tunes: A New Look," *Early Music* 14: 346–57.

———. 1991. "How Fast Do You Want the Quadernaria?" *Marriage of Music and Dance: Papers from a conference held at The Guildhall School of Music and Drama, Silk Street, Barbican, London EC2, 9th–11th August 1991*. London: National Early Music Association (NEMA).

———, trans. and ed. (1993) 1999. *Guglielmo Ebreo of Pesaro: De Pratica Seu Arte Tripudi*. Reprint, Oxford: Clarendon Press.

Sutton, Julia, with Barbara Sparti. 1998. "Ballo and Balletto." In *International Encyclopedia of Dance*, edited by Selma Jeanne Cohen, 1:351–52. New York: Oxford University Press.

Vecellio, Cesare. (1589) 1977. *Vecellio's Renaissance Costume Book: All the 500 Woodcut Illustrations from the Famous Sixteenth-Century Compendium of World Costume by Cesare Vecellio.* Reprint, New York: Dover Publications.

Wilson, D. R. 2006. *Domenico of Piacenza (Paris, Bibliothèque Nationale, MS ital. 972)* Rev. ed. Cambridge: Early Dance Circle.

Zingarelli, Nicola. 1973. *Vocabolario della lingua italiana.* Decima edizione minore. Bologna: Zanichelli.

Dance and Identity in Fifteenth-Century Europe

Jennifer Nevile

In early modern Europe there is ample documentation that people distinguished between dances which originated from different regions. Contemporary sources, such as chronicles, letters, comments in dance treatises, dance titles, and even publication titles, all reveal that dance practices across Europe were categorized and labeled. For example, when Robert Coplande translated a *basse danse* treatise from French into English in 1521, he called his work, "Here followeth the manner of dancing of bace dances after the use of France and other places." Guglielmo Ebreo, dance master in fifteenth-century Italy, proudly asserts in his treatise on the art of dancing that any dance student who has diligently studied all the exercises provided by him in his treatise will be able to dance perfectly any German, Greek, or Slavonic (that is, Croat) dance,[1] or indeed any dance from whatever country he wishes.[2] As far as Guglielmo was concerned, different regions had different identifiable styles of dance.

The question which fascinates us today concerns what criteria people used in the fifteenth century when they labelled one dance as French, another as Italian, a third as German. This essay takes Guglielmo's comments as its starting point, addressing the question: what identified dances in fifteenth-century Europe as belonging to one country or another? Various criteria are discussed which might have been used to distinguish between dances: choreographic structure, choreographic style, the gestures and qualities of the movements executed by the dancers, the costumes of the dancers, and the musical style of the accompanying music. These criteria are examined with regard to Italian, French, and English dance practices.

The second half of this essay focuses on the significance of this differentiation between dance styles. Historians such as Peter Burke have argued that in fifteenth-century Europe identity was expressed through rituals, myths, and material culture. Dance was an important part of social ritual at this time, and as such was one way in which people expressed their identity. Movement, gesture, deportment, and facial expressions were believed to be a mirror of each person's soul. Given the significance of an individual's movements for her or his own spiritual identity, it is not surprising that dance, an organized system of movements, was one of the vehicles society used for expressing a larger, communal identity. The way in which this larger group identity was expressed through the dance is discussed in relation to fifteenth-century Italian society.

Guglielmo's comments in his treatise are not the only indication we have that people at that time differentiated between dance practices in the various areas of Europe. Contemporary sources, chronicles, and letters often describe the occasions at which dancing occurred, including private entertainments; public functions to welcome or honour visiting dignitaries, ambassadors, or rulers of neighbouring states; celebrations of weddings, births, and military victories; or as part of theatrical performances. Sometimes these accounts include a comment on the nationality of the dances which were performed, especially, it seems, when festivities were held to honour a delegation from another court or country. For example, in 1494 Bianca Maria Sforza visited Innsbruck for the coronation of the Holy Roman emperor, Maximillian I. Her companion wrote of how Bianca Maria Sforza expertly performed French, Italian, and German dances, with the comment that performing German dances was an easy task because they were similar to Hungarian dances (Padovan 1985, 32). The Ferrarese chronicler Bernardino Zambotti records how on October 17, 1476, a ball was held in the ducal palace at Ferrara in honour of Beatrice d'Aragona who was about to be married to the king of Hungary, Matthias Corvinus. At this ball a group of Hungarian gentlemen danced in their own style before the assembled court (Zambotti 1928, 23).

In 1490 the wedding of Isabella d'Aragona (the daughter of Ippolita Sforza) to the Duke of Milan, Giangaleazzo Sforza, produced a glittering array of international dance styles. Groups of four to twelve dancers from Poland, Germany, France, Spain, and Hungary, all dressed in the costume of their country, performed their own dances to honor the bridal couple. A number of Isabella's ladies-in-waiting entertained the company by dancing Neapolitan and Spanish dances (Sparti 1993, 52). This was followed by an invitation to the Spanish contingent to entertain the company with "dui balli a la spagnola." The French gentlemen and ladies then performed "dui balli a la franzosa" to the delight of Isabella (Padovan 1985, 33).[3]

We even have hints that in fifteenth-century Italy dance styles from different cities were distinguished from each other. For example, in 1459 Galeazzo Maria Sforza visited Florence. After an evening with the Medici family at their country villa in Careggi, Galeazzo wrote to his father: "When [dinner] was over, a charming little show was given by the ladies. The wives of Piero [di Cosimo] and of Giovanni, a grown daughter of Piero's, the wife of Pierfrancesco [di Lorenzo, brother of Cosimo], a young Strozzi, ... and a few country women took part in it. They all did dances *in the Florentine manner* [emphasis added], skipping and shifting in refined fashion."[4] Galeazzo, a product of Milanese society, implies in his letter that the dancing of his Florentine hosts was in a different style to that to which he was accustomed. Exactly how the Florentine style of dancing differed from the Milanese is almost impossible to determine from such a description, yet it is clear that Galeazzo was easily able to make such a distinction. David Wilson has suggested that regional differences may also have existed within the French *basse danse* genre, for example, between Burgundy and northern and central France (Wilson 2008, 172).

In these reports there is specific mention of Italian, French, German, Slavonic, Polish, Hungarian, Spanish, and Neapolitan dances, but no indication of how these dances were differentiated from each other. Even Guglielmo did not specify the criteria he used to differentiate between a German, Greek, or Italian dance. The important question is: what was it about these dances which caused those who saw them to be able to identify and categorize them as belonging to one particular region or country? There are a number of possible features which people in the fifteenth century might have used to differentiate between their own and other, foreign, dances. These features include: the choreographic structure of the dance; the choreographic style—that is, the precise manner in which individual steps were performed; the dancers' gestures and the quality of their movements when dancing; the costumes of the dancers; and the music that accompanied the dances. By "choreographic structure" I mean the step vocabulary of the choreographies and how these steps were combined into sequences. "Choreographic style" encompasses the different manner in which the steps common to several European dance practices were used in each practice, and the way in which steps from predominantly one practice were used occasionally in another.

Choreographic Structure

Perhaps the most obvious method of discriminating between dances is on the basis of their choreographic structure. This would entail the step vocabulary of the dances and the way individual steps were combined into sequences. The fifteenth-century French *basse danse*, for example, had an ordered choreographic structure with rules that defined the ways in which a *mesure* could be constructed from a sequence of simples, doubles, reprises, branles, and reverences. There were also rules that ordered the way *mesures* were combined to form a dance.[5] The choreographic structure of the fifteenth-century French *basse danse* is shown in table 1. The Italian *bassadanza*, however, had a far more flexible choreographic structure, with many alternatives in the way individual steps were combined into sequences.

Table 1. Choreographic Structure of the Fifteenth-Century French *Basse Danse*

Imperfect Measures - Step sequence	Perfect Measures - Step sequence
reverence	reverence
↓	↓
branle	branle
↓	↓
2 simples	2 simples
↓	↓
1/3/5 double	1/3/5 double
↓	↓
↓	2 simples
↓	↓
1/3* reprise	1/3* reprise
↓	↓
branle	branle

*An alternative pattern for 3 reprise was reprise, double, reprise.

The number of doubles determined the type of *mesure*, according to the following rules:
  1 double = *petite mesure*
  3 doubles = *moyenne mesure*
  5 doubles = *grande mesure*

Table 2 shows the structure of an Italian *bassadanza* with the most common step sequence in the central column, and the numerous alternatives to this step sequence shown to the right and left. The key difference between the choreographic structures of these two genres is that the Italian *bassadanza* lacked the fixed units of the French *mesure*. The Italian *bassadanza* was, as a result, more free-flowing and continuous. More variation was possible at the individual step level due to the absence of the fixed structure of the *mesure*.

The Italian treatises record several dances in which the Italian dance masters were deliberately imitating the French *basse danse* style; that is, the *balli* "Fraza mignion franzesse" (NY, fol. 31r) and "Franzese Amoroso" (P*a*, fol. 58v–59r), and the *bassadanze* "Bassa Franzesse" (NY, fol. 31r) and "Borges Francese" (P*a*, fol. 43v). In these dances the usual choreographic structures of the Italian dance genres were altered so that they conformed to the choreographic structure of the French *basse danse*. The choreography of "Bassa Franzesse" fits exactly within the complicated system of *mesures* that regulated the French *basse danse*, since, although Italian, it is constructed of a *grande parfaite mesure*, a *moyenne parfaite mesure*, and then a *petite imparfaite mesure* (although the last two *continentie* are missing from this *mesure*). The choreographer of "Bassa Franzesse" has even replaced the usual Italian *riprese* with *riprese françese*. After the three *mesures* are completed, "Bassa

Table 2. Choreographic Structure of the Italian *Bassadanza*

Options Before		Main Step Sequence		Options After
doppio	→	sempio ↓	→	ripresa
riverenza ripresa	→	doppio ↓ ↓	→	sempi riverenza
volta tonda	→	ripresa or meza volta ↓	→	doppio
doppio	→	riverenza or continenza or volta tonda ↓ sempio	→	doppio

Franzesse" ends with eight *tempi* of *saltarello*, or *passo brabante*, that is, the *pas de brébant*, the after dance of the fifteenth-century French *basse danse*. Thus, in order to imitate the French style in this dance, the choreographer has followed the French choreographic structure (the system of *mesures* and the concluding *pas de brébant* section) as well as changing some of the steps to French versions.[6]

In the *ballo* "Fraza mignion franzese," the Italian choreographer was also trying to imitate the French style. In this case the dance begins with a *riverenza* and two *continentie*, which is extremely unusual for an Italian *ballo* but is quite normal for a French *basse danse*. Once again the choreography is structured according to French rules (a *petite imparfaite mesure*, then two *mesures* of a *moyenne* variant), even though it has been modified to allow for the introduction of sections of different *misura* (in this case *piva misura*). The dance ends in the same manner as the "Bassa Franzesse," with eight *tempi* of *saltarello*.

These examples where the Italians were imitating the style of their northern neighbours clearly illustrate at least one of the criteria by which the Italian *maestri di ballo* discriminated between their dances and those of the Franco-Flemish practice, that is, by choreographic structure and the use of certain steps associated with the French practice, such as the *riprese françese*.

If choreographic structure was one way of differentiating between the French and Italian dance practice, it could also be used to identify fifteenth-century English dance style.[7] The variable step sequences of English dances lie at the opposite extreme from the regulated choreographic structure of the French *basse danse*. The dances found in the Gresley papers do not exhibit any marked tendencies to follow one particular step with another—apart from two exceptions.[8]

There are no common step combinations for the opening sequences of the dance, and, similarly, the conclusion of the dances shows no adherence to a closing formula.

Choreographic Style

Another possible indicator of national identity in dance practice is the choreographic style—that is, the manner in which steps common to various dance practices were performed in each different country, and the way they were used in the step sequences. Single and double steps and the bow or reverence occur in Italian, French, and English choreographies in the fifteenth century. The names of these steps are consistent in all three countries, yet the manner of their execution could well have been one of the criteria which caused them to be labeled as "English," "Italian," etc. Certainly the manner in which the steps "single" and "double" are used in the English choreographies also distinguish these dances from continental practices. In English dances singles are grouped in multiples of three—three, six, or nine—and are specifically mentioned in nineteen dances. Therefore one can assume that this grouping was probably standard. Doubles, on the other hand, are only mentioned in four dances, and on each occasion are in groups of "2 doblis."[9] This is in direct contrast to the French and Italian genres in which double steps are used in every dance, whether it is a *ballo*, *bassadanza*, or *basse danse*. In the fifteenth-century French *basse danses*, singles occur only in pairs[10] and doubles in groups of one, three, or five, with only a few exceptions.[11] In the Italian *bassadanze* and *balli*, *sempi* almost always occur in pairs, while *doppi* in the body of the choreographies occur mostly in sequences of one or two.[12]

The use of the reverence also differs between the English, French, and Italian practices. The *obeysaunce* is found in very few of the English dances (only three in fact). This differs enormously from the French *basse danse* tradition, in which every dance begins and ends with a *reverence*, and also from Italian practice, where half of the *balli* and nine-tenths of the *bassadanze* contain a *riverenza*.

The English choreographies also contain the *brawl* (*branle*), a step which is firmly associated with the French *basse danse* tradition but is not used in the same manner. The *brawl* does not form part of the opening sequence, nor is it used to delineate the end of each *mesure*, as in the French *basse danse*. Rather it occurs at irregular intervals throughout the dances, just as do the other steps. For example, in the dance "Talbott," for two performers, the first person moves forward, the second person moves in the opposite direction, and then they turn to face each other. The instructions then read: "brawle at onys and then com togydder" (Gresley, 55). Similarly, in "Northumberland de tribus," in the middle of the dance all three participants turn to face each other and "brayll" (Gresley, 72). Furthermore, in the English dances the *brawl* is used in only one-fifth of the choreographies. It is not an invariable part of every dance as it is in the French *basse danse*. Indeed the step is used far less than other steps which are unique to these choreographies; that is, *rakis*, *trett*, *retrett*, and *flowerdelice*, whose usage varies from just under 40 percent to just over 70 percent.[13]

Gestures and Quality of the Dancers' Movements

Since dance at this time was an activity in which the gestures and deportment of the participants played an important part, a third possible criterion used to differentiate between dances from different countries is the posture and gestures of the dancers and the quality of the movements executed by them. While Domenico and Guglielmo mention that the gestures of the dancers should be moderate and in harmony with the music, they do not elaborate on what these gestures involved.[14] Given the relatively undeveloped state of research into gesture in fifteenth-century Europe, it is difficult to state definitively how the gestures and quality of movement would have differed between Italians performing a *bassadanza* at Milan, Ferrara, or Florence, and Burgundian nobles performing a *basse danse* at the court of Burgundy. Two hundred years later, in the seventeenth century, there is evidence of an increasing awareness of gesture and the ways in which it varied between different social situations and locations (Burke 1991, 74–76). This is illustrated by John Bulwer's 1644 publication on the "Naturall Language of the Hand" (Bulwer [1644] 1974, 250). As Robert Toft explains in his summary of Bulwer's views: "According to . . . Bulwer, the Italians used too much gesture of the hand, and French action was full of 'quick and lightsome expressions.' But in Germany and England, countries with similar national complexions, 'moderation and gravity in gesture is esteemed the greater virtue.' The Spaniards, however, although equally disposed to moderate and grave action, use the hands 'as often [as] principals as accessories to their proud expressions'" (Toft 1993, 111–12).

One cannot say that the same recognition and interest in *national* gestural characteristics were necessarily present in fifteenth-century Europe. It was certainly the case, however, that in Italy both the dance masters and the humanist intellectual elite regarded a person's movements as a mirror of their soul. A person's character and disposition were revealed by the way in which they moved, walked, danced, or stood in repose. Francesco Barbaro said in *De re uxoria* (1415–16) that "the character of men's minds is ascertained from facial expression and carriage" (Fermor 1990, 69). Movement should be measured and moderate, since excessive movement, or a total lack of movement, was regarded as unnatural, ugly, and a sign of the vices or defects in a person's character. Moderation in movement signified a virtuous soul, a person who was not dominated by an excess of vice nor skewed by an excessive amount of one particular virtue.[15]

Writing in the late 1430s, the humanist Matteo Palmieri repeated the belief that the nature of a person's soul was revealed by their movements and facial expressions.

> Now I will discuss that which is appropriate to the body, both in its movements and when at rest. . . . One must flee from every movement and whatever condition of the body which deforms it from its natural use and makes it appear ugly to look at. . . . Often it happens that by small signs one recognizes great vices, and these signs give to us a true indication of the state of our soul, as for example, an elevated glance signifies arrogance, a lowered mien signifies humility, while to lean to one side indicates sorrow. . . . In walking one must consider one's age and rank. One must not walk too upright, nor make one's steps slow, hesitant and with such gravity that one appears proud, like those in a procession of ecclesiastical dignitaries. Neither should one spread one's clothes or walk so swollen and rounded that it appears that the street is not capable of holding you. . . . Neither does one wish to walk too quickly, as this signifies fickleness, and demonstrates that one is lacking in constancy, but rather every movement should express an ordered modesty, in which is observed one's proper dignity, having nature always as our teacher and guide.[16]

In his treatise Domenico expressed similar sentiments to Palmieri. He insisted on moderation in the movements of the dance, of keeping to the mean at all times (P*d*, fol. 1v). Given the importance placed on gesture, the carriage of the body, and the appropriate facial expressions, and on having control over one's movements at all times in fifteenth-century Italy it would not be surprising if society invested specific bodily movements with the added significance as a sign of identity.

Costume of the Dancers

A fourth criterion which might have been used to differentiate between dances from different countries is costume, a part of the spectacle that is almost invariably commented upon in the descriptions of important public occasions. In his autobiography Guglielmo discusses the various occasions at court at which he was present as *maestro di ballo*, or as a participant. One of these was a banquet given in Naples by the duke of Calabria in honor of the ambassador of the duke of Burgundy: "And then, in the middle of the meal, the duke of Calabria and Don Federico came in with a group of masked dancers dressed in the French fashion; that is, in fine, new gold cloth fringed with ermine, and a sleeve of embroidered, grey damask so long that it almost reached the ground. There, right in the middle of the banquet they danced French *balli* with Madonna Duchessa [Ippolita Sforza] and with Madonna Lionora."[17] In this context the French costume and dances were a compliment to the guest of honor at the banquet, the ambassador of the Duke of Burgundy, Charles the Bold. The fact that the costume was identified as French indicates that dress was one method by which the Italians differentiated themselves from the French.

Clothing in the fifteenth century was used to express many things: the status or rank of the wearer; their age, occupation, and gender; and the region in which they lived. Clothes, especially the fabric from which they were constructed, were intimately connected with the industry of local regions. For example, around 1500 the doge of Venice, Leonardo Loredan, introduced "ornately designed and richly threaded damask and velvet" as the fabrics for his formal costume. This decision was part of a conscious program to advertise Venice's silk industry, which produced luxury garments coveted by all of Europe (Jardine 1996, 119–20). As Stella Mary Newton comments: "the dress of the doge could mark the exact importance of the occasion and this could apply to not only the annual festivals but also the precise standing (in the eye of the Republic) of any foreign guest or Venetian returning from abroad. When an official welcome was given by the doge, the warmth of that welcome could be noted not only from his words but from the exact quality of the crimson he had put on" (Newton 1988, 29).

It is not surprising, then, that clothing was used as an expression of identity in Renaissance Europe. Ambassadors were often advised to dress according to the style of the court at which they were present so as not to offend the sensitivities (or prejudices) of their hosts. The English and Flemish, for example, had no wish to be identified with either the Germans or the French (Bertelli 1988, 186–87). In *Strong Words: Writing and Social Strain in the Italian Renaissance*, Lauro Martines argues for the importance of clothing as an indicator of the wearer's social position.

> [M]y sense is that everyday dress in Italian Renaissance cities told a more complete story by representing social differences in finer detail, so that people were able at a glance to pick out married women, maidens, and widows, as well as merchants, attorneys (*notai*), shopkeepers, such as apothecaries, and the varieties of craftsmen and workers, not to speak of peasants and rural noblemen. When in a verbal exchange with a stranger, how would you know which pronoun of address to use, if not by the way the other was dressed? You did not use the deferential forms *voi* and *signore* with everyone, for they were not merely polite terms, . . . but rather terms of social identification and of tribute paid to status. (Martines 2001, 173)

If, as Martines argues, the fine details of everyday dress were used by fifteenth-century Italians in their daily interactions with others as a means of discriminating

among persons of different rank and status, then it seems reasonable to assume
that clothing was also used by them as a means of differentiating between the different dance practices which they watched or performed themselves.

Music

A fifth possible way in which people in the fifteenth century might have distinguished between their dances and those of other countries is by the music that
accompanied the dance. If this was the case, then one has to ask what defined
French, German, or Italian music as such. This subject, still being debated among
musicologists, includes aspects such as melodic structure, cadential patterns,
instrumentation and performance style, methods of harmonization, the language
of the text, poetic structure, and the birthplace of the composer. Based on statements by the fifteenth-century Italian dance masters where they mention that
new *balli* were composed to French chansons, yet give no indication that the
new dances were anything other than Italian,[18] it is tempting to conclude that
the possibility that music defined the national identity of the dance which it
accompanied is not a strong one. This is not to say that music itself was not recognized as having national characteristics. Indeed, given the strong Neoplatonic
influences on Renaissance thought, one would expect a fundamental connection between music and "ethos," that is, national or regional identity. Rather, no
national characteristic of the music was central to the identification of the dance
that it accompanied.

Dance as a Sign of Identity

From the preceding discussion it is clear that people in fifteenth-century Europe
did distinguish their dances from those of other regions and countries, and that
they used a variety of different criteria to make these distinctions. In the second
half of this essay I argue that these distinctions had significance, and indeed that
different dance styles contributed to people's sense of identity. Burke has argued
that in the fifteenth to the seventeenth centuries European identities came from
multiple sources—the city in which people lived and worked, the group or class
in society to which they belonged[19]—and that these multiple local identities were
expressed not by language but in "civic rituals, images, and myths" (Burke 1993,
73). The way in which people moved, walked, and danced, and the gestures they
used while involved in all these activities helped to contribute to the total effect of
their rituals and images.

   One of the main genres of dance that was used to express communal identity in Italy was the *moresca. Moresche* were frequently performed during formal
state occasions such as banquets, triumphal entries, jousts and tournaments,

marriage celebrations, and theatrical performances, and were danced by courtiers as well as by "professional" dancers. Thus *moresche* were more than private
entertainments.[20] They were elaborate stage shows with sumptuous costumes and
opportunities for display. The *moresche* were all part of public spectacles where this
dance form was used as an aid in the establishment of the identity of a city—or
state—and also as a means of perpetuating and unifying these two civic bodies.
Such public events were part of the way a city or state negotiated its relationship
with other states and, in the process, realized its own identity. The spectacles in
which the *moresche* occurred were public rituals in which every action, no matter how small, had enormous implications.[21] Every aspect of a visit by foreign
dignitaries was carefully planned and controlled by the host city. Dance, a major
component of public spectacle, would not be ignored by the festival planners.

The way a city's identity was asserted by a *moresca* was through its choreographic aspects, such as danced combat; pantomimic devices depicting agricultural work and exotic characters such as wild men; as well as characteristic
costumes, such as blackened faces and clothes made of silk or other precious
fabrics. Stylized combat, for example, was often a feature or theme of *moresche*.
Agonistic scenes were often portrayed by courtiers and dancing masters on spe-
cially built platforms or stages, either outside in the main piazza or in the *sala
grande* of the ducal palace. Combat was either between Moors and Christians (as
in 1378 and 1389 at the French court in Paris; see Heartz 1960, 334); between
knights and wild men (as happened at the English court in 1515) or even two
groups of knights (Heartz 1960, 338); or between mythological personae such as
centaurs and Hercules, as seen in a *moresca* which formed part of the wedding
celebrations of Ercole d'Este and Eleonora d'Aragona in 1473. Three years later,
also in Rome, a *moresca* performed during a banquet consisted of a fight between
"virtues and vices" (Cruciani 1983, 164 and 166). At the sumptuous and extravagant wedding banquet in Pesaro in 1475 there was a *moresca* where a wild man,
"hairy and horrid," fought with a lion, that is, with a man dressed in the skin of a
lion (De Marinis 1946, 34).

Another common theme of the *moresca* was a depiction of rural activities, particularly in the later fifteenth century when the *moresca* became almost
synonymous with the *intermedio*. For example, in the marriage festivities of
Costanzo Sforza and Camilla d'Aragona, held in Pesaro in 1475, beautifully
dressed and adorned young men, carrying diverse agricultural implements of
gold and silver, enacted the pursuits of sowing (by scattering flowers from gilded
baskets) and harvesting the grain in time with the music (De Marinis 1946, 38).
In all the descriptions of rural *moresche*, the costumes of the dancers are sumptuous and the agricultural implements they carry are made (or gilded) with gold
or silver.

Part of the purpose of these spectacles was the impact they made on foreign visitors. As Trexler has argued, the public nature of the rituals was a way to consolidate and enhance the "image" or "honor" of the state. One way of defining who one is, is to state what one is not. Thus the *feste* and the *moresche* in particular were "danced dramas" in the sense that they represented society dramatically defining who it was before the eyes of foreigners: their civilized identity was demonstrated by showing scenes of both civilization and barbarism. The scenes of the wild men, savages, or barbarians in the *moresche* were one way of declaring: "This is what we are not."[22] This type of statement was not new, as it was part of the tradition inherited from the ancient Greeks (Gillies 1994, 8–9). For the spectators and participants at festivals, the wild men (the "other") would be "exotic," that is, "outlandish, barbarous, strange and uncouth" (Gillies 1994, 25). Part of the Renaissance sense of the "exotic" was blackness.[23] Thus the blackened faces and hands of the *moresca* dancers could be seen as representing the barbarian, the person who exists outside the limits of society.

The pantomimes of agricultural society were also a way of expressing the civilized identity of the participants. Today we think of urban and rural lifestyles as being quite distinct, with the stereotypical image of the city as more sophisticated and therefore more "civilized." But in the Renaissance agriculture was seen as the oldest of all the civilized arts, and therefore the key to civilization itself (Gillies 1994, 180). The country was seen as civilized because it was the place where one retired for reflection and philosophical thought, and to escape the polluting influences of the city, a place primarily devoted to commerce. The rural world was seen as embodying serenity and order, a place full of "pleasure, wholesomeness, loveliness and grace" (Puppi 1991, 47); while the urban life was viewed as essentially disordered and artificial, a place of confusion, intrigue, and conflict—an attitude inherited from the ancient Roman tradition. Therefore, when the courtiers mimed the labors of the field in their silken garments and golden mattocks, they were creating a scene which implied that even though the center of their political organization was urban, their society was truly civilized because it was based on agriculture. They were identifying not with the reality of the average farm laborer's daily grind of poverty but with agriculture as civilization.

Every human civilization confronts the basic uncertainty of existence and has to construct a social order to mitigate against this uncertainty. One way of doing this is to construct "symbolic boundaries of personal and collective identity" (Eisenstadt 1992, 68). Through rituals the boundaries of personal and collective identity are established and reinforced by an expression of group identity. Thus rituals "demarcate, emphasize, affirm [and] solemnize . . . social relationships" (Lewis 1988, 136). Even in our society today celebrations are concerned with defining the group. For example, the decision concerning which members of the family to invite to a wedding is a decision about defining who is considered a member of the family group and who is not. The rituals, or spectacles, of the various Italian city-states and courts, of which the *moresca* was a part, can also be seen in this way. The fact that dance was used as an expression of identity may be one of the reasons why in Italy there was more interest in Italians choreographing and performing their own dances than in performing dances from other countries. Certainly in fifteenth-century Italy there does not seem to have been a demand from the social elite for choreographies by non-Italians. This is in contrast to their demand for foreign, especially northern European, musical compositions. Italian dance manuals do not have sections of "foreign" choreographies in them, yet we know that the Italian dance masters were well aware of the French dance style since, as we have seen, they imitated it. Italian dance masters traveled widely throughout Italy, yet so far there are no records of their working outside the country. There are also no letters from Italian rulers to their counterparts at northern courts asking to borrow their dance masters for an important celebration. It seems that on important state occasions the Italian social elite wanted to perform Italian choreographies.

On the other hand, composers, singers, and musicians traveled and worked throughout Europe in the fifteenth century. The composers whose work survives in Italian manuscript collections are mostly foreign—that is, English, Franco-Flemish, and Spanish. Thus the collections of music that were copied at the Italian courts, as opposed to the collections of dances, contain works from composers of different nationalities writing in different styles. In the fourteenth century the north Italian musical manuscript collections contain equal numbers of French and Italian songs; of the approximately six hundred Italian songs, all except two are by Italian composers (Fallows 1996b, 432). After 1415 the situation changes, as from 1415 to 1440 four hundred and fifty French polyphonic songs are found in the manuscript collections, but less than forty Italian polyphonic songs. Furthermore, "virtually no indigenous Italian composers can be named between about 1430 and 1480" (Fallows 1996b, 433).

Obviously one of the reasons for the lack of documentation of Italian composers during this fifty-year period was the popularity and success of improvisatory practices by Italian musicians. But my point here is that this is in contrast to the dance practice at exactly the same time—a practice which also involved improvisatory genres, but yet was recorded in manuscript collections with names of the choreographers included. Thus this same period, 1430 to 1480, saw the rise and flowering of the Italian dance masters, men who emerged from the shadow of anonymity which still engulfed their northern counterparts, and who left practical descriptions of over three hundred dances.

Notes

1. It is interesting to note that the non-Italian dance practices mentioned by Guglielmo in his treatise belong to the same groups of non-Italian native speakers who had significant communities in Italy in the fifteenth century. According to Peter Burke (1993, 77), these groups "affirmed their separate cultural identity by speaking languages other than Italian."

2. "Et piu che habiando in voi tal pruova & experienza potreti perfettamente danzare Todescho, grecho, schiavo et moresco & di qual si vuole altra natione & comporre anche balli" (P*g*, fol. 22r).

3. Padovan is quoting from Solmi 1904, 86.

4. Trexler 1991, 426. Trexler cites a nineteenth-century German source by B. Buser (1879, 347). The letter in question is found in Paris, Bibliothèque Nationale de France, MS fonds it. 1588, fol. 226r, and is translated in the collection edited by Stefano Ugo Baldassarri and Arielle Saiber (2000, 322–24). In this translation the authors describe the dancing as "Everyone danced fine quadrilles in the Florentine manner" (324).

5. For a more detailed discussion of the choreographic structure of the *basse danse*, see Wilson 1983 and 1984–85; Wilson 2008; Wilson and Daniels, unpublished manuscript; Heartz 1958–63. The analysis has been simplified for the purposes of this essay, as a full discussion is beyond its scope.

6. The other *bassadanza*, "Borges," does not follow the structure of a French *basse danse* so exactly, as it lacks the opening *reverence* and *branle* steps, and the three *riprese* are replaced with three *sempi*, not with *riprese françese*. It does, however, still follow the French choreographic structure as it consists of two *mesures*: *grande parfaite* and *petite imparfaite*.

7. At present the fifteenth-century English dance practice is represented by the twenty-six choreographies, thirteen dance tunes, and a list of ninety-one dance titles found in the papers of the Gresley family of South Derbyshire. For a transcription of this material, see Fallows 1996a; and for an analysis and evaluations of these dances, see Nevile 1998, Nevile 1999, and Wilson 1999.

8. The two exceptions to this flexibility in step sequences are the position of the term *trace*, and the steps *trett* and *retrett*. In the margin, along with the name of each dance, there are manuscript addenda: *trace, with trace,* or *doubll trace*. Sixteen dances begin with a *trace*, and seven with a *doubll trace*. Three dances do not have these marginal addenda but two of them—*Leben disinens* and *Aras*—still commence their choreographic descriptions with the phrase "After the end of the trace" (Gresley, 63 and 64). The other exception is the step *trett*, which forms a sequence with the step *retrett*. The step *trett* occurs eighty-two times in seventeen dances, and in seventy-six of those eighty-two occurrences it is followed by the step *retrett*. No other step in these dances has anything like this regular association with another step.

9. One could hypothesize that the double step was common in English dances, but for some reason in the Gresley dances it is not specifically mentioned by name and is hidden in phrases such as "forth," "go forth," "bak" etc. If one counted all these cases, then the number of doubles would increase dramatically, as twenty-two dances have phrases such as "forth" or "bak" in their choreographic descriptions. The situation is more complicated, however, as many of the occurrences of "forth," "bak," etc., are prefaced by the number three. Given the overwhelmingly triple grouping of singles mentioned above, one has to take into consideration that on these occasions the phrase "3 forth" might be shorthand for "3 singlis." Therefore, when one excludes the occurrence of the phrases "3 forth" and "3 bak" from one's

calculations, one finds that in just over half the dances the double step is mentioned. This figure of 50 percent, while greater than the 15 percent of dances which specifically mention a double step, is still far below the 100 percent occurrence rate of the double step in the Italian and French practices.

10. The one exception to this "rule" that singles only occur in pairs is the "Basse dance de Bourgogne," one of seven dances found on a flyleaf of a copy of the *Geste des nobles francois* belonging to Jean d'Orléans, Comte d'Angoulême (ca. 1445). Significantly, in this dance the singles appear in groups of three (Wilson 1984–85, 5).

11. The Salisbury collection has one dance with a sequence containing two doubles, and another dance with two occurrences of a four double sequence. Wilson feels that the sequences of paired doubles are so uncommon in the *basse dance* repertory that to presume they are errors is "extremely improbable" (Wilson 1984–85, 7).

12. This figure applies to the *doppi* in the body of the *balli* choreographies only. For the opening sequence the *doppi* range in an even manner from sequences of one to sixteen steps.

13. *Rakis* = 11/26 (42 percent): *Trett* = 17/26 (65 percent): *Retrett* = 20/26 (77 percent): *Flowerdelice* = 10/26 (38 percent).

14. One example is from P*a*, fol. 31r–v. A discussion continues among dance scholars of exactly what was meant by the dance masters in the passages where they discuss the necessary gestures and movements of the dancer's body; see Fermor 1990, Franko 1986, Nevile 1991, Pontremoli 1990, and Sparti 1985.

15. For a detailed discussion of fifteenth-century Italian dance masters' views on moderation in dance movements, see Nevile 2004, 75–103.

16. Palmieri 1982, 95–97: "Seguita dire quello che ne' movimenti e riposi del corpo si convenga. . . . Ogni moto e qualunque stato del corpo, il quale disforma dal naturale uso e pare a vedere brutto si de' fuggire. . . . Spesso adviene che per piccoli cenni si consoce maximi vitii e dàssi inditii veri di quello sente l'animo nostro, come per elevato guatare si significa arrogantia; pel dimesso, humilità, per restrignersi in su il lato, dolore. . . . In nello andare si de'considerare l'età il grado: non andare intero, né muovere i passi tardi, rari e con tanta gravità che si paia pomposo et simile alle processioni delle degnità sacerdotali; non si de' e'spandere i vestimenti et andare gonfiato e tondo, siché apaia non capere per la via. . . . Non vuole però anche l'andare essere si presto significhi leggereza, et dimonstri non essere in ella persona constanzia, ma ogni movimento si referisca a una ordinata vercundia, in nella quale s'osservi la propria degnit, avendo sempre la natura per nostra maestra e guida."

17. P*a*, fol. 79v: "Et poy in meçço del pasto venne el ducha de Calabbria & don Federicho con una mommaria de maschare vestite a la francese cioe de panno doro fino dala peçça con una balça de armelliny. Et una manicha era de damaschino berectino longha squase fino interra arachamata & li loro facti bally francesi con madonna duchessa & con madonna lionora in meçço del pasto propio." (I wish to thank Giovanni Carsaniga for his advice on the translation of this passage.)

18. P*d*, fol. 7r. Domenico states that he composed all the tunes for the dances he records—except for "La fia guielmina," which is a French ballata. It also seems reasonable to assume that the *ballo* "Franco cuore gentile" (for which no music exists in the dance treatises) would have been danced to the music of Dufay's chanson *Franc cueur gentil*. In spite of their accompanying French music these two dances are not singled out as *françese* in the dance treatises: their choreographies do not reveal any affinities with the French style, nor are they in any way different from all the other *balli* as they conform to the basic structural pattern of that Italian genre.

19. Burke says that people constructed their identity from belonging to the city in which they lived and worked, belonging to one class or another in society, and belonging to a larger territorial grouping—to one country or another. For example, city-dwelling Italians divided society into three groups (or classes): there were "the rich, or more exactly the 'fat', the *popolo grasso*; the 'little people', or *popolo minuto*; and those in the middle, the *mediocri*" (Burke 1993, 75). In some Italian cities, such as Florence, the populace also had loyalty to specific areas within the city in which they lived (Burke 1993, 73).

20. For descriptions of *moresche* in fifteenth-century Italy, see Pontremoli and La Rocca 1987, 219–31. For a discussion of *moresche* and their significance in early sixteenth-century Roman carnival celebrations, see Cummings 2007, 289–341.

21. Richard Trexler has argued that every step in the visit by a foreign prince or ambassador to Florence was very carefully choreographed. For example, at which point would the visiting party be met? If outside the city, how far outside the city; if inside the city, would it be at the entry gate, or at the main piazza? At which location would the visitor dismount from his horse on the *Loggia dei Lanzi*? What would be the number and social standing of the citizens who would meet the foreign visitor? All these questions, and many more, were carefully debated, as each of them had precise nuances of meaning for the Florentine citizens and the visiting party (Trexler 1991, 306–18).

22. "[W]hen men were uncertain as to the precise quality of their sensed humanity, they appealed to the concept of wildness to designate an area of subhumanity that was characterized by everything they hoped they were not" (White 1978, 152).

23. "[W]ildness is identified with the wandering life of the hunter (as against the stable life of the shepherd and farmer), the desert (which is the Wild Man's habitat), linguistic confusion (which is the Wild Man's as well as the barbarian's principal attribute), sin, and physical aberration in both color (blackness) and size" (White 1978, 162).

References

Manuscripts Cited

Gresley   Gresley of Drakelow papers. Derbyshire Record Office, D77 box 38, pp. 51–79.

Pa   Guglielmo Ebreo da Pesaro. *Domini Iohannis Ambrosii pisauriensis de pratica seu arte tripudii vulgare opusculum*. Paris, Bibliothèque nationale de France, MS fonds it. 476.

Pd   Domenico da Piacenza. *De arte saltandj & choreas ducendj: De la arte di ballare et danzare*. Paris, Bibliothèque nationale de France, MS fonds it. 972.

Pg   Guglielmo Ebreo da Pesaro. *Guilielmi Hebraei pisauriensis de pratica seu arte tripudii vulgare opusculum*. Paris, Bibliothèque nationale de France, MS fonds it. 973.

NY   Guglielmo Ebreo da Pesaro. *Ghuglielmi ebrei pisauriensis de praticha seu arte tripudi vulghare opusculum*. New York, New York Public Library, Dance Collection, *MGZMB-Res. 72-254.

Secondary Sources

Baldassarri, Stefano Ugo, and Arielle Saiber, eds. 2000. *Images of Quattrocento Florence: Selected Writings in Literature, History, and Art*. New Haven: Yale University Press.

Bertelli, Sergio, Franco Cardini, and Elvira Garbero Zorzi. 1986. *The Courts of the Italian Renaissance.* Translated by Mary Fitton and Geoffrey Culverwell. New York: Facts on File Publications.

Bulwer, John. (1644) 1974. *Chirologia: Or the Naturall Language of the Hand and Chironomia; or the Art of Manual Rhetoric.* Edited by James W. Cleary. London. Reprint, Carbondale: Southern Illinois University Press.

Burke, Peter. 1991. "The Language of Gesture in Early Modern Italy." In *A Cultural History of Gesture*, edited by Jan Bremmer and Herman Roodenburg, 71–83. Cambridge: Polity Press.

———. 1993. *The Art of Conversation.* Cambridge: Polity Press.

Buser, B. 1879. *Die Beziehungen der Mediceer zu Frankreich: Während der Jahre 1434–1490, in ihrem Zusammenhang mit den allgemeinen Verhältnissen Italiens.* Leipzip: Duncker & Humblot.

Cruciani, Fabrizio. 1983. *Teatro nel Rinascimento: Roma, 1450–1550.* Rome: Bulzoni.

Cummings, Anthony M. 2007. "Leo X and Roman Carnival (1521)." *Studia musicali* 36: 289–341.

de Marinis, Tammaro, ed. 1946. *Le nozze di Costanzo Sforza e Camilla d'Aragona celebrate a Pesaro nel maggio 1475.* Florence: Vallecchi.

Eisenstadt, S. N. 1992. "The Order-Maintaining and Order-Transforming Dimensions of Culture." In *Theory of Culture*, edited by Richard Münch and Neil J. Smelser, 64–87. Berkeley: University of California Press.

Fallows, David. 1996a. "The Gresley Dance Collection, *c.* 1500." *RMA Research Chronicle* 29: 1–20.

———. 1996b. "French as a Courtly Language in Fifteenth-Century Italy: The Musical Evidence." In *Songs and Musicians in the Fifteenth Century*, 429–41. Aldershot: Variorum.

Fermor, Sharon. 1990. "Studies in the Depiction of the Moving Figure in Italian Renaissance Art, Art Criticism and Dance Theory." PhD diss., Warburg Institute, University of London.

Franko, Mark. 1986. *The Dancing Body in Renaissance Choreography (c. 1416–1589).* Birmingham, AL: Summa Publications.

Gillies, John. 1994. *Shakespeare and the Geography of Difference.* Cambridge: Cambridge University Press.

Guglielmo Ebreo da Pesaro. 1993. *De practica seu arte tripudii: On the Practice or Art of Dancing.* Edited and translated by Barbara Sparti. Oxford: Clarendon Press.

Heartz, Daniel. 1958–63. "The Basse Dance: Its Evolution circa 1450–1550." *Annales musicologiques* 6: 287–340.

———. 1960. "Un Divertissement de Palais pour Charles Quint à Binche." In *Les Fêtes de la Renaissance*, edited by Jean Jacquot, 2:329–42. Paris: Centre National de la Recherche Scientifique.

Jardine, Lisa. 1996. *Worldly Goods: A New History of the Renaissance.* London: Macmillan.

Lewis, Ioan Myrddin. 1988. *Social Anthropology in Perspective: The Relevance of Social Anthropology.* 2nd ed. Cambridge: Cambridge University Press.

Martines, Lauro. 2001. *Strong Words: Writing and Social Strain in the Italian Renaissance.* Baltimore: Johns Hopkins University Press.

Nevile, Jennifer. 1991. "'Certain Sweet Movements': The Development of the Concept of Grace in 15th-Century Italian Dance and Painting." *Dance Research* 9, no. 1: 3–12.

———. 1998. "Dance in Early Tudor England: An Italian Connection?" *Early Music* 26: 230–44.

———. 1999. "Dance Steps and Music in the Gresley Manuscript." *Historical Dance* 3, no. 6: 2–19.

———. 2004. *The Eloquent Body: Dance and Humanist Culture in Fifteenth-Century Italy.* Bloomington: Indiana University Press.

Newton, Stella Mary. 1988. *The Dress of the Venetians, 1495–1525.* Aldershot: Scolar Press.

Padovan, Maurizio. 1985. "Da Dante a Leonardo: La danza italiana attraverso le fonti storiche." *La Danza italiana* 3: 5–37.

Palmieri, Matteo. 1982. *Vita civile.* Edited by Gino Belloni. Florence: Sansoni.

Pontremoli, Alessandro. 1990. "Estetica dell'ondeggiare ed estetica dell'aeroso: Da Domenico a Guglielmo, evoluzione di uno stile coreutico." In *Guglielmo Ebreo da Pesaro e la danza nelle corti italiane del xv secolo*, edited by Maurizio Padovan, 159–68. Pisa: Pacini.

Pontremoli, Alessandro, and Patrizia La Rocca. 1987. *Il ballare lombardo: Teoria e prassi coreutica nella festa di corte del XV secolo.* Milan: Vita e Pensiero.

Puppi, Lionello. 1991. "Nature and Artifice in the Sixteenth-Century Italian Garden." In *The History of Garden Design: The Western Tradition from the Renaissance to the Present Day*, edited by Monique Mosser and Georges Teyssot, 47–58. London: Thames and Hudson.

Solmi, E. 1904. "La festa del Paradiso di Leonardo da Vinci e Bernardo Bellincione." *Archivio storico lombardo* 1.

Sparti, Barbara. 1985. "Stile, espressione e senso treatrale nelle danze italiane del' 400." *La Danza italiana* 3: 39–53.

———, ed. and trans. 1993. Introduction to *De practica seu arte tripudii: On the Practice or Art of Dancing*, by Guglielmo Ebreo da Pesaro, 3–72. Oxford: Clarendon Press.

Toft, Robert. 1993. *Tune thy Musicke to thy Hart: The Art of Eloquent Singing in England 1597–1622.* Toronto: University of Toronto Press.

Trexler, Richard C. 1991. *Public Life in Renaissance Florence.* Ithaca, NY: Cornell University Press.

White, Hayden. 1978. *Tropics of Discourse: Essays in Cultural Criticism.* Baltimore: Johns Hopkins University Press.

Wilson, David R. 1983. "Theory and Practice in 15th-Century French Basse Danse." *Historical Dance* 2, no. 3:1–2.

———. 1984–85. "The Development of the French Basse Danse." *Historical Dance* 2, no. 4: 5–12.

———. 1999. "Performing Gresley Dances: The View from the Floor." *Historical Dance* 3, no. 6:20–22.

———. 2008. "The *Basse Dance c.* 1445–*c.* 1545." In *Dance, Spectacle, and the Body Politick, 1250–1750*, edited by Jennifer Nevile, 166–81. Bloomington: Indiana University Press.

Wilson, David R., and Véronique Daniels. "The Basse Dance Handbook." Unpublished manuscript.

Zambotti, Bernardino. 1928. *Diario ferrarese dall'anno 1476 sino al 1504.* Edited by Giuseppe Pardi. In vol. 24, pt. 7 of *Rerum italicarum scriptores*, ed. Lodovico Antonio Muratori, rev. Giosue Carducci and Vittorio Fiorini, 1–501. Bologna: N. Zanichelli.

Reevaluating the Repertory

Acoustics, Liturgy, and Architecture
in Medieval English Cathedrals

William Peter Mahrt

The architecture of a medieval cathedral formed an impressive site for the liturgy and thus for music, since the liturgy was entirely sung.[1] The building was structured to provide a significant number of differentiated spaces (see figure 1) in which different liturgical actions took place, particularly the choir (6) and presbyterium (4), nave (11) and side aisles (10), lady chapel (1) and other side chapels (3, 5, 8, & 9), and cloister (12) with chapter house (13). These spaces were structured to suit the liturgical actions that took place within them, and certain aspects of the architecture are inexplicable without reference to the requirements which the liturgy made upon the architecture.[2]

It is the concrete elements of the floor plan that constitute the point of intersection between liturgy and architecture, and they must be distinguished from the superstructure of the building, including the elevation (the arcades, triforium, and clerestory), as well as the crossing. In my view, the latter elements symbolize aspects of the heavenly liturgy and are only indirectly related to those of the floor plan. The crossing is a good example: the cruciform shape of the building finds its epitome in the point where the nave and the transepts intersect; there is often a lantern tower there with an intricate geometric design on its ceiling. I speculate that the geometric design of this highest point in the building depicts the geometry of the heavens beyond. There is, curiously, no single way in which the floor plan relates to this crossing. In secular cathedrals the choir screen, and thus all of the choir, is most often at the eastern boundary of the crossing; but in monastic cathedrals the choir more frequently extends farther west into the nave, and the crossing stands over the choir, as, for example, at Winchester.

An interesting example of the variability of this interrelation is Ely. In the Norman cathedral, the choir extended back into the nave. In the fourteenth century the unique and justly famous lantern over the crossing was constructed, but below it remained quite a clutter of choir stalls and all that pertained to them. It was only in 1771 that the choir was moved eastward beyond the crossing,[3] leaving

Figure 1. Salisbury Cathedral Floor Plan.

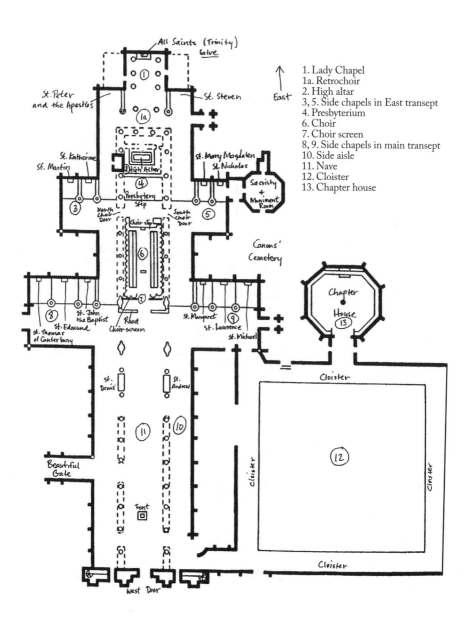

1. Lady Chapel
1a. Retrochoir
2. High altar
3, 5. Side chapels in East transept
4. Presbyterium
6. Choir
7. Choir screen
8, 9. Side chapels in main transept
10. Side aisle
11. Nave
12. Cloister
13. Chapter house

the impressive open space beneath the lantern and giving the beauty and symbolism of the crossing priority over the liturgically functional aspect of the placement of the choir, a very long time after it had ceased to be a *monastic* choir.

While such things as the arrangement of the elements of the floor plan and their division by screens are evident spatial articulations that relate to liturgical function, another differentiation of liturgical space, which receives less attention from architectural and liturgical historians but is crucial to the music sung in them, is the acoustics of these spaces. My purpose here is to address the way in which acoustics differ from space to space within an English Gothic cathedral and how these differences may relate to the way the space met the demands of the liturgy and its music, even how they may have related to the repertory of polyphonic music sung in them. This study is an outgrowth of trips taken with singers through the cathedrals of southern England, centered at Salisbury, study days on which the spaces of various cathedrals and abbey churches were explored acoustically. My principal point of departure is the observation of remarkable acoustical differences between the spaces. I will address the spaces themselves and their liturgical functions, and then turn to their acoustics.

But first, for England, a particular distinction must be emphasized between secular and monastic cathedrals. A secular cathedral had chapters of canons, whose function was the conduct of the divine offices; the chapter was headed by a dean, who was supported by three other principal officers: the precentor, chancellor, and treasurer. Individual canons could hold property, and their income came from endowments of church property; in some cases they were quite well-to-do. These cathedrals included York, Lincoln, Salisbury, St. Paul's, Hereford, Wells, Chichester, Exeter, and Lichfield (Harrison 1963, 3). In monastic cathedrals the function of the chapter was carried by a community of monks, with the bishop of the diocese functioning as abbot of the community, while the prior exercised the most important authority within the community. The monastic cathedrals included Canterbury, Winchester, Durham, Norwich, Coventry, Bath, Worcester, Ely (Benedictine), and Carlisle (Augustinian) (Harrison 1963, 3). From the distinction between secular and monastic cathedrals flowed a few important architectural differences, some of which depended upon the enclosure of the community from outside attendance at services, the details of which I give below.

The liturgical focal point of the cathedral was the high altar facing east (2), the traditional direction of prayer; it was, together with its surrounding spaces—the presbyterium immediately before it (4) and the choir to the west of it (6)—bounded by a screen which surrounded these spaces as a unit and emphasized their unity and their being set apart from the larger spaces of the building, an *ecclesiola in ecclesia*.[4] In the presbyterium and at the altar, the ministers conducted the ceremonies of the liturgy, particularly of the Mass. In the choir stalls the choir

sang their part of the principal services of the day, seated in facing stalls and singing antiphonally from side to side. One of the most interesting features of this
area is the presence of the choir screen at the west end (7). On the one hand, the
choir screen divided the choir space from the nave and emphasized its particular
functionality and sacrality; on the other hand, it seems to a modern observer to
have created an undesirable separation from the congregation in the nave.

What congregation? Theoretically, the cathedral was the location of the
liturgy of the cathedral clergy, and no general provision was made for the laity.
They had parish churches where they attended services; sometimes a space within
the cathedral itself was set aside for their services. If they did attend the cathedral's
own services, it may have been at ancillary altars or in the lady chapel, or they may
even have come into the presbyterium (as they do today) or observed the services
from the choir aisles. Indeed, the place of the laity must have varied considerably from cathedral to cathedral. In monastic cathedrals they were most likely
not admitted to the services at all; recall that the present-day cathedral at Bury
St. Edmunds was a splendid parish church in the Middle Ages, on the grounds of
the monastery, while the much larger monastery church, now in ruins, stood just
behind it. On the other hand, in secular cathedrals such as Salisbury, the laity may
have been given much greater access to cathedral services: at Salisbury a rubric
for the asperges, the sprinkling with water just before the Sunday Mass, provided
that once the clergy had been sprinkled, the laity standing in the presbyterium
should also then be sprinkled ("Post aspersionem clericorum laicos in presbyterio
hinc stantes aspergat," Henderson [1882] 1969, 4.) Likewise, the Masses at side
altars and chantries were to be scheduled in succession so that in the course of the
morning a Mass was being said at any time, and laity who came into the cathedral
in the hope of attending a Mass would be able to do so.

Choir screens in parish churches were often constructed differently, being
"pierced"; that is, while they still functioned to mark a clear delineation of the
space between the nave and the choir, they were a kind of grillwork through which
the congregation in the nave could easily see the proceedings in choir and presby-
tery. Nineteenth-century restorations of choir screens in cathedrals were often of
this grillwork sort, but were replacements of stone choir screens, as at Salisbury,
presumably as a response in the structure to the changed role of the congregation.

The lady chapel was the location of the Lady Mass, celebrated daily in the
Sarum rite. In the secular cathedrals this chapel was usually in the easternmost
position, east of the high altar; it was also usually a separate space, with lower ceilings and separated from the high altar by a retrochoir, an ample area that often
contained the shrine of the principal saint of the locality. It is interesting that in
some monastic cathedrals and abbeys the lady chapels were to the side or at the
back of the building: for example, at Glastonbury and at Durham at the west end,

at Ely and Bristol off the north transept, at Canterbury in the crypt, and at Rochester in the south aisle. (At Norwich, Winchester, Gloucester, and Worcester they were in the easternmost position, as in secular cathedrals.) These non-easternmost positions may well have reflected a reluctance to admit the laity beyond the choir area, since it was a part of monastic enclosure; conversely, they attest to the often-stated desire to provide for the laity's attendance at the Lady Mass. When the dedication of the entire cathedral was to the Blessed Virgin, as at Salisbury, then at least liturgical propriety dictated that the easternmost chapel have a dedication other than to Mary: at Salisbury, it was to the Trinity and All Saints; still, descriptions of this chapel also include the designation "Salve," the first word of the introit of the most widely sung Lady Masses, indicating that it did function normally as a lady chapel.[5]

Numerous side chapels, all facing east, were the location of a Mass each day; the medieval protocol was that only one Mass be said at each altar in a day. These chapels were also the goal of a procession once in the year, usually after vespers on the eve of the day of the saint to whom the altar was dedicated.

Processions were an important part of the medieval liturgy, and before Mass every Sunday, a procession was made in the Sarum rite; on ordinary Sundays it went around the altar, down the North aisle, around the baptistery, and then up the center of the nave, through the choir screen door, and into the choir. The nave was thus the location of an important part of the Sunday observance; scholars have sometimes speculated that this is the principal function of the nave. In the English cathedrals, length is the important dimension (in contrast to the French, where height is what is cultivated). The processional movement from west to east, from less sacred to more sacred, into the choir through an imposing portal, the choir screen door, is certainly a very significant aspect of the medieval English liturgy, and an important means of defining, observing, and celebrating the Gothic sense of hierarchically organized sacred spaces.

If the feast day were a very important one, the procession went through the cloister and outside and around the church. The cloister is sometimes identified principally with monastic churches, and is where the monks study. In the face of this, some scholars contend that the cloister is a nonfunctional item in secular cathedrals. But, in most English cathedrals, the cloister forms a kind of forecourt to the chapter house, which stands to the east of the cloister and is most often placed symmetrically in relation to it. The commemoration of this sacred space by processions on the most important days may imply the importance of the cathedral chapter in relation to the liturgy celebrated.

The chapter house itself is a very important part of the architecture, a beautiful building with impressive foyers and entryways. What takes place there, however, is usually not the formal liturgy but chapter business. On only one day in the

Sarum rite does the chapter house play a role in the liturgy—Holy Thursday, for the washing of the feet. This ceremony consists of the bishop or dean washing the feet of members of the chapter, after which food and drink is had; it is a kind of family affair for the chapter, expressed by its unique location in the chapter house.

Just as these architectural spaces are differentiated according to their function, so the acoustics of these spaces also differ; it is my point here that these differences relate in various ways to the music that was sung in the spaces, and to its liturgical function.

The most remarkable acoustic in these buildings is that of the lady chapels. In my observation, it is the most perfect environment for the singing of a small ensemble. If you sing here a piece of fourteenth-century polyphony in three parts, one singer to a part, you wonder why it ever occurred to anyone to write in four parts. These spaces have a unique balance between fullness and clarity. Modern acoustic spaces are either full and resonant at the expense of clarity (as at Grace Cathedral in San Francisco or the Stanford Memorial Church), so singers love them but audiences complain that they cannot discern the words; or they have an almost clinical clarity (such as Campbell Auditorium at Stanford, a very dry acoustic about which the consulting acoustician said that was exactly what he wanted), where audiences do not object to them but singers complain that they cannot hear themselves well in them. The lady chapels—for example, at Salisbury, Wells, Chichester, Exeter, and many others—are characterized by a kind of focus that returns a good bit of the sound back to its source, allowing the singer to hear well, giving a sense of fullness, but not creating the diverse reverberation that works against clarity. This focus is the result of several factors: First, they are not very large, and the shape is somewhat enclosed; this cultivates both a full resonance and limits over-reverberation. Second, the rib-vaulting in the ceilings must play a role in the returning the sound back to the source. Tim Tatton-Brown, consulting archeologist for Salisbury Cathedral, has proposed that it is the nearly paraboloid shape of the ceilings which contributes to this focus. While the angle of most of them is a bit too steep for that to be a simple explanation, it must be a contributing factor. Curiously, in the very active musical life of these cathedrals today, the lady chapels are not very often used for music: they are most often the location of spoken services.

The acoustic of the choir contrasts strikingly with that of the lady chapel, the choir being the location of most of the musical liturgy, both in the Middle Ages and today. The requirement for resonance was not so critical there, since the principal music was plainsong and a fair number of singers participated. In the choir stalls one can observe a reinforcement of the lower voices and the suppression of the upper voices. If you sing from the bottom of the bass clef upwards, you hear a full resonance, which begins to thin out about middle C and becomes much less resonant by G or A above that. This can be observed both in churches which retain their medieval choir screens and in those from which they have been removed. It took me a while to realize what was going on, because I was quite unprepared for the phenomenon. I have not yet analyzed the components of this peculiar acoustic or its history, but Tim Tatton-Brown speculates that the wooden frames upon which the choir stalls rest serve some acoustic function. I can only point to the evident institutional advantage of such an acoustic: it requires the cultivation of quite a number of children's voices in relation to the number of adult men. In recent usage at Salisbury there have been eighteen children—boys or girls sing on alternate days—and they sing only the soprano part; there are six men, two each singing alto, tenor, and bass. I would propose a distinct advantage of having to cultivate that many children's voices: this justifies a critical mass for a choir school, and it educates a significant number of future musicians and clergy in a superb musical tradition; conversely, the expense of paying adult singers is minimized.

There is an additional observation to be made about the acoustic of the choir: observers in the nave noticed quite a difference between the places where there was a solid choir screen and those in which the choir was open to the nave. It was an unexpected result: they could hear the choir better in the places where there was a choir screen. Perhaps the choir screen helps to focus the sound of the choir upwards to the vaulting, which then reflects it into the nave

The acoustic of the nave has a very interesting liturgical effect. If the function of the nave is principally for processions, then the aspect of motion through space is an important feature, and the shift of acoustic through the nave underscores the progress of that procession. As one processes down the side aisle, there is just a bit of enclosure of the space that reflects the sound back from the aisle vaulting, but there is also a more remote reverberation which returns from the nave itself; upon moving into the nave, the change in sound is notable: it opens up, being the resonance of the largest space in the entire building, and is slightly more focused, since the spaces around the procession are laterally symmetrical. Upon reaching the choir screen, the procession moves through the choir screen door and enters the choir; at this point the change of acoustic is remarkable—from the large open space of the nave to the more concentrated sound of the choir. The motion into the space that is the object of the procession is reinforced by acoustic shift that increases the sound.

A more remarkable contrast can be heard between the acoustic of the nave and that of the cloister. Generally, the cloisters are quite low and enclosed, and the reverberation there is thrilling to singers; it gives no hint, however of the change that awaits them when they move into the nave from the cloister, again, an opening up of the sound that is the exact acoustical result of the passage from a low enclosed space to the high and grand space of the nave. It is true that the direct passage from cloister into nave occurs infrequently in the Sarum processions; more frequently, the procession moves out of the cloister into the open air and then into the nave through the west portal. Even there, the succession of widely differing acoustics reinforces the sense of progress in the procession.

There is an interesting counterexample of functional musical acoustics. When we first approached the authorities at Wells to make such experiments, they were enthusiastic and suggested we should not overlook the chapter house, since they hold their concerts there. I thought this strange, for there was very little sung historically in the chapter house, but we tried it anyway. It was awful! There was plenty of reverberation, but rather little clarity; the sound swirled around the space in a somewhat uncontrolled fashion. It must be conceded that in a concert this effect is ameliorated somewhat by seating an audience throughout the floor of the building, but that was never done in the Middle Ages. Instead, the members of the chapter sat in the seats at the edge of the space. Moreover, the proper use of the space must have been for speech. We thus experimented with speech, with another interesting result. If you raised your voice and spoke in a rhetorical fashion, you could be heard clearly from any point around the periphery of the room; if you spoke in a lower voice, however, your voice did not carry at all—a perfect solution for a meeting of a chapter, in which a smaller group of canons might want to confer without being heard and then address the whole body and be heard.

This is a report in progress; there is much more to study and observe and to begin to measure. What emerges quite clearly is that the spaces differ remarkably, and many of these differences serve important liturgical purposes. How much of this was deliberate, and at what stage in its history it was controlled deliberately, remains to be studied. Suffice it to say, it cannot have all been an accident.

Notes

1. The best account of this remains Harrison 1963; also valuable for the matters at hand is Harper 1991, especially chap. 2, "Liturgy and the Medieval Church," 24–42, and chap. 8, "Processions and Other Liturgical Observances," 127–38; the details of the processions of the Sarum rite are best studied in Frere (1898–1901) 1969; the processions are given extensive treatment in Bailey 1971; for the architecture of Salisbury Cathedral, see Cocke and Kidson 1993, and Binski 2004, chap. 3, "Mary's Great Churches, Lincoln and Salisbury," 62–77.

2. Draper (2006, 197–215) explores this relationship extensively.

3. Cocke 2003, 215; Maddison 2000, 117.

4. In another paper I address the hierarchical treatment of sacred space in these buildings; see Mahrt, forthcoming.

5. At Salisbury, the guides to the cathedral constantly point out that this is NOT a lady chapel but rather Trinity chapel; technically they are correct, unless you define lady chapel as the place where the Lady Mass is sung, and then it is indeed a lady chapel.

References

Bailey, Terence. 1971. *The Processions of Sarum and the Western Church.* Toronto: Pontifical Institute of Medieval Studies.

Binski, Paul. 2004. *Becket's Crown: Art and Imagination in Gothic England, 1170–1300.* New Haven: Yale University Press.

Cocke, Thomas. 2003. "The History of the Fabric from 1541 to 1836." In *A History of Ely Cathedral,* ed. Peter Meadows and Nigel Ramsay, 213–23. Woodbridge: Boydell Press.

Cocke, Thomas, and Peter Kidson. 1993. *Salisbury Cathedral: Perspectives on the Architectural History.* Royal Commission on the Historical Monuments of England. London: HMSO.

Draper, Peter. 2006. *The Formation of English Gothic: Architecture and Identity.* New Haven: Yale University Press.

Frere, Walter Howard. (1898–1901) 1969. *The Use of Sarum: The Original Texts Edited from the MSS.* 2 vols. Cambridge: Cambridge University Press; Reprint, Farnborough: Gregg.

Harper, John. 1991. *The Forms and Orders of Western Liturgy from the Tenth to the Eighteenth Century: A Historical Introduction and Guide for Students and Musicians.* Oxford: Clarendon Press.

Harrison, Frank Ll. 1963. *Music in Medieval Britain.* 2nd ed. London: Routledge & Kegan Paul.

Henderson, W. G., ed. (1882) 1969. *Processionale ad usum insignis ac præclaræ ecclesiæ Sarum.* Leeds: McCorquodale; Reprint, Farnborough: Gregg.

Maddison, John. 2000. *Ely Cathedral: Design and Meaning.* Ely: Ely Cathedral Publications.

Mahrt, William Peter. Forthcoming. "Sacred Space, Sacred Time, and Music in the Processions of the Sarum Rite."

"Haec est nimis": A Trope-Transcription Puzzle

Greta-Mary Hair

Introduction

The introductory Introit trope melody for the Mass on Easter Feria II, "Haec est nimis" from Paris, Bibliothèque nationale de France, MS fonds lat. 903 (fol. 153v, see figure 1)[1] is a challenging melody to transcribe, and solutions are unlikely to be found in consultation and comparison with concordant manuscripts alone. This article presents these problems and suggests solutions that underline the necessity for an editor to investigate the scribal practice of writing the trope melodies, a practice which is found to be consistent across the manuscript concerned, in this case, BnF 903.[2]

The host chant for the trope is "Introduxit vos," with Psalm verse incipit "Confitemini Domino," written in the Gradual section of the manuscript (fol. 77v, see figure 2). The edited texts with translations are set out below. The spelling in the manuscript is maintained, rubrics given in the manuscript are in capitals, and editorial rubrics and additional material are enclosed in square brackets.

FERIA II
[Text References: Exodus 13:5 & 9; Psalm 105:1]
    [Tropus]
    Haec est nimis prefulgida festa,
    potentissimus[3] in qua servitute populum eruit suum.
        (This is an exceedingly illustrious festal [day]
        on which the most powerful ruler rescued his people from slavery.)
    Iam paschalis occisus est agnus
    cuius mors nostra fuit vita.
        (The Paschal Lamb has now been slain
        whose death has been our life.)
    Divina pavit quos manna,
    Xristo psallite laudes et odas.
        ([You] whom divine manna has nourished,
        sing praises and odes to Christ,)

Alleluia!
  (Alleluia!)
Morte calcata, unicus Patri perditam ovem
reduxit ad gregem, atque:
  (Death, having been trampled underfoot,
  The Father's only Son has led the lost sheep back to the fold, and so:)

  [Antiphona]
  Introduxit vos Dominus in terram fluentem lac et mel [Ex.13:5],
  alleluia, et ut lex Domini semper sit in ore vestro. [Ex. 13:9]
  Alleluia, alleluia!
    (The Lord has led you into a land flowing with milk and
    honey, alleluia, so that the law of the Lord might be on your
    lips forever. Alleluia, alleluia!)

  PSALMUS
  Confitemini Domino, [quonian bonus,
  quoniam in seculum] misericordia eius.[4]
    (Acknowledge the Lord for he is good,
    for his mercy [extends] into eternity.)

  [Gloria Patri]
  Gloria [Patri, et Filio, et Spiritui Sancto:
  sicut erat in principio, et nunc, et semper,
  et in secula] seculorum. Amen.
    (Glory be to the Father, and to the Son,
    and to the Holy Spirit:
    as it was in the beginning, is now and forever shall be,
    and into the ages of ages. Amen.)

Before moving to the technical aspects of transcription central to this study, a brief review of the symbolic significance of the text of the Introit antiphon for this Easter Feria II (Easter Monday) Mass will place this chant in its historical and liturgical context.

In "The Italian Neophytes' Chants," Kenneth Levy (1970) refers to an ancient custom within the pre-Carolingian single Easter Mass that was celebrated in the Lateran up until as late as the sixth or seventh century. The liturgy was centered not only on the Resurrection but also on the First Communion of those who had been baptized in the Easter Vigil baptismal ceremony. He describes the custom as:

the offering to the newly-baptized on Easter eve of a chalice containing milk and honey, as a symbol of the fulfillment through baptism of the Lord's promise to Moses: *educam* [*vos*] *in terram quae fluit lacte et melle* (Exodus: 3, 8, 17). This was administered at Communion between the consecrated bread and wine. . . . It is first mentioned explicitly in the *Apostolic Tradition* attributed to Hippolytus of Rome (c. 170–c. 236). There may be an earlier reference in Tertullian, and there is a probable reference later on in Jerome. The custom is still alive at the beginning of the sixth century, when it is described in a letter of the Roman deacon John (later [?] Pope John I [523–26]) to Senarius.[5]

Although a chant with the text "Introduxit vos" is not among the surviving neophyte chants cited by Levy from early Italian traditions associated with Milan, Benevento, and Ravenna, the text is reminiscent of the ancient custom. Levy cites an Alleluia verse, "Eduxit Dominus" (Levy 1970, 181n1), from the Easter Vigil Mass in the Rheinau Gradual (Hesbert 1935, lxi, 98); and a version of the Benediction of Milk and Honey in as late a source as the mid-tenth century Romano-Germanic Pontifical of Mainz (Levy 1970, 215), the text of which is edited by Andre Wilmart (1933, 14–15) and Pierre-Marie Gy (1959, 209–10). With the decline in adult baptism, the shift to infant baptism, and the implementation of appropriate changes in the liturgy, the rite of milk and honey became obsolete. The Vigil Mass, now placing greater emphasis on the expectation of the Resurrection, was moved from dawn back to midnight, and an additional Mass was introduced whose focus was firmly placed on the Resurrection (Levy 1970, 182). "Introduxit vos" may be a remnant from (or a reminder of) the milk and honey ceremony, perhaps via the Alleluia verse removed from its original liturgical function within the Easter ceremonies and reworked to become the Introit for the Mass for Feria II. In the Ambrosian "Ante-Evangelium" for Christmas, an example of one such move "from Christmas to St. Stephen's Day" is given by Levy (1970, 189n19, acknowledging Michel Huglo) in what he describes as "an attempt to hold on to an older regional usage by proximity, after its traditional place is pre-empted by the standard Gregorian practice." Whether the chant originates from the ancient milk and honey ritual or not, the allegorical significance conveyed in the use of the Old Testament text to communicate the topological levels of meaning across the Judaic/Christian tradition illustrates the manner in which the medievals read and interpreted biblical texts, and the use they made of them in their selection of texts for liturgical use. However, to trace and verify this suggestion would be the subject of another study.

The Scribe's Method of Writing Melodies, Unique to BnF 903

The melodic shape of the Psalm verse incipit "Confitemini Domino" in both troper and gradual, and the "Gloria [Patri]" incipit with "Seculorum amen" differentia in the troper function not only as cues but also as the psalm-tone fragments which enable one to recognize the modal assignment of the antiphon (mode 8) and to identify the pitch-at-line as G for the antiphon (see figures 1 and 2). During the preparation of the manuscript, the odd-numbered, horizontal lines ruled by the scribe with a dry-point stylus (not visible in figures 1–3) were intended as central reference points for writing the melodies between the

Table 1

Mode		Pitch-at-Line*	Final	Reciting-Tone
Protus (authentic)	1	F	D	A
Protus (plagal)	2	D	D	F
Deuterus (authentic)	3	G	E	C
Deuterus (plagal)	4	F	E	A
Tritus (authentic)	5	A	F	C
Tritus (plagal)	6	F	F	A
Tetradus (authentic)	7	B	G	D
Tetradus (plagal)	8	G	G	C

*I have adopted the convenient phrase "pitch-at-line" from Frasch 1986, 43.

even-numbered lines on which the texts were written. In common with other, similar Aquitanian manuscripts, the neumes that were placed on the dry-point line (henceforth DPL) were assigned a particular pitch in relation to the mode (see table 1).[6]

In addition, the scribe of BnF 903 selected certain neumes to represent the semitone: the *quilisma*, *semicircular virga*, and a form of the *porrectus*. The *virga cornu* (horned virga) represents the pitches E, A, or B-natural, according to melodic context. As an aid to identifying and confirming the mode of a chant, these particulars are unique to BnF 903. This carefully worked out system rendered the tonary obsolete, at least for its earlier, principal raison d'être as a source of reference for checking and confirming the modal assignment of chants.

The conventional *custos* and *equaliter* ("eq" or "e"), also commonly found across Aquitanian sources, is retained in BnF 903. The former, placed at the end of each line within a single chant, anticipates the pitch of the first neume in the following line (see the flag-shaped sign at the end of lines 1 and 2–7 in figure 3), and the latter alerts the observer to a change in the pitch level at which the melody is written and, consequently, to a change in pitch for the pitch-at-line. Both the custos and equaliter could effect this change, analogous to a change of clef in staff notation (Frasch 1986, 37–56, esp. 43–46).

Transcribing "Haec est nimis"

Having established from the Psalm verse incipit, the "Gloria" cue, and the "Seculorum amen" differentia that the chant melody is assigned to mode 8, one realizes that in the troper the neumes of the antiphon cue "Introduxit," D–D–DFG–GF with E as pitch-at-line (figure 1, line 5 from top), are not placed in the correct

Figure 1. Easter Feria II Introit trope, "Haec est nimis," BnF 903, fol. 153v.
(Photo reproduced by permission of Bibliothèque nationale de France.)

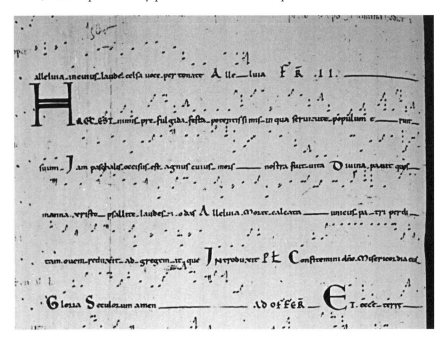

Figure 2. Easter Feria II Introit, "Introduxit," BnF 903, fol. 77v.
(Photo reproduced by permission of Bibliothèque nationale de France.)

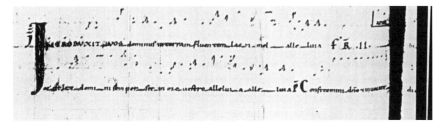

positions for a mode 8 melody with G as pitch-at-line, see table 1, "Tetradus (pla-gal)." Compare the "Introduxit" incipit in the Gradual (figure 2), where the pitches are correctly placed, with the cue in the troper placed a third higher. If an equaliter sign had been placed in the troper above the "PL" (abbreviation for the Psalm verse rubric), the pitches for the psalm incipit, "*Confite*mini" would read correctly as F–AG–GC, with G as the pitch-at-line. Although there is no equaliter, there is an erasure mark. It is possible that the scribe who wrote the main text underlay left a tiny cue, "PL," for the rubricist to insert the abbreviated psalm verse rubric in larger capitals, and that the rubricist erased the equaliter by mistake together with the cue, after inserting the rubric.

Transcribing backwards from the chant cue with E as pitch-at-line, the results agree with the transcription by Günther Weiss (1970, 336–37; hereafter cited as MMMAe) from the same source, until the word "vita" (figure 1, line 3 from the top). The *quilisma* neume in line 4 at "unic*us*" is correctly placed, effecting the semitone, A–B-flat. Again, there is no equaliter to indicate a change for the pitch-at-line, but Weiss has interpreted a change to F. His solution is that the pitch-at-line is F from the trope incipit "Haec est nimis" to "vita," after which it changes to E from "Divina" for the rest of the trope melody and also for the antiphon cue, "Introduxit," changing to G only for the following psalm-tone fragments: "Confitemini Domino," "Gloria," and "Seculorum amen" (which are not transcribed in Weiss's edition)—fragments which confirm that the chant melody is assigned to mode 8 (see figure 1 and example 3; also MMMAe, 336–37).

There are three concordant Aquitanian sources: BnF 1871 (fol. xviir), BnF 1084 (fol. 132r), and BnF 1118 (fol. 48r), which are cited in Weiss's critical notes. In Apt 17 (5) (pp. 149–50), "Haec est nimis" is divided into three parts as interpolatory trope elements. Weiss has also edited this version (MMMAe, 431–33). In addition, there are two Italian sources: Vich, Biblioteca episcopale, MS 105 (111), fol. 4r; and Vich, Biblioteca episcopale, MS 106 (31), fol. 53v.

In BnF 1871, considered to be a reliable source for the pitch accuracy of heightened neumes (figure 3, line 8, and example 4, last line), the pitches for the chant cue incipit, "Introduxit," are placed at a level comparable with the incipit in the gradual of BnF 903, where the pitch-at-line is G (figure 2, line 1, and example 3, line 10). Transcribing the melody backwards from the chant cue, the pitch level for G remains until the custos indicates a change after "*Divi*-na" at the end of the third line above the chant cue, "Introduxit." The custos is placed one step above the level at which G is placed—on the following line at "Divi-*na*"— but the first neume on *na* is placed one step lower. Therefore the pitch level for G from "atque" (transcribing backwards) to "[Divi]-*na*" becomes the pitch level for F, in the preceding section. This change occurs close to the place where Weiss interprets a similar change in the melody of BnF 903, although in the latter manuscript, according to Weiss, the change occurs between "vita" and "Divina," with F as pitch-at-line up to and including "vita," and E from "Divina" onwards (figure 1 and example 3).

Continuing to transcribe the version in BnF 1871 backwards, the pitch level continues for F until the custos between "Iam" and "pascalis" again indicates a change. This custos, referring to the first pitch in line four, is placed two steps above the pitch level for F (as from "pascalis" onwards), but the first pitch in line

Figure 3. Easter Feria II Introit trope, "Haec est nimis," BnF 1871, fol. xviir.
(Photo reproduced by permission of Bibliothèque nationale de France.)

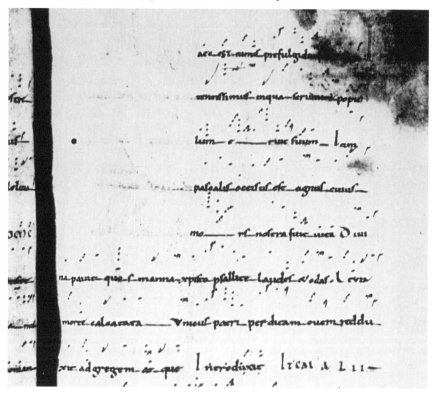

four is placed only one position above, which is G. Therefore the pitch level for F
becomes the level for E prior to "pascalis."

In summary, according to my reading, the melody in BnF 1871 is written
so that:

1. The incipit, "Haec est nimis," begins on C: C–CD–DE–DC
2. There is a change of pitch level at "pascalis": G–A–G
3. There is a change of pitch level at "[Divi]-na pavit": G–GA–A

I calculate that, according to Weiss, the melody in BnF 903 is written as follows:

1. From "Haec" to "vita" inclusive, pitch-at-line = F
2. From "Divina" to "Introduxit" inclusive, pitch-at-line = E
3. [From "Confitemini" onwards, pitch-at-line = G, not transcribed]

In the melody of BnF 1118, the pitches for the chant cue, "Introduxit," are also
placed in the correct positions for a melody assigned to mode 8. Although there
are no DPLs ruled for pitch-at-line, and neither custodes nor equaliters are in

this trope melody—the manuscript apparently having been produced in Saint-Martial at Limoges before the introduction of custodes attributed to Adémar of Chabannes (Grier 2005, 68)—the heighted neumes do appear to communicate some degree of pitch placement, especially at the beginning and end of a phrase. According to my calculation, the notation for the first trope line, "Haec est nimis . . . qua," is placed a fourth higher than in BnF 903, BnF 1871, and Apt 17 (5), which suggests that G is placed at more or less the center point between the text lines. Accordingly, the first phrase of the melody in transcription would read as follows:

Example 1. Introit trope, "Haec est nimis," BnF 1118, fol. 48r.

The question arises, does the pitch level for the melody in BnF 1118 offer a clue to an authentic reading of the melody in BnF 903 from the trope incipit "Haec est nimis" to "vita" inclusive? If so, the pitch-at-line in BnF 903 would be B, and the opening melody, in transcription, would be almost identical with the passage quoted above from BnF 1118. B is assigned to the pitch-at-line for mode 7 melodies, the authentic form of the tetradus mode and, therefore, closely related to mode 8 by their common final, G. If the phrases ending on "suum" and "vita" terminate on G in BnF 1118, B would be placed at more or less center point in lines two and three up to "vita." To have found a melody in BnF 1118 offering such a clue, indefinite but suggestive, to the pitch level at which the opening section of the melody in BnF 903 is written, was extraordinarily unexpected.

A Survey of the Pitch-at-Line

It is well known that across the repertoire as a whole, certain chants in both the Mass and Office (for example, Graduals and Offertories, and Office Responsories) are written partly in the authentic mode and partly in the plagal; for example, authentic for the melody of the respond and plagal for the verse, or vice versa. Single phrases within a chant or trope melody may suggest the authentic form where the overall assignment is plagal, and vice versa. In the Aquitanian sources with heighted neumes and DPLs, the pitch-at-line frequently changes for such Gradual and Offertory verses with no indicative equaliter or custos. The same practice is observed between trope and chant melodies. Of the total number of 103 tropes in BnF 903 for Introits, Offertories, and Communions (fols. 147v–163r), ninety are written from their incipits (but not always continuing throughout) with the

Table 2

Feast	Trope & Folio No.	Chant & Folio No.	Mode (Chant)	Pitch-at-Line (Chant)	Pitch-at-Line (Trope)
1. St. Stephen	Alme Dei fol. 149r	Elegerunt (Off.) fol. 12r	8	G	E
2. Holy Innocents	Hodie parvulorum fol. 149v	Ex ore (Int.) fol. 13r	2	D	F
3. Holy Innocents	Psallite sanctorum fol. 150r	Vox in Rama (Com. fol. 14r)	7	B	D
4. Ascension	Elevatus est fol. 155r	Viri Galilei (Off. fol. 90v)	1	F	D
5. St. Marcial	Marcialis meritum fol. 158r	Statuit ei (Int.) fol. 19r	1	F	D
6. St. Andrew	Alma dies fol. 161r	Michi autem (Int.) fol. 27v	2	D	F–D
7. St. Andrew	Ut meruit fol. 161v	Dicit Andreas (Com) fol. 116r	8	G	F (mode 6)
8. The Apostles	Nobile apostolicum fol. 161v	Michi autem (Int.) fol. 27v	2	D	F–D
9. More than One Martyr	Summa Dei fol. 162r	Multitudo (Com.) fol. 21v	2	D	F
10. Virgin	Ad est nunc fol. 162r	Dilexisti (Int.) fol. 3r	8	G	B–G
11. Church Dedication	Celebremus fol. 162v	Terribilis est (Int.) fol. 132r	2	D	D–F
12. Church Dedication	Donum istam fol. 163r	Domus mea (Com.) fol. 133r	5	A	F

same pitch-at-line as their host chants. If the trope melody is not written with the same pitch-at-line as its host chant, it is often written from the incipit in reference to the pitch-at-line associated with its authentic form (if the host chant is plagal), or vice versa. With the exception of two, the examples in table 2 illustrate these relationships.

In numbers 2, 4–6, and 8–12, the trope melodies are written, in some cases partially, with the pitch-at-line associated with the other form of the mode to which the host chant in assigned (authentic if plagal, or vice versa).

The trope "Psallite sanctorum" (no. 3) is written with D as pitch-at-line, associated with mode 2 and the final in that mode. But the host chant "Vox in Rama" is assigned to mode 7, in which melodies D functions as the reciting tone. In this context, one may consider D to function as a pivotal pitch common to both the trope and host chant melodies. It is interesting that in this particular trope, the melody would probably have been sung an octave higher to connect with the chant incipit which begins on D, the reciting tone for the chant assigned to mode 7. In number 1, E—the final for mode 3 melodies—is the pitch-at-line for the trope melody, and C is the common reciting tone for modes 3 and 8.

"Dicit Andreas," the Communion chant for the feast of St. Andrew (no. 7), is assigned to mode 8, with G as pitch-at-line. But the trope, "Ut meruit," is written at a pitch level associated with mode 6—namely, F as pitch-at-line. This variation is explained not through an authentic/plagal relationship but through a change in the modal assignment for this chant as observed in the entries for it across the tonaries (Huglo 1971, 91). The same chant in BnF 776 (fol. 328r or fol. 123r) is written in mode 6, but the pitches of the psalm-tone cue for mode 6 are superimposed over a poor attempt to erase the pitches of the mode 8 psalm tone, the modal melodic shape of which remains discernible.

Thus, the majority of trope melodies in BnF 903 that are not written with the same pitch-at-line as their host chants are written in reference to the pitch-at-line associated with the plagal mode (if the host chant is assigned to the authentic form, and vice versa).

Returning to "Haec est nimis" (figure 1, and example 3), the interpretation that the pitch-at-line for the melody in BnF 903 is B in the passage from "Haec" to "vita" inclusive is supported by:

1. The level at which, in my calculation, the opening section of the melody in BnF 1118 may be written with G placed more or less at center point in a similar way in which the host chant, assigned to mode 8, is also written in BnF 903.
2. The level at which the opening melody is written in BnF 1084c (fol. 132r), which has a different melodic configuration, GF–FG–GA–GF[7].
3. The majority of trope melodies in BnF 903 that are not written from

Example 2. Introit trope, "Haec est nimis," and chant incipit, "Introduxit," BnF 903, fols. 153v and 77v.

their incipits in reference to the same pitch-at-line as their host chants but are written with the pitch-at-line associated with the plagal if the host chant is authentic (or vice versa), a practice which is also common between the responds and their verses in Responsories of the Office, and in Gradual and Offertory chants of the Mass.

The melodies in Vich 105 (fol. 4r) and Vich 106 (fol. 53r) appear to begin at the lower pitch level on C in agreement with the melodies in BnF 1871 and Apt 17 (5).[8]

If one accepts my reading from "Haec est nimis" to "vita," one observes the following:

1. Phrase beginnings, melodic direction between the pivotal pitches G, D, and C, and cadences (predominently on G, one on D, and one on F) suggest that the melody lies across modes 7 and 8. From "Haec" to "suum" the ambitus ranges from F to D, the subfinal and reciting tone for mode 7. C (the reciting tone for mode 8) also features as a pitch goal, but C is less dominant.

2. From "Iam paschalis" to "vita," the melody moves into a higher register; the ambitus, G–G, and the emphasis given to D suggest mode 7.

3. The pitches and melodic shape of the trope's opening phrase are similar to those of the antiphon, exemplifying a manner of melodic relationship known to exist between some tropes and their host chants (Evans 1970, 95).

4. In the transcription (see example 3), the first two trope lines both terminate on G. The second trope line, ending at "vita," connects smoothly at the unison on G with the beginning of the third trope line, at "Divina." This would be the most likely place for an equaliter to indicate a change of pitch-at-line from B to E. (In BnF 1871 the change in pitch level is indicated by a custos placed at the end of the line between the syllables *vi* and *na* of "Divina"—see figure 3, lines 5–6, and example 4, lines 5–6.)

Concluding Remarks

Observations 1 and 2 above reveal and note features which are characteristic of the tetradus mode, characteristics which are not present in the same passage of the melody I have transcribed from BnF 1871, where the melody centers around D and A. A similar pattern is observed in Weiss's transcriptions of the melodies from BnF 903 and Apt 17 (5). (MMMAe 336–37; 431–33).

My suggestion concerning the missing equaliter between "vita" and "Divina" is questionable. But I think it not unreasonable to suggest that the scribe may have omitted to place an equaliter between "vi*ta*" and "*Di*vina." Normally he would have left a small *D* as a cue for the rubricist to insert the capital for "Divina." A thoughtful scribe might think it unwise to place the permanent *e* so close to the temporary rubricist's cue. Did he consider it best to return and insert the *e* after the rubricist had inserted the capital *D*? And did he forget to do this? There are many instances in the manuscript where the presence of an equaliter would solve a problem, but it is not present. Whatever may have happened when the manuscript was prepared in the eleventh century, an equaliter understood between "vita" and "Divina" is a solution to this editorial problem confronting us today. From this point (from "Divina" to the end), my transcription

1. follows the clue given by the pitch level at which the "Introduxit" cue is written in the troper, where the pitch-at-line is E;
2. confirms the semitone (A–B-flat) for the *quilisma* sung to "uni*cus*" (figure 1, line 4);
3. agrees with the same passage in Weiss's edition and, variants excepted, with the similar passage in Apt 17 (5) (MMMAe, 431–33).

The section from "Divina" on in both BnF 903 and Apt 17 (5) terminates on the final, G, allowing for a descending, connecting interval of a fourth G–D, characteristic of mode 8, between the trope ending and chant incipit. BnF 1871 terminates on A, effecting an interval of a perfect fifth, characteristic of mode 1.

If one accepts my suggested equaliter as a scribal omission between "vita" and "Divina," the resulting melody in transcription

1. effects a connection at the unison on G, the final, between "vita" and "Divina," marking the two sections of the melody;
2. reveals the overall character of the tetradus mode with respect to the final, G, as the dominant pitch goal, and a division of the melody into authentic mode 7 (from "Haec" to "vita") expressed through D, the reciting tone as pitch goal and the ambitus G–G (with additional lower F as subfinal) followed by a shift to the plagal in the second part ("Divina" to "atque"), where the melodic emphasis lies in the lower tetrachord G–D, ambitus D–C;

Example 3. Transcription of Easter Feria II Introit trope,
"Haec est nimis," BnF 903, fol. 153v.

Example 4. Transcription of Easter Feria II Introit trope, "Haec est nimis," BnF 1871, fol. xviir.

Haec est ni - mis pre - - ful - gi - da fes - ta. Po -

-ten - tis - si - mus in qua ser - vi - tu - te po - pu -

[Custos]

-lum e - - - - ru - it su - um. Iam

pas - ca - lis oc - ci - sus est ag - nus cu - ius

[Custos]

mors nos - tra fu - it vi - ta. Di - vi -

*

- na pa - vit quos man - na. Xris - to psal - li - te lau - des et o - das

al - le - lu - - ia.

Mor - te cal - ca - ta u - ni - cus Pa - - tri

per - - di - tam o - vem re - du -

[Antiphona]

- xit ad gre - gem at - - - que: In - tro - du - - xit.

* laudes : B GF MS, likely scribal error

3. highlights the frequently recurring descent to D, as in the melodic fragment GA–FD–FG–G sung to "Alleluia." The fragment in BnF 1871 is
placed up one tone but retains the intervals. (If the custos between "*Divina*" was misplaced a step too high, the melodic level would be in agreement with BnF 903 and Apt 17 [5].)

Frasch views BnF 903 as a kind of tonary, but "not a tonary of the type that
lists chants under modal headings; rather, the modal classifications are implicit
in its notational system" (Frasch 1986, 4). Since the manuscript was produced
to enable singers to identify the mode of a chant without reference to a tonary,
the communication of modal clarity for the scribe would have been a priority,
especially for an opening passage. The first part of the trope melody lies in the
authentic tetradus region, and this he appears to have articulated by choosing B
as pitch-at-line.

As the discussion above concerning melodies from table 2 shows, not all
the trope melodies in BnF 903 conform as closely to these modal boundaries:
some demonstrate more distant, inter-modal relationships. In Leo Treitler's discussion of the "first mode character" of the "Dulciter agnicole" trope melodies also
composed for the "Introduxit vos" mode 8 Introit (in BnF 909, BnF 1120, BnF
1121, and Apt [17] 5), he writes concerning:

> the idea of a melodic matrix defined by range, pitch collection, and
> preferred melodic interval progressions, within which more than one
> modal configuration could be differentiated. . . . The means of modal
> differentiation partly control the progress of melodies, but not entirely.
> So that while modal identification is possible, common features remain
> between melodies of different modes. . . . But to think of this at all in
> terms of mode would be to refer it to a system that may have little
> relevance for the relation between a plainchant and its trope. In the
> *Apt* version the tropist appears to have pursued a greater modal consis-
> tency, or again we may say simply that he remained more narrowly in
> the melodic track of the introit. In any case the result is a composition
> that is less dynamic, and less shaped by an idea of the whole; it is more
> uniform, but less unified. The question that comes to mind is whether
> this sort of difference between the two versions is displayed consis-
> tently throughout the respective collections of tropes. That question
> calls for systematic study of whole collections from such points of view.
> The pursuit of such a study promises to enhance our understanding of
> the background of melodic resources and systems against which tropes
> (and music in other new genres) were composed and transmitted. As
> for the modal system, the study of trope transmission from the view-
> point of modal affinities promises to enhance our understanding of
> modality in that time as a compositional parameter beyond its narrow
> regulating role for the plainchant. (Treitler 1982, 21, 22)

While I believe that this study of "Haec est nimis" has achieved an interpretation of the melody that more closely reflects the intentions of the scribe of BnF 903 in relation to the project aims of producing the manuscript, Treitler's study calls for rigorous analytical attention to the role of transmission in the task of editing. The "Haec est nimis" melodies in BnF 903 and BnF 1871 would seem to parallel, at least to some degree, those of "Dulciter agnicole" in Apt 17 (5) and the Aquitanian sources cited, respectively.

Around the time that BnF 903 was produced (ca. 1025), Guido d'Arezzo cut through these complexities of communicating music in a written medium by inventing the four-line staff with clefs. With the acceptance and dissemination of his system throughout Europe, many problems, especially with regard to communicating pitch accuracy, passed into oblivion, and the notational system of BnF 903 became obsolete almost as soon as the manuscript appeared.

Notes

I acknowledge, with thanks to the British Academy, a grant to consult materials in the Corpus Troporum archives (hereafter CT) in Stockholm and to check manuscript sources in the Bibliothèque nationale de France in Paris in 1998. I am also indebted to Ritva Jacobsson and Bodil Asketorp of Stockholm, and to Graham Hair for his computer expertise.

1. fol. 153v : 154v (folio is numbered incorrectly).
2. This central manuscript, and other similar sources consulted, are abbreviated throughout the article, as for example, BnF 903.
3. potentissimus : potentissimis; CT III, 2, 108.
4. "Confitemini Domino [. . .] misericordia eius," Ps. 105:1, Troper, fol. 153r; cf. "Confitemini Domino et invocate," Ps. 104:1, Gradual, fol. 77v.
5. Levy 1970, 213–14. For references concerning Hippolytus, Tertullian, Jerome, and John the Roman deacon, see Levy 1970, 214nn71–73; and for relevant liturgical articles, nn.70 and 74–77.
6. See Ferretti 1925, 160–61; Frasch 1986, 43.
7. The diastematy of BnF 1084c is unreliable with regard to pitch. The opening incipit and certain melodic fragments excepted, the melody as a whole is difficult to transcribe.
8. I am indebted to Bodil Asketorp, with whom I discussed this paper, and who kindly transcribed and gave me not only the Vich melodies (which at the time I did not have) but those from all currently known concordant sources.

References

Manuscripts cited

Asterisks refer to sources consulted on microfilm.
Apt 17 (5)   Apt, Basilica of St Anne, MS 17 (5)

BnF 776   Paris, Bibliothèque nationale de France, MS fonds lat. 776
BnF 903   Paris, Bibliothèque nationale de France, MS fonds lat. 903
BnF 1084c   Paris, Bibliothèque nationale de France, MS fonds lat. 1084c
BnF 1118   Paris, Bibliothèque nationale de France, MS fonds lat. 1118
BnF 1871   Paris, Bibliothèque nationale de France, MS nouv. acq. lat. 1871
Vich 105   *Vich, Biblioteca episcopale, MS 105 (111)
Vich 106   *Vich, Biblioteca episcopale, MS 106 (31)

Books, Articles, and Communications

Asketorp, Bodil. n.d. "A Table of Transcriptions of the *Haec est nimis* Trope Melodies."
     Personal communication of unpublished material.
Björkvall, Gunilla, ed. 1986. *Corpus Troporum.* Vol. 5, *Les deux tropaires d'Apt, MSS 17 et 18:
     Inventaire analytique des MSS et édition des textes uniques.* Studia Latina Stockholmien-
     sis 32. Stockholm: Almqvist & Wicksell. [CT V]
Björkvall, Gunilla, Gunilla Iversen, and Ritva Jonsson, eds. 1982. *Corpus Troporum.* Vol.
     3, *Tropus du propre de la messe 2, Cycle de Pâques.* Studia Latina Stockholmiensis, 25.
     Stockholm: Almqvist & Wicksell. [CT III]
Le Codex 903 de la Bibliothèque nationale de Paris (XIe siècle): Graduel de Saint-Yrieix. 1925.
     Paléographie musicale 13. Solesmes: Abbey of St Peter.
Evans, Paul. 1970. *The Early Trope Repertory of Saint Martial de Limoges.* Princeton Studies
     in Music 2. Princeton: Princeton University Press.
Ferretti, Paolo. 1925. "Étude sur la notation Aquitaine d'après le graduel de Saint-Yrieix."
     Introduction to *Le Codex 903 de la Bibliothèque nationale de Paris (XIe siècle)*, 54–211.
Frasch, Cheryl Crawford. 1986. "Notation as a Guide to Modality in the Offertories of
     Paris, B.N. Lat. 903." PhD diss., The Ohio State University, 1986.
Grier, James. 2005. *The Musical World of a Medieval Monk: Adémar of Chabannes in Eleventh-
     Century Aquitaine.* Cambridge: Cambridge University Press.
Gy, Pierre-Marie. 1959. "Die Signung von Milch und Honig in der Osternacht." In *Pas-
     chalis Sollemnia*, ed. Balthasar Fischer and Johannes Wagner, 206–11. Basel: Herder.
Hesbert, René-Jean, ed. 1935. *Antiphonale Missarum Sextuplex.* Brussels: Vromant.
Huglo, Michel. 1971. *Le tonaires: Inventaire, analyse, comparaison.* Paris: Société française
     de musicologie.
Levy, Kenneth. 1970. "The Italian Neophytes' Chants." *Journal of the American Musicological
     Society* 23: 181–227.
Treitler, Leo. 1982. "Observations on the Transmission of Some Aquitanian Tropes." In *Actu-
     elle Fragen der musikbezogenen Mittelalterforschung: Text zu einem Basler Kolloquium des
     Jahres 1975*, ed. Wulf Arlt et al., 11–60. Forum Musicologicum 3. Winterthur: Amadeus.
Weiss, Günther, ed. 1970. *Introitus-Tropen.* Vol. 1, *Das Repertoire der südfranzösischen Tro-
     pare des 10. und 11. Jahrhunderts.* Monumenta Monodica Medii Aevi 3. Kassel: Bären-
     reiter. [MMMAe]
Wilmart, André. 1933. "La Bénédiction Romaine du lait et du miel dans l'euchologe Bar-
     berini." *Revue Benedictine* 45: 10–19.

Compositional Method and Inspirational Guesswork: Reconstructing the Latin Motets of Martin Peerson (ca. 1572–1651)

Richard Rastall

Introduction

The common use of partbooks in the performance of English music from the sixteenth century onwards, together with the loss of many pre-Restoration musical sources, has led to a curious situation in which a significant proportion of the repertory survives in only an incomplete state. Consequently, some music of even the best-known composers must now be reconstructed before it can be performed.[1] Martin Peerson is among the less famous composers whose music is affected by this problem; some of his finest music has been unavailable for this reason.[2]

Peerson's fifteen Latin motets survive in a unique source, manuscripts F. 16 through F. 19 at the Bodleian Library, Oxford. This is a set of four partbooks, out of an original five, the cantus book being missing. The copying was probably completed in 1655–56, but most of the repertory is clearly much older than that. The music contained in these books, including sacred consort songs by Peerson and others, mostly survives elsewhere; Peerson's Latin motets do not, and so must be reconstructed from this source.

Reconstructing an incomplete musical texture may be considered, broadly speaking, on three levels:

1. "Mechanical": the texture must be made to work at the most basic musical level.
2. Stylistic: the music must be made to conform to the musical style of the period and the genre concerned.
3. Individual: the compositional methods and stylistic "fingerprints" of the particular composer must be considered.

Of these, the last demands a detailed analysis and discussion of the composer's extant work, and this is not yet possible for Peerson because his music is not readily available. There is five-part music that might be considered stylistically very close, certainly: the *Grave Chamber Musique* (published 1630) uses a homogeneous imitative style, and so does the string fantasia "Attendite."[3] The latter is itself incomplete and in need of reconstruction; however, for all of this music there is a problem of chronology: the *Grave Chamber Musique* seems to have been composed at various times after the beginning of the century, and neither the motets nor "Attendite" can be dated. In addition, the *Grave Chamber Musique* is a setting of poetic texts in English, not of Latin prose. A direct comparison of these repertories may therefore lead to assumptions that will distort our view of the motets.

My reconstruction of Peerson's motets has been largely without reference to other works, and in what follows here I shall concentrate on the first two levels mentioned: the musical mechanics of the texture, and the general musical style of the Latin motet in England around the turn of the seventeenth century. Some of the more obvious fingerprints of Peerson's personal style will of course become apparent and will form an important part of the discussion; but I shall not try to treat them systematically. At some later date it will no doubt be possible to discuss the styles of Peerson's music in detail.

"Mechanical" Considerations

A reading of the existing four-part texture of Peerson's motets immediately faces the reader with an obvious but important requirement. Music of the early seventeenth century uses incomplete triads very little, and in particular the third is rarely missing. In almost any place in an incomplete texture where there is no third—or a fourth as the third's displacement—we can assume that the missing voice will supply it. While this situation seems almost too basic to merit much consideration, it is very important in dealing with one of the most difficult problems of reconstruction: namely, when to leave the reconstructed voice silent.

Leaving aside passages in which a phrase in three or four parts is repeated quasi-antiphonally, it is often difficult to be sure when a reduced texture is in operation. Of the surviving voices, the quintus (voice II) sometimes rests for several bars together, whereas the lower three voices (altus, tenor, and bassus) rarely rest for more than a bar (four minim beats) at a time.[4] Since the cantus often works in tandem with the quintus and must have had roughly the same range, it seems likely that the cantus, too, sometimes rested for several bars together. But the existence of a complete texture without it does not mean that the cantus is silent: other factors must be considered before that conclusion is reached. The identification of silences remains one of the editor's biggest problems in reconstructing a part, so that the demand for an extra note—as when the third is missing from a chord—may be a vital indicator of cantus activity.

Whether the third should be supplied on the strong beat or displaced by the fourth (usually by suspension) is to be determined by the context. One of the

Example 1. "Levavi oculos meos" (motet 4), 30–32.

most important contexts is that of cadences: these can be addressed early on in the process of reconstruction because they involve melodic and harmonic characteristics that are largely conventional in terms of the general musical style. Example 1 shows a cadence from "Levavi oculos meos" (motet 4) in which the melodic outline to be added is defined precisely by the missing thirds. It is a relatively easy decision that the leading note should be delayed—the dissonance on the pretonic chord is such a strong convention in this style that one would need very good reason to reach the F-sharp on the third beat of bar 31. The rhythm added above the cantus staff is therefore used. The details of rhythm and embellishment are, however, much more open to discussion; I have left this cadence plain, but a singer might well decide to embellish it.

The lack of a third is not the only indicator of a missing note. Peerson's distribution of notes in chords is sometimes unusual—one might say bizarre—compared to that of more "mainstream" composers, in relation to both spacing and doubling. The harmony "rules" that one learns as a student are in fact very limited, being based mainly on the most accessible music of J. S. Bach and Palestrina (the chorales and certain Mass movements, respectively). From these pieces one learns that some doublings are better than others—e.g., that of the major third in the chord being generally unacceptable—and that a wide gap between adjacent voices is poor spacing, except that the tenor and bass can be separated by an octave or more. But a working knowledge of the music of these and other composers shows that such "rules"were often broken. Indeed, they are not rules at all but limitations imposed as a relatively easy way of controlling a student's stylistic development.

Nevertheless, the stylistic norms for major composers are not always those of the minor composers, and this phenomenon needs investigation. I suspect that Chapel Royal composers such as Tallis, Parsons, Byrd, Gibbons, and Tomkins developed an efficient and recognisable style that they knew would work in the circumstances in which their music was performed; that they passed this on to their pupils and younger colleagues; and that this dissemination involved some composers (John Ward is a likely example) who were never Gentlemen of the Chapel. One result is that the music of a nonestablishment composer often looks crude or simply wrong to those of us brought up to study the major figures. One could not imagine Byrd writing a passage such as that in example 2(a), for instance: the wide spacing between voices III and IV, the blatant evasion of consecutive fifths in bar 41 (voices II and IV), and the apparently uncontrolled chording and voice leading of bars 43–44 would certainly have brought out my teacher's red pen.

Yet on any objective criteria we must accept this as being within the general style. The music sounds perfectly good if well performed, and the features that I have just identified can be viewed positively as characteristic of the composer. It simply happens that the boundaries of this individual style are recognisably far removed from those of our "mainstream" composers: and one reason for this is that the more extreme spacing here makes the music harder to perform, because the notes are more difficult to pitch accurately than in a homogeneously spaced texture with more "vocal" melodic intervals.[5] Because of our relative unfamiliarity with this style, the reconstruction of these bars would be difficult were it not for the particular structural principle in use here. Fortunately, it is clear that Peerson repeats at this point of the cantus a phrase that has already appeared as a sort of ostinato in other voices (example 2[b]).

This example warns us to take careful note of what is actually in the four-part texture that survives, and not to introduce preconceived notions of what *ought* to be there. Such reconstruction is, after all, often a process of problem solving, and that demands that we look at the evidence. From the particular features of what survives we can often gain a view of what is missing—the lack of a third in the chord is a specific version of this principle. To give one of many possibilities, example 3(a) shows a cadence from "Hora nona" (motet 8) in which the quintus line ends rather abruptly: one can imagine that the final F-sharp could have been held for two beats, the dissonant altus E appearing on the half beat and being treated as a dissonance only on the fourth beat when the bass gives the texture a rhythmic boost (see example 3[b]). In fact, the crotchet F-sharp shows that an

Example 2(a). "Laboravi in gemitu meo" (motet 13), 40–44.

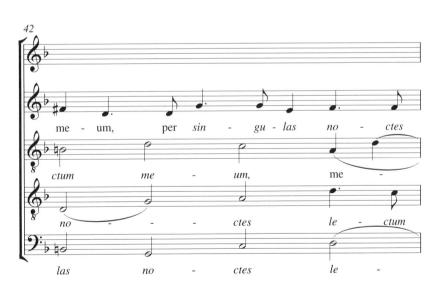

Example 2(a) (*continued*)

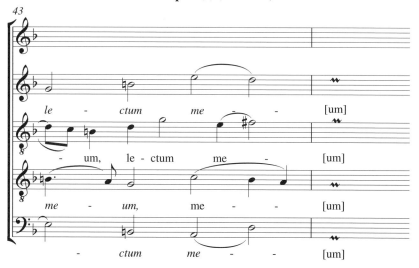

Example 2(b). "Laboravi in gemitu meo" (motet 13), 40–44.

Example 2(b) (*continued*)

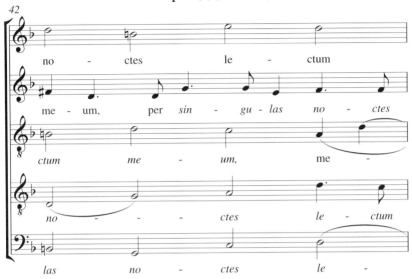

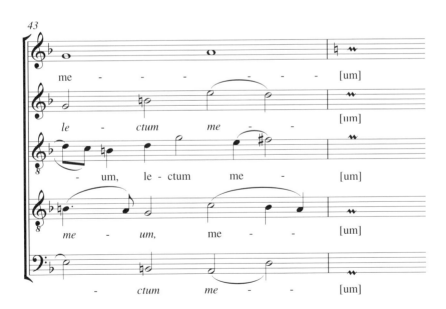

Example 3(a). "Hora nona" (motet 8), 29–31.

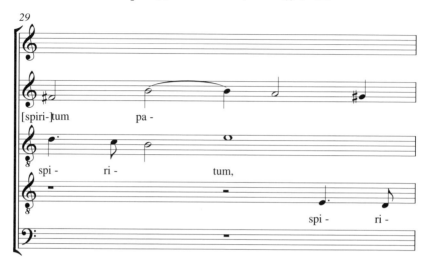

Example 3(b). "Hora nona" (motet 8), 29–31.

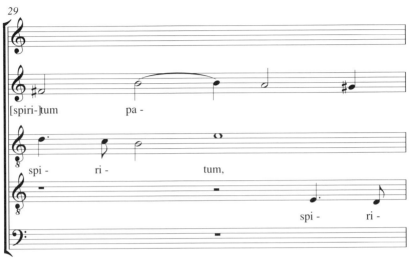

Example 3(c). "Hora nona" (motet 8), 29–31.

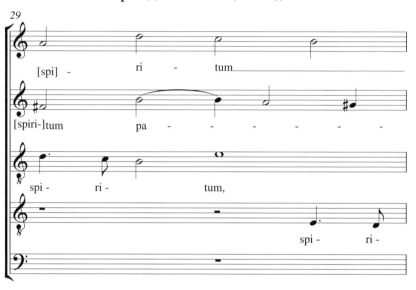

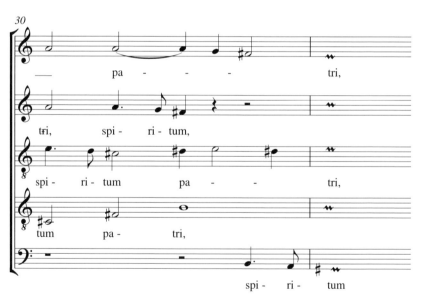

incompatible note is about to arrive in another voice. This must be in the cantus. Considering that the dissonant E (altus) on the fourth beat can best be forced to resolve by an F-sharp, it is clear that the incompatible note is probably a G. The result is shown in example 3(c). The rest of the cantus line shown in example 3(c) is dictated by the need to provide the dissonances implied by the quintus in bar 29.

General Style: Imitative Entry Groups

Even quite advanced counterpoint students deal mainly with questions of pitch, and it is tempting to approach any reconstruction by asking what note one should write in any particular place. But writing good counterpoint demands a wider and more musical view. Rhythm is a vital ingredient; indeed, in teaching counterpoint I always found myself insisting that rhythmic counterpoint is a basic requirement of the skills to be developed. Another aspect is that of not writing free counterpoint all the time, but reusing what has already been seen to work. This brings us to one of the most helpful considerations of what survives: the construction of paragraphs of imitative polyphony, and especially of expositions—or, as I think we should call them in a nonfugal context, initial entry groups.

The placing of entries in the "standard" four-part fugal or other imitative exposition may be expressed as

$$T \times D \, y \, T \times D$$

where adjacent T[onic] or D[ominant] entries, shown by the pitch name of the starting note, are separated by x or y beats.[6] Since y is normally larger than x, because of the need to confirm the tonal starting point after a move away, this scheme is effectively two pairs of entries. At the start of motet 4, shown in example 4, the cantus must start the piece, since all other voices have a rest; a tonic entry in the cantus not only works well but shows a conformity to the standard pattern: D 2 G 4 D 2 G. "Tonic" and "dominant" entries in this case actually start on the dominant and tonic notes, respectively, and in fugal terms the "answer" is "tonal"; the fourth entry appears delayed by one beat because the first note is shortened (as is quite common) for rhythmic reasons. As is potentially the case in all of the motets, this initial entry group is actually in five parts. In any such case the fifth part provides a challenge to the composer, since a creative way must be found to integrate it into what would otherwise be a symmetrical structure. In the present case the fifth (quintus) entry is nonstandard. Indeed, it is not an entry of the imitative point at all, but a piece of free counterpoint: only the initial rising interval gives any suggestion of imitation.

The great majority of Peerson's motets start imitatively, but only the last two, which are linked as *prima* and *secunda partes*, could be said to begin with a

Example 4. "Levavi oculos meos" (motet 4), 1–5.

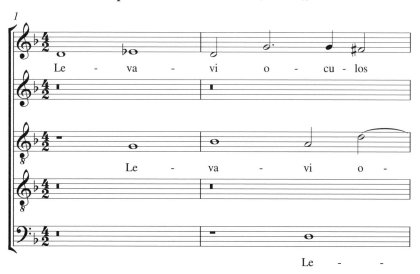

Le - va - vi o - cu - los

Le - va - vi o -

Le - - -

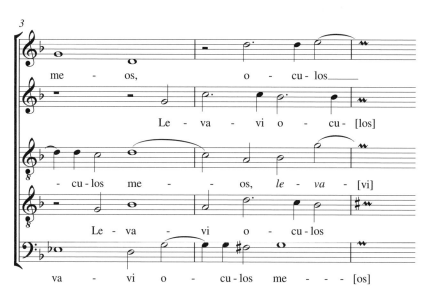

me - os, o - cu - los_____

Le - va - vi o - cu - [los]

- cu - los me - - os, *le - va* - [vi]

Le - va - vi o - cu - los

va - vi o - cu - los me - - - [os]

regular five-part "exposition." In both cases the group is based on two pairs but with the fifth entry attached to the first pair to form a 3+2 grouping of entries:

14	D 2 G 4 D 8	D 2 G
15	D 2 G 2 C 6	D 2 G

In "Multa flagella peccatoris" (motet 15) the cantus starts the piece, and its role is inescapable (example 5); the opening of "Nolite fieri" (motet 14) is also so clearly regular that the cantus is not in doubt (example 6).

Of the other motets that start with an imitative entry group, several are based on two (more or less regular) pairs of entries. The fifth or "extra" entry may be found between the pairs (nos. 2 and 6) or at the start of a second entry group (no. 3), or there may be two extra entries between the pairs (no. 5). One motet (no. 13) shows four fairly regular entries (GG CG) before moving to other material, while another (no. 12) has only three regular entries before melodic and rhythmic variation makes further entries impossible; and one (no. 7) becomes irregular after only two entries (the second an inversion of the first). The last of these motets with imitative openings (no. 10) both varies the initial interval and changes the continuation, so that although the entries are recognizable because the initial interval is large, the group is not structured as one would expect. This is probably an area that needs to be explored eventually in some depth.

As is always the case in imitative structures, second and subsequent entry groups are even less regular than the initial ones. Peerson tends to follow the common principles: he shortens the imitative material, brings it together with itself in stretto, uses voice exchange, and moves whole textures around and repeats them in a quasi-antiphonal manner. All of these make the reconstruction of the cantus relatively simple. Peerson also uses a technique that is very much his own and has been labelled "chain canon" imitation. This uses multiple repetitions of melodic material over a single harmony or a simple repeating harmonic pattern, typically with some exciting rhythmic detail that makes up for the loss of forward harmonic impetus. This is not the place to explore chain canon in detail, but an example from "Nolite fieri" (motet 14) will show the extent to which the technique aids the reconstruction of the missing part (example 7).

Informing the guesswork

The discussion of Peerson's compositional strategies has so far focused on methods common to many composers, but it will be obvious that some of his individual preferences could be considered in a similar way. His use of chain canon is one example; a less radical one is his habit of falling onto a tonic or dominant note from above, temporarily displacing the expected note, as seen in example 1 (bar 30, voice III, 3rd beat). The latter is a less clear-cut technique than the former,

Example 5. "Multa flagella peccatoris" (motet 15), 1–5.

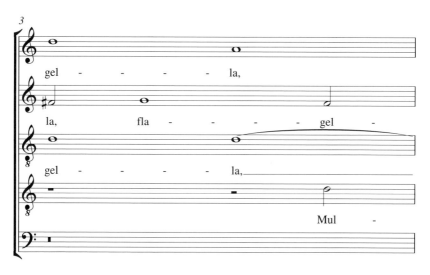

Example 5 (*continued*)

Example 6. "Nolite fieri" (motet 14), 1–6.

Example 6 (*continued*)

Example 7. "Nolite fieri" (motet 14), 39–42.

Example 7 (*continued*)

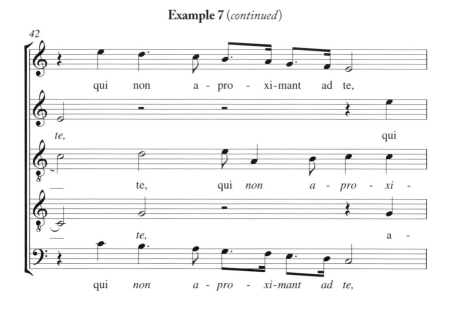

however, and for that reason offers a greater degree of uncertainty as to the composer's intention in detail. The fact that the details of Peerson's music often cannot be foreseen does not, however, make them unimportant: they can have a medium-term effect on the flow of the music.

While I do not intend a full discussion of his individuality here, it will be useful to rehearse the nature of the problems that arise and to say something of the ways in which they can be addressed. Broadly speaking, the reconstructor's difficulties arise because of Peerson's use of rhythmic and melodic variation, resulting in a flexible free counterpoint that is difficult to categorise.

His use of rhythmic variation is an alternative to imitation as a means of forging building-blocks. At a local level the technique is useful in retaining the interest of the performer and listener in music where the text setting is largely syllabic. The generally irregular nature of even his initial entry groups, already noted, stems as much from rhythmic as from melodic variation. It is a technique that demands, and in Peerson's case clearly demonstrates, a compositional mind that is both richly inventive and carefully controlled. Occasionally he uses rhythmic variation to make possible the larger-scale repetition of a very limited text. One example of this is his thirteen-bar setting of the word "obediens" in "Christus factus est" (motet 7, bars 25–38); another, which demonstrates considerable inventive virtuosity, is the setting of "dicit eis Jesus," quickly reducing simply to "Jesus," in "Quid vobis videtur" (motet 11, bars 36–50).

Such passages deserve close examination, for they are musically highly sat-isfying paragraphs that do not rely on the usual constructional methods. For our present purposes, however, I want only to demonstrate the problems of rhythmic reconstruction and to suggest ways of arriving at acceptable solutions.

We can start with the nonimitative opening of "Deus omnipotens" (motet 1), shown in example 8. From bar 2 onwards the cantus can be reconstructed by reference to material repeated in other voices, but the cantus must start the piece and bar 1 presents a problem. Peerson uses various rhythms for the word "Deus": while it seems likely that the pitch of the cantus should be the note d", the rhythm of the word is not obvious. There are several possibilities (shown above the cantus staff in example 8), all affecting the flow of the music in the first bar. This is a par-ticular kind of gesture, and it is strong enough not to be seriously compromised by any of these solutions. But those that continue the cantus line into the second bar also affect the rather different gesture that begins there. Should the bassus be allowed to start this gesture alone? If not, is a bare fifth an appropriate way of starting it, and will the cantus d" spoil the effect of the second-beat entries?

My own inclination is to end the cantus entry in bar 1, but not everyone will agree. The similar opening of "Hora nona" (motet 8) does not help, unfortu-nately, for several reasons (example 9). There is more text, and in bars 1–2 the four syllables group themselves into triple rhythms in voices III and IV. The impact of the second entries is distinctly less powerful than in "Deus omnipotens," for obvi-ous textual reasons, and the early entry of voice II further softens the effect. Voice II's triple rhythm, too, continues that of voices III and IV. There is thus a metrical and rhythmic continuation from the first phrase to the second, so it is relatively unimportant whether or not the cantus rests before its second entry. My decision to let it do so stems mainly from a recognition that the two beats between its triple-time phrases (voice I, bar 2, beats 3 and 4) are extrametrical.

These two openings offer some insight into the care with which Peerson delivered his musical gestures. Two further examples, from "Quid vobis videtur" (motet 11), may be useful in demonstrating how questions of word setting—in this case, of direct speech—can suggest approaches to reconstruction.

Early in "Quid vobis videtur" the bystanders answer "David" in reply to Jesus's question "What do you say of the Christ? Whose son is he?" Although they all give the same answer, they do not do so with one voice: rather, some answer ear-lier than others, the answer approaching unanimity as individuals gain confidence from other answers in the group. Peerson represents this by setting the phrase "Dicunt ei omnes David" in freely imitative polyphony in which the appearances of "David" become increasingly concentrated and closer together (bars 25–36). Example 10 shows the beginning and the ending of this process. At the same time, Peerson uses a related technique at the narrative level by progressively (but not

Example 8. "Deus omnipotens" (motet 1), 1–3.

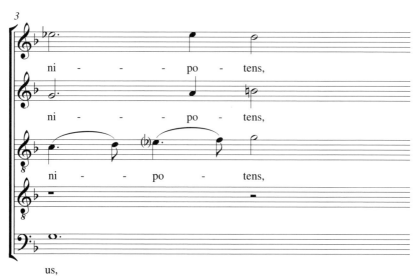

Example 9. "Hora nona" (motet 8), 1–4.

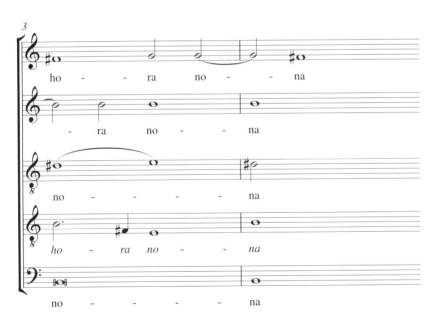

Example 10(a). "Quid vobis videtur" (motet 11), 25–29

Example 10(a) (*continued*)

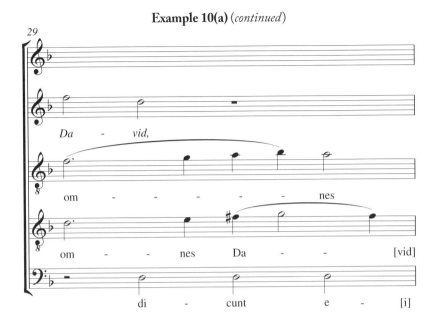

too obviously) highlighting the word "omnes" in the conventional homorhythmic way: this can be seen in example 10(a), bar 27, and example 10(b), bars 32 and 34. Clearly, the cantus must conform to these processes.

In contrast to this, Peerson begins Christ's next question—"How is it that David calls him Lord?"—in a devastatingly direct way (example 11).[7] Although there is the possibility of some rhythmic embellishment (at the start of bar 51, for instance), it is clear that the cantus should basically confirm this homophonic outburst. (My solution is the simplest available, in order to make the effect of this passage as strong as possible.)

When rhythmic variation and pitch variation come together, the result is free polyphony of a kind that is very hard to replicate precisely. Here, if anywhere, the reconstructor may be required to compose new material, inventing a line in the general context of the given material where no useful specific context exists. The general contexts, obviously, include the probable pitch range of the voice, the appropriate pitch range for the portion of the text being set, and stylistic characteristics such as features considered earlier in this section.

Conclusion

In reconstructing a missing voice one must first identify the criteria that will enable appropriate choices to be made in a reasoned way. The process is largely one of limiting the possibilities so that the most credible solution emerges. Where

Example 10(b). "Quid vobis videtur" (motet 11), 32–36

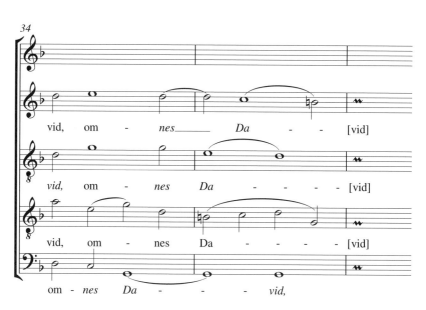

Example 11. "Quid vobis videtur" (motet 11), 49–52.

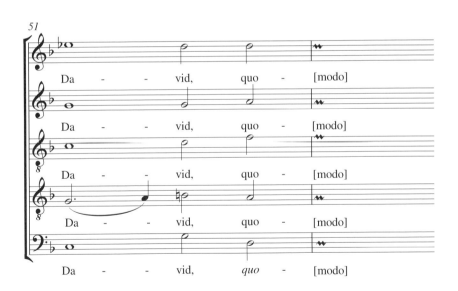

this is impossible, one must make the best-informed guess that one can, often choosing between equally valid possibilities.

Much depends on gaining a knowledge of the composer's mind, which can be done only by noting and analyzing the visible and audible results of the composing activity. The conventions of this activity offset the freedom of the composer's individual mind, so that one can often rely on the composer doing something in the "normal" way—effectively, within the melodic, harmonic, and rhythmic norms that together make up the common musical styles of the period. Where the reconstructor cannot depend on these styles, the process of reconstruction becomes one of active invention: in this case the reconstructor is likely to change the relationship between the expected and the unexpected in the composer's work.

This relationship is important in several ways. It helps to define the character of a composer (for instance, Haydn's unexpectedness is often witty, while Beethoven's can be dramatic); it is one factor in the control of the composer's invention, allowing the music to be constructed logically, so that it sounds coherent without being predictable; and it controls some of the composer's choices that determine the musical flow, the gestures, and what one might term the rhetorical effect of the music.

This relationship is, ultimately, the key to a successful and credible reconstruction. While the composer can—indeed, must—do unexpected things in the music, the reconstructor can rarely do so with impunity. The dilemma is that the composer's unexpectedness is unquestionable both as a feature of the music and as a characteristic of the composer: one may think the music successful or unsuccessful, the effect of it good or bad, but never as valid or invalid in terms of the composer's output. If the reconstructor does something unexpected, however, it is likely to be characteristic of the reconstructor rather than of the composer, and therefore invalid. A reconstruction is therefore often less interesting than the original because the reconstructor has "played safe";[8] this is sensible, not only for the stylistic reasons just given but because, in most cases, the reconstructor will not be as good a composer as the composer of the music. In any case, no one will be as good as the composer at composing *his own* music.

The logical conclusion must be that no reconstruction can do justice to the original. One might of course produce a very fine piece of music that has no pretensions to be the work of the original composer, but that is a different matter.[9] In the case of Peerson's motets 80 percent of his work survives, a reconstruction of the missing voice is possible, and the result needs to be as close as we can get to what Peerson wrote. While a 100 percent success in this is clearly impossible, and in any case we should not know if it had been achieved, it is a goal worth aiming for. More importantly, perhaps, the process of reconstruction is the opportunity to examine a composer's work closely, to follow the mental processes involved in its construction, and to come to a deeper understanding of the music.

Notes

1. The recent history of Byrd's *Great Service* comes to mind in this regard; see Monson 1982, p. v. The whole pre-Reformation repertory of Cambridge, Peterhouse MSS 471–74 is another case in point: the preface to Sandon (1992–) includes a useful analysis of the problem of incomplete partbook sets.

2. See Peerson 2002. All examples in this essay Copyright © Nick Sandon, Antico Edition, 2002.

3. The five-part sacred consort songs must be excluded from consideration here. They are largely in a similar imitative style, but—the "full" sections apart, perhaps—it must be assumed that the requirements of mixed instrumental and vocal textures affected details of the style.

4. A bar in my edition is of four minim beats, and thus it is in all examples shown here; the motets contain only one short section in triple mensuration.

5. This is greatly simplified and could be debated, but I believe that systematic study of specific examples will show it to be correct.

6. This is based on the system introduced in Kerman (1966) 1978, 519–37, esp. 521. The article is reprinted in Kerman 1994, 90–105, see esp. 92–93.

7. This text, which is a Magnificat antiphon, is taken from Christ's confrontational questioning of the Pharisees reported in Matthew 22:41–44.

8. And, conversely, critics often point to the more bizarre moments in a reconstruction to say, "X would never have written that," only to find that that is precisely what X *did* write.

9. It is interesting that Anthony Payne—undoubtedly a fine composer—did not claim to have reconstructed Elgar's Third Symphony, but only to have elaborated Elgar's sketches. This is perhaps partly because the symphony never existed as a complete or even partly-completed work. "Elaborated" considerably understates a very remarkable achievement, but Payne's terminology is a proper, if modest, distinction.

References

Duffin, Ross W., ed. 2006. *Cantiones Sacrae: Madrigalian Motets from Jacobean England.* Middleton, WI: A-R Editions.

Ex Cathedra Consort, Jeffrey Skidmore, conductor. 2005. *Martin Peerson (c1572–1651): Latin Motets.* Hyperion CDA67490. [Sound Recording.]

Kerman, Joseph. (1966) 1978. "Byrd, Tallis, and the Art of Imitation." In *Aspects of Medieval and Renaissance Music: A Birthday Offering to Gustave Reese*, ed. Jan LaRue, 519–37. New York: Norton; Reprint, New York: Pendragon Press.

———. 1994. *Write All These Down: Essays on Music.* Berkeley: University of California Press.

Monson, Craig, ed. 1982. *The English Services II.* The Byrd Edition, vol. 10b. London: Stainer and Bell.

Peerson, Martin. 2002. *Complete Works I: The Latin Motets.* Edited by Richard Rastall. Newton Abbot: Antico Edition.

Sandon, Nick, ed. 1992– . Ongoing 40-volume edition of Cambridge, Peterhouse MSS 471–74. Renaissance Church Music, vols. 101–. Newton Abbot: Antico Edition.

Dance and Historiography:
Le Balet Comique de la Royne, an Italian Perspective

Barbara Sparti

No single court ballet of the Renaissance and early Baroque has had as much spe-cialized literature dedicated to it as has Balthasar Beaujoyeux's *Le Balet Comique de la Royne*, or Allegory of Circé. Carol and Lander MacClintock's English trans-lation of 1971, including a modern transcription of the music, followed the pio-neering works of Henry Prunières ([1914] 1970) and Frances Yates ([1947] 1968, 1959). A slightly abridged English translation was included in Selma Jeanne Cohen's 1974 dance history source readings. Margaret McGowan published a facsimile of *Le Balet* in 1982, presenting it in its historic, political, and artistic contexts. An analysis of the music and dancing was made by Pierre Bonniffet in 1992, and in the following year Mark Franko, in his *Dance as Text*, devoted more than one chapter to the work.[1] A modern production of the entire *Balet Comique*, including the dances, was mounted in Geneva in 1997.[2] An Italian translation by Mariateresa Dellaborra, including an edition of the music and introductory essays, appeared in 1999;[3] and, a year later, at an International Early Dance conference in Ghent, Anne Daye and Jeremy Barlow analyzed the *Balet*'s dance and dance music and presented a reconstruction.

In the following essay I will examine the dance in the *Balet Comique*, ques-tioning some of the more frequent statements and assumptions that continue to be transmitted about this allegory of *Circé*, and offering another point of view. Furthermore, because of Beaujoyeux's Italian origins, because of Prunières's con-viction that the French *entremets* and *ballet de cour* were directly influenced by the fifteenth- and sixteenth-century Italian *moresche* and *intermedi*, and because most of those who have studied *Circé* and given it a place of primacy have done so without seeing it in a context beyond that of French court spectacles,[4] I shall also look at the *Balet Comique* in the light of the dancing that preceded and followed it in Italy.

Livret

The most important reason for the frequent study of the *Balet Comique*, performed in Paris October 15, 1581, is the fortuitous availability of its *livret*, or program of the spectacle—a unique documentation of this court entertainment in which poetic text, music, dance descriptions, and stage directions were noted down, illustrated, and published four months later. It is this source on which dance historians and other specialists have based most of their research. Since, however, the *livret* was written by "the man in charge" of the *Balet*, Balthasar de Beaujoyeux (né Baldassare da Belgioioso), and since it was also the official description of a magnificent royal spectacle, it goes without saying that the purpose of this account was to remind those who had been present, and impress those who would, instead, only read about it, of the novelty and marvel of the entertainment, and the great expense involved. The occasion was the marriage of the king's favorite, the Duke of Joyeuse (Monsieur Anne d'Arcques), of the queen's sister, Marguerite of Lorraine, known also as Mademoiselle de Vaudemont. The underlying political motive for the spectacle is stated by Beaujoyeux: the allegory was to reflect the benign, just, and strong rule of Henri III (at a highly critical time for France). Thus, the king and his court are honored in the *livret* as are, in passing at least, those who composed *Circé*'s text, music, and décor.[5] It is, however, the author of the *livret*, the *corago*[6] himself, who is especially lauded, with all four of the dedicatory poems singing his praises. Publication of the *livret* hopefully meant renown and prestige beyond the occasion itself. Given this, it is difficult to know how much of Beaujoyeux's commentary we can trust. Certainly we must bring a critical eye to bear. As art historian Giuseppe Bertini points out in his excellent discussion of the *livret* describing the marriage festivities of Alessandro Farnese in Brussels in 1565, "there is a general diffidence surrounding this type of publication . . . and in order to evaluate its historic substance, a laborious task of verification is necessary" (Bertini 1997, 13).[7]

　　Beaujoyeux's claim in the *Balet Comique*'s preface that "nine to ten thousand spectators" of the court were assembled for the occasion was clearly an exaggeration (McGowan 1982, fol. 7v). While most readers today recognize this, they might be surprised at one scholar's conclusion that, because of the size of the hall, the figure may well be reducible to a mere five hundred (Woodruff 1986, 123). Why, one needs to ask, should this have been the only license in the *livret*? Elsewhere, Beaujoyeux's ambiguity comes into play. His "la grande salle de Bourbon" (McGowan 1982, fol. 3v) has given rise to different hypotheses regarding where the *Balet* took place: in the Grande Salle du Louvre or the Salle de Bourbon in the Palais du Petit Bourbon (Woodruff 1986, 98–102)? Furthermore, considering Beaujoyeux's concern with possible plagiarists, his assertion (McGowan 1982, fol.

3r–v) that the plot of the *Circé* allegory was his own is more than open to question, some scholars believing that the story was instead by Agrippa d'Aubigny (Mac-Clintock 1971, 12; McGowan 1982, 37).

Other contemporary sources dealing with the *Balet Comique* carry their own biases. McGowan (1982, 39–42) reports the (predictably) enthusiastic correspondence of diplomats who had been in the audience, and, on the other hand, the comments of satirists who "caution those analyzers who succumb too wholeheartedly to the assembled magical forces of music, dance, verse and décor" (McGowan 1982, 40).[8]

A "First"

The other reason for the various studies of the *Balet Comique* is that it is considered to be "the first *ballet de cour*" in which poetry, music, décor, and dance "combine to support a single dramatic action . . . [and] first in the long list of precursors of the *tragédie lyrique*" (Anthony [1980] 1995, 88, 90).[9] However, while McGowan points out (1982, 23) that the particular combination of words, song, dance, and spectacular décor (with no distinction in subject matter) was "unique," she suggests that it was neither new nor, since it was not taken up again "for more than a century," innovative. James Anthony ([1980] 1995, 90) confirms that the *Balet Comique* was not a "first" in terms of setting a precedent: "The structural significance of *Circé* apparently had little effect on the following generation of those responsible for the *ballet de cour*. Their works, based largely on 'mascarades à l'italienne,' included unrelated *entrées* of colourful and grotesque characters." There is no question that, as McGowan states, the *Balet Comique* "was not going to pass on many ingredients and its discoveries to the future" (1982, 23). Nevertheless, perhaps too little importance has been given by historians (after Prunières) to the court festivals—in France and in Italy—*before Circé*, as well as to the lack of import and influence it brought to bear *after* its performance.

Dance in *Circé*: Title and Definition of "Balet"

James Anthony raised the question, "How many writers of later generations [seventeenth and eighteenth centuries] were actually familiar with the text and music of *Circé* and how many were echoing, often verbatim, the opinion of others" (Anthony 1981, 28). The query is applicable to many writers of the twentieth century. Considering how often the *Balet Comique* is cited by dance (and other) specialists, it is remarkable how little is known about the actual dance involved. For those who take the time to read the *livret*, it comes as a considerable surprise to discover just how exiguous the dance really is in the *Balet* and that what dance there is, is of one sort only.

The first point to clarify is that the *Balet Comique* is not a ballet—in the modern, or classical interpretation—as so often it is assumed to be. It is not at all clear why Beaujoyeux called this mixture of different arts around a central theme a "balet," but by combining the term with "comique," in the sense of theatrical drama, he arrived at a definition for a composite spectacle of music, poetic text, dance, and scenery. One might ask why he did not use another term. I suggest that then, as now, a name for this kind of spectacle is not easily found: pageant, review, masque, musical comedy? I wonder, furthermore, if *Le Balet Comique de la Royne* had been entitled "Allegory of Circe"—without the soubriquet of "balet"—would it have received the amount and kind of attention it has from dance historians.

What is even more confusing is that Beaujoyeux uses the same word, "balet," for the two "dances" or choreographies that occur within the work. He claims to have "given the first title and honor to the dance, and the second to the story, which I designated 'Comic'" (Cohen 1974, 20). Despite this honorary title, "balet" was limited for Beaujoyeux: "being, in truth, no more than the geometrical groupings of people dancing together, accompanied by the varied harmony of several instruments" (Cohen 1974, 19). This oversimplified definition of "balet" hardly sounds like the words of a choreographer, even one writing for a nonspecialized audience. One would think that Beaujoyeux the choreographer would have wanted to impress the spectators and readers with the importance of his dances in particular by alerting them explicitly to the compositions' complexity, significance, and worth.

Beaujoyeux: Choreographer of *Le Balet*?

Beaujoyeux has been referred to in modern studies as a "dancing" or "ballet master" though there is no evidence whatsoever for this (for example, Daye 2000, 72; MacClintock 1995, 324). He was Catherine de' Medici's *valet de chambre*, and was considered to be an outstanding violinist (Anthony 1981, 29). Due to the ambiguity of the term "balet," it is not clear if Beaujoyeux was indeed the choreographer of the dances in *Circé* or, as perhaps with the *Balet des Polonais* (1573), the choreographer-*corago* (McGowan 1982, 37, 48n96), impresario-stage manager, and "master planner" (Anthony 1981, 29) of the entire *Balet*. This is certainly what emerges from the *livret* where his name appears on the title page.[10] The king's publisher of the *livret* refers to Beaujoyeux as "Geometrician, inventive and unique in your science" (McGowan 1982, 26), another instance where clarity is lacking. If we take Beaujoyeux literally and limit the dance to geometric forms only, then as "geometrician" it seems more than likely that he was the theoretical inventor-choreographer of the *Circé* dances, though probably not the "practical" dancing master.[11] Given the contemporary praise (in the *livret* poems) and the great esteem in which modern scholars hold him, it may come as a surprise—and is certainly worthy of note—that Beaujoyeux's name does not appear again in any of the ten or so "ballets" and *mascarades* that took place at the French court after the *Balet Comique* (McGowan [1963] 1978, 251–52) and before his death, which was perhaps in 1587.[12] It is true that the experiment of a composite spectacle was not reproduced in those years, in part at least for financial reasons, and while the names of poets and musicians for ballets have come down to us, not untypically, no choreographer's name has (McGowan [1963] 1978, 49–52).

The Two "Ballets"

Both "ballets" in the *Balet Comique* are composed entirely of geometric figures. This type of dance, also called "horizontal dance" (McGowan [1963] 1978, 36), was not a novelty in France having already made its appearance in the earlier (simpler and less studied) *Balet des Polonais*. "Horizontal dance" contrasted with "imitative" or pantomimic dance that was present in the French *mascarades* both before and after *Circé*.[13]

The first "ballet" in *Circé*, danced by twelve naiads, consisted of twelve figures, "toutes diverses l'une de l'autre" (McGowan 1982, fol. 22v). Only the starting position of the first entrée is described: that is, a line of six dancers with lines of three in front and behind, respectively, forming a kind of diamond from which the naiads then moved in and out among each other in different directions until the ending, when they assumed the same starting position. The other dance was the final "grand Balet," introduced by an entrée of "15 passages" and made up of forty "passages ou figures Geometriques" (McGowan 1982, fols. 55v–56r). Here, the twelve naiads, joined by four dryads, performed a variety of large and small geometric figures, all different and including squares, circles, and triangles. Beaujoyeux points out that as soon as the naiads, dressed in white, had traced out ("marquées") a figure, the dryads, clad in green, "broke" it, so that as one figure ended, the next began immediately. The music changed from "grave" to "gai," from binary to ternary, and was accompanied by "pas doux & alenti [slow]." Halfway through the *Balet* the dancers did a chain, with four different "interlacings" that resembled "a battle array, so well was the order kept, and so dextrously [did] each endeavor to observe her rank and cadence" (Cohen 1974, 30; McGowan 1982, fol. 56r).

This is the total extent of the choreographic information.

Importance and Meaning of the Two "Ballets"

There is no hint, as the MacClintocks somewhat hesitatingly suggest (1971, 16–17), that "the geometrical figures . . . are supposedly symbolic of the themes of the story." Going further, I question the words of Frances Yates, that the final ballet was "intended as an artistic expression and reinforcement of the Pythagorean-Platonic core of the [Baif] Academy—that all things are related to number, both in the outer world of nature and in the inner world of man's soul" (Yates [1947] 1968, 248). Nor do I find confirmation for McGowan's claim that the dance figures "intended to mirror the harmony of celestial bodies" (1998, 285). What I am proposing here is that none of the above statements emerge from either the *Balet*'s choreographies or text, and that modern specialists have tended to place their own interpretations on the material, often creating a "humanistic mystique," reiterating long-established clichés and seeing symbolism in the dances where none exists. If, as some modern scholars hold, it was commonplace by the 1580s that geometric figures in dance were symbols of the cosmos, in Italy, at least, figured dance consisted of either abstract figures or figures of specific images and devices. Moreover, if there was no need for Beaujoyeux to spell out the dances' geometric and number symbolism in words in the *livret*—inasmuch as this had been an accepted part of an educated person's world view for much of the Renaissance—why include four commentaries on the well-known allegory of *Circé*?

Is it not significant that in the *livret* less than one page each is devoted to the two dances, particularly in comparison to Beaujoyeux's lengthy and detailed descriptions of, for example, the moveable scenery or "floats," such as the fountain (four pages) or Minerva's chariot?[14] I thus cannot see, as does McGowan (1982, 27), that Beaujoyeux has "emphasize[d] that part of the occasion for which he was principally responsible, [giving] considerable expansion in his account to these geometric dances." Furthermore, why, among the twenty-seven engravings by Jacques Patin, were these "floats" and the *intermedi* scenes of the tritons and the satyrs reproduced in the *livret*, while there are none showing either the dancers or their geometric figures? On the other hand, in the *livret* of Beaujoyeux's earlier *Balet des Polonais* (1573), an engraving reproduces sixteen nymphs in a "frozen" moment of a geometric figure of their (supposedly) one-hour-long ballet (Franko 1993, 22), though we have to wait for the 1610 *Ballet de M. de Vendosme*[15] (Prunières [1914] 1970, 39) and even later in Italy (see below) for published depictions of geometric figures, floor patterns, and symbolic representations.

To impress further the readers of the *livret* with the quality of the entertainment, Beaujoyeux points out that he has written down the music of the "grand Balet" so that everybody should know what a variety of airs was necessary, "and so that nothing should be lacking or imperfect in the description of what occurred" (McGowan 1982, fol. 56r). What follows is a complete transcription of Lambert de Beaulieu's music, which actually highlights the absence of a similar record of the choreography.[16]

Hence, I raise the question whether the spare and nonspecific choreographic accounts in the *Circé livret*, together with the iconographic omissions, truly support the conviction that dance was of primary importance in the *Balet Comique*, and that Beaujoyeux, author of the *livret* and director of the whole, was also—except in a generic and theoretical sense—the choreographer. The danced interludes were important because of the participation of the queen and her ladies, but the choreography was neither novel nor as complex or elaborate as that in previous court fêtes (McGowan 1981, 27). Furthermore, these "ballet portions" did in no way "continue the unfolding plot," as the MacClintocks have asserted (1971, 16). The dance was "part of the action" *only* when interrupted by Circé.

Performance Viewing: Reading Figured Dance

In France, as modern writers tell us, geometric figured dances were supposed to be seen from above (McGowan [1963] 1978, 36), in order that the audience could "decipher or . . . read choreographic patterns" (Franko 1993, 16; see also 21, 39). McGowan states (1982, 30) that the king "seated on his throne, was probably the only spectator/player who could view the designs correctly." However, if we look at Patin's "Figure de la Salle," we note that the king (together with the queen mother, Catherine de' Medici, on his right) is really only slightly raised (McGowan 1982, fol. 4r). How much could he have seen and "deciphered" from the dais which Beaujoyeux had had built "close to the ground, only three 'degrees' high" (McGowan 1982, fol. 4v)?[17] Why should the best of all perspectives (at least for the modern viewer) have been that of the court ladies, seated behind the king on forty ascending tiers, rather than that of the various ambassadors who were, instead, apparently at ground level, not to mention that of the gentlemen (and ladies) in the side galleries who, though raised, had a distorted vision of the geometric patterns? It is certainly worth taking into consideration Dianne Woodruff's suggestion that "where people sat and what they saw or didn't see from various vantage points reveals an aesthetic tolerance different from our own" (Woodruff 1986, 125).

Figured Dance in Italy

Whether or not Beaujoyeux was the choreographer of the two "ballets" in the *Balet Comique de la Royne*, or rather the *corago* of the entire spectacle, it is apparent that he did not draw on his Italian antecedents for the dance or its music. Abstract figures, formations, and floor patterns were a feature of the *bassedanze* and *balli* created by Guglielmo Ebreo, Domenico da Piacenza, and other fifteenth-century dancing masters.[18] These consisted of horizontal, vertical, and "snake-like" lines and chains. Choreographies from Fabritio Caroso's *Il Ballarino* (1581) and Cesare Negri's *Gratie d'Amore* (1602) include hays ("chains") in lines, circles, and Z-shapes; files of dancers crisscrossing; "figure eights"; arch ("duck-and-dive") figures; "half-moons" or crescents; a snail-like "winding up the ball of yarn"; "cast offs" (called "fountain figure" by present-day Italian folk dancers); and, as with the fifteenth-century choreographic formations, dancers in triangles, circles, and squares. These features were found in traditional dances, "modernized" by Renaissance dance masters (see, for example, the "Chiaranzana" [Caroso (1581) 1967, fols. 176v–178v] and the "Catena" and "Caccia d'Amore" [Negri (1602) 1969, 277–80, 281–84], as well as in two staged choreographies composed by Negri and performed by six ladies and six gentlemen with lighted torches in the theatre of Milan's Ducal Palace in 1599 (Negri [1602] 1969, 271–76). Figured floor patterns, limited because of space, were also a major feature of "O che nuovo miracolo," Emilio de' Cavalieri's *ballo* for the final *intermedio* of *La Pellegrina*, produced for the marriage of Grand Duke Ferdinando de' Medici and Christine of Lorraine in 1589.[19]

"Geometric dancing," similar to that of the *Balet Comique*, was adopted in early seventeenth-century Italy by the musical theatre where figured floor patterns were, for the most part, used by the chorus. An initial hint of this appears in the final *ballo* of Cavalieri's *La Rappresentazione dell'Anima e del Corpo* ([1600] 1967) that was to be sung and danced with dignity, "with chain figures and 'passings' of all the couples."[20] Very similar are the instructions given to the chorus in the anonymous *Il Corago o vero alcune osservazioni per metter bene in scena le composizioni drammatiche* (The *corago* or some advice about how to stage dramatic works), written sometime between 1628 and 1637, where we are told, more than once, that the chorus can proceed doing various "spasseggi [*sic*] et intrecciamenti," the more participants, the better (Fabbri and Pompilio 1983, 98). However, *Il Corago* specifies that these various movements should lead into and conclude with symbolic representations and the portrayal of princely devices or monograms. In order that the figures be clearly recognized and understood, it was necessary to make a short pause as each one was formed (99).

Examples of musical productions that used these precepts—even before they were written down in *Il Corago*—were those of the Jesuit College of Nobles in Rome. In 1597 and again in 1620, the tragedy *Crispo* was performed. "[T]he chorus was made up of sixteen lads . . . who, guided by the *corifeo* [leader of the chorus], performed their exits and entrances, the dances and counter-dances and pauses . . . singing and playing" (Sardoni 1986, 22–23). A published edition included drawings of some of the chorus's floor patterns: a two-headed eagle (representing the Holy Roman Empire); a cross encircled by a snake which took form during a prayer to Christ; the rays of an eye and ear symbolizing Fame; and a labyrinth and a cross denoting divine power (Sardoni 1986, 17, 18, 23). In 1623 another production at the Collegio Romano had the chorus, "for variety and embellishment . . . ," do "passages representing the ancient chorus in its heavenly movements . . . with labyrinths, knots, spires . . . and other figures of stars, moons, lilies and devices of the Ludovisi family" (Sardoni 1986, 24).

To date we know of only one geometric figure dance in Italy that was not performed by a chorus but by dancers only. This is the "Ballo de' [24] Cavalieri" which appeared in *La Festa a Ballo "Delizie di Posillipo Boscarecce, e Maritime"* (The sylvan and maritime delights of Posilipo), performed in Naples in 1620 (Jackson 1978). The twenty-four figures were neither symbolic nor representative as in *Crispo*, but were abstract geometric designs. (Could this not be the case also with the geometric patterns in the dances in the *Balet Comique*?) The choreographer is known, one Giacomo Spiardo. He also included mimed *balletti*, with "stravaganti gesti" featuring swans, apes, and satyrs. It is historiographically significant that this court spectacle—with its music (instrumental only for the dances, as in *Circe*) written by several different composers and its mythological theme drawn largely from Tasso's *Gerusalemme Liberata*—has attracted so little attention from dance and theatre historians, despite its availability in a facsimile edition.

It is possible that the "geometric dance" used in court ballet (for the first time, as far as can be determined, in the *Balet des Polonais*), influenced not only the *Balet Comique* and the *Balet de M. Vendosme* but also Italian court spectacle, at least the Neapolitan *Festa a Ballo*. In France these figured court choreographies were performed by noble ladies (*Balet des Polonais* and *Balet Comique*) or gentlemen (*M. Vendosme*), and not by professional *ballerini*/dance masters. This is also the case in Spiardo's final Neapolitan *Ballo* (for twenty-four gentlemen), as well as in Negri's torch dances and his "Brando Alta Regina" (danced by both ladies and gentlemen). In all other known Italian examples, chain and geometric figures were employed by members of the chorus who danced and formed figures while singing. Giovanni Battista Doni, in his *Musica scenica* (1974, 60, 95–96), makes a distinction between dancers in a ballet (*Ballo*) and the singers in moving choruses (*al passeggio*) who "may wish to represent an occasional labyrinth" but should limit themselves to a moderate number of figures—simple circles (like the round choirs of the ancients), lines, and square figures—performed well and in tempo. Is it not significant that Doni specified that steps and figures were to reflect the poetic text and the particular characters being represented, while Beaujoyeux, so often presented by modern scholars as patron and inventor of figured dance and particularly of a type which interpreted the *balet*'s dramatic verse, makes no such references?

Dance for Italian Spectacles Prior to the *Balet Comique*: Pantomimic Dance

Both *Il Corago* and Doni's *Musica scenica* refer to the presence of pantomimic dance in the first decades of Italian opera.[21] The roots for this type of "narrative" or "imitative" dance can be found in the numerous *balli/balletti* with mythological and allegorical themes—often called *moresche* or *intermedi*—which were produced in the fifteenth and sixteenth centuries (Sparti 2002). In the *moresche*, or "panto-mimic ballets," the allegories are danced out, while in the *Balet Comique* the dances are abstract even though the story, through its spoken and sung text, is an allegory. On the other hand, "imitative dance" was part of the French fifteenth-, sixteenth-, and even seventeenth-century *mommeries*, *mascarades*, and *entremets* (before and after *Circé*),[22] and one might well ask why there is no such dance in the *Balet Comique*, especially for the *intermedi* of the Tritons and of the Satyrs. (Think of the magnificent and detailed descriptions—costumes, gestures, and instruments—for the "Ballo dei Satiri e Baccanti" that ended the *intermedii* for the 1539 wedding festivities of Eleonora of Toledo and Cosimo de' Medici [Minor and Mitchell 1968, 349–53]). The *moresche* were described by ambassadors and chroniclers present at events such as princely wedding banquets, plays, and carnival spectacles. A few excerpts will serve as examples:

1. In 1473 in Rome during a seven-hour banquet a "*ballo* of Hercules" was performed as an allegorical homage to Eleonora of Aragon's new spouse, Ercole d'Este. The "ballet" portrayed a group of centaurs disrupting a wedding celebration and trying to abduct the nymphs with whom Hercules and other classical heroes were dancing. After a "fine battle, the centaurs, defeated by Hercules, retreated and the festive dancing recommenced."[23]

2. A *moresca* about Jason, described by Balthasar Castiglione, was performed in Urbino in 1513 between the acts of the *Calandra*: "Jason appeared at one side of the stage dancing, armed in the ancient manner, handsome, with a sword and wonderful shield. On the other side were two bulls who seemed real ... and spewed fire from their mouths ... Jason harnessed them, had them plow, and he sowed the dragon's teeth, from which little by little men armed *all'antica* grew out of the stage ... and they danced a proud *moresca* to kill Jason ... Jason entered with the golden fleece and he danced marvelously" (Dovizi 1985, 205). Castiglione, author of *The Book of the Courtier*, was in charge of the *intermedi* and may have "invented" (designed) the *moresca*. However, he was not the choreographer/dance master. Does this help to clarify Beaujoyeux's role in the *Circé* dances?

3. A more complete *moresca*, an entire spectacle which included recitation, took place in Rome at carnival and was reported by Castiglione to Federico Gonzaga in 1521. "Eight young Sienese *moreschanti* performed a *moresca* in the courtyard of Castel Sant'Angelo. ... The Pope, and many other gentlemen, looked on from the windows" (Cruciani 1983, 491–92). The characters were a young woman, eight "hermit-friars," and Cupid. In between the spoken text were five different danced parts: the hermits

leading a chained Cupid; the hermits and Cupid fighting; the hermits dancing around Cupid, all in love with the young woman thanks to Venus's potion and Cupid's arrow; the hermits, dressed now as gallants, dancing the *moresca* another time; and finally, two *moresche* performed with swords—the music for all the dancing provided by pipe and tabor.[24] For Prunières ([1914] 1970, 24), this "ingenious association of dance, poetry, music with dramatic action . . . is a veritable prototype of the *ballet du cour.*"

An Allegorical Fable Performed in Bologna in 1487: Parallels with the *Balet Comique*

Even if the pro-Italian Prunières calls the Castel Sant'Angelo 1521 *moresca* a "veritable prototype," he nonetheless gives Beaujoyeux the honor of having created the first *ballet de cour* through his uniting poetic text, music, scenic décor, and dance around a common dramatic action ([1914] 1970, 82–86). It is, at this point, worth looking at a Bolognese allegorical spectacle from 1487 which is so rich in parallels to *Circé* as to do away with all claims as to the latter's primacy and uniqueness, except as concerns France.[25]

The festive occasion during which this untitled allegorical fable was performed was also, as in Paris one hundred years later, a dynastic marriage—in this case between Annibale Bentivoglio, son of the lord of Bologna, and Lucrezia d'Este, daughter of the Duke of Ferrara and half-sister of Isabella d'Este. The grandiose celebrations lasted for several days, as did those for the Duke of Joyeuse, culminating in the allegorical spectacle. The underlying political reason was Bologna's desire and determination to keep its own *signoria*, independent of the Papal States and of Este expansionist pressures. Hence, the various festive events were devised to confer a dignity on the Bentivoglio family equal to that of such magnificent courts as those of Ferrara, Mantua, and Florence (Bortoletti 2002, 322–23).

There are several eyewitness accounts of the allegorical fable, besides the official version (which was written in Latin). The most detailed is by Giovanni Sabadino degli Arienti, a literato in the employ of the lord of Bologna (the groom's father). Unimpeded by limits of length and official purpose, he clearly wished to express his gratitude and esteem to his lord, and thus was able to give free rein to his description. Sabadino claims to have sat for nine hours viewing the spectacle "with great bliss" from the musicians' platform. (This is clearly an exaggeration and outdoes that of the five-and-a-half hours of the *Balet Comique*.) Similarly to *Circé*, the important viewers were raised: illustrious guests and the newlyweds themselves were seated on a tribune and looked down on the performance, which took place in the great hall of the Bentivoglio palace.

The allegorical fable, with poetic texts by the erudite humanist Domenico Fusco Arimenense, has as its theme chastity, love, and marriage. The story revolves around a lost nymph (personifying the bride, Lucrezia d'Este) at grips with the insidious wiles of Venus and the determination of Diana. Each in her own way suggests pleasure on the one hand, chastity on the other, seeking to divert the nymph-Lucrezia from marriage. Finally Juno counsels her to unite with a certain youth (Annibale) in holy matrimony. The allegory-spectacle included dance, mime, vocal and instrumental music, dramatic-poetic text (spoken and sung), scenic effects (moveable stage machinery), and, of course, costumes and accessories, minutely described. The mythological figures and classical gods were representative of a "well-tried and immediately recognized imagery" (Bartoletti 2002, 327). Dance was ever present within the performance of the fable itself and, furthermore, nicely ensconced between a prelude—featuring the extraordinary dexterity of a six-year-old Tuscan girl dancing alone and with a male partner to the accompaniment of pipes and tabor—and a postlude, with dancing for all the assembled company. Moreover, the important stage props, a tower, a palace, a mountain with a cave near a wood, a rock or crag, each made its appearance "dancing." Each was so large that it held several performers, some hidden inside.[26] Unfortunately, there are no specific drawings illustrating any aspect of the spectacle, nor has any music survived.

A brief description of how the allegory unfolds will indicate the various kinds and moments of dance as they occurred, and how they fit together with the music, props, and poetic text. The "fabula" began with "tube" (probably shawms and trombones) introducing an old wood-god who, in turn, made room for the dancing tower. After each of the above-mentioned stage props appeared and danced—"as if by itself"—to its place in the scene, Diana and one of her nymphs addressed the Bentivoglios in verse. A wild lion (which fiercely jumped about "as if real") was presented to the lord as a symbol of vice dominated by the virtue of Diana (Bortoletti 2002, 329). Following this, a dance called "La Caccia" (The hunt), sung by a chorus of six, was performed by Diana and her nymphs.[27] When they had finished, they began dancing a *bassadanza* in a ring accompanied by instrumental music. Cupid's shooting an arrow and striking one of the nymphs, Lucrezia (the bride's namesake), interrupted the *bassadanza* and caused the other nymphs to flee. (This brings to mind Circé's interruption of the naiad's dance.) Venus, with Infamy and Jealousy close by, then tried in verse to woo the nymph to her court. Juno warned "Lucrezia" about Venus's wiles, and presented to her "Annibale," her future husband. In Cupid's presence the two performed a dance called "Vivolieta" (Live happily).[28] Three different sorts of celebratory dances followed. The first, to sung music, was performed by the four "Emperors of the world" who, with their ladies, appeared from out of the [Bentivoglio] palace. After this, another

of Cupid's arrows struck the rock and brought forth a lady holding a flower and
a quince (symbol of fertility). Eight men with black faces, wearing Moorish dress
and bells, danced around her "in *moresca* fashion" to the sound of pipe and tabor
and other instruments: a propitiatory rite dedicated to both Love and to the young
bride.[29] Lastly, many couples from the Butchers Guild, wearing the Bentivoglio
device,[30] performed a dance with garlanded hoops. No choreographic description
is known, though there is a contemporary image.[31] The finale-postlude consisted
of round and couple dances, which grew faster and faster, and in which all those
present at the entertainment took part. Having the noble onlookers dance after a
spectacle was quite usual in sixteenth-century France, as were circle dances—yet
the Bologna festivity is the only known occasion in Italy that included audience
participation,[32] and one of the few where courtiers danced in the round.

We do not know who the performers—the actors, dancers, and singers—in
the "Love, Chastity, and Marriage" allegory were. They almost certainly were not
nobility or they would have been named,[33] and the real Lucrezia and Annibale
were in the audience. No mention is made of a *corago*, for either the general festivities or for the allegory. Nor do we have a name for the choreographer, although
Lorenzo Lavagnolo—the highly esteemed dancing master who had taught dancing to the Este sisters, Isabella, Beatrice and Lucrezia, in Ferrara—had been
sought by the Bentivoglio court to prepare the wedding entertainments (Bortoletti 2002, 336–38).

The similarities between the Bologna 1487 *fabula* and the 1588 *Balet
Comique* are worth reiterating: (1) the occasion—the "royal" marriages and
the strong political motives; (2) the place—a hall in the palace; (3) the seating
arrangements—the audience raised; (4) the mobile sets with their cargo of goddesses, dancers, and other personages; (5) the introductory speech and the recitation throughout in verse; (6) the interruption of the dancing; (7) the finale with
dancing for all; and (8) the uncertainty regarding the choreographer. Some of the
main differences between the two productions, which help to explain why one has
been more studied than the other, are the absence of a *livret* for the Bologna allegory and the lack of any extant written music. Text and description are, however,
available in manuscript accounts and in a published version from 1891 (Zannoni),
discussed, furthermore, by Gabriele Cazzola in 1979 and by F. Alberto Gallo in
1982. That these sources have not been examined, to even half the extent of that of
the *Balet Comique*, can perhaps be explained by the relative inaccessibility of two
of these secondary sources (Zannoni and Gallo), and further, I suggest, by unfamiliarity on the part of non-Italian dance and theatre historians with the Italian
language and Italian dance, particularly that of the fifteenth century.

Examining the differences in dance between the two spectacles, we have
that of the *Balet Comique* consisting of two sole "ballets," both geometric and both

performed, to instrumental music only, by female members of the French court. In the Bologna allegory, the "introductory" dance is performed by a six-year-old Florentine girl whose grace was outstanding and whose technique included many high jumps and leg beats. The fable itself begins with the dancing in each of the sets, and then the miming and leaping about of the fierce lion. A variety of different ent dance types are performed including a *bassadanza*, a *moresca*, and dances with titles not found in the contemporary repertoire as it is known to date, possibly composed for the occasion. These are performed to sung music, pipe and tabor, and other unspecified instruments. The dancers in Bologna, both men and women, are anonymous and presumably from different social strata—including pages and members of the Butchers Guild, and possibly the occasional courtier. It is worth noting that circle dances, which ended the evening in both Paris and Bologna, are never described by the quattrocento dance masters whose treatises tend to contain their own original "art" choreographies, designed mostly for a couple or trio. Round dances were performed in villages as traditional ("folk") dances and also occasionally in *moresche* and choreographed allegories, but this is, for the present at least, the only text that has nobles doing circle dances.[34]

Conclusion

A myth has grown up around the *Balet Comique de la Royne*, and myths are difficult to dismantle. Criticism has been raised about the limits of this work but it has not been heard, partly because it has been hidden by further mystification. Selma Jean Cohen, for example, admits that "the author of this libretto devotes far more space to the texts of the speeches and songs and to descriptions of the decorations than he does to the dances," but the reason she gives for this is that "after all, most of his readers knew the steps from their own experience in court ballrooms" (Cohen 1974, 19). We have seen, however, that for those interpreting the humanistic (and political) meanings of the two ballets, the steps were the least important factor. As to the music of *Circé*, James Anthony states that "the intrinsic musical value of the *Ballet comique* is not commensurate with its historical position. The choral music is square and rigidly homophonic with only an occasional cross relation to lend some harmonic interest" (1981, 30).[35] Piero Gargiulo (1999, xv) confirms this, suggesting that the music is "certainly not thrilling [and is] outstanding only in sporadic episodes." As for the text, Prunières ([1914] 1970, 87) says that the poetry was far too mediocre to be by d'Aubigné. Given this, why should the dance alone be admirable and worthy of note?

The myth of the importance of the *Balet Comique* is based, as we have seen, on the survival of its *livret*—a rare (if not unique) extant example of a sixteenth-century court entertainment replete with its notated music, poetic text, staging directions, and illustrations. It is the absence of similar documentation for other spectacles that has inspired so many studies of *Circé*, more than for any other contemporary work. The same lack of documentation makes it impossible to compare the *Balet Comique*'s artistic worth with that of the various court productions of the time.

I suggest that if the *Balet* is studied, the quality of its various parts (music, dance, text, and scenery) must also be evaluated, as must the artistic-historic success (or failure) of the experiment of the *musique-danse-poésie mesurés à l'antique*. Future research should also attempt to keep in mind the context of the spectacles that came before and after it in both France and Italy. Most of these have not been considered worthwhile to investigate because their danced and mimed *moresche*, *mommeries*, *intermedi*, or *ballets* were not structured around a single dramatic intrigue. It is the importance given to the *Balet Comique*'s unified plot, by Beaujoyeux himself and up through the ages to the present, which also requires reexamination. This aesthetic value continues to give an unquestioned place of honor to unified works as being superior to those composed of episodes. As a result, other court ballets, even those in which music and text survive, are dismissed by scholars as being of little interest. Are we ready to clip away at the historiography that has grown up around *Circé*, and make way for the emergence and the study of other dance spectacles?

Notes

1. See References for these and the following texts.
2. Gabriel Garrido directed the Ensemble Elyma; choreography was by Bruna Gondoni and Véronique Daniels (the *grand Bal*); regisseur was Alain Carré.
3. Besides Dellaborra, who offers chapters on Belgioioso (Beaujoyeux) and on the performance of the *Balet*, other contributions to the volume include those by musicologist Piero Gargiulo, dance historian Claudia Celi, and early music performer Sergio Balestracci.
4. Prunières ([1914] 1970) and Anthony (1981) are notable exceptions.
5. La Chesnaye, Lambert de Beaulieu and Jacques Salmon, and Jacques Patin, respectively.
6. In sixteenth- and seventeenth-century Italy, the *corago* was stage manager, director, impresario, movement coach, and more. See Savage and Sansone, 1989, 495–96.
7. All translations are my own unless otherwise noted.
8. McGowan recognizes that, in the end, the extravagant costs, rather than working for the court in this critical period for France, produced censure, so that the *Balet Comique* was actually "a political failure" (1982, 42).
9. The *Balet Comique* also attempted to recreate the measured music, poetry, and dance of antiquity (see Franko 1993, 34–35; Yates [1947] 1968, 56–58; Walker 1948; Daye 2000, 73).
10. "Balet Comique de la Royne, faict aux nopces de Monsieur le Duc de Ioyeuse & madammoyselle de Vaudemont sa soeur. Par Baltasar de Beauioyeulx, valet de cambre du Roy, & de la Royne sa mere."

11. See below in text for Castiglione as inventor of *moresche*.

12. According to the MacClintocks (1971, 11), after having served as *valet de chambre* to Henri III, Marie Stuart, Charles IX, and the duc d'Alençon, Beaujoyeux was again in Catherine's service in 1587 "and had been made *Écuyer* and *seigneur des Landes*." His date of death is still unconfirmed.

13. See n. 22 below.

14. The *livret*, after 15 introductory pages (dedications, preface, etc.) has 75 folios (150 pages) of which 27 are full-page illustrations and 53 almost all full-pages of music. The final 3 1/2 pages dedicated to commentaries on the *Circé* allegory are printed in a much smaller character-type.

15. See Franko (1993, 18) for a reproduction of the twelve figures that were based, in theory, on the alphabet of the ancient druids.

16. About half of the music for the *Balet Comique* is dance music.

17. "[u]n Dez pres de terre, ayant troi *degrez* de haulter." McGowan (1982, 29) assumes this to mean three *feet* high, though in the next pages "pieds" is used more than once to describe the scenery.

18. For the masters, choreographies, and dance types, see Guglielmo Ebreo 1993.

19. See Nevile 1999, esp. 124 and footnote, and 127–30.

20. Final paragraphs of the *Avvertimenti per la presente Rappresentatione* (Cavalieri [1600] 1967).

21. *Il Corago*'s promised chapter on "pantomimo," a mode of recitation without "the human voice and by means of gesture and dance in time to music," is not included; perhaps it was lost or never written (Fabbri and Pompilio 1983, 40).

22. See Prunières ([1914] 1970, 9–16) and McGowan ([1963] 1978, 37–40) for the fifteenth and early sixteenth centuries where many pantomimes, similar to those in Italy, were being performed, featuring heroes like Jason and Hercules as well as fiery dragons. Also note Pierre de Brach's description of the *Masquarade du Triomphe de Diane* performed in Bordeaux around 1575–76 (McGowan [1963] 1978, 34–36). Finally, see Anthony (1981, 33) for ballets and court *fêtes* between 1596 and 1607 that "borrowed liberally from the 'mascarades à l'Italienne.'"

23. See Sparti 1996, 42, 43–44, 60.

24. Besides references to pipe and tabor players (*tamburini*), there is little information regarding the music for these mimed *balletti*.

25. Though this source was known, Bortoletti (2002) is the first to have examined it from the point of view of the dance involved.

26. *Circe*'s moveable decor carried dancers and actors, but neither the fountain nor chariot "danced."

27. There is no way of knowing if the choreography of this "Caccia" was at all similar to sixteenth century choreographies of the same name (See Negri [1602] 1969, 281–84; and Compasso 1995, 5).

28. No dance or contemporary music by this name is known.

29. Two illustrations come to mind: "morescanti" wearing bells (and accompanied by a pipe player and a drummer) exuberantly dance around a woman holding a fruit (in the Freydal MS of Maximilian I; also in Brainard 1981, 722); and an anonymous Florentine engraving with naked men (bells on wrists) acrobatically and wildly dancing round a Venus holding, possibly, a quince (Istanbul, Sérail Museum, reproduced in Bortoletti 2002, 332).

30. The Bentivoglios had been butchers in past centuries and their *signoria* in the 1400s was strongly supported by the Butchers and other Guilds.

31. See the graffiti fresco (attributed to Girolamo Ristori, 1455–1512) now in the Mural Painting Museum, Prato, and reproduced in Bortoletti 2002, 334.

32. At the end of the *Balet Comique*, the dancers (queen, princesses, ladies, maidens) all chose a prince or gentleman to dance with and performed together "le grand Bal," followed by branles in lines and circles. "Le grand Bal" may well have been "la Chiaranzana," a dance for many couples that was often performed at weddings including that of Henri IV and Maria de'Medici in Lyons in 1600 (D'Ancona 1913, 426). It was composed of many figures and supposedly could last an hour or more.

33. On what was a rare occasion for a prince or courtier, in 1502 Cesare Borgia performed in a *moresca* in the Pope's court in Rome. Though masked, he was richly enough dressed to be recognized by the chroniclers (Guglielmo Ebreo 1993, 53).

34. See the miniature by Taddeo Crivelli in the Bible of Borso d'Este representing the court of Solomon, the only known contemporary depiction of nobles—three courtiers and their ladies—dancing in a circle. Is this a rare but realistic image, or a decorative, perhaps symbolic one? (Guglielmo Ebreo 1993, 59, and 60, pl. 15.)

35. Anthony ([1980] 1995, 30) adds that "The ['musics' for the] dances . . . have a formal charm despite the almost geometric regularity of phrase groupings."

References

Anthony, James R. 1981. *French Baroque Music from Beaujoyeulx to Rameau.* Rev. ed. New York: W. W. Norton.

———. (1980) 1995. "Ballet de cour." In *The New Grove Dictionary of Music and Musicians,* edited by Stanley Sadie, 2:88–90. Reprint, London: Macmillan.

Balestracci, Sergio. 1999. "L'uso degli strumenti nel *Balet comique de la Royne*." In Dellaborra 1999, 9–28.

Barlow, Jeremy. 2000. "*Honneur à la Dance*: A Musical Analysis of *Le Premier Ballet* in *Le Balet Comique de la Royne*." In *Terpsichore 1450–1900: Proceedings of the International Dance Conference, Ghent, Belgium, 11–18 April 2000,* edited by B. Ravelhofer, 65–70. Ghent, Institute for Historical Dance Practice.

Bertini, Giuseppe. 1997. *Le nozze di Alessandro Farnese: Feste alle corti di Lisbona e Bruxelles.* Milan: Skira.

Bonniffet, Pierre. 1992. "Esquisses du ballet humaniste (1572–1581)." In *Le Ballet aux XVIe et XVIIe siècles en France et à la Cour de Savoie,* edited by Marie-Thérèse Bouquet-Boyer, 16–49. Cahiers de L'I.R.H.M.E.S. 1. Geneva: Slatkine.

Bortoletti, Francesca. 2002. "An Allegorical *Fabula* for the Bentivoglio-d'Este Marriage of 1487." *Dance Chronicle* 25/3: 321–42.

Brainard, Ingrid. 1981. "An Exotic Court Dance and Dance Spectacle of the Renaissance: *La Moresca*." In *Report of the Twelfth Congress of the International Musicological Society, Berkeley 1977,* edited by Daniel Heartz and Bonnie Wade, 715–29. Kassel: Bärenreiter.

Caroso, Fabritio. (1581) 1967. *Il Ballarino.* Venice. Facsimile reprint, New York: Broude.

Cavalieri, Emilo de'. (1600) 1967. *La Rappresentazione dell'Anima e del Corpo.* Rome. Facsimile reprint, Bologna: Forni.

Cazzola, Gabriele. 1979. "'Bentivoli machinatores': Aspetti politici e momenti teatrali di una festa quattrocentesca Bolognese." *Biblioteca Teatrale* 23/24: 14–38.

Celi, Claudia. 1999. "Le metamorfosi di Circe e l'arte del sovrano dominio." In Dellaborra 1999, 3–8.

Cohen, Selma Jeanne, ed. 1974. "Balthasar de Beaujoyeulx, *Ballet Comique de la Reine* Paris, 1582." In *Dance as a Theatre Art: Source Readings in Dance History from 1581 to the Present*, edited by Selma Jeanne Cohen, 19–31. New York: Dodd, Mead.

Compassio, Lutio. (1560) 1995. *Ballo della Gagliarda*. Introduction by Barbara Sparti. Facsimile reprint, Freiburg: "fa-gisis" Musik- und Tansedition.

Cruciani, Fabrizio. 1983. *Teatro nel Rinascimento: Roma 1450–1500*. Biblioteca del Cinquecento 22. Rome: Bulzoni.

D'Ancona, Alessandro. 1913. "Descrizione di un banchetto del 1600." In *Mélanges offerts a M. Émile Picot par ses amis et ses élèves*, 1:421–27. Paris: Librairie Damascène Morgand.

Daye, Anne. 2000. "*Honneur à la Dance*: A Choreographic Analysis of the Ballet Entries of *Le Balet Comique de la Royne*." In *Terpsichore 1450–1900: Proceedings of the International Dance Conference, Ghent, Belgium, 11–18 April 2000*, edited by B. Ravelhofer, 71–83. Ghent: Institute for Historical Dance Practice.

Dellaborra, Mariateresa. 1999. *"Une Invention Moderne": Baldassare da Belgioioso e il "Balet Comique de la Royne."* Lucca: Libreria Musicale Italiana.

Doni, Giovanni Battista. (1763) 1974. *Trattato della musica scenica*. In *Lyra Barberina*, edited by Antonio Francesco Gori, vol. 2: lines 1–202. Florence. Facsimile reprint, Bologna: Forni.

Dovizi, Bernardo. 1985. *La Calandra: Commedia elegantissima per messer Bernardo Dovizi da Bibbiena*. Edited by Giorgio Padoan. Medioevo e umanesimo 57. Padua: Antenore.

Fabbri, P. and A. Pompilio, eds. 1983. *Il Corago, o vero, Alcune osservazioni per metter bene in scena le composizioni drammatiche*. Studi e testi per la storia della musica 4. Florence: Olschki.

Franko, Mark. 1993. *Dance as Text: Ideologies of the Baroque Body*. RES Monographs in Anthropology and Aesthetics. Cambridge: Cambridge University Press.

Gallo, F. Alberto. 1982. "La danza negli spettacoli conviviali del secondo Quattrocento." In *Spettacoli conviviali dall'antichità alle corti italiane del '400*, 261–67. Rome: Centro de studi sul teatro medioevale e rinascimentale.

Gargiulo, Piero. 1999. "Prefazione." In Dellaborra 1999, xi–xvi.

Guglielmo Ebreo of Pesaro. 1993. *De pratica seu arte tripudii: On the Practice or Art of Dancing*. Edited, translated, and introduced by Barbara Sparti. Oxford: Clarendon Press.

Jackson, Roland. 1978. *A Neapolitan Festa a Ballo: "Delizie di Posilipo Boscarecce, e Maritime" and Selected Instrumental Ensemble Pieces from Naples Conservatory MS 4.6.3*. Recent Researches in the Music of the Baroque Era 25. Madison: A-R Editions.

MacClintock, Carol. 1995. "Beaujoyeux, Balthasar...," In *The New Grove Dictionary of Music and Musicians*, edited by Stanley Sadie, 2:324. Reprint, London: Macmillan.

MacClintock, Carol and Lander MacClintock, transl. and ed. 1971. *Le Balet Comique de la Royne 1581*. Musicological Studies and Documents 25. New York: American Institute of Musicology.

McGowan, Margaret M. (1963) 1978. *L'Art du Ballet de Cour en France 1581–1643*. Paris: Centre national de la recherche scientifique.

———. 1982. *Le Balet Comique by Balthazar de Beaujoyeulx*. Medieval & Renaissance Texts

& Studies 6. Binghamton, NY: Center for Medieval and Early Renaissance Studies, State University of New York at Binghamton.

———. 1998. "Ballet de Cour." In *International Encyclopedia of Dance*, edited by Selma Jeanne Cohen, 1:285–87. New York: Oxford University Press.

Minor, Andrew C., and Bonner Mitchell. 1968. *A Renaissance Entertainment: Festivities for the Marriage of Cosimo I, Duke of Florence, in 1539*. Columbia, MO: University of Missouri Press.

Negri, Cesare. (1602) 1969. *Le Gratie d'Amore*. Milan. Facsimile reprint, New York: Broude.

Nevile, Jennifer. 1998. "Cavalieri's Theatrical *Ballo* 'O che nuovo miracolo': A Reconstruction." *Dance Chronicle* 21/3: 353–88.

———. 1999. "Cavalieri's Theatrical *Ballo* and the Social Dances of Caroso and Negri." *Dance Chronicle* 22/1: 119–33.

Prunières, Henry. (1914) 1970. *Le Ballet de cour en France avant Benserade et Lully*. Paris: Henri Laurens. Reprint, New York: Johnson Reprint Corp.

Sardoni, Alessandra. 1986. "La sirena e l'angelo: La danza barocca a Roma tra meraviglia ed edificazione morale." *La Danza Italiana* 4: 7–26.

Savage, Roger, and Matteo Sansone. 1989. "*Il Corago* and the Staging of Early Opera: Four Chapters from an Anonymous Treatise circa 1630." *Early Music* 17: 495–511.

Sparti, Barbara. 1996. "The Function and Status of Dance in the 15th-Century Italian Courts." *Dance Research* 14/1: 42–61.

Sparti, Barbara. 2002. "The Moresca and Mattaccino in Italy—circa 1450–1630." In *Proceedings of the Symposium Moreska Past and Present*, 1–11. Zagreb: Institute for Ethnology and Folklore Research.

Walker, D. P. 1948. "The Influence of *musique mesurée à l'antique*, Particularly on the Airs de Cour of the Early Seventeenth Century." *Musica Disciplina*, 2:141–63.

Woodruff, Dianne L. 1986. "The 'Balet Comique' in the Petit Bourbon: A Practical View." In *Proceedings of the Society of Dance History Scholars*, 91–129. University of California, Riverside: SDHS.

Yates, Frances A. (1947) 1968. *The French Academies of the Sixteenth Century*. London: Warburg Institute. Reprint, Nendeln, Liechtenstein: Kraus Reprints.

———. 1959. *The Valois Tapestries*. London: Warburg Institute.

Zannoni, Giovanni. 1891. "Una rappresentazione allegorica a Bologna nel 1487." *Atti Reale Accademia dei Lincei*, ser. IV/7: 414–27.

Mutanze, Divisions, and *Diferencias*:
Variation Form in Late Renaissance Dance

G. Yvonne Kendall

Dance does not exist in a vacuum. Any study of source contents for *la danza* will be incomplete without making reference to its partner discipline—*la musica*. The conjunction of the disciplines of music and dance has vital implications for both, particularly in the areas of form and performance. This study will address one of the most prominent and influential forms in both its musical and choreographic incarnations: variation form.[1] The examination of this specific example from the sixteenth century will advance understanding of one aspect of the relationship between dance and music.

Variation form, a vibrant creative structure, first appeared in music and dance in sixteenth-century Italy when much of Italy was under Spanish rule. During this era, the most prolific output of cinquecento dance manuals was produced in northern Italy and Naples, regions largely controlled by Spanish governors. Once their tours of duty had ended, these governors often returned to Spain accompanied by Italian dance masters who were also responsible for introducing Italian style at the courts of France, Austria, Poland, and Savoy, among others.[2] However, Italy also received influence from Spain, as did these other countries. Every major dance manual of the period includes mention of Spain and contains dances that refer to that Iberian nation.

Dances found in variation form have been identified in England, France, Italy, and Spain, all countries known for rich music sources. They include works by such notable musicians and publishers as Pierre Attaingnant, William Byrd, Antonio de Cabezón, and Antonio Gardano. The published volumes of French dance master Thoinot Arbeau, and Italians Fabritio Caroso and Cesare Negri, are well represented in the search for variation-form choreographies; and the relatively unknown dance manuscripts of England and Spain add a new and exciting depth to this study. This essay defines variations as found in late Renaissance choreographies and identifies the dance types that appeared in those forms. A listing of music and dance resources consulted can be found under References, below.

Sixty-six choreographies related to variation form are preserved in twelve dance sources and more than twenty music sources, containing in excess of seven hundred concordant tunes that I have identified from the sixteenth and early seventeenth centuries. These surprisingly copious source materials reveal a rich mine of information. Examining the choreographies and music found in variation form as preserved in these sources makes it possible to specifically identify: (1) the dances that appear in variation form in both music and choreographies, (2) the frequency of their appearances, (3) the formal elements shared by both disciplines, and (4) the formal elements that are discipline-specific.

The Music

The music search was limited to documents from those countries that produced dance manuals. They represent lute and keyboard variations primarily from Italy and Spain, as well as sources from France and England where Italian and Spanish influences were strongly felt.[3] Consort music in simple homophonic settings was excluded in order to provide a clearer comparison with the dance sources. Although dance sources that contain music present it in simple homophonic settings, all of the actual choreographies in these sources are typically as elaborate as the most elaborate dances in the purely music sources. The remaining choreographies (those without music) at least imply choreographies much more complex than the simplest music settings, therefore the most apt comparisons between the two arts can only be found by comparing choreographies and music that are equivalent in complexity.

The first example of variation form to be published was Joanambrosio Dalza's *Intabulature di lauto*, by eminent Venetian music printer Ottavio Petrucci in 1508. The Italian origins of variation form provided in lute tablature are only one reason for the use of these sources for analysis. Lute sources were also chosen because they represent both common practice and the cutting edge; they are abundant in the repertoire of late renaissance Italy and, most appropriate for the purposes of this study, lute tablature is the most common means by which music is presented in the choreographic sources.[4]

That these musical and choreographic sources reflect the influences of Italy and Spain was an important supplementary factor in the repertoire choices made for this study. It must be noted, however, that in the case of England the term "lute sources" includes all plucked string instruments such as the lute, cittern, and bandora (also "pandora"). Similarly, in Spain this term is generic for music playable on lute, harp, vihuela, or on keyboard instruments.[5]

The decision to include keyboard music in this study was primarily made because such sources—particularly those from England—are often cited as the zenith of variation-form composition. These English sources, however, show a clear relationship to the major progenitors of the form. Their inclusion allows us to see these pieces in the context of their time, not as virtuosic deities residing on Olympian peaks above mundane, earthly dance, but as typical representatives of the period: not *musica caelestis* but *musica instrumentalis*. In addition to individual printed sources, I have also included monumental studies—Coelho (1995) is a catalog of Italian lute manuscripts, while Esses (1992) contains manuscript and printed sources representing variation form dances from Spain, and Sabol (1978) contains manuscript sources of English dance.

Regarding form, music variations of this period take a preexisting tune, commonly a dance tune, and vary it in an assortment of ways. The melody can be changed while the harmony remains the same; the harmony or other accompanimental figures can be changed while the melody remains the same; or both can change while a characteristic rhythmic figure remains the same. In each case, some familiar quality remains as the anchor for the variations. In music all of these types of variation can be found in the same piece. The macroform of musical variations is much the same from piece to piece. The theme is presented, followed by a series of variations that sometimes end with another statement of the theme. The dances found in this form are the *canario*, *gagliarda*, *passamezzo*, *tordiglione*, and *pavan/pavaniglia* (see table 1 for variation dances found in music sources).

The Choreographies

For variation choreographies, I searched all known sources from England, France, Italy, and Spain for any references to musical or choreographic variation: terms such as *mutanza* in Italian, "variation" or "division" in English, and *diferencia* or *mudança* in Spanish (see table 2 for variation dances in dance manuals). Not surprisingly, the only sources that routinely met the search requirements were from Italy and Spain. Manuscript sources from England, France, and Spain also contain variation choreographies.

These choreographic sources include four major volumes from France and Italy, each containing at least forty dances with their music. This basic musical form has choreographic counterparts. In fact, the word *mutanza* or a variant of it appeared as one of the following three types of choreographic structures (the designations are my own).

Type 1: Major-Section Variation

In type 1, the variation-related word appears at the head of major sections of choreographies that are overwhelmingly variation based. This is the category of some

Table 1. Variation Dances Found in Music Sources.

	canario	gagliarda	passamezzo	pavane	pavaniglia	tordiglione
			Printed			
Abondante		12	10			
Attaingnant		16		7		
da Crema			3			
Dalza				9		
Fitzwilliam		36	7	28	1	
Gardane		16	6	1		
Holborne				11		
Le Roy, 1551		5		2		
Le Roy, 1568		2	1	2		
Molinaro		11	11	10		
Ladye Nevels		9	1			
Phalese		14	10			
Rotta		7	7			
Terzi		31	9			
			Manuscript			
Coelho	13	220	123	8	21	9
Esses		3		12	3	
Sabol		2	3	2	1	
			Totals			
	13	384	191	92	26	9

of the most common choreographic and musical dance variations: the *canario*, *pas-samezzo*, and *tordiglione*. In Negri's *tordiglione*, each section after the two opening *tempi* has the word *mutanza* in its heading. There are four *mutanze* per person in this choreography, each with this heading. As is the case here, the music for major-section variations is generally a simple sixteen-measure tune that is repeated for each choreographic strain. A repetition of eight to ten times surely makes a case for improvised variations among the musicians.

The major dance variation forms of type 1 begin with what the Spanish sources regularly, and Negri occasionally, call an *entrata*. In this *entrata* the dancers do a forward-moving entry passage together before the actual *mutanze* begin. The variations, then, consist of alternating solos for each dancer. During these solos the other dancer does a choreographed strolling pattern, known as a *passeggio*, in order to avoid standing like "una statua" (a statue), as Caroso says in *Nobiltà* (1600, 164). Negri's *tordiglione* choreography also ends with a passage together, very much like the repetition of the theme at the end of some musical variations.

Table 2. Dances in Choreographic Sources.*

	1) Major Section Variation	2) Minor Section Variation	3) Internal Variation
Caroso, *Ballarino*	Amor mio	Alta Vittoria	Alta Ruissa
	Canario	Barriera nuova	Ardente sole
	Chiara stella	Bassa Pompilia	Austria Gonzaga
	Gloria d'amore	Bassa Savella	Barriera
	Leggiadra Ninfa	Chiaranzana	Bassa e Alta
	Passamezzo	Contrapasso nuovo	Bassa Ducale
	Pavana Mathei	**Gagliarda** di Spagna	Bassa Toscana
	Piantone	Nuova Fenice	Bentivoglio
	Tordiglione		Cesarina
			Cesia Orsina
			Coppia Capelli
			Felice Vittoria
			Fiamma d'Amore
			Florido Giglio
			Fulgente stella
			Gentilezza d'Amore
			Giunto m'ha Amore
			Gracca Amorosa
			Laccio d'Amore
			Leggiadra d'Amore
			Maraviglia d'Amore
			Nobiltà
			Ombrosa Valle
			Pavaniglia
			Spagnoletta
			Villanella
			Vita e quanto haggio
Caroso, *Nobiltà*	**Gagliarda** di Spagna	Alta Vittoria	Bassa e Alta
	Passamezzo	Altezza d'Amore	Amorosina Grimana (**pavaniglia**)
	Tordiglione		
	Piantone		
Jaque	Billano		
	Folias		
	Pabana		
Lupi	**Canario**		
	Gagliarda		
	Passamezzo		
	Tordiglione		
Negri	**Canario**	Ballo per 8 cavalieri	**Pavaniglia** Romana
	Catena d'Amore		**Pavaniglia** di Milano
	Tordiglione		
Reglas	**Pavana** Italiana		

*Dance types are in bold print.

It is important to note that even though *passeggi* are not themselves variations, they have a vital function in choreographic variations. They serve a role much
like the underlying harmony or ground bass in musical variations by providing
regular continuity of motion against which the changes in the soloist's *mutanza*
are contrasted. The *passeggio* is, in fact, a term exclusive to variation choreographies. Like slight chord changes in the harmony of music variations, the *passeggi*
can also have "ornaments" added for interest. For example, the male *passeggio* for
the first woman's variation in Negri's "Tordiglione" has instructions for doing the
steps in two different ways in order to vary it.[6]

Beyond the formal similarity between music and choreographies displayed
in major section form, choreographic variations are much more diverse. With the
rare exception of free-form instrumental pieces like preludes or fantasias, variations are not found in music as sections within single-movement compositions.
But the second type of choreographic variation form does just that.

Type 2: Minor-Section Variation

Type 2 choreographies are often multipartite structures with an opening section (Caroso's *tempo* or Negri's *parte*) similar to an *entrata*, a middle section (or
sections) of alternating variations, and a faster ending section(s). These ending
sections usually have different music and even differing meters. For this type of
choreography, the variation term is found as a header for a variation phrase that is
only one section or *tempo* of a larger choreography that may not be set predominantly to a single variation tune. In "Alta Vittoria," a couple dance in Caroso's *Il
Ballarino,* there is an opening *entrata* performed by both dancers, followed by two
gagliarda variations per dancer, a *saltarello* section (called *sciolta* in Caroso's music)
performed together, and then a *canario* section that is also in variation form.[7] The
music is in duple meter, even the *gagliarda*, until after the variations, where Caroso
indicates triple meter in the lute tablature.

Type 3: Internal Variation

Here, the variation term appears *within* the text of a choreography section. In
the fifth, seventh, and fourteenth *tempi* (sections) in the *pavaniglia* from Caroso's *Nobiltà* entitled "Amorosina Grimana," the instructions are given and then
referred to as a variation, as follows: "In the fifth section, they both will do said
variation again, opposite one another, backwards—the man beginning with the
right foot, and the woman with the left."[8]

"Said variation" refers to the passage given in the fourth *tempo* of this choreography. Type 3 is the choreographic category to which the *pavaniglia* (also
known as the "Spanish Pavan") belongs. Each variation is in ternary form (ABC).

Each A section serves as an anchoring figure that opens individual variations while remaining essentially unchanged throughout the dance. The B section is the variation proper, where the steps and floor patterns change. In this type 3 category each variation ends with a different anchoring section—the C section that, like the A sections, rarely changes. What changes that do occur in the A and C sections are akin to ornaments added to the themes of music variations. There are two versions of this choreography in Negri that have forms and music unmistakably related to the Caroso examples, only lacking the use of the actual word "mutanza."

In John Ramsey's Inns of Court manuscript, *The Practise of Dauncinge*, he claims that the Spanish Pavin "must be learnd by practise & demonstration, beinge performd with bounds & capers & then ye end honour."[9] The only other dances this source cites as needing to be learned by example are the *gagliarda* and the *volta*, a *gagliarda* variant. This provides further confirmation for a sixteenth-century view of these dances as variations. Arbeau's French version has opening (A) and closing (C) sections that remain stable while the middle (B) section has the instructions, "And [in] other passages of this Spanish Pavane, here in the place of these *fleurets*, the dancer does other gestures."[10]

Jaque (Spain) and Lupi (Italy), both virtually unknown sources, focus on variation choreographies. Of Jaque's six choreographies, three are variations. Lupi confirms the prominence of the *canario*, *gagliarda*, *passamezzo*, and *tordiglione* as important examples of variation form, as they hold a major place in his publication.[11] Additions to the three choreographic types I have identified are found in Compasso and Lutij, sources containing lists of variations that are not arranged as formal choreographies. There are also lists in Negri of variation choices specifically designated for women.

The Gagliarda

The *gagliarda* (Fr. *gaillarde*, Eng. galliard, Sp. *gallarda*) is a vigorous leaping dance normally found in triple meter with steps that are grouped in odd numbers of five, seven, eleven, etc. The basic step pattern, called the *cinque passi*, has a characteristic rhythm mirrored in many of the musical versions of this dance (see example 1)[12]:

Example 1. *Gaillarde.*

Arbeau, *Gaillarde*

As seen in table 1, the *gagliarda* is by far the most commonly occurring dance in music sources of the period, although not all instances of it are in variation form. One of the most versatile dances of the period, the *gagliarda* functioned in a number of different contexts including major- and minor-section variations with variants on these forms. In major- and minor-section contexts the *gagliarda* is nearly always presented as variations; however, in internal sections, it may only be represented by the basic five step.

Negri makes note of several dance masters for whom this dance was their crowning glory as a solo professional specialty. One of these dance masters, Lutio Compasso, was himself the author of a book that contains *gagliarda* variations.[13] His *Ballo della gagliarda* is composed of over one hundred variations including *mutanze* divided into sections called *scempie* ("simple"), *doppie* ("double"), and *piu difficili* ("more difficult"). These sections consist of suggested lists of steps that could be combined to make a variation of from one to six *gagliarda* measures. He ends his book with instructions for hops (*salti*) and capriols.

In this context dance masters were expected to improvise variations, hence their choreographies were not notated. Compasso, who, according to Negri, was noted as "valenthuomo nella professione del ballare" (valiant gentleman in the dance profession) for his *gagliarda* variations, provided ideas that dancers could introduce into a pattern of their own (Negri 1602; Negri [1602] 1969, 3). Additionally, both Negri and Caroso give examples of a similar expectation for talented amateurs.[14] Lists of *gagliarda* variations, such as those found in Compasso, Lupi, Lutij, and Treatise 2 of *Le gratie* (Negri 1602) were probably intended for these talented amateurs.

The *gagliarda* is present in all the major dance manuals. Arbeau has eight *gagliarda* variations with nine tunes. Of the over eighty dances in Caroso's *Ballarino*, eight refer to the *gagliarda* in whole or in part. *Nobiltà* has a higher percentage with nine of its 49 choreographies related to the *gagliarda*. In Caroso's volumes, the *gagliarda* is found only in single couple dances, with one exception, *Barriera*, which is for three couples. Negri's *Le gratie* has the highest percentage with nearly half eighteen of its forty-three dances containing *gagliarda* sections.

In dance manuals the *gagliarda* is sometimes found as a type 2 choreography with a section where the music changes to *gagliarda* rhythms, and the basic *cinque passi* is danced. Negri's "Biscia Amorosa" for two couples is one example of this treatment. In the fifth of six *parti* the dancing couple does this basic step (Negri 1602; Negri [1602] 1969, 165–68).

Another minor-section choreographic form for the *gagliarda* is the change of music to *gagliarda* rhythms coupled with the identification of a choreographic change to a *gagliarda* section, but one having no *cinque passi* steps. *Ballarino*'s "Lucretia Amorosa" displays this pattern (Caroso 1581; Caroso [1581] 1967, fols.

84v–86r). The choreography is in two general sections: the first duple, the last in the standard *gagliarda* triple meter.

The *gagliarda* can also be found as a major-section choreography; Caroso's "Gagliarda di Spagna" is one such example. Its form is typical for choreographic variations. In this case the couple performs three opening *tempi* together. Then, beginning with the man, they alternate solo variations, the woman repeating what the man has done. The choreography ends with a final variation performed together. While this choreography contains only two variations, its format would make the addition of more variations quite simple; this type most clearly matches the variation form found in music compositions.

Although the *gagliarda* frequently occurred as part of *balletti*, proving the *gagliarda*'s importance in ensemble choreographies, it rarely appears as pure type 1 variation choreography. This is interesting in view of its ubiquitous appearances in music variation. The virtuoso nature of many of these music variations is in all likelihood a reflection of the fact that the extempore creation of *gagliarda* variations was a noted professional specialty among dance masters. In Treatise 1, chapter 1, Negri relates the experience of taking his more expert students to dance the *gagliarda* before several Milanese nobles. In addition to this, the *gagliarda* is one of only four dance types cited as a professional specialty for specific dance masters, the others being *canario*, *mattachins*, and *moresca*. Of the twenty-two instances where specialties are mentioned in this section, seventeen are for the *gagliarda* (Negri 1602; Negri [1602] 1969, 2–6). The relative absence in these sources of the most virtuoso professional dance as type 1 variations presents strong evidence that the dance manuals were intended for amateurs.

In dance manuals the most common appearance of *gagliarda* choreographic variations is as type 2 choreography providing one or more *gagliarda* sections in a *balletto* that has other dance sections. Negri's "Galleria d'amor" demonstrates this form (Negri 1602; Negri [1602] 1969, 189–91). There are six *parti*: In opening *parti* 1–3 the two couples dance together, each *parte* ending in a choreographic refrain. Likewise in the closing *parti* 5–6 both couples dance together, but this time with a lively *canario*.

The middle *parte* is where the *gagliarda* appears. Treated as a dance within a dance, *parte* 4 begins with a complete opening sequence featuring the *riverenza* followed by two flirtatious *continenzia*. This sequence is normally found only at the very beginning of a choreography. Next come the *cinque passi*, which occur four times. This opening sequence and *cinque passi* phrase match the bipartite music when played once through. Because the music instructions require two iterations of the music, that leaves the second playing for what Negri specifies as the *mutanza* of eleven actions. This variation can be performed to the A section of the music, leaving the B section for four more *cinque passi*.

Example 2. *Passo e mezzo.*

Ballarino, *Passo e mezzo*

The Passamezzo

The *gagliarda* is followed in frequency by the *passamezzo* (also *passo e mezzo*; Eng. "passing measures"; Fr. *passemeze*) which, according to Arbeau, is a somewhat faster version of the slow duple-metered *pavane* (see example 2). Describing this relationship in more detail he says: "The instrumentalists play it several times less slowly and in a lighter measure . . . calling it the passamezzo."[15] As with all Arbeau choreographies, his version of the *passamezzo* is minimalist, especially when compared to the florid Italian versions.

The English measure is clearly a type of *passamezzo*, which would confirm Arbeau's description of the *passamezzo* as a moderate-tempo processional dance similar to many surviving English country dances.[16] In fact the step vocabulary used in the measures is the same as those used in Arbeau's *passemeze*. It would thus seem that the measures and the *passamezzo* can be grouped in a class of processional dances that would also include the pavane and almain, all of them duple in meter. Lupi's treatise stands alongside the massive Caroso volumes in containing elaborate choreographies for this dance.

Unlike the *gagliarda* which, as stated, appears in a variety of contexts, the *passamezzo* is exclusively found as a type 1 choreography in variation form (Lupi 1607, 218–24).[17] Caroso's "Passo e mezzo" choreography is a case in point. Located in *Il ballarino*, this dance by an anonymous choreographer begins with the couple dancing an *entrata* together (Caroso 1581; Caroso [1581] 1967, 46–49). They then go through a series of three sets of variations in each of which the man does a variation first, while the woman performs a *passeggio*, and vice versa, with the woman performing this same *passeggio* during each male variation. Each time the man finishes his variation the woman follows with hers which, in this dance, is different from his in each instance. During her variations he does his own *passeggio* which is repeated during each of the woman's variations. Interestingly, Compasso's list of *gagliarda* variations also has some more elaborate *passeggi*. "Mutanza 88," for example, has a heel-toe movement followed by a capriol, which is a scissoring movement of the legs performed during a jump (Compasso 1560, fol. Br). This is done to one side, then to the other, its active nature giving a stronger sense of visual counterpoint to the couple's movements.

Before three additional sets of variations in this *passamezzo*, the couple performs a *passeggio* together. This one, like the first, is more elaborate than those solo *passeggi* that accompany the solo variations, but is not complex enough to be considered a joint variation. Furthermore, the clear labeling of the dance's *tempi* as either *mutanza* or *passeggio* would seem conclusive. Once sets 4–6 of the solo variations are finished, the couple performs one more section that is labeled *passeggio insieme* ("passage together"), as the previous two sections were also labeled. Conversely, this situation is quite different. The two dancers who have thus far performed the same steps together, or more elaborate steps as soloists, are now performing separate variations, for each dancer, occurring simultaneously. They come together with an opening *riverenza* pattern that is reversed, the *continentie* coming before the final bow.

It is in this dance that Caroso (or the anonymous choreographer) shows a clear differentiation of male and female roles. The male variations have more actions than those for the female and include more flourishes (*fioretti*) for the foot and more capriols. For example, in the third variation set, the man does sixteen actions while the woman does only twelve. In his variation there are eight *fioretti* and a hop, among other steps; in the woman's the majority of the steps keep low to the ground, consisting of basic steps, *riprese* (sideways posing steps), and a few *trabuchetti* (a light sideways hop onto one foot). It is only in the final *passeggio* that the woman dances her more active steps with a variation mostly comprised of *fioretti* and *trabuchetti*. The man's actions are ratcheted up even more. He has not only *fioretti* and *trabuchetti* but also five capriols.

The Pavane/Pavaniglia

Next in frequency is some version of the *pavane* (Eng. pavan/paven/pavin; It. *pavana*; Sp. *pabana/pavana)*, or *pavaniglia* (Eng. "Spanish Pavan"; Fr. *pavane d'Espagne/pavane espagnolle*; Sp. *pavanilla/pavana italiana*). The *pavane* is a slow duple-meter dance often used as a processional. Like the *gagliarda*, the *pavane* has a characteristic rhythm as seen in Arbeau's *pavane* chanson "Belle qui tiens ma vie" (Arbeau 1588, fols. 28v–33v; see example 3a). Because of its slow tempo and simple steps that did not require a great deal of concentration, the *pavane* was considered dangerous, as slow dances throughout the ages have been and still are—perhaps because assignations could be planned while dancing.

The *pavaniglia*, a more specific type of *pavane*, has music that assumes great importance as it is the one dance tune that is concordant in all regions that produced choreographies for this period (see example 3b). Additionally, although tunes for several dances have concordances in many countries, for countries with extant choreographic sources the *pavaniglia* has the only choreographic concordance common

Example 3a. *Pavaniglia.*

Ballarino, *Pavaniglia*

Example 3b. *Pavane.*

Arbeau, "Belle qui tiens ma vie"

to all. The first known notation of this tune, named only as "Pavana," appeared in a Spanish source from 1546 by Alonso Mudarra. A Spanish dance source by Jaque also contains a *pabana* that is clearly a version of the Italian *pavaniglia* as found in the Italian sources. In fact, a study of the musical sources in Esses (1992) shows that *pavaniglia* music was often known in Spain simply as *pavana* or *pabana*, especially after 1580. Perhaps this is why the *pavaniglia* is a dance associated with Spain everywhere except Spain itself where, paradoxically, it was known as the *pavana italiana*. Another possibility is that the tune and its harmony are originally Spanish, while the variation choreography is originally Italian.

The term "pavane" is more common for music in England and, to a lesser extent, Spain. Both are, however, regularly found in variation form. When the term "pavaniglia" is used, whether choreographically or musically, the specific "Spanish Pavan" tune and/or harmony are always in evidence.

Arbeau's *pavane* shows the most fundamental format for the dance. Several couples line up behind one another and process forward using the same basic step pattern—that is, two single steps (*simple*) and one double step (*double*) (Arbeau 1588; Arbeau 1967, fol. 27r–v).[18] This pattern equals four measures of music. It is repeated several times.

Caroso's *Ballarino* has the only extant full-length choreography for the *pavana*. "Pavana Matthei" by M. Battistino is a type 1 choreography beginning with an opening section which the couple performs together (Caroso 1581; Caroso [1581] 1967, 112). In dual meter this part moves from the *riverenza* to Italy's more stylish version of Arbeau's basic steps—two *passi puntati* and one *seguito* (Negri 1602; Negri [1602] 1969, 105–6).[19] This is followed by two regular steps (*passi*) forward and two *riprese*.[20]

Next, the music changes to triple meter and the man and woman alternate variations as in the *passo e mezzo*. While the solo dancer performs, the other dancer strolls the *passeggio*. There are two differences in *Ballarino*'s choreography.

One is that the man and woman do the same *passeggio* steps, and the other is that each of the two variation sets ends with the dancers doing a brief wheeling passage together in order to change places. When the solo *mutanze* are done, the dancers do simultaneous *mutanze* that then lead to a *passeggio* together to end the dance.

Pavaniglia choreographies are far more common. One appears in every major source and several minor ones. Arbeau's minimal example is in ternary (ABC) form, with the instruction that the B section is to be varied with each repetition of the whole. Negri's "Pavaniglia alla romana" displays the same type 3 format (Negri 1602; Negri [1602] 1969, 132). The sixteen-measure tune is divided into three sections. Section A is always five measures long and, after the first *parte* which contains the opening *riverenza pattern,* comprises three steps, a *cadenza,* and a *sottopiede*. Section C has two steps, a hop, and a *cadenza.* In both sections A and C the couple is always dancing together.

Each of the ten B sections contains a different variation. Unlike the *gagliarda, passamezzo,* and *pavana,* these *parti* are performed by the dancers as a couple, that is, the same steps at the same time. The only exceptions are *parti* 3 and 7 when the steps of the B section are done first by one dancer and then, when the entire *parte* is repeated, by the other.

The Canario

Almost without exception, the *canario* appears in music as variations. The *canario* (Eng. canaries; Fr. *canarie*) is a sturdy triple meter dance with a distinctive stamping movement. Musically, it tends to have a great deal of repetition using a few stock rhythms (see example 4). Frequently, it is seen in type 2 *balletti* as a final dance section, but in some sources, particularly Italian, the *canario* also occurs as an autonomous type 1 choreography.

Nobiltà's "Alta Vittoria" includes four dance sections: the opening unnamed dance, a *gagliarda,* a *saltarello,* and, as an ending, the *canario* (Caroso 1600; Caroso [1600] 1980, 296; see example 5). For the opening section and *saltarello,* the couple dances together. Appropriately, the two variation dance types found in this choreography are in variation form. The *canario* begins with a section of dancing together. At the end of this section, to avoid just standing there the woman is instructed to make gracious motions while the man performs his solo variation. The man is not so instructed.

The man then performs a variation of his own choosing, ending it with a refrain that Caroso specifies. The woman does her own variation, ending with the same refrain. They then dance together before executing another solo variation after which each ends together, as is typical.

Example 4. *Canario.*

Negri, *Il Canario*

Example 5. *Tordiglione.*

Nobiltà, *Tordiglione*

Negri's "Il Canario" (Negri 1602; Negri [1602] 1969, 198) is an example of a major-section choreography. The couple dances together before doing four alternating solo variations. Each variation then ends with a *riverenza* done together. After the second variation set they do a *passeggio* together, after which come two more solo variations and a *passeggio* together. One remarkable part of this choreography is the length and complexity of each *mutanza*. While most variations have twelve to sixteen actions, these have over twenty actions each.

The Tordiglione

The *tordiglione* (Eng. tordion; Fr. *tourdion*) is also a couple dance that, unusually, is common in either duple or triple meter. It is almost exclusively found in variation form whether in musical or choreographic sources. Arbeau defines this dance as a kinder, gentler *gagliarda* that omits the vigorous leaps, therefore allowing for a faster tempo. More specifically, he says "the tune for the *tourdion* and the tune for the *gaillarde* are the same, and the only difference is that the *tourdion* is danced low to the ground and in a lighter quicker measure, and the *gaillarde* is danced high in a slower heavier measure" (Arbeau 1588; Arbeau 1967, fols. 49r–51v). He in fact uses the same triple meter tune for both (see example 1, above).

Although, generally, the differences between these two dances appear to be more extensive in Italian sources, Caroso corroborates Arbeau in his description of "Tordiglione" from *Nobiltà* (Caroso 1600; Caroso [1600] 1980, 319). In discussing the proper ending of any *tordiglione* variation Caroso says that the reader must do it exactly as described because "it behooves one to end *gagliarda* variations with a *cadenza*."[21] Any other ending "non stà bene" (is not good). Caroso's insistence on the proper performance of this dance is reiterated at the end of the dance when he adamantly states that the reader must "do it in the manner I have said" in order to have the "true rule, perfect theory" and be *giustissima* (Caroso 1600; Caroso [1600] 1980, 324).

Example 6. Excerpts from "Alta Vittoria."

Nobiltà, "Alta Vittoria" opening

Gagliarda

Sciolta

Canario

Nobiltà's "Tordiglione" begins with two *tempi* danced together (see example 6). At the end of the second of these Caroso includes an ending pattern called a *creanza*. John Florio, author of a sixteenth-century Italian-English dictionary, defines this word as "manners, education, civilitie."[22] Caroso's *creanza* consists of one *sottopiede*, two *trabucchetti*, and three simple steps.

The dancers then alternate variations, the woman sometimes repeating the man's variation (sets 1 and 3) and sometimes doing a different one. The *passeggio* that each does for the first variation set is the same for both, but after the second they join hands to do the *creanza*, changing places. It is possible to add this *creanza* because the *passeggio* is short and repetitive, so all the dancers need do is substitute the *creanza* for a repetition of the *passeggio* pattern. The third variation set is accompanied by a different *passeggio* which recurs after the fourth and last set with the added *creanza*.

Conclusions

The close structural relationship between music and choreographies is easily established by the fact that the same dances were viewed as most appropriate for variation treatment in both dance and music sources. These dances—the *canario*, *gagliarda*, *passamezzo*, *pavane/pavaniglia*, and *tordiglione*—each have individual characteristics of form, rhythm, or melody that are found in both disciplines, and differences that clearly represent the need to make the form idiomatic to the discipline. The differences are found in formal approach and in the tempo indications found in dance instructions.

The importance of this study for those concerned with performance practice cannot be underestimated. Musicians and dancers need to be aware of the relationships between their arts, because these relationships can serve as guidance for the interpretation of the dances discussed in this study. Relationships of form, tempo, and even the articulation of the dance steps can provide important material for reflection when performing these dances as a solo musician, as a dancer, or as a musician providing accompaniment for dancers.

The intricate variations of the English virginalists and Spanish organists, for example, have often been viewed as unrelated to actual dancing because of their virtuoso complexities. This purported distancing has allowed some performers to play dance variations as if they were unmeasured preludes by Louis Couperin or rubato-laden études by Chopin. The results of my research clearly show that these dances were no more and no less representative of the variation form as it was practiced in dance and music during the period under examination, thus providing no foundation for performing these pieces as if unrelated to dance. But more than that, the results prove that understanding the conjunction of these two arts has vital implications for both in the areas of transmission history, form, and performance.

Notes

At the twentieth annual meeting of the Society of Dance History Scholars, held in 1997 at Barnard College, New York, eminent Renaissance dance scholar Julia Sutton led a session entitled "Form in Dance and Dance Music from 1400–1720." This noteworthy session contributed to placing Western dance/dance-music analysis in a more prominent place by highlighting historical dance from its earliest treatises through the baroque treatises of eighteenth-century France. This paper is a direct outcome of that session. The author is responsible for all translations throughout the article except as otherwise indicated.

1. For standard information on variation form in music see: Sisman 1986; Drees and von Fischer 1998; Hudson 1981, 169–70. The article in the *New Grove Dictionary of Music and Musicians* (von Fischer 1980) is a shorter version of von Fischer 1966.

2. Treatise 1 of Cesare Negri's tripartite dance manual *Le Gratie d'Amore* (Negri 1602 and Negri 1969) lists numerous dance masters of his acquaintance who served outside Italy. Among these were: Francesco Legnano (1532–1602), who served at the courts of Charles V and Philip II in Spain; Virgilio Bracesco (fl. 1546–68), who served Henry II in France; Giovanni Ambrosio Valchiera (fl. 1587), who served Emanuel Filibert, Duke of Savoy; Alessandro Barbetta, who served the Duke of Bavaria; Giovanni Ambrogio Landriano, who served the Duke of Poland; Giovanni Stefano Martinello, who served the Archbishop of Cologne; and Cesare Agosto Parmegiano, who served the nobility of Flanders.

3. Spanish organist Antonio de Cabezón traveled to England in 1554 with Philip II of Spain for the festivities surrounding Philip's marriage to Queen Mary. The "Spanish Pavan" is found in English music and choreographic sources only after this date. As one small example of Italian influence in England, Thomas Morley's appropriations of the vocal dance music of Italian composer Giovanni Gastoldi is well documented. Much of the exposure of English composers to continental music and dance undoubtedly occurred during the "grand tour" taken by many an English gentleman.

4. The well-known French treatise *Orchesographie* by Thoinot Arbeau (facsimile in Arbeau 1972; translation by Mary Stewart Evans in Arbeau 1967) presents only the melodies of most of its dance tunes. The three major Italian sources—Caroso's *Il Ballarino* (facsimile Caroso 1967), Caroso's *Nobiltà di Dame* (translation by Julia Sutton in Caroso 1995; facsimile Caroso 1980), and Negri's *Le Gratie* (facsimile Negri 1969)—all include mensural melodies, lute tablature, and, in the case of *Nobiltà*, there are even separate bass lines for some of the dances. Lesser-known Italian dance sources include only tablature; most English and Spanish sources have no music whatsoever, although many have titles that match those of extant instrumental and vocal music.

5. Representative sources would include: Antonio de Cabezón, *Obras de música para tecla, arpa y vihuela* [Works of music for keyboard, harp, and vihuela], (Madrid, 1578); Luys Venegas de Henestrosa, *Libro de cifra nueva para tecla, arpa y vihuela* [Book of new tablatures for keyboard, harp, and vihuela], (Alcalá, 1557); Tomás de Santa María, *Arte de tañer fantasia, assi para tecla como vihuela* [The art of playing fantasias for keyboard as well as vihuela], (Vallodolid, 1565).

6. In the male *passeggio* for the woman's first variation in Negri's "Tordiglione," he suggests two patterns in order to add interest: "Il cavaliero in questo tempo passagiando farà quattro sequiti finti per fianco. . . . Si fanno questi seguiti in duo modi per variar li detti passi. À chi piacerà a passeggiar essi passi senza voltarsi intorno si puo far' as suo piacere." The gentleman, at this time, goes on to do four false *sequiti* sideways. These steps may be done in two ways in order to vary said steps. Whoever wants to do these steps without turning around may do as they please. (Negri 1602; Negri 1969, 194.)

7. "Alta Vittoria" (Caroso 1581, 103). *Sciolta* is a term used in Italian dance manuals for generic triple-meter music.

8. "Pavaniglia" (Caroso 1600, 103). "Nel quinto tempo, faranno amendue un'altra volta detta *mutanza* per contrario in dietro; principiandola l'huomo col piè destro, & la Dama col sinistro" (Caroso 1581; Caroso 1967, 38).

9. [John Ramsey], *The Practise of Dauncinge* [London, ca. 1606], Bodleian Library, MS Douce 280.

10. "Et aultres passages de ceste pavane d'Espagne, en lieu de ces fleurets icy, le danceur fait d'aultres gesticulations tant en marchant que retrogradant" (Arbeau 1588; Arbeau 1972, fol. 96v). This instruction is placed beside the music notes at the actual place where the variation would begin, matching the positioning of the "variation" section in the Italian sources. In the opening instructions he also makes it clear that each time that B section is done "aultres noveaulx mouvements" (other new movements) must be performed, then repeated backwards and so on for the repeats that follow.

11. Livio Lupi, *Libro di gagliarda, tordiglione, passo è mezzo, canario, è passeggi* (Palermo: Maringo, 1607).

12. The *cinque passi* is a six-beat step pattern beginning with four one-beat leaps forward, with the last leap used to launch the dancer from the ground with the dancer remaining

suspended until cadencing on the last beat. It is called the five step because there are five actions in the pattern.

13. "Lucio Compasso Romano, è stato valenthuomo nella professione dell ballare alla gagliarda; hà scritto diverse mutanze della gagliarda, ha fatto scuola in Roma, & Napoli fioritissima" (Lucio Compasso, Roman, has been a valiant gentleman in the profession of dancing the *gagliarda*. He has written diverse *gagliarda* variations [and] has truly flourishing schools in Rome and Naples) (Negri 1602; Negri 1969, 3).

14. For information on renaissance dance improvisation, see the "Dance" section of McGee (2003, 117–92), featuring the following articles: G. Yvonne Kendall, "Ornamentation and Improvisation in Sixteenth-Century Dance"; Jennifer Nevile, "Disorder in Order: Improvisation in Italian Choreographed Dances of the Fifteenth and Sixteenth Centuries;" and Barbara Sparti, "Improvisation and Embellishment in Popular and Art Dances in Fifteenth- and Sixteenth-Century Italy."

15. "Les jouers d'instruments la sonnent aulcunes fois moins pesamment, & d'une mesure plus legiere . . . lapellent passemeze" (Arbeau 1588; Arbeau 1967, fol. 33r).

16. See Payne 2003; see also Kendall (2005) for a review of this book.

17. Lupi's dance "Passo, e mezzo in gagliarda" is curious because it has the names of two dances in its title. It has the same format as Caroso's "Passo e mezo." Both dances open with the couple dancing an opening section together. This section is then followed by alternating *mutanza/passeggio* pairs, where each dancer does a *mutanza* while the other does a simple *passeggio*.

18. The *simple* steps are just that. One foot takes a step forward; the other comes up beside it in what Arbeau calls a *joint*. This "joining" is called a *cadence*. The foot that has just joined then steps forward. The *double* takes four counts. There are three steps followed by a *cadence*.

19. The definition for the *passo puntato* in its *grave* and *ordinario* forms are in Rule 4 of Treatise 1. The *passo puntato* is similar to Arbeau's single step where one foot takes a step forward and the other moves up to join it side by side. The difference with the Italian two-count step is that it is "stopped"—i.e., the dancer takes one step forward onto the ball of the foot (which raises the body), then stays in that raised position until the last half of the second count. At that point the body is lowered as the other foot joins its partner. The *seguito* is a modified *double* using four counts. For the first three beats the dancer takes simple steps forward, each foot following (*segue*) the other. The third beat is interrupted by a *spezzato*—a movement that breaks (*spezza*) the step and finishes the pattern on beat four.

20. The Italian *passi* are similar to Arbeau's *pas simple* but without the *cadence*. The Italian steps just keep the feet passing one another.

21. "le mutanze de gagliarda convien che si finiscano in cadenza" (Caroso 1600; Caroso 1980, 320).

22. John Florio, *A worlde of wordes* (London, 1598); quoted here from Florio (1598) 1972, 90.

References

Music: Primary Sources

Abondante, Giulio. 1546, 1587. *Intabulatura sopra el lauto*. Books 1, 5. Venice: Gardane.

Attaingnant, Pierre, ed. 1531. *Quatorze Gaillardes, neuf pavannes . . . en la tabulature du jeu d'orgues, epinettes. . . .* Paris: Attaingnant.

Byrd, William. 1591. *My ladye Nevells Booke*. Great Britain. Owned privately.

Cabezón, Antonio de. 1578. *Obras de Musica para Tecla, Arpa y Vihuela*. Madrid.

da Crema, Joan Maria. 1546. *Intabolatura de lauto*. Venice: Gardane.

Dalza, Joanambrosio. 1508. *Intabulatura de lauto*. Venice: Petrucci.

The Fitzwilliam Virginal Book. [16th century.] Cambridge Fitzwilliam Museum Mu.Ms. 168.

Gardane, Antonio, ed. 1551. *Intabolatura nova di varie sorte di balli*. Venice: Gardane.

Holborne, Anthony. 1597. *The Cittharn School*. London: Peter Short.

LeRoy, Adrian. 1551. *Premier Livre de Tablature de Luth*. Paris: Le Roy & Ballard.

———. 1568. *A Breife and easye instruction. . . .* London: Kyngson.

Milán, Luís. 1536. *Libro de musica de vihuela de mano*. Valencia.

Molinaro, Simone. 1599. *Intavolature di liuto*. Book 1. Venice: Amadino.

Mudarra, Alonso. 1546. *Tres libros de musica en cifras para vihuela*. Seville: Juan de Leon.

Narváez, Luis de. 1538. *Los seys libros del Delphin de musica de cifras para tañer Vihuela*. Valladolid: Diego Hernandez de Cordova.

Phalèse, Pierre. 1571. *Theatrum Musicum*. Louvain: Phalèse & Ballero.

Pisador, Diego. 1552. *Libro de musica de vihuela*. Salamanca: Guillermo Millis.

Rotta, Antonio. 1546. *Intabolatura de lauto*. Book 1. Venice: Gardane.

Terzi, Giovanni Antonio. 1599. *Intavolatura di liutto*. Books 1, 2. Venice: Vicenti.

Valderrábano, Enriquez de. 1547. *Libro de musica de vihuela, intitulado Silva de Sirenas*. Valladolid: Francisco Fernandez de Cordovo.

Venegas de Henestrosa, Luis. 1557. *Libro de cifra nueva para tecla, harpa, y vihuela*. Alcala: Joan de Brocar.

Music: Modern Collections

Coelho, Victor. 1995. *The Manuscript Sources of Seventeenth-Century Italian Lute Music*. New York: Garland.

Esses, Maurice. 1992. *Dance and Instrumental* Diferencias *in Spain during the 17th and 18th Centuries*. Stuyvesant NY: Pendragon. (Contains Cabezón, Milán, Mudarra, Narváez, Valderrábano, Venegas de Henestrosa, and Pisador as cited above, and numerous Spanish manuscripts from the sixteenth century.)

Heartz, Daniel, ed. 1965. *Keyboard Dances from the Earlier Sixteenth Century*. Rome: American Institute of Musicology. (Contains Gardane and Attaingnant cited above).

Sabol, Andrew. 1978. *Four Hundred Songs and Dances from the Stuart Masque*. Providence, RI: Brown University Press.

Dance: Primary Sources

[Anthoine Emeraud?] [Ca. 1600.] "Instructions pour dancer." Hesse, Hessiche Hochschul- und Landesbibliothek HS 304.

Arbeau, Thoinot. 1588. *Orchesographie*. Langres: Jehan des Prez.

Caroso, Fabritio. 1581. *Il Ballarino*. Venice: Ziletti.

———. 1600. *Nobiltà di Dame*. Venice: Il Muschio.

Compasso, Lutio. 1560. *Ballo da gagliarda*. Florence.

Esquivel Navarro, Juan de. 1642. *Discursos sobre el arte del dancado*. Seville: Gómez de Blas.

Jaque, Juan Antonio. [17th century]. *Libro de danzar*. Madrid, Biblioteca Nacional MS 18580/5.

Lupi, Livio. 1607. *Libro di gagliarda, tordiglione, passo è mezzo, canario, è passeggi*. Palermo: Maringo.

Lutij, Prospero. 1589. *Opera bellissima nella quale si contengono molte partite et passeggi di gagliarda*. Perugia: Orlando.

Negri, Cesare. 1602. *Le Gratie d'Amore*. Milan: Pontio and Piccaglia.

[Ramsey, John]. [ca. 1606.] *The Practise of Dauncinge*. Oxford, Bodleian Library, MS Douce 280. London.

Reglas de danzar. [Ca. 1600.] Madrid, Real Academia de la Historia, Colección Castro y Salazar, Vol. N-025. Fol. 149v.

Tarragó, Jatot. [Ca. 1580]. *Aquesta carta de dansas es feta*. Barcelona, Biblioteca de Catalunya M.1410/2.

Other: Primary Sources

Cotgrave, Randle. (1611) 1950. *A Dictionarie of the French and English Tongues*. London: Islip. Facsimile reprint, Columbia: University of South Carolina Press.

Florio, John. 1598. *A Worlde of Wordes*. London: Arnold Hatfield.

Secondary Sources and Facsimile Editions

Antón Priasco, Susana. 1998. "'Reglas del danzar': Edición de un manuscrito español de danza del siglo XVI." *Revista de Musicologia* 21: 239–45.

Arbeau, Thoinot. 1967. *Orchesographie*. Translated by Mary Stewart Evans. New York: Dover.

———. (1588) 1972. *Orchesographie*. Langres. Facsimile reprint, Geneva: Minkoff.

Caroso, Fabritio. (1581) 1967. *Il Ballarino*. Venice. Facsimile reprint, New York: Broude.

———. (1600) 1980. *Nobiltà di Dame*. Venice. Facsimile reprint, Bologna: Forni.

———. 1995. *Nobiltà di Dame*. Translated by Julia Sutton as *Courtly Dance of the Renaissance: A New Translation and Edition of the Nobiltà di dame (1600)*. New York: Dover.

Coelho, Victor. 1995. *The Manuscript Sources of Seventeenth-Century Italian Lute Music*. New York: Garland.

Drees, Stefan, and Kurt von Fischer. 1998. "Variation." In *Die Musik in Geschichte und Gegenwart*, edited by Ludwig Finscher, 2nd ed., 9:1238–46. Kassel: Bärenreiter.

Esses, Maurice. 1992. *Dance and Instrumental Diferencias in Spain during the 17th and 18th Centuries*. Stuyvesant, NY: Pendragon.

Florio, John. (1598) 1972. *A worlde of wordes*. London. Facsimile reprint, Hildesheim: Georg Olms.

Heartz, Daniel, ed. 1965. *Keyboard Dances from the Earlier Sixteenth Century*. Rome: American Institute of Musicology.

Hudson, Richard. 1981. *Passacaglio and Ciaccona: From Guitar Music to Italian Keyboard Variations in the Seventeenth Century*. Studies in Musicology 37. Ann Arbor: UMI Research Press.

Kendall, G. Yvonne. 1999. "Dance." In *Encyclopedia of the Renaissance*, 118–22. New York: Scribners.

———. 2003. "Ornamentation and Improvisation in Sixteenth-Century Dance." In McGee 2003, 117–44.

———. 2005. Review of *The Almain in Britain, c.1549–c.1675*, by Ian Payne. *Music & Letters* 86: 109–114.

———. 2011. *The Music of Arbeau's "Orchesographie"*. Hillsdale, NY: Pendragon.

McGee, Timothy, ed. 2003. *Improvisation in the Arts of the Middle Ages and Renaissance*. Kalamazoo, MI: Medieval Institute Publications.

Negri, Cesare. (1602) 1969. *Le Gratie d'Amore*. Milan. Facsimile reprint, New York: Broude. Translated by Gustavia Yvonne Kendall, PhD diss., Stanford University, 1985.

Nevile, Jennifer. 2003. "Disorder in Order: Improvisation in Italian Choreographed Dances of the Fifteenth and Sixteenth Centuries." In McGee 2003, 145–69.

Payne, Ian. 2003. *The Almain in Britain, c.1549–c.1675: A Dance Manual from Manuscript Sources*. Aldershot: Ashgate.

Sabol, Andrew. 1978. *Four Hundred Songs and Dances from the Stuart Masque*. Providence, RI: Brown University Press.

Sisman, Elaine. 1986. "Variation." In *The New Harvard Dictionary of Music*, ed. Don Randel, 902–7. Cambridge, MA: Belknap Press of Harvard University Press.

Sparti, Barbara. "Improvisation and Embellishment in Popular and Art Dances in Fifteenth- and Sixteenth-Century Italy." In McGee 2003, 170–92.

von Fischer, Kurt. 1966. "Variation." In *Die Musik in Geschichte und Gegenwart*, edited by Friedrich Blume, 13:1274–1309. Kassel: Bärenreiter and Metzler.

———. 1980. "Variations." In *The New Grove Dictionary of Music and Musicians*, ed. Stanley Sadie, 19:537–55. 20 vols. London: Macmillan.

Notes on Contributors

RICHARD J. AGEE is Professor and Chair of the Music Department at Colorado College. He was awarded a PhD from Princeton University in 1982 and has received numerous grants to pursue his continuing research in Italian music of the cinquecento and seicento. He has written articles that have appeared in the *Journal of the American Musicological Society, Early Music History, Music Library Association Notes, Studi Musicali,* and *Rivista Italiana di Musicologia.* In 1997, A-R Editions released his major edition of *Costanzo Festa, Counterpoints on a Cantus Firmus,* and 1998 saw the publication of his book *The Gardano Music Printing Firms, 1569–1611* (University of Rochester Press).

ELEONORA M. BECK is Associate Professor of Music at Lewis & Clark College in Portland, Oregon. She has published widely in the field of medieval and Italian music, including two books: *Singing in the Garden: Music and Culture in the Tuscan Trecento,* Bibliotheca Musicologica 3 (Lucca: Libreria Musicale Italiana Editrice, 1998), and *Giotto's Harmony: Music and Art in Padua at the Crossroads of the Renaissance* (Florence: European Press Academic Publishers, 2005).

CLYDE BROCKETT, Professor Emeritus of Musicology at Christopher Newport University, earned his MA and PhD degrees in Musicology at Columbia University. He is well known for his scholarly work on chant. His volume *Letania and Preces: Music for Lenten and Rogations Litanies,* was issued by the Institute of Mediaeval Music, Ottawa (2006), and his edition of the anonymous eleventh-century tonary, *On the Formulas of the Modes,* was published by the American Institute of Musicology (1997). He has written a number of articles concerning the music of medieval church drama and has directed and performed in four dramas. Currently he is collecting and transcribing the repertory of processional antiphons extant before 1200.

ANN BUCKLEY is a Research Associate at the Centre for Medieval and Renaissance Studies, Trinity College, Dublin. She was awarded a PhD in Musicology from the University of Cambridge on the topic of the Old French lyric *lai* and its relation to Latin song (1991). Her research interests include medieval song, music iconography, and music in medieval Ireland. She is a member of the Medieval Song Network (http://www.medievalsongnetwork.org/), and of the editorial board of the *Encyclopaedia of Music in Ireland* (UCD Press, forthcoming), and a contributor to the *New Grove*. Other publications include "Abelard's Planctus and *lai* Melodic Style," in *The Poetic and Musical Legacy of Heloise and Abelard*, ed. David Wulstan (Westhumble and Ottawa: Plainsong and Medieval Music Society/Institute of Mediaeval Music, 2003); and "Music in Ireland to c. 1500," *A New History of Ireland: Prehistoric and Early Ireland*, vol. 1, ed. Dáibhí Ó Cróinín (Oxford University Press, 2005), 744–813. Among her current projects is a study of the surviving corpus of liturgical propers for Irish saints throughout medieval Europe (initially funded by the Irish Research Council for the Humanities and Social Sciences); an edited volume on this topic is in preparation (to be published by Brepols). She has collaborated with the Scottish early music ensemble, Canty, in CD recordings of the offices for St. Brigit (Sanctuary, 2005) and St. Patrick (Divine Art, 2008), and in public lecture-recitals also with Schola Hyberniae, Altramar, the Choir of Saint Patrick's Cathedral, Dublin, and Norwich Cathedral Choir.

ALICE V. CLARK is Associate Professor and Coordinator of Music History at Loyola University New Orleans. Her research focuses on aspects of the medieval motet, especially that of Guillaume de Machaut and his contemporaries. A student of Margaret Bent, she has published in *Plainsong and Medieval Music*, *The Journal of Musicology*, *Fauvel Studies*, and the *On-Line Reference Book in Medieval Studies*, among other places, and is currently working on an essay on the motet in the fourteenth century for the forthcoming *Cambridge History of Medieval Music*. In addition to her scholarship, she teaches widely, especially in medieval studies and opera. She is active in the American Musicological Society and the International Machaut Society, among other organizations, and for a number of years she served as chair for Musicology at Kalamazoo, the organization that took over organizing music sessions at the International Congress on Medieval Studies after Ingrid Brainard's death.

VINCENT CORRIGAN has been on the faculty of Bowling Green State University since 1973 where he teaches harpsichord and graduate and undergraduate music history courses. He holds bachelor's degrees in music education, piano, and harpsichord from Carnegie-Mellon University and a PhD in musicology from

Indiana University. His primary interests lie in medieval music with an emphasis on music of the troubadours and trouvères, polyphony of the twelfth and thirteenth centuries, and early liturgies, as well as harpsichord performance. His awards include an NEH Summer Stipend for work on the Medieval Lyric, and an Andrew W. Mellon Fellowship for the study of medieval liturgies. Corrigan has studied harpsichord with Fernando Valenti and Marie Zorn, and musicology with John Reeves White, Edward Roesner, and Hans Tischler. Publications include *The Feast of Corpus Christi* with Barbara Walters and Peter Ricketts, a facsimile edition of the manuscript Paris, BNF lat. 1143, and articles on modal transmutation, the rhythm of trouvère song, hemiola, and the Codex Calixtinus. Corrigan has also released a CD, *The Young Scarlatti*, which features several of the composer's earlier works for harpsichord.

CYNTHIA CYRUS is an Associate Dean as well as Associate Professor of Musicology and Affiliated Faculty in Women's and Gender Studies at the Blair School of Music at Vanderbilt University. She received her doctorate from the University of North Carolina at Chapel Hill in 1990 with a dissertation on the Florentine Chanson Reworking. She has published and spoken widely on the circulation of music in the later Middle Ages and Renaissance, focusing particularly on musical volumes owned or used by women in late medieval France and Germany. Her book, *The Scribes for Women's Convents in Late Medieval Germany*, was published by the University of Toronto Press in 2008. She has articles in *Early Music, Sewanee Medieval Studies, Plainsong and Medieval Music, College Music Symposium*, and is both author and editor for *ORB: On-Line Reference Book for Medieval Studies*. In addition, she has published an edition of late fifteenth and early sixteenth century chansons: *De tous biens plaine: 28 Settings of Hayne van Ghizeghem's Chanson*, Recent Researches in the Music of the Middle Ages and Early Renaissance 36 (Madison: A-R Editions, 2000).

JOSEPH DYER taught music history at the University of Massachusetts Boston until his retirement in 2001. His research interests have included various topics in the fields of chant, liturgy (especially Rome in the Middle Ages), monasticism, and medieval music theory. His most recent articles include: "Roman Processions of the Major Litany (*litaniae maiores*) from the Sixth to the Twelfth Centuries," in *Roma Felix: Formation and Reflections of Medieval Rome*, ed. Éamonn Ó Carragáin and Carol Neuman de Vegvar (Aldershot: Ashgate, 2007), 112–37; "Raymund Schlecht: A Forgotten Nineteenth-Century *Choralforscher*," in *Studies in Medieval Chant and Liturgy in Honour of David Hiley*, Musicological Studies 87 (Budapest: Institute for Musicology; and Ottawa: Institute of Mediaeval Music, 2007), 149–78; "The Place of *Musica* in Medieval Classifications of Knowledge," *Journal*

of Musicology 24 (2007), 3–71; and "The Offertory: An Introduction and Some
Hypotheses," in *The Offertory and Its Verses: Research, Past, Present and Future; Proceedings of an International Symposion at the Centre for Medieval Studies, Trondheim,
25 and 26 September 2004*, ed. Roman Hankeln (Trondheim: Tapir Academic
Press, 2007), 15–40. He is a Fellow of the Royal School of Church Music.

CATHY ANN ELIAS is an Associate Professor in the School of Music at
DePaul University. She received her MA in library science and her PhD in musicology from the University of Chicago. Her research focuses on two areas: compositional process in sixteenth-century Franco Flemish composers' masses, and
performance practice based on medieval and Renaissance Italian literary sources.
She has published in journals such as *Early Music*: "Musical Performance in Sixteenth Century Italian Literature: Straparola's Le piacevoli notti." She also has
numerous chapters in books including "Mid-Sixteenth Century Chanson Masses,
A Kaleidoscopic Process," in *Early Musical Borrowings*, ed. Honey Meconi; and,
an article on musical entertainment in the fourteenth century in Gloria Alliare,
ed., *The Italian Novelle*, both published by Routledge Press; as well as an article, "A
New Look at *Cantus Firmus* Process in Crecquillon's *Missa Kein adler in der Welt
so schön*," in *Uno gentile et subtile ingenio: Studies in Renaissance Music in Honour of
Bonnie J. Blackburn* (2009) published by Brepols. She also reviews for *Notes* and
The Journal of the American Musicological Society.

GRETA-MARY HAIR is an Honorary Fellow in the School of Literatures,
Languages and Cultures at The University of Edinburgh. While the present article
focuses on material following on from her PhD thesis on eleventh-century troped
chants from Aquitaine, her most recent publications are editions of the music
and liturgy of Scottish saints' offices, jointly edited with Betty I. Knott (texts and
translations) from the thirteenth-century Sprouston Breviary—"The Office of St
Andrew, Patron Saint of Scotland" (2005), and *Vespers, Matins & Lauds for St Ken-
tigern, Patron Saint of Glasgow* (2011)—published by The Musica Scotica Trust.
Hair has held lecturing positions at the Riverina College of Advanced Education
(now Charles Sturt University) and at LaTrobe University. Together with Robyn
E. Smith, she edited *Songs of the Dove and the Nightingale: Sacred and Secular Music
c. 900–c. 1600* (1995).

G. YVONNE KENDALL is currently an Associate Professor of Music in Hous-
ton, Texas. Her main field of research is historical dance in the late sixteenth
and early seventeenth centuries. Dr. Kendall has published in *Encyclopedia of the
Renaissance, Renaissance Quarterly, Dance Research, Early Music*, and *Music & Letters*, among others. Dr. Kendall wrote the newly revised and expanded chapter on

dance in the newest edition of *A Performer's Guide to Renaissance Music*, edited by Jeffrey Kite-Powell.

WILLIAM MAHRT grew up in Washington State and attended Gonzaga University and the University of Washington; he completed a doctorate at Stanford University in 1969. After teaching at Case Western Reserve University and the Eastman School of Music, he returned to Stanford in 1972, where he teaches musicology and directs the Stanford Early Music Singers, which presents quarterly concerts of music from the late Middle Ages through the early Baroque. He is president of the Church Music Association of America and editor of its journal *Sacred Music*. Dr. Mahrt has published articles on the relation of music and liturgy and music and poetry; his most recent scholarship concerns the liturgical use of English cathedrals in the Middle Ages. Since 1964 he has directed the St. Ann Choir in Palo Alto, which sings Mass and vespers in Gregorian chant for the Sundays of the year, with polyphonic Masses of Renaissance masters for the holy days. He frequently leads workshops in the singing of Gregorian chant and the sacred music of the Renaissance.

NONA MONAHIN is currently completing her PhD in musicology (with a focus on Renaissance dance) at Monash University, Australia. She resides in Massachusetts, USA, where she teaches Renaissance and Baroque Dance in the Five College Early Music Program, and works in the Robert Frost Library at Amherst College. She is a former member of The Cambridge Court Dancers, and has choreographed for the Hampshire Shakespeare Company and the Five College Opera Project. She has published a paper, "Leaping Nuns? Social Satire in a Fifteenth-Century Court Dance," in *Proceedings of the Society of Dance History Scholars Joint Conference with The Congress on Research in Dance, New York, 11–13 June 1993* (Riverside: SDHS, 1993).

JENNIFER NEVILE is currently an Honorary Research Fellow in the School of English, Media and Performing Arts at the University of New South Wales. Her research on fifteenth- and sixteenth-century dance practices and their relationship with other contemporary artistic practices has been published in many book chapters and journal articles, including *The Cambridge Companion to Ballet* (2007), *Early Music*, *Renaissance Quarterly*, and *Dance Research*. 2004 saw the publication of her monograph on the relationship between dance and humanism in fifteenth-century Italy, *The Eloquent Body: Dance and Humanist Culture in Fifteenth-Century Italy* (Indiana University Press). In 2008 Indiana University Press published *Dance, Spectacle, and the Body Politick, 1250–1750*, her edited collection of essays on dance, music, and theater during this period.

RICHARD RASTALL is Emeritus Professor of Historical Musicology at the University of Leeds, and a Fellow of the Society of Antiquaries. Among his published works are a successful book on notation, a two-volume work on music in early English drama, musical editions and reconstructions, and articles on various aspects of early music. He is currently engaged in editing the complete works of Martin Peerson (ca. 1572–1651) and John Milton (ca. 1563–1647), both for Antico Edition. The founder of the Manton Consort of Viols, in which he plays tenor viol, he has a particular interest in domestic music making in the Jacobean period.

JULIA WINGO SHINNICK is Assistant Professor at the University of Louisville in Louisville, Kentucky. She earned her PhD in historical musicology in 1997 at the University of Texas at Austin with a dissertation entitled "The Manuscript Assisi, Biblioteca del Sacro Convento, MS 695: A Codicological and Repertorial Study." Dr. Shinnick's research at present focuses on violence in the trouvère pastourelle in light of the mimetic theory of René Girard. Her publications include: "Mimetic Crisis in the Medieval Mass: The Educative Role of a Sequence for Saint Thomas of Canterbury," in *Violence in Medieval Courtly Literature: A Casebook*, edited by Albrecht Classen (New York: Routledge, 2004); and "Violence in the American Musical," in *Violence in America: An Encyclopedia* (New York: Charles Scribners Sons, 2000).

BARBARA SPARTI is a dance historian specializing in fifteenth- to seventeenth-century Italian dance. She was Distinguished Visiting Professor at UCLA, and guest lecturer-choreographer in Israel, University of California at Santa Cruz, and Princeton. Besides her edition-translation of Guglielmo Ebreo's 1463 dance treatise (*De pratica seu arte tripudi*, Oxford University Press 1993), and her introduction to Ercole Santucci's *Mastro da ballo, 1614* (Olms 2004), her publications deal with musical questions in Renaissance and Italian Baroque dance, especially dance sources and their socioeconomic, political, and aesthetic contexts. Her recent publications include "*Balli* to Dance and Play in a Sixteenth-Century Miscellany" (with F. Carbone and A. Ziino), in *Music Observed: Studies in Memory of William C. Holmes*, ed. C. Reardon & S. Parisi (Harmonie Park Press, 2004); "Isabella and the Dancing Este Brides, 1473–1514," in *Women's Work: Making Dance in Europe Before 1750*, ed. L. Brooks (University of Wisconsin Press, 2007); and "Hercules Dancing in Thebes, in Pictures and Music," *Early Music History* 26 (2007). Ms. Sparti, who founded and directed the Gruppo di Danza Rinascimentale (1975–88), has choreographed period works for stage and TV.

ELIZABETH RANDELL UPTON is an Assistant Professor in the Department of Musicology at UCLA. She received her PhD from the University of

North Carolina at Chapel Hill in 2001 with a dissertation entitled "The Chantilly Codex (F-CH 564): The Manuscript, Its Music and Its Scholarly Reception." She is completing a book on Dufay chansons, *Song Culture: Guillaume Dufay and the Early Fifteenth-Century Chanson*, has recently published "Editing Chantilly Chansons: Scribal Procedures for Text Placement and Larger Questions of Musical Style," in *A Late Medieval Songbook and Its Context: New Perspectives on Codex Bibliothéque du Château de Chantilly, 564*, ed. Anne Stone and Yolanda Plumley (Turnhout: Brepols, 2009), and has several articles forthcoming.

BARBARA R. WALTERS is Associate Professor of Sociology, Kingsborough Community College, City University of New York, and a Consortial Faculty member for the CUNY Online Baccalaureate in Communication and Culture. She has a PhD in sociology and an MA in both sociology and musicology from the State University of New York at Stony Brook. Her recent publications include: "Women Religious Virtuosae from the Middle Ages: A Case Pattern and Analytic Model of Types," *Sociology of Religion* 63 (2002); "Church-Sect Dynamics and the Feast of Corpus Christi," *Sociology of Religion* 65 (2004); The Politics of Aesthetic Judgment (Rowman & Littlefield, 2003); and *The Feast of Corpus Christi*, with Peter T. Ricketts and Vincent Corrigan (Penn State Press, 2006).

Index

Typeset in 10/13 Adobe Caslon Pro
Designed and composed by Tom Krol
Manufactured by Cushing-Malloy, Inc.

Medieval Institute Publications
College of Arts and Sciences
Western Michigan University
1903 W. Michigan Avenue
Kalamazoo, MI 49008-5432
http:/ /www.wmich.edu/medieval/mip

 WESTERN MICHIGAN UNIVERSITY